NATIONAL DEFENSE RESEARCH INSTITUTE

Cross-Agency Evaluation of DoD, VA, and HHS Mental Health Public Awareness Campaigns

Analysis of Campaign Scope, Content, and Reach

Joie D. Acosta
Jennifer L. Cerully
Eunice C. Wong
Elizabeth L. Petrun Sayers
Mikhail Zaydman
Lisa S. Meredith
Ilana Blum
Nupur Nanda
Terri Tanielian
Rachel Ross
Asa Wilks

Prepared for the Psychological Health Center of Excellence
Approved for public release; distribution unlimited

For more information on this publication, visit www.rand.org/t/RR1612

Library of Congress Cataloging-in-Publication Data is available for this publication.
ISBN: 978-0-8330-9936-5

Published by the RAND Corporation, Santa Monica, Calif.
© Copyright 2020 RAND Corporation
RAND® is a registered trademark.

Support RAND

Make a tax-deductible charitable contribution at
www.rand.org/giving/contribute

www.rand.org

Preface

This report contains the methods and results of an empirical cross-agency evaluation of the scope, content, and dissemination of four public awareness campaigns that aim to overcome negative perceptions and promote awareness of mental illness and its treatment. These campaigns are currently implemented at the U.S. Department of Defense (DoD), U.S. Department of Veterans Affairs (VA), and U.S. Department of Health and Human Services (HHS). This cross-agency evaluation of mental health public awareness campaigns was conducted to determine progress toward the Barack Obama administration's Cross-Agency Priority Goal of improving mental health outcomes for service members, veterans, and their families. A cross-agency evaluation looks across campaigns to understand their collective reach, areas of alignment or overlap, and collective impacts. There are two phases for the cross-agency evaluation: evaluation design and evaluation of campaign scope, content, and reach (i.e., the cross-agency evaluation). The DoD campaign progressed to a third phase—an efficacy test of the campaign messages. In this report, we focus on the cross-agency evaluation. The report contains a detailed description of how the evaluation design—including plans for the cross-agency evaluation and forthcoming efficacy test of the DoD campaign—was developed through literature review, consultation with campaign staff, and feedback on evaluation design from experts. In addition, this report provides findings from the cross-agency evaluation of the four mental health public awareness campaigns, which was conducted between June 2015 and June 2016. Because of a major revision of the Defense Health Agency, the report publication was significantly delayed. The four campaigns are the Real Warriors Campaign (from DoD), Make the Connection and Veterans Crisis Line (both from VA), and National Recovery Month (from HHS). All share overlapping short- and long-term goals to improve knowledge of mental health symptoms and promote positive perceptions of individuals with mental health conditions and of mental health treatment. The cross-agency evaluation focuses on assessing

- each campaign's scope and content to identify any overlapping target populations, messages, or desired outcomes, as well as any unique contributions
- campaign dissemination to determine reach to target populations
- each campaign's degree of alignment with best practices for design and dissemination.

To conduct the evaluation, we convened an expert panel, performed a content analysis of the campaign's materials, analyzed process data collected by the campaign, and analyzed social media data.

The contents of this report will be of particular interest to national policymakers and health policy officials within DoD, VA, and HHS, as well as policymakers in other sectors who sponsor or manage media campaigns to support mental health more generally.

This research was conducted within the Forces and Resources Policy Center of the RAND National Defense Research Institute, a federally funded research and development center sponsored by the Office of the Secretary of Defense, the Joint Staff, the Unified Combatant Commands, the Navy, the Marine Corps, the defense agencies, and the defense Intelligence Community.

For more information on the Forces and Resources Policy Center, see www.rand.org/nsrd/ndri/centers/frp or contact the director (contact information is provided on the webpage).

Contents

Boxes

Figures

Tables

Summary

More than 2.7 million service members have deployed to support operations in Iraq and Afghanistan since 2001 (Watson Institute for International and Public Affairs, 2015). Many who return report mental health problems, such as depression, posttraumatic stress disorder, and problematic substance use. Without appropriate treatment, these problems can have wide-ranging and negative effects on service members' quality of life and their social, emotional, and cognitive functioning and can negatively affect their relationships with family and friends (Denning, Meisnere, and Warner, 2014; Ramchand et al., 2015).

One deterrent to seeking appropriate treatment is the prevalence of negative perceptions, often referred to as *stigma*,[1] surrounding mental illness and treatment (Acosta et al., 2014; Clement et al., 2015; Evans-Lacko et al., 2013). Mental health public awareness campaigns have been used as one strategy to combat stigma and promote treatment-seeking. Evaluations of mental health–focused public awareness campaigns implemented in both the United States and other countries suggest that such campaigns can reach large audiences; increase mental health knowledge; reduce negative attitudes, beliefs, and perceptions toward those with mental illness; and act as cost-effective strategies for reducing mental illness stigma (Gaebel et al., 2008; Jorm, Christensen, and Griffiths, 2005; Wyllie and Lauder, 2012; Collins et al., 2015; Livingston et al., 2014; Dietrich et al., 2010; Evans-Lacko et al., 2014).

In 2015, the Barack Obama administration designated the improvement of mental health outcomes for service members, veterans, and their families as a Cross-Agency Priority Goal (CAP-G). An interagency task force cochaired by representatives from the Executive Office of the President, DoD, VA, and HHS was formed to determine progress toward the CAP-G and achieve the following objectives: (1) reduce barriers to mental health care; (2) enhance access for service members, veterans, and family members with mental health care needs; and (3) support research on effective diagnosis and treatment.

The task force formed workgroups to focus specifically on each of the objectives. To help address the first objective of reducing barriers to care, the task force asked the CAP-G Barriers to Care Working Group to secure an evaluation of federally funded public awareness campaigns aimed at overcoming negative perceptions of mental health conditions and treatment and promoting awareness of available resources. DoD, VA, and HHS all operate public awareness campaigns that predate the CAP-G, and the RAND National Defense Research Institute was asked to conduct a comprehensive empirical cross-agency evaluation of four of these campaigns. The evaluation would focus not on the individual campaigns themselves but on the campaigns' collective reach, areas of alignment or overlap, and collective impacts.

The four campaigns in the evaluation are the following:

1. Real Warriors Campaign (RWC), operated by DoD, is a "multimedia public awareness campaign designed to encourage help-seeking behavior among service members, veterans, and military families coping with invisible wounds" (RWC, undated-d).

2. Make the Connection (MTC), operated by VA, is "a public awareness campaign that provides personal testimonials and resources to help Veterans discover ways to improve their lives" (VA, 2015).

3. Veterans Crisis Line (VCL),[2] also operated by VA, conducts outreach to promote its confidential telephone, chat, or text-based counseling for veterans in crisis, their families, and their friends (VCL, undated-b).

4. National Recovery Month (also referred to as Recovery Month), operated by HHS and sponsored by the Substance Abuse and Mental Health Services Administration (SAMHSA), conducts events and outreach each September and throughout the year "to increase awareness and understanding of mental and substance use disorders and celebrate the people who recover" (National Recovery Month, undated).

Purpose of the Report

The purpose of this report is twofold. First, it provides a detailed description of how the evaluation design—including plans for this cross-agency evaluation and a forthcoming efficacy test of the DoD campaign—was developed through literature review, consultation with campaign staff, and feedback on evaluation design from experts. Second, the report contains findings from the cross-agency evaluation of the campaigns' collective scope, content, and dissemination.

To align with the CAP-G objective of reducing barriers to care, the evaluation design and cross-agency evaluation focused on the target populations (i.e., service members, veterans, and their families) named in the campaigns' goals and on shared desired outcomes across agencies and campaigns. This report on the cross-agency evaluation will be followed by a report on the efficacy test of the DoD campaign.

---

[2]   The evaluation focused on the public awareness campaign materials used to promote VCL. We did not attempt to evaluate the operations or effectiveness of the crisis line itself.

Approach to Conducting a Cross-Agency Evaluation

To design the campaign evaluation activities (Figure S.1), we conducted a systematic literature review of prior evaluations of public awareness campaigns and solicited input on evaluation design from experts and campaign staff. We then conducted a cross-agency evaluation of the campaigns' collective scope, content, and dissemination, using four methods that do not rely on primary data collection:

- secondary analysis of campaign process data to determine campaign reach
- content analysis exploring whether campaign materials align with stated messages, target populations, and desired outcomes, and identifying overlapping and unique content
- expert panel to determine whether campaigns align with best practices and to solicit recommendations for campaign improvement
- analysis of social media data to determine how campaigns are being disseminated and whether campaigns are reaching influential social media users.

The cross-agency evaluation (and the bulk of this report) answers questions about

- **scope and content:** How do campaigns align or complement each other? Where are there overlaps and gaps in their scope and content? What are the unique contributions of each campaign?

Figure S.1
Campaign Evaluation Activities

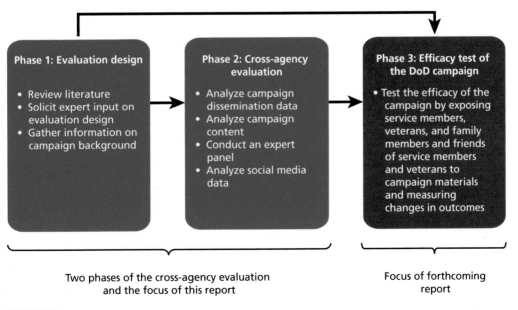

Phase 1: Evaluation design	Phase 2: Cross-agency evaluation	Phase 3: Efficacy test of the DoD campaign
• Review literature • Solicit expert input on evaluation design • Gather information on campaign background	• Analyze campaign dissemination data • Analyze campaign content • Conduct an expert panel • Analyze social media data	• Test the efficacy of the campaign by exposing service members, veterans, and family members and friends of service members and veterans to campaign materials and measuring changes in outcomes

Two phases of the cross-agency evaluation and the focus of this report

Focus of forthcoming report

RAND RR1612-S.1

- **dissemination:** What is the collective reach of the campaigns via different channels?
- **efficacy:** Do the campaigns follow best practices in their design and dissemination? Is it therefore likely that campaigns as designed and implemented will achieve their goals?

A forthcoming report will provide results of the efficacy test of the DoD campaign.

Key Findings and Recommendations

The following sections summarize RAND's findings and recommendations in four areas of interest: messaging, content of campaign materials, dissemination and reach, and inclusion of direct connections to care. At the end of each recommendation, we have noted in parentheses who should take the lead—a federal partner group (such as the existing interagency task force that can work cross-agency) or the campaigns themselves.

Efficiency and Coordination of Mental Health Messaging

At the time of our evaluation, the four campaigns, which have distinct yet overlapping audiences, shared desired outcomes (to improve knowledge of mental health symptoms and promote positive perceptions of individuals with mental health conditions and of mental health treatment). They offered a variety of messages—for those at risk of mental illness, considering treatment, in need of immediate support, or in recovery, and for those who support those experiencing mental illness or in recovery—to their common audiences and unique messages when appropriate. The majority of campaign content (82 percent across all four campaigns) aligned with shared goals, and the individuals pictured in the materials reflected the target audiences of each of the campaigns.

Despite these similarities, DoD, VA, and HHS could expand the campaigns' collective coordination and point individuals to unique resources specific to their mental health issues by working together across campaigns and possibly with a set of 32 national and regional organizations that partner with at least two of these agencies. Similarly, the campaigns could cross-reference each other more as resources—a quick and easy strategy that could improve service members' and veterans' access to services. Because campaigns were initiated at different points in time, the agencies lack consistent metrics across campaigns to measure campaign performance—which could help improve them in context with the other campaigns.

Efficiency and Coordination of Mental Health Messaging Recommendations

    1.1   Cross-reference other campaigns more when presenting resources in campaign materials (campaigns).

1.2   Convene national and regional partners to help define a strategic national direction for public mental health education that DoD, VA, and HHS can use to guide their efforts (federal partner group, working with the campaigns).

1.3   Clearly define the unique contributions and intentional overlap in messages and target populations across the campaigns (federal partner group, working with the campaigns).

1.4   Monitor coordination of current and new campaign efforts to promote strategic coordination of messaging and dissemination (campaigns, working through the federal partner group).

1.5   Develop a targeted set of performance measures that cuts across campaigns (federal partner group).

1.6   Explore the development of cross-campaign and cross-platform measures to fully capture exposure and synergy across campaigns (federal partner group).

Findings on Campaign Content

Most campaign content aligned with best practices; clearly communicated the messages; and used credible, positive messengers. However, the could be improved in several areas. For example, some experts who reviewed the campaigns thought that the materials could be clearer about how service members' anonymity and/or confidentiality is protected. Also, about half of the campaign webpages did not specifically cite the source used to generate content for the page. Staff from campaigns report that although the content is rooted in the research evidence base, they intentionally chose to omit source information to avoid being overly technical and to appeal to target audiences. However, this design choice could make it difficult for users to judge material credibility or to seek out more information.

Though all campaigns contained some content that addressed substance use, Recovery Month more heavily emphasized substance use in its materials. In addition, campaigns that tried to serve multiple audiences often had content for secondary audiences (such as family members and health professionals) that our experts thought was limited and less developed than the materials developed for primary audiences.

Recommendations for Campaign Content

2.1   Determine whether source information should be clearly marked on more campaign materials (campaigns).

2.2   Review campaign content that does not align with a specific campaign's desired outcome (or shared desired outcome) and consider modification or deletion (campaigns).

2.3   Review content and links to ensure they are all current (campaigns).

2.4   Specify what level of anonymity and/or confidentiality is guaranteed by self-assessment and direct connections to mental health care (e.g., call lines, chat lines, direct connections to a local medical center) (campaigns).

2.5   Enhance materials targeting support networks (and other target audiences, as relevant)—but also consider whether to serve a smaller audience in order to develop more and richer content for the main target of service members and veterans (campaigns).

Dissemination and Reach

Campaigns used multiple approaches to disseminate their materials and messages, including websites, public service announcements, social media, television, radio, and in-person engagement. While the reach of all campaigns (except for Recovery Month[3]) increased between 2012 and 2015, it was impossible to measure the degree to which campaigns reached their specific target audiences because campaigns were not collecting those data.

The campaigns' websites played host to more than 4 million sessions in 2015. A significant share of visitors spent only a brief amount of time on the websites. It is unclear based on the data available for this evaluation whether the brevity of site visits is due to low user interest or engagement or to effective design of material that is easily and quickly processed. Each site housed some faulty links or outdated content that should be updated.

The analysis found that, in 2015, the campaigns may have reached as many as 5.6 million people through Facebook, YouTube, and Twitter. VA's MTC campaign had the greatest reach on these platforms, providing more than 90 percent of the campaigns' collective Facebook fans and YouTube views. Although campaigns used Twitter in a very limited way, they still managed to connect with users who have above-average influence in mental health.

The campaigns aired more than 400,000 combined radio and television public service announcements, resulting in more than 42.9 billion impressions—90 percent of them from DoD's RWC. Other outreach in 2015 resulted in campaign attendance at more than 250 events, distribution of more than 10 million materials (most raising awareness of VCL), and partnering with more than 700 organizations and agencies.

The timing of campaign outreach varied, with some campaigns highly active during certain time periods (particularly Recovery Month). It is unclear to what degree campaigns coordinated the timing of their activities with each other.

Dissemination and Reach Recommendations

3.1   Develop strategies to use Twitter more effectively (campaigns).

---

[3] From 2012 to 2015, the Recovery Month website analytics program was revamped and migrated from Webtrends to Google Analytics. The systems calculate user interaction metrics differently. In addition, the site metrics changed yet again, to the standardized SAMHSA Google Analytics tracking code. In March 2015, a new Recovery Month website launched as a new internal site within SAMHSA.gov. It contained 75 percent less content than the previous site and provided access to only 2014 materials and some 2015 materials—unlike the prior version, which had offered more than 15 years of content.

3.2   Modify campaign websites to be more engaging and meet the needs of brief visitors (campaigns).

3.3   Consider whether the campaigns should intentionally time their active outreach to occur in different months to increase the likelihood of reaching overlapping target populations or whether to time outreach at the same time of year to achieve more saturation in a shorter period (campaigns, working through the federal partner group).

Inclusion of Direct Connections to Care

These recommendations focus on enhancements that could allow service members, veterans, and their families to make a direct connection to some form of care as a result of viewing campaign materials. Though all campaigns offered general resources on mental health problems and treatment (e.g., locator tools that allowed users to find locations to get care in their geographic area, outreach phone lines that provide resources but not any direct mental health care), just 27 percent of campaign materials provided *direct connections* to care (defined as resources that provided a connection to a crisis line or chat or directly to a specific medical center to make an appointment). We recognize that providing these direct connections to care may be a difficult task, but we provide these recommendations because a shared long-term goal across all campaigns (as shown in the campaign logic models) is to encourage target audiences to seek care if they need it.

Inclusion of Direct Connections to Care Recommendations

4.1   Ensure that a direct connection to mental health care (i.e., phone line, live chat line, direct connection to a local medical center) is included on relevant campaign materials (campaigns).

4.2   Determine whether a centralized call line that allows users (not in immediate crisis, but in need of care) to make an appointment for mental health care is a resource that should be offered by campaigns. Though this is not feasible for any individual campaign to execute, we urge consideration of such a service to remove barriers to care for service members and veterans (federal partner group).

Limitations of the Cross-Agency Evaluation

In alignment with the fact that the evaluation is to respond to a CAP-G, the cross-agency evaluation was intentionally designed to address goals, messages, and processes shared across multiple agencies and campaigns. As a result, the evaluation presented here is not intended to serve as a full and comprehensive evaluation of each campaign. In addition, this cross-agency evaluation examined only the scope, content, and dissemination of the campaigns; we did not examine whether the campaigns are effective or cost-effective. Many campaigns take an integrative approach to their design, aiming to create a campaign in which the "whole that is greater than the sum of the parts and the optimal message impact is achieved" (Cheng, Kotler, and Lee, 2011, p. 10; Schultz and Schultz, 2004). Given that we did not evaluate campaign efficacy or effectiveness for the cross-agency evaluation, we are unable to draw any conclusions about this aspect of campaigns.

Each method used to conduct the evaluation is subject to its own limitations. The content analysis is limited in that all campaign materials were treated equally. That is, when determining characteristics of materials, we did not distinguish between them or weight them differently—for example, between content intended to be more educational (e.g., an infographic) and content intended to be less so (e.g., a social media graphic that is not intended to convey the same amount of information). Also, the content analysis does not include campaign content developed in the time since the analysis was conducted. The secondary analysis of process data relied on data available from all campaigns and thus does not include process data unique to a single campaign. The process data we used to determine reach did not allow us to identify unique users, so much of the data reported (e.g., the number of page views on a website) represent an upper bound on the number of possible individuals who could have been exposed. The expert panel findings are not generalizable to all mental health public awareness campaigns because of the explicit focus on military and veteran populations and because they reflect the feedback of a targeted group of experts. In addition, the best-practices checklist that expert panel members used to assess campaigns was developed as part of this evaluation and was not available to campaign developers during the creation of the campaigns. Thus, campaigns may not have been aware of some best practices on the list. Finally, just two of the campaigns—RWC and Recovery Month—have active Twitter accounts, which limits the usefulness of Twitter data for examining the campaigns' reach and influence via social media. Finally because of a major reorganization at the Defense Health Agency, which is responsible for overseeing this work, the publication of this report was significantly delayed. By the time this report was released, the interagency task force that requested this evaluation was dissolved and the federal emphasis on the CAP-G was diminished.

Conclusions

The cross-agency evaluation of the four DoD, VA, and HHS mental health public awareness campaigns detailed in this report relied on three assumptions: (1) to align with CAP-G, the evaluation should focus on service members, veterans, and their families; (2) to be efficient, the evaluation should focus on shared desired outcomes across campaigns; and (3) to be comprehensive, the evaluation should assess the effectiveness and efficiency of campaigns. The results of the evaluation allowed us to generate a number of recommendations regarding campaign scope, content, and reach, as well as cross-agency efficiency and coordination of mental health messaging. Had we designed an evaluation under a different set of assumptions (e.g., by focusing on the most influential pieces of each campaign rather than shared elements across campaigns), we might not have come to the same conclusions. This raises the issue of precisely which assumptions should guide a cross-agency evaluation of this type. Contemplating this issue leads to broader, overarching questions: What should each agency's role be in promoting greater access to care for service members and veterans? To what degree should efforts overlap or be unique? Continuing to take a cross-agency approach to answering these questions and understanding the success of campaigns individually and collectively will be important to improving mental health outcomes for service members, veterans, and their families. Improving mental health outcomes for these populations remains a priority, despite the fact that the CAP-G and associated interagency task force and working group that commissioned this report no longer exist.

Acknowledgments

We gratefully acknowledge the assistance of the campaign staff and administrators who provided support during the evaluation: (1) Real Warriors Campaign—Rick Black, Lauren Wilson, and Kathryn Duthaler from Booz Allen Hamilton, and MAJ Demietrice Pittman from the Defense Health Agency's Healthcare Operations Directorate; (2) Make the Connection and Veterans Crisis Line—Wendy Tenhula, Kacie Kelly, Caitlin Thompson, Elizabeth Karras, Koby South, and Rhett Herrera from the U.S. Department of Veterans Affairs; and (3) National Recovery Month—Cicely Burrows-McElwain, Ivette Torres, Michele Monroe, Roger Brawn, Terence Rose, Stephanie Weaver, and CAPT Wanda Finch from the Substance Abuse and Mental Health Services Administration.

We also thank Clara Aranibar, Nina Ryan, and Jamie Greenberg for the administrative support they provided preparing this document. Alyson Youngblood, Courtney Kase, Doug Yeung, and Luke Matthews provided valuable insights in the processing of web analytics and social media data; and Coreen Farris, Thomas Trail, and Lane Burgette provided critical input on the evaluation design. In addition, we thank our project monitor at the Psychological Health Center of Excellence (formerly the Defense Centers of Excellence for Psychological Health and Traumatic Brain Injury), LT Evette Pinder, as well as CAPT Anthony Arita, Katherine McGraw, and Mark Bates for their support of our work. We also appreciate the valuable insights we received from Rebecca Collins and Ellen Beckjord. Their constructive critiques were addressed as part of RAND's rigorous quality assurance process to improve the quality of this report.

Finally, we thank the members of the expert panel, convened as part of the evaluation, for sharing their time and feedback: Patty Barron, Joseph Capella, Elisia Cohen, Emily Falk, Tony Foleno, Vicki Freimuth, Howard Goldman, Madelyn Gould, Anara Guard, Nancy Harrington, Kate Hoit, Gary L. Kreps, Annie Lang, Tessa Langley, Xiaoli Nan, Seth Noar, Mark Olfson, Ronald Rice, John Roberts, Karen Roberts, Alex Rothman, Barbara Van Dahlen, David L. Vogel, Cynthia Wainscott, and Rick Zimmerman.

Abbreviations

24/7	24 hours a day, seven days a week
ADHD	attention deficit hyperactivity disorder
AFSP	American Foundation for Suicide Prevention
AUC	area under the curve
AUSA	Association of the United States Army
CAP-G	Cross-Agency Priority Goal
DAV	Disabled American Veterans
DCoE	Defense Centers of Excellence for Psychological Health and Traumatic Brain Injury
DoD	U.S. Department of Defense
EV	eigenvector
FAQ	frequently asked question
HBM	Health Belief Model
HHS	U.S. Department of Health and Human Services
HIV/AIDS	human immunodeficiency virus, acquired immunodeficiency syndrome
IAVA	Iraq and Afghanistan Veterans of America
IP	internet protocol
M	mean
MCL	Military Crisis Line
Md	median
MH	mental health
MTC	Make the Connection
NAMI	National Alliance on Mental Illness
OCD	obsessive-compulsive disorder

OEF	Operation Enduring Freedom
OIF	Operation Iraqi Freedom
OND	Operation New Dawn
PRO-ACT	Pennsylvania Recovery Organization–Achieving Community Together
PSA	public service announcement
PTSD	posttraumatic stress disorder
R	range
RWC	Real Warriors Campaign
SAMHSA	Substance Abuse and Mental Health Services Administration
SVM	support vector machine
TTC	Time to Change
USO	United Service Organizations
VA	U.S. Department of Veterans Affairs
VCL	Veterans Crisis Line

CHAPTER ONE

Introduction

More than 2.7 million service members have deployed to Iraq and Afghanistan since 2001 (Watson Institute for International and Public Affairs, 2015). When they return, many report mental health challenges, such as depression, posttraumatic stress disorder (PTSD), and problematic substance use. A 2008 study estimated that roughly half of those who need treatment for these conditions seek it. Of those who get treatment, slightly more than half receive minimally adequate care (e.g., at least eight visits with a mental health professional in the past 12 months), and the proportion that receives high-quality care is thus likely to be even smaller (Tanielian and Jaycox, 2008). Without appropriate treatment, these mental health problems can have wide-ranging and negative impacts on service members' quality of life; on their social, emotional, and cognitive functioning; and on their relationships with family and friends (Denning, Meisnere, and Warner, 2014; Ramchand et al., 2015).

Need for a Cross-Agency Evaluation of Mental Health Public Awareness Campaigns

In 2015, the Barack Obama administration designated the improvement of mental health outcomes for service members, veterans, and their families as a Cross-Agency Priority Goal (CAP-G) ("Cross-Agency Priority Goal: Service Members and Veterans Mental Health," undated). An interagency task force cochaired by representatives from the Executive Office of the President, U.S. Department of Defense (DoD), U.S. Department of Veterans Affairs (VA), and U.S. Department of Health and Human Services (HHS) was formed to determine progress toward the CAP-G and achieve the following objectives: (1) reduce barriers to mental health care; (2) enhance access for service members, veterans, and family members with mental health care needs; and (3) support research on effective diagnosis and treatment.

The CAP-G Barriers to Care Working Group was formed to address the goal of reducing barriers to seeking mental health treatment and support through a series of activities that included an evaluation of federally funded public awareness campaigns aimed at overcoming negative perceptions of mental health conditions and treatment and promoting awareness of available resources.

Public awareness campaigns are a relatively common approach to increasing knowledge and changing behaviors. They have been defined as efforts that are

- intended to generate specific outcomes in a relatively large number of people
- implemented over a specified period of time
- composed of a set of organized communication activities that push out a set of specific messages via an array of media outlets
- often coordinated with interpersonal and community-based communication efforts (Coffman, 2002; Rogers and Storey, 1987).

Evaluations of mental health–focused public awareness campaigns implemented in both the United States and other countries suggest that such campaigns can yield outcomes that align with the CAP-G. Specifically, evaluations indicate that public awareness campaigns focused on mental health can reach large audiences; increase mental health knowledge; and reduce negative attitudes, beliefs, and perceptions toward those with mental illness, and they can be cost-effective strategies for reducing mental illness stigma (Gaebel et al., 2008; Jorm, Christensen, and Griffiths, 2005; Wyllie and Lauder, 2012; Collins et al., 2015; Livingston et al., 2014; Dietrich et al., 2010; Evans-Lacko et al., 2014).[1] Because stigma may deter people from seeking mental health treatment, these campaigns may help promote help-seeking behavior (Acosta et al., 2014; Clement et al., 2015; Evans-Lacko et al., 2013).

DoD, VA, and HHS have each implemented one or more public awareness campaigns that predate the release of the CAP-G. However, to date, no comprehensive empirical cross-agency evaluation of the scope, content, dissemination, or impact of these public awareness campaigns has been conducted to determine how well the agencies' combined efforts are accomplishing the aforementioned CAP-G objectives. To inform the federal government about the overall effectiveness of its mental health public awareness campaigns, a cross-agency evaluation is needed—one that focuses on understanding the campaigns' collective reach, areas of alignment or overlap, and collective impacts.

Purpose and Organization of This Report

To help assess the effectiveness of federal mental health public awareness campaigns, the RAND National Defense Research Institute was asked to design and conduct a

---

[1] Throughout the report, we use *stigma* to broadly refer to a range of negative attitudes and beliefs and incorrect or lacking knowledge about mental illness and/or its treatment. The academic literature, DoD, and VA commonly use this term. However, the Substance Abuse and Mental Health Services Administration (SAMHSA) within HHS is moving away from this term.

cross-agency evaluation of campaigns that DoD, VA, and HHS have implemented to reduce negative perceptions about mental health conditions and treatment and increase awareness of resources available to service members, veterans, and their families. Each agency was asked to identify its relevant public awareness campaign(s) most in alignment with the CAP-G. Four campaigns were selected for the cross-agency evaluation:

1. Real Warriors Campaign (RWC), operated by DoD, is a "multimedia public awareness campaign designed to encourage help-seeking behavior among service members, veterans, and military families coping with invisible wounds" (RWC, undated-d).
2. Make the Connection (MTC), operated by VA, is "a public awareness campaign that provides personal testimonials and resources to help Veterans discover ways to improve their lives" (VA, 2015)
3. Veterans Crisis Line (VCL),[2] also operated by VA, conducts outreach to promote its confidential telephone, chat, or text-based counseling for veterans in crisis, their families, and their friends (VCL, undated-b).
4. National Recovery Month (also referred to as Recovery Month), operated by HHS and sponsored by SAMHSA, conducts events and outreach each September and throughout the year "to increase awareness and understanding of mental and substance use disorders and celebrate the people who recover" (National Recovery Month, undated).

The cross-agency evaluation has two phases: evaluation design and evaluation of the campaign content, scope, and reach (i.e., the cross-agency evaluation). The DoD campaign progressed to a third phase—an efficacy test of the campaign messages. In this report, we focus on the evaluation design and cross-agency evaluation. This report contains a detailed description of how the evaluation design—including plans for the cross-agency evaluation and forthcoming efficacy test of the DoD campaign—was developed through literature review, consultation with campaign staff, and feedback on evaluation design from experts. In addition, this report shares the findings of the cross-agency evaluation of the campaigns' scope, content, and dissemination. The evaluation focused not on the performance of the individual campaigns themselves but on the campaigns collectively.

To align with the first objective under the CAP-G (reducing barriers to care), the evaluation plan design and cross-agency evaluation focused on the target populations (i.e., service members, veterans, and their families) named in the goals and on shared desired outcomes across agencies and campaigns. This report focusing on the cross-

---

[2] The evaluation focused on the public awareness campaign materials used to promote VCL. We did not attempt to evaluate the operations or effectiveness of the crisis line itself.

agency evaluation of campaigns will be followed by a forthcoming report describing the efficacy test of the DoD campaign.

Chapter Two describes the approach used to design the evaluation and the methods used for the cross-agency evaluation of the campaigns' scope, content, and dissemination. Chapter Three presents the goals, key messages, theoretical basis, dissemination methods, and ongoing tracking of various metrics for each campaign. Chapter Four describes the scope of each campaign and highlights areas where they align, as well as each campaign's unique contributions. Chapter Five presents findings from our content analysis detailing how campaign content aligns with stated goals and target populations and highlighting areas of overlap or gaps in campaign content. Chapter Six presents findings from our expert panel and secondary analysis of campaign process data, which describe campaign reach and how users interact with campaigns. Chapter Seven summarizes key findings, draws conclusions, and offers recommendations for how to improve campaigns' scope, content, and dissemination. Detailed methods are provided in Appendixes A–F.

CHAPTER TWO

Approach to Evaluating Campaigns

This chapter describes the two phases of the cross-agency evaluation: design and evaluation of campaign content, scope, and reach (Figure 2.1), as well as plans for a third phase efficacy test with the DoD campaign. This report focuses on the cross-agency evaluation. We began Phase 1 by conducting a systematic literature review of prior evaluations of public awareness campaigns and soliciting input on evaluation design from experts and campaign staff (described in greater detail in Appendixes A and B) to inform the development of the overall evaluation approach. Second, we conducted a cross-agency evaluation of the campaigns' scope, content, and dissemination (discussed in Chapters Three through Six) using four methods that do not rely on primary data collection: a secondary analysis of cam-

Figure 2.1
Three Phases of the Cross-Agency Evaluation

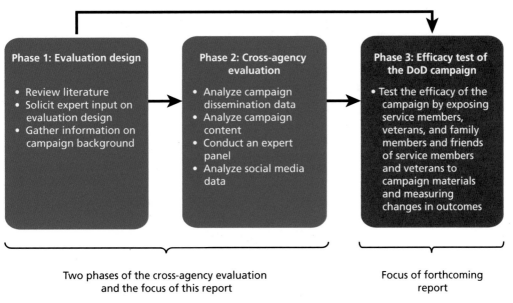

Phase 1: Evaluation design

- Review literature
- Solicit expert input on evaluation design
- Gather information on campaign background

Phase 2: Cross-agency evaluation

- Analyze campaign dissemination data
- Analyze campaign content
- Conduct an expert panel
- Analyze social media data

Phase 3: Efficacy test of the DoD campaign

- Test the efficacy of the campaign by exposing service members, veterans, and family members and friends of service members and veterans to campaign materials and measuring changes in outcomes

Two phases of the cross-agency evaluation and the focus of this report

Focus of forthcoming report

RAND RR1612-2.1

paign process data; a content analysis exploring whether campaign materials align with stated messages, target populations, and objectives; an expert panel to determine whether campaigns align with best practices; and an analysis of social media data to determine how campaigns are disseminating their message and materials over Twitter and whether campaigns are reaching influential social media users. A forthcoming report will detail the efficacy test of campaign messages for the DoD campaign (Real Warriors).

Phase 1: Design the Campaign Evaluation Approaches

Review Evaluation Literature

We conducted a systematic literature review of prior evaluations of public awareness campaigns. The campaigns selected for evaluation were aimed at overcoming negative perceptions of mental health conditions and treatment and promoting awareness of available resources. These goals were reminiscent of those shared by existing mental health public awareness and stigma reduction campaigns, so we began our literature search by reviewing relevant resources used in several earlier literature reviews related to mental health stigma: (1) *Mental Health Stigma in the Military* (Acosta et al., 2014); (2) an in-progress review of literature on the effects of stigma on various treatment-related behavior (e.g., care-seeking, completion of care plans) and other positive outcomes (e.g., social functioning) (Cerully, Acosta, and Sloan, 2018); and (3) a RAND report on the content, design, and dissemination of RWC (Acosta, Martin, et al., 2012). Both the narrative and articles from these literature reviews were reviewed and coded, and details relating to the focus of our study were abstracted. Abstracted information included intervention and survey periods, evaluation design, measures of barriers to care, outcomes assessed, and the effects of perceived stigma and other barriers to care on relevant treatment outcomes.

To update and augment these prior reviews, we performed our own web-based search of peer-reviewed literature from May 2014 to July 2015 in relevant databases. The articles we identified underwent successive rounds of screening—including a title and abstract review followed by a full-text review—to exclude unsuitable articles (Table A.3). Articles selected for inclusion were then reviewed and coded using the same process as for the earlier literature reviews (Acosta et al., 2014; Cerully, Acosta, and Sloan, 2018). We then reviewed the coded information from all identified literature and summarized this into a series of recommendations for evaluating mental health public awareness campaigns. These recommendations, as well as search strategies and coding processes, are detailed in Appendix A of this report.

Solicit Expert Input on Evaluation Design

We also sought recommendations from recognized national and international experts in the fields of barriers to mental health treatment and evaluation of public awareness campaigns. These experts were selected because they had expertise in stigma and these areas, or they were knowledgeable about existing data sources (or running a large-scale evaluation or survey related to stigma or barriers to mental health care). To elicit feedback, we used two primary strategies. First, for RAND's in-house experts, we organized a video conference with ten attendees from the three main RAND offices and other sites. Before the video conference, attendees were given a short document summarizing the evaluation goals and giving background information on the selected campaigns. The two-hour panel discussion was moderated, and a semistructured interview guide was used to stimulate conversation about gold standards in public awareness campaign evaluation, advantages and disadvantages of identified evaluation methods, appropriate variables for evaluating intermediate and long-term outcomes, and recommendations for assessing cross-agency outcomes. Second, we conducted semistructured telephone interviews of 30–60 minutes with eight experts external to RAND. The interviews covered the same topics, and the external experts were provided the same short background document prior to their interviews. A research team member took detailed notes during the video conference and each interview. Another research team member reviewed the notes to identify evaluation recommendations and organized and summarized those recommendations into a single list. Appendix B contains detailed information about the recommendations that emerged from our consultation with the experts. The processes by which we elicited expert input were determined by the RAND Human Subjects Protection Committee to be exempt from human subjects review under federal guidelines.

Gather Information on Campaign Background

We consulted with campaign staff to gain a thorough understanding of each campaign selected for evaluation. We also gathered information about any metrics of campaign performance that they were collecting. Prior to consulting with campaign staff, we collected publicly available information on each campaign, including goals, key messages, barriers to mental health care addressed by the campaign, target audiences, and dissemination strategies. We met with staff of each campaign to review this information, correct any errors, and incorporate any additional information that they provided. We then used the information to generate logic models for each campaign showing their activities and desired short- and long-term outcomes. Our consultations with campaign staff were determined by the RAND Human Subjects Protection Committee to be exempt from human subjects review under federal guidelines.

Develop Options for Conducting the Cross-Agency Evaluation

Reviewing the literature and seeking expert input yielded a number of recommendations for approaching an evaluation of the efficiency, effectiveness, and efficacy of public awareness campaigns. While generating evaluation options, we operated under the following three assumptions: (1) to align with the CAP-G, the evaluation should focus on service members, veterans, and their families; (2) to be efficient, the evaluation should focus on shared desired outcomes across campaigns; and (3) to be comprehensive, the evaluation should assess the effectiveness and efficiency of campaigns. The resulting evaluation options were designed to evaluate whether the selected campaigns reach their intended target population and achieve shared desired short- and long-term outcomes. Thus, the options were organized around evaluating campaign *scope and content* (goals, messages, target audiences, and associated materials), *dissemination* (how campaign materials reach target audiences), *efficacy* (the likelihood that the campaigns, as designed, would achieve their desired outcomes), *effectiveness* (whether the campaigns actually achieved the desired short- and long-term outcomes with the intended target populations), and *efficiency* (whether campaigns were able to achieve their desired outcomes in ways that were cost-beneficial or cost-effective). These options were designed based on recommendations from experts and the literature review (Table 2.1) and tailored based on the shared target populations and desired outcomes common across campaigns (described in detail in Chapter Four). While these recommendations guided the design of the options, it is important to note that issues related to timeline and available resources also factored into the final evaluation design. Table 2.2 summarizes the evaluation options and the types of evaluation questions each option is intended to answer.

Because of timeline demands and resource constraints, the cross-agency evaluation used methods that did not require primary data collection. These included an evaluation of the scope and content of campaigns to determine their alignment, over-

Table 2.1
Evaluation Recommendations from Experts and the Literature Aligned with Evaluation Methods

Key Evaluation Questions	Related Recommendations	Source of Recommendation
Cross-agency evaluation methods		
Scope and content: How do campaigns align with or complement each other?	• No recommendations	
Dissemination: Do campaigns reach their target audiences?	• Incorporate social media into evaluation, given the role social media plays dissemination.	Experts
	• Assess campaign reach by incorporating measures of message exposure and number of people who have contact with campaign materials.	Literature review

Table 2.1—Continued

Key Evaluation Questions	Related Recommendations	Source of Recommendation
Outcome evaluation methods		
Efficacy: Is it likely that campaigns, as designed and implemented, will achieve their outcomes?	• Consider efficacy trials, which can provide useful information but test artificial conditions.	Experts
Effectiveness: Did the campaigns achieve their goals?	• Administer repeated assessments over time in the target population. • If feasible, incorporate a control or comparison population into an effectiveness trial of the campaign. • Examine the impact of mental health campaigns on individuals with unmet mental health needs (i.e., the desired target population vs. the general public). • Evaluate the impact of mental health public awareness campaigns on initiation of treatment-seeking (i.e., the desired target behavior).	Both experts and literature review
	• Assess campaign exposure using measures that guard against false memories. • Positive attitudes toward individuals with mental health conditions and mental health treatment are important to measure but are not necessarily linked to help-seeking. • Knowledge of mental illness signs and symptoms and available resources may be a prerequisite to help-seeking. • Social norms may be linked with help-seeking, so they should be measured. • Measures of behavioral intentions and self-efficacy may serve as helpful intermediate outcomes. • Measures of treatment engagement, mental health, and quality of life may be too distal to capture. • Evaluations of public awareness campaigns targeting substance use should assess the stigma specific to substance use.	Experts
	• Employ rigorous sampling procedures.	Literature review
Efficiency: Are campaigns able to achieve outcomes in a cost-effective or cost-beneficial way?	• Consider cost analyses, which can more accurately represent the contributions of campaigns.	Experts

Table 2.2
Campaign Evaluation Designs

Key Evaluation Questions	Detailed Subquestions	Evaluation Options That Answer Each Question
Cross-agency evaluation methods		
Scope and content: How do campaigns align with or complement each other?	• Where are there overlaps or gaps in campaign scope and content? • What are the unique contributions of campaigns?	Categorize the content of campaign messages.
Dissemination: Do campaigns reach their target audiences?	• What is the reach of campaigns? Are those who are reached part of campaigns' target audiences? • How is reach related to campaign desired short- and long-term outcomes?	Conduct secondary analysis of process data.
	• Were campaigns or associated resources mentioned among those engaged in discussion of mental health and mental health treatment on Twitter?	Assess content shared about mental health on Twitter.
Efficacy: Is it likely that campaigns, as designed and implemented, will achieve their desired outcomes?	• Does the campaign follow best practices in its design and dissemination?	Conduct expert panel assessment of alignment between campaign design and best practices.
Outcome evaluation methods		
Efficacy: Is it likely that campaigns, as designed and implemented, will achieve their goals?	• Does exposure to campaign materials affect desired short-term outcomes as intended?	Test the efficacy of campaign messages.
Effectiveness: Did the campaigns achieve their goals?	• What is the association between campaign exposure and identified desired short- and long-term outcomes?	Conduct a survey to compare those exposed to the campaign with those not exposed.
Efficiency: Are the campaigns able to achieve desired outcomes in a cost-effective or cost-beneficial way?	• Do the benefits of the campaign outweigh the costs? • What amount of change in treatment-seeking is needed to yield a positive economic return?	Assess campaigns' cost relative to outcomes.

lap, or unique contributions, as well as an assessment of their dissemination efforts. These methods were all determined by the RAND Human Subjects Protection Committee to be exempt from human subjects review under federal guidelines.

Phase 2: Conduct a Cross-Agency Evaluation of Campaigns

For this cross-agency evaluation, we conducted a multimethod assessment of the scope, content, and dissemination of each selected campaign with an intentional emphasis on exploring approaches to identifying summary measures or findings across campaigns that speak to the campaigns' collective efficiency (i.e., whether they work together). Neither alignment nor efficiency was an intentional part of the campaigns' design, but because of the campaigns' common goals (i.e., to get service members and veterans access to mental health care) and the national push for these supports, it is critical to determine their collective contribution and ways in which they can work together better in the future. The cross-agency evaluation relied on four complementary methods:

1. Categorize the content of campaign messages.
2. Analyze process data collected by campaigns.
3. Assess content shared about mental health on Twitter.
4. Assess whether campaigns follow best practices in design and dissemination.

This evaluation provided information about whether campaigns are reaching the intended target populations, are part of national Twitter conversations about mental health, and are following best practices in campaign messaging and design. Because these evaluation methods did not use primary data collected from campaign target populations, this phase does not provide an empirical evaluation of campaign effectiveness. However, the Phase 3 evaluation will use primary data collection to assess efficacy of the DoD campaign. The cross-agency evaluation methods are briefly summarized here, with more-detailed description of the methods appearing in Appendixes C–F.

Categorize Campaign Content

This method was used to identify gaps and overlap in messaging within and across the mental health public awareness campaigns. Between November 2015 and January 2016, RAND staff conducted an analysis of all available campaign content, including RWC, MTC, VCL, and Recovery Month websites, articles, video and audio content, and print materials. All content was systematically coded according to a set of criteria based on the social marketing and communication literature. We created a database to capture the coding, organized by campaign. Specifically, we adapted a strategy used in coding informational resources for previous RAND studies (Tanielian and Jaycox, 2008; Meredith et al., 2008) to code all content on the following: (1) relevance to the target populations; (2) alignment with campaign goals; (3) function within the campaign (e.g., educational information, resources to promote help-seeking, promotion of RWC); and (4) whether the content provided connections to services, additional information, or support. We also reviewed campaign content to determine how campaigns cross-referenced or linked to one another. A summary of the content reviewed and a more detailed description of the review process are included in Appendix C.

Analyze Process Data Collected by Campaigns

All of the agencies routinely collect various process metrics to track the dissemination of their mental health public awareness campaigns. Agencies regularly maintain process metrics on their campaign websites, social media sites (e.g., Facebook, YouTube), public service announcements (PSAs), attendance at conferences and events, dissemination of campaign materials, and collaborations with partner organizations. To assess dissemination efforts, we requested a limited set of process data that were collected across agencies in December 2015. We focused our analysis on types of process data that were available from at least two campaigns, and individual campaigns may have other process data that are not reported here.

Given that campaign websites serve as the central hub for storing and disseminating information and resources, we analyzed website process metrics for multiple years (2012–2015[1]) to examine longitudinal trends.

For all other vehicles of campaign dissemination, we obtained process metrics for 2015 only. As shown in Table 2.3, agencies collected process data on similar dissemination vehicles, with the exception of social media. RWC and Recovery Month use Facebook, YouTube, and Twitter and have associated data. MTC uses Facebook and YouTube (but not Twitter) and collects associated data. In contrast, VCL does not use social media, so it does not track such metrics.

We analyzed available process metrics for each campaign to answer the following questions about their collective campaigns: (1) How many people were reached by the mental health public awareness campaigns? (2) How did users engage with the mental health public awareness campaigns? and (3) Who are the users of the mental health public awareness campaigns? We could not determine the degree to which the campaigns reached their target audiences because the campaigns do not collect information

Table 2.3
Campaign Process Data Sources

Data Source	RWC	MTC	VCL	Recovery Month
Website	x	x	x	x
Radio PSAs	x	x	x	x
Television PSAs	x	x	x	x
Conferences or events	x	x	x	x
Campaign materials	x	x	x	x
Partner organizations	x	x	x	x
Facebook	x	x		x
YouTube	x	x		x
Twitter	x			x

about whether those exposed to the campaigns are part of their target audiences. More

---

[1]   Though website analytic data were available for 2011, we chose not to analyze them because the agencies did not all use the same website analytics tracking program at that time and different analytics packages may determine metrics differently.

details on the methods used to analyze secondary process evaluation data can be found in Appendix D.

Assess Content Shared About Mental Health on Twitter

To better understand the dynamic relationship between campaign communication and social media, we assessed the content generated by those discussing mental health–related topics on Twitter. We selected Twitter as the social media platform to explore because Twitter data are publicly accessible in a way that other platforms' data are not, so Twitter is best suited to this type of analysis. Specifically, Twitter messages ("tweets") were coded to determine whether they were relevant to mental health (i.e., contained mental health–specific language or referenced mental health status or treatment). Once a tweet was coded as mental health–relevant, it was then further coded by

- type: whether the tweet (1) communicates about the thoughts or feelings of the author or a person other than the author (i.e., self-disclosure), (2) offers information about a topic or resource to help address mental health problems, or (3) appropriates or borrows mental health language to describe a non–mental health event (e.g., "the weather is bipolar today")
- topic: the specific mental health content or condition(s) referenced in the tweet, such as depression, PTSD, or anxiety
- presence of stigmatizing content: whether the tweet used mental health terminology in a derogatory way (e.g., "psycho") or negatively referred to mental health–related topics (e.g., people with mental health disorders, the treatment process, or service providers).

The coding scheme was designed to help describe the content of mental health tweets and was iteratively developed using small sets of pilot data that were hand-coded and then analyzed to find a set of codes that would provide detailed information on the content of tweets, without compromising the reliability of the computer-automated coding model.

To understand the mental health discussion on Twitter, we acquired Twitter data, then coded them for content. We developed independent search strategies for identifying tweets that contained content relevant to mental health or related to the campaign, then used a third-party service to apply the search and provide resulting data sets. Coding the tweets involved having researchers code a set of approximately 5,000 tweets by hand and then developing a computer-based automated coding model to use on the full data set of tweets. Three researchers hand-coded 4,760 tweets using a set of standardized codes. We calculated rater agreement using a mean of pairwise Cohen's kappa, a common metric of coding consistency, and achieved fair to excellent agreement for most codes. We then used the results of this coding to create a set of automated coding models that could replicate the human coding on the full data set of 13.4 million tweets. Frequently occurring tweet characteristics could be modeled successfully, but infrequently occurring tweet characteristics could not be modeled successfully.

To determine how campaign content is being used, we also examined the social network structure of Twitter users and retweets around the four campaigns, as well as the posting of campaign-related information on Twitter. Specifically, we assessed whether agencies are connecting with users who have the greatest reach (e.g., greatest number of followers and retweets) and are able to further spread the campaigns' key messages. In our data set of 13.4 million tweets, we identified 2.3 million that were relevant to mental health. Among the relevant tweets, we identified 570,000 "directed" tweets (i.e., ones that explicitly mentioned another user). We used the presence of a directed tweet as an indication of connection between users. We combined these connections to map out the network of users who tweet about mental health and then computed how central each user was to the network. This computation takes into account the number of connections a user has and the number of connections that their connections have. We used this centrality measure to assess the influence of users who engaged with the campaign content. More information on the methods used to analyze Twitter data can be found in Appendix E.

Assess Whether Campaigns Follow Best Practices in Design and Dissemination

Incorporating expert input into evaluations is common practice (Fitch et al., 2001; Nevo, 1985; Wroblewski and Leitner, 2009), and we opted to use a modified version of the RAND/UCLA Appropriateness Method to use expert input to develop a checklist of best practices for mental health public awareness campaigns. Experts then rated each evaluated campaign against a subset of the checklist items. The RAND/UCLA Appropriateness Method (Fitch et al., 2001; van het Loo and Kahan, 1999) is a widely used systematic technique for obtaining expert judgment on topics that lack formalized guidelines to direct practice, such as mental health public awareness campaign design.

To generate a preliminary checklist of best practices for mental health public awareness campaigns, we began with a list developed previously for an evaluation of RWC (Acosta, Martin, et al., 2012). We then conducted a supplemental literature review to identify any missing best practices and crafted additional potential checklist items. A panel consisting of experts in five key areas (applied communication campaigns, behavior change, health communication, mental health and barriers to mental health care, and military mental health) rated each proposed checklist item on two dimensions: its validity (i.e., having adequate scientific evidence or professional consensus to support a link between the checklist item and campaign effectiveness) and its importance (i.e., critical influence on the development or implementation of a campaign). Items receiving average validity and importance ratings of at least 5 (on a Likert scale of 1–7, with 7 being very important or very valid) were included in a final checklist. Experts then rated each of the campaigns using the final checklist items. Following each rating, we held a virtual meeting of experts to discuss and finalize their ratings and to gather qualitative feedback on additional areas for improvement for each campaign that were not covered in the checklist rating exercise. More information on the methods used for the expert panel can be found in Appendix F.

Limitations of the Cross-Agency Evaluation

In alignment with the notion that the evaluation is to respond to a CAP-G, the cross-agency evaluation was intentionally designed to address goals, messages, and processes shared across multiple agencies and campaigns. As a result, the evaluation presented here is not intended to serve as a full and comprehensive evaluation of each campaign. In addition, this cross-agency evaluation examined only the scope, content, and dissemination of the campaigns; it was not able to determine whether the campaigns are effective or cost-effective. Many campaigns take an integrative approach to their design, aiming to create a campaign in which the "whole is greater than the sum of the parts and the optimal message impact is achieved" (Cheng, Kotler, and Lee, 2011, p. 10; Schultz and Schultz, 2004). Given that we did not evaluate campaign efficacy or effectiveness for the cross-agency evaluation, we are unable to draw any conclusions about this aspect of campaigns.

Each method used to conduct the evaluation is subject to its own limitations. The content analysis is limited in that it does not include campaign content developed in the time since the analysis was conducted. The secondary analysis of process data relied on data available from all campaigns and thus does not include process data unique to a single campaign. The process data we used to determine reach did not allow us to identify unique users, so much of the data reported (e.g., the number of page views on a website) represent an upper bound on the number of possible individuals who could have been exposed. The expert panel findings are not generalizable both because of the explicit focus on military populations and because they rely on the feedback of a targeted group of experts. In addition, the best-practices checklist that expert panel members used to assess campaigns was developed as part of this evaluation and was not available to campaign developers during the creation of the campaigns. Thus, they may not have been aware of some best practices on the list. Finally, just two of the campaigns—RWC and Recovery Month—have active Twitter accounts, which limits the usefulness of Twitter data for examining the campaigns' reach and influence. The publication of this report was significantly delayed because of a major reorganization at the Defense Health Agency, which is responsible for overseeing this work. By the time this report was released, the interagency task force that requested this evaluation was dissolved and the federal emphasis on the CAP-G was diminished.

Phase 3: Conduct Outcome Evaluation

As mentioned previously, this report focuses on the cross-agency report, which does not rely on any primary data collection. Initially, there was to be a Phase 3 cross-agency evaluation to : (1) test the efficacy of campaign messages in changing undesirable attitudes and behaviors and (2) assess campaigns' benefits relative to outcomes. A first step was to assess the feasibility of conducting a cost-benefit evaluation of the four campaigns. To calculate the necessary sample size for the evaluation, we obtained campaign costs, and determined the number of treatment seekers needed for the campaign to break even with its cost and the associated population change that an evaluation would need to detect. This feasibility test determined that the sample size needed for an evaluation with 80-percent power was greater than the total population of military personnel and veterans. Given that the necessary sample size exceeds the population to be sampled, an appropriately powered cost-benefit evaluation was not feasible. Therefore, it was determined that an efficacy test was the most appropriate and feasible way to evaluation cross-agency campaign outcomes. However, because of a major reorganization of the Defense Health Agency, the regulatory approvals to conduct the efficacy test were significantly delayed, and thus the VA and SAMHSA campaigns decided to withdraw from the Phase 3 evaluation. In April 2019 it was determined that only the Real Warriors campaign, DoD's campaign, would move forward with the efficacy test. Results from this study will be forthcoming.

CHAPTER THREE

Campaigns Selected for Cross-Agency Evaluation

This chapter describes the goals, target populations, key messages, theoretical basis, dissemination methods, and campaign-tracking efforts of the four campaigns selected for the cross-agency evaluation.

Real Warriors Campaign

Despite attempts from DoD and VA to enhance mental health services, many service members do not seek care when they have mental health problems (Tanielian and Jaycox, 2008). To address this issue, DoD instituted RWC in 2009. RWC is a large-scale "multi-media public health awareness campaign designed to encourage service members, veterans, and their families coping with invisible wounds to reach out for appropriate care or support" (RWC, undated-d). The Psychological Health Center of Excellence (PHCoE) within the Defense Health Agency oversees the campaign. At the time of evaluation, PHCoE was known as the Deployment Health Clinical Center, within the Defense Centers of Excellence for Psychological Health and Traumatic Brain Injury (DCoE), and thus we refer to DCoE throughout this report. RWC supports multiple target audiences and encourages them to "reach out for help to cope with invisible wounds" (RWC, undated-d). Various digital and traditional marketing platforms are leveraged with the aim of encouraging help-seeking behavior among service members and veterans coping with psychological wounds. Figure 3.1 shows a logic model summarizing the broad goals, the target populations, and the specific desired short- and long-term outcomes of the campaign. (The achievement of desired outcomes is an indicator of whether a campaign is meeting its goals.)

Goals and Target Population
RWC has five goals:

1. Reduce misperceptions and combat myths of mental health concerns and treatment through education.

2. Foster a culture of support for psychological health—i.e., that seeking help is a sign of strength.
3. Restore faith in the Military Health System.
4. Improve support systems (e.g., friends, family) for services members and veterans with mental health concerns.
5. Empower behavior change among service members and veterans.

These goals, expanded from goals initially set in 2009, further clarify and direct campaign activities. The campaign targets primary audiences of active duty service members ages 18–29, active duty service members of other ages, members of the National Guard and Reserve, veterans, and military families, as well as secondary audiences of health care professionals and line leaders.

Key Messages

RWC maintains six core messages in support of outlined campaign goals. The core messages are:

1. Experiencing psychological stress as a result of deployment is common.
2. Unlike visible wounds, psychological wounds and brain injuries are often invisible and can go untreated if not identified.
3. Successful treatment and positive outcomes are greatly assisted by early intervention.
4. Service members and their families should feel comfortable reaching out to their units and chain of command for support.
5. Reaching out is a sign of strength that benefits service members, their families, their units, and their services.
6. Warriors are not alone in coping with mental health concerns (i.e., there is a vast network of support and resources throughout each of the services).

RWC augments these messages, as needed, based on current military trends (e.g., troop drawdown), how stigma is being discussed in DoD reports, and other current events that are being discussed in traditional or social media.

Theoretical Basis

The goals of RWC are guided by the Health Belief Model (HBM). The HBM explains which beliefs should be targeted in communication campaigns to cause positive health behaviors (Carpenter, 2010). The theory behind the model posits that if individuals perceive a negative health outcome to be severe, believe that they are susceptible to the negative outcome, perceive the benefits to behaviors that reduce likelihood of that outcome to be high, and perceive the barriers to adopting those behaviors to be low, then those individuals are likely to engage in those behaviors

Figure 3.1
Real Warriors Campaign Logic Model

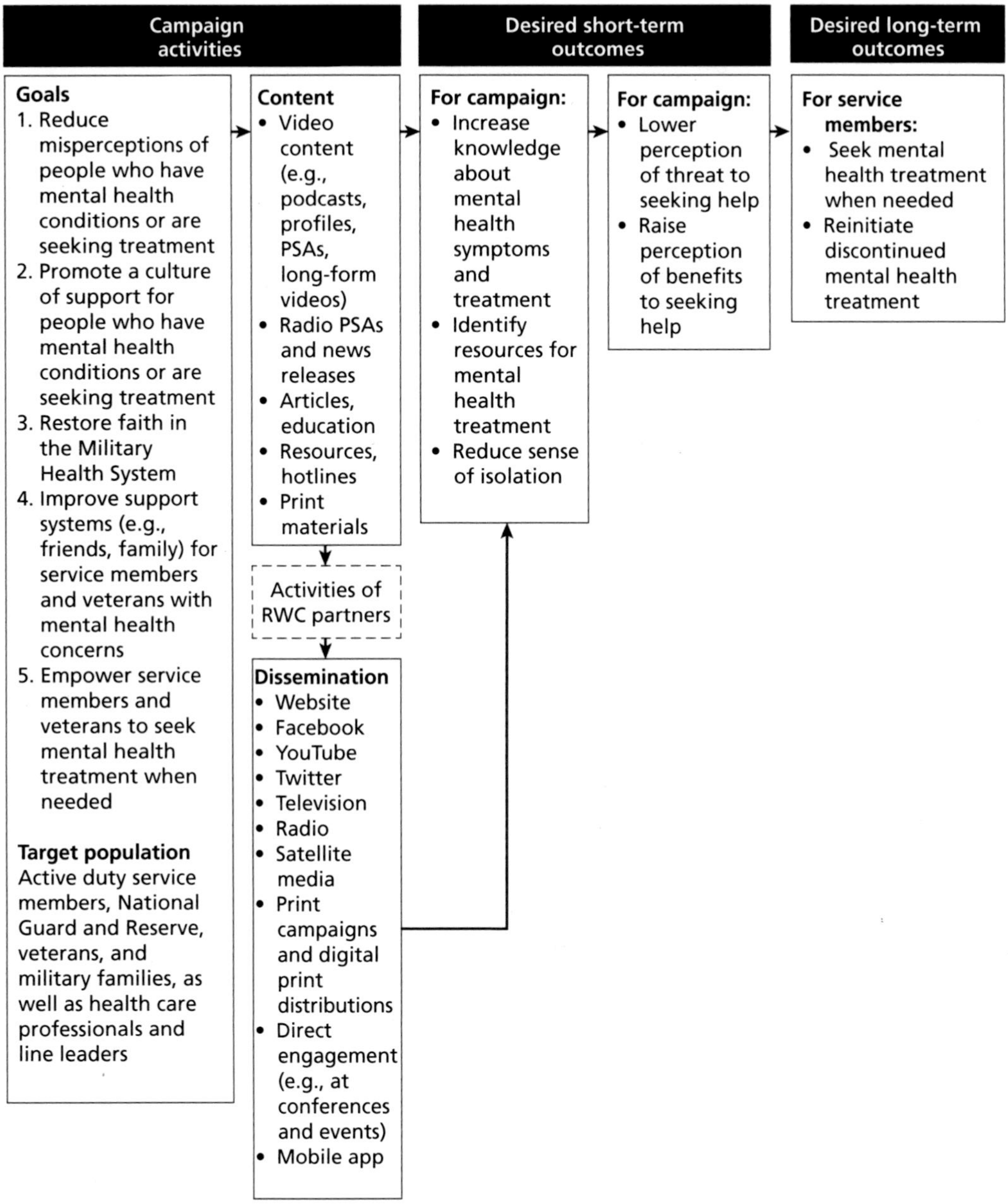

Campaign activities		Desired short-term outcomes		Desired long-term outcomes
Goals 1. Reduce misperceptions of people who have mental health conditions or are seeking treatment 2. Promote a culture of support for people who have mental health conditions or are seeking treatment 3. Restore faith in the Military Health System 4. Improve support systems (e.g., friends, family) for service members and veterans with mental health concerns 5. Empower service members and veterans to seek mental health treatment when needed **Target population** Active duty service members, National Guard and Reserve, veterans, and military families, as well as health care professionals and line leaders	**Content** • Video content (e.g., podcasts, profiles, PSAs, long-form videos) • Radio PSAs and news releases • Articles, education • Resources, hotlines • Print materials ┌─────────────┐ Activities of RWC partners └─────────────┘ **Dissemination** • Website • Facebook • YouTube • Twitter • Television • Radio • Satellite media • Print campaigns and digital print distributions • Direct engagement (e.g., at conferences and events) • Mobile app	**For campaign:** • Increase knowledge about mental health symptoms and treatment • Identify resources for mental health treatment • Reduce sense of isolation	**For campaign:** • Lower perception of threat to seeking help • Raise perception of benefits to seeking help	**For service members:** • Seek mental health treatment when needed • Reinitiate discontinued mental health treatment

RAND RR1612-3.1

(Carpenter, 2010). The model organizes these assumptions into four constructs: (1) perceived susceptibility, (2) perceived severity, (3) perceived barriers, and (4) perceived benefits. In 2015, the campaign evaluated the use of the HBM (and examined alternative behavior change models) and determined that the HBM was still an appropriate guiding theory for RWC.

Dissemination Methods

RWC uses both digital and coalition-building platforms to reach target audiences. Primary dissemination methods are a website (including a mobile version), social media platforms, a mobile application, traditional media (television and radio PSAs), partnership activities, conferences, and events. The campaign's website serves as a central location that houses information, resources, and links to corresponding social media websites. Resources include downloadable materials, e-cards, video profiles of service members, PSAs, a live chat function (with an outreach center), and articles that provide tools, tips, and resources for each target population. The site also contains personal "vignettes" (profiles) of service members that allow target populations to learn from the experiences of the profiled service members. The website features a shopping cart that visitors can use to order free print materials. RWC uses television and radio to reach audiences. RWC also connects to target populations through Facebook, Twitter, YouTube, Scribd, RSS web feeds, message boards, podcasts, widgets, and banners.

RWC collaborates with a variety of DoD, service-specific, and federal organizations, as well as national and local not-for-profits that share the campaign's mission and assist with reaching target audiences. In addition to partnerships, RWC disseminates information and materials to target populations through public outlets such as installation events (e.g., "Game Day" events), speaking engagements, and exhibitions at military and health industry conferences and events.

Campaign Tracking

RWC tracks metrics for media relations, outreach, interactivity (e.g., page views, downloads, emails), social media, and multimedia. Media relations metrics include the number of news clips and PSAs shared by national or statewide media, the cumulative views and downloads of video profiles, and feedback from interviews with RWC leadership and volunteers. Outreach metrics capture data for partnership engagement (e.g., the number of partners linking to the campaign website, the total partner networks), conferences and events (e.g., total number of events attended, total number of audience members), and materials dissemination (e.g., number of materials orders, cumulative number of installations, command units and other organization requesting materials). Interactivity metrics collect information on website visitors, visits to the mobile website, page views to resources, and referral website traffic. The campaign collects metrics for all social media and digital platforms (e.g., Facebook page likes,

Twitter followers, snapshots of digital audiences). Finally, RWC tracks the number of video profiles produced or updated, radio or television PSAs produced, and podcast listeners for its multimedia activities. The campaign also collects data on clicks to its "Seek Help" and "Find Care" buttons that connect target audiences to TRICARE, VA, and immediate crisis resources, such as the Military Crisis Line (see the "Veterans Crisis Line" section later in this chapter). When tracking metrics, RWC purposefully avoids collecting information about user characteristics in an effort to protect confidentiality.

Make the Connection

MTC is a VA public awareness campaign designed to promote mental health to veterans and their supportive networks through education and outreach, and to motivate and facilitate help-seeking among veterans with mental health needs. Launched in 2011, MTC includes personal testimonials from fellow veterans that describe help-seeking experiences, emphasizing recovery and conveying positive treatment outcomes. Information on symptoms, conditions, and treatment options is organized by life experiences and challenges rather than primarily focusing on diagnosis or illness. Information on VA and community resources are made readily available on MTC to facilitate treatment-seeking. Videos that target family and friends of veterans are also included in the testimonials. A summary of the broad goals, the target population, and the specific desired short- and long-term outcomes can be found in Figure 3.2.

Goal and Target Population

MTC was developed to target the following primary goals (Tenhula, 2016):

- Foster positive conversations about mental health and engage veterans in sharing stories of mental health challenges and recovery with other veterans.
- Reduce barriers to help-seeking, such as stigma, and improve attitudes and beliefs related to mental health conditions and use of treatment services among veterans.
- Educate veterans and their supportive networks by presenting accurate information on common life events, mental health symptoms, and conditions in non-clinical, easy-to-read language.
- Promote help-seeking by increasing awareness of VA and community resources among veterans and their supportive networks.

Secondary goals include the following:

- Encourage audiences to share video testimonials and campaign materials with veterans and their families.

Figure 3.2
Make the Connection Logic Model

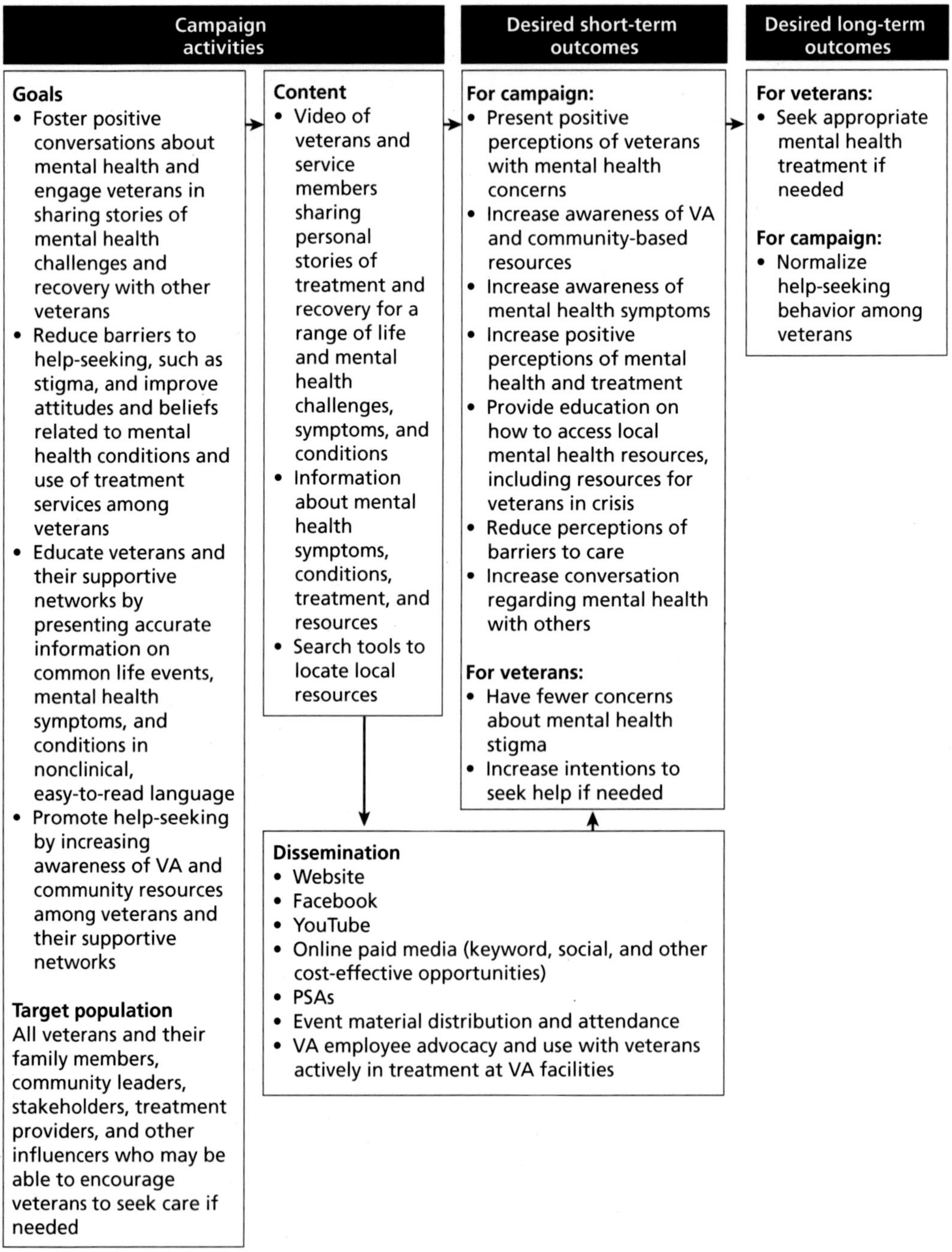

Campaign activities		Desired short-term outcomes	Desired long-term outcomes
Goals • Foster positive conversations about mental health and engage veterans in sharing stories of mental health challenges and recovery with other veterans • Reduce barriers to help-seeking, such as stigma, and improve attitudes and beliefs related to mental health conditions and use of treatment services among veterans • Educate veterans and their supportive networks by presenting accurate information on common life events, mental health symptoms, and conditions in nonclinical, easy-to-read language • Promote help-seeking by increasing awareness of VA and community resources among veterans and their supportive networks **Target population** All veterans and their family members, community leaders, stakeholders, treatment providers, and other influencers who may be able to encourage veterans to seek care if needed	**Content** • Video of veterans and service members sharing personal stories of treatment and recovery for a range of life and mental health challenges, symptoms, and conditions • Information about mental health symptoms, conditions, treatment, and resources • Search tools to locate local resources **Dissemination** • Website • Facebook • YouTube • Online paid media (keyword, social, and other cost-effective opportunities) • PSAs • Event material distribution and attendance • VA employee advocacy and use with veterans actively in treatment at VA facilities	**For campaign:** • Present positive perceptions of veterans with mental health concerns • Increase awareness of VA and community-based resources • Increase awareness of mental health symptoms • Increase positive perceptions of mental health and treatment • Provide education on how to access local mental health resources, including resources for veterans in crisis • Reduce perceptions of barriers to care • Increase conversation regarding mental health with others **For veterans:** • Have fewer concerns about mental health stigma • Increase intentions to seek help if needed	**For veterans:** • Seek appropriate mental health treatment if needed **For campaign:** • Normalize help-seeking behavior among veterans

- Invite health care professionals to incorporate video testimonials into clinical practice.
- Increase social media engagement through "likes," comments, and shares, and increase the number of subscriptions to the MTC YouTube channel.

MTC's target audience includes veterans of all ages, service branches, and eras of service. The campaign has a special emphasis on trying to reach veterans who are not already active users of VA services. The campaign also seeks to provide informational resources to the general public, family members, treatment providers, and other influencers who may be able to encourage veterans to seek care if needed.

Key Messages

Key messages of MTC focus on "connectedness" among veterans, leveraging the power of peer-to-peer influence among veterans to create a new dialog centered around normalizing help-seeking, and conveying that recovery is possible and treatment works.

Theoretical Basis

The outreach strategy of MTC is theoretically grounded in a contact-based approach to stigma reduction (Corrigan et al., 2012). According to this approach, behavior change is more likely when the message is delivered by a person to whom the recipient can relate—someone the recipient can recognize as having gone through similar experiences and having similar interests and goals. MTC applies this contact-based approach to both content and the web experience. While videos are designed to convey messages "by veterans for veterans," the user can also create a customized web experience and access personal video narratives of veterans describing their mental health recovery based on their particular gender, service era, service branch, and combat experience. As already indicated, videos are also available for supportive networks. Exposure to these individualized, personal narratives is intended to instill trust, credibility, and a sense of community.

Dissemination Methods

MTC maintains a collection of over 600 videos of more than 400 veterans (and loved ones) sharing their personal stories of mental health recovery. This large collection allows for relatively precise matching between users and the videos to which they are exposed. The website allows for tailoring the user's experience based on his or her characteristics (gender, service era, military branch, and combat experience). Personal vignettes are used to help educate veterans—via the experiences of other veterans—on how to understand and navigate mental health challenges. The video testimonials depict veterans discussing a wide variety of mental health symptoms or challenging life events, including personal, financial, medical, or legal issues. In addition, the campaign website provides a variety of resources, including e-books, mental health self-assessment tools, links to a mobile app for mental health, and search tools to locate local mental health resources. The resource locator is linked to VA resources, the National Resource Directory, and SAMHSA's Behavioral Health Treatment Services Locator. Television and radio advertisements and social media channels are utilized to disseminate MTC information. The campaign also reaches health professional audiences by disseminating materials through national conference participation and through health care organizations and by providing a designated section on the website for clinicians.

Consistent with the campaign's primary goals, VA created content with the intention of providing a broad range of information on mental health and treatment (primarily from existing VA resources) in nonclinical, nonstigmatizing language that target audiences would find easy to read. As part of this process, a team of subject-matter experts was engaged to develop, review, and refine materials. Campaign content intentionally does not include citations or other source information in an effort to use plain language and appeal to veterans who may seek to avoid mental illness–related labels.

Campaign Tracking

Tracking user information is not an aim of MTC. To build trust, MTC purposefully avoids tracking the characteristics that users provide to customize their web experience. Many conventional web metrics are recorded, however, provided they do not conflict with the campaign's commitment to user confidentiality. For example, the campaign tracks page views, time spent on the website, and whether users access search tools to locate local resources. MTC also tracks social media web traffic and monitors these platforms continuously for the purpose of responding to user requests for information. Additionally, the MTC social media platforms are monitored 24 hours a day, 365 days a year to ensure that visitors who appear to be in crisis are acknowledged, supported, and directed to crisis intervention resources, such as VCL (see the next section) or SAMHSA's National Suicide Prevention Lifeline. Furthermore, MTC social media moderators have direct connections with VCL and will request support when a social media user appears to be suicidal.

Veterans Crisis Line

VCL is a free, confidential service available 24 hours a day, 365 days a year that provides specialized care to veterans in crisis and resources to their families and friends. VCL can be accessed by telephone and using text and online chat platforms. A proportion of responders on the crisis line are veterans themselves, further personalizing the experience for callers. VCL provides immediate crisis intervention and, when necessary, connects veterans with local services, such as VA suicide prevention coordinators or emergency services. The call center was established as a partnership among VA, SAMHSA, and SAMHSA's National Suicide Prevention Lifeline. Through this collaboration, there is one central phone number. When the line is answered, veterans (or service members) are prompted to press "1" for transfer to VCL. Responders address caller concerns and assess risk, connect the caller with appropriate available resources, and work to help overcome barriers to treatment-seeking (e.g., transportation issues). VCL is also co-branded as the Military Crisis Line (MCL) for active duty service members and marketed as such by DoD.

This evaluation focused on the public awareness campaign for promoting awareness and use of VCL, not the actual operations of the crisis line. Further, we focused only on the public awareness campaign that intends to increase awareness and use of VCL among veterans and their families (not of MCL among active duty service members). The campaign logic model (Figure 3.3) summarizes goals, target population, and desired short- and long-term outcomes.

Goal and Target Population

The goal of the VCL campaign is to increase awareness and use of VCL among veterans in crisis, and the campaign places particular emphasis on disseminating information to specific subgroups in the veteran population (e.g., women, veterans under age 20 and over age 45) identified as being at epidemiological risk. Family members of veterans in need are also targets of this campaign.

Key Messages

The key campaign messages are as follows:

- If you are in crisis, contact VCL.
- One call, one text, one conversation can save a life.

In addition to these key messages, VCL has since 2014 used the key theme of "the Power of One" to focus on "the importance of connection, interpersonal relationships, community, and outreach to Veterans" in providing support to veterans (Herrera, 2016). This theme emphasizes how single individuals performing singular acts can make a difference in terms of enabling veterans to feel supported and empowered.

Theoretical Basis

VCL staff did not report a theoretical basis for their efforts to raise awareness of the campaign.

Dissemination Methods

VCL campaign materials are disseminated primarily through grassroots outreach, online advertising, and event attendance; however, such media efforts as out-of-home marketing (i.e., billboards, television and radio PSAs) are also used in select markets. VCL also uses social media channels to disseminate information. Each VA suicide

Figure 3.3
Veterans Crisis Line Logic Model

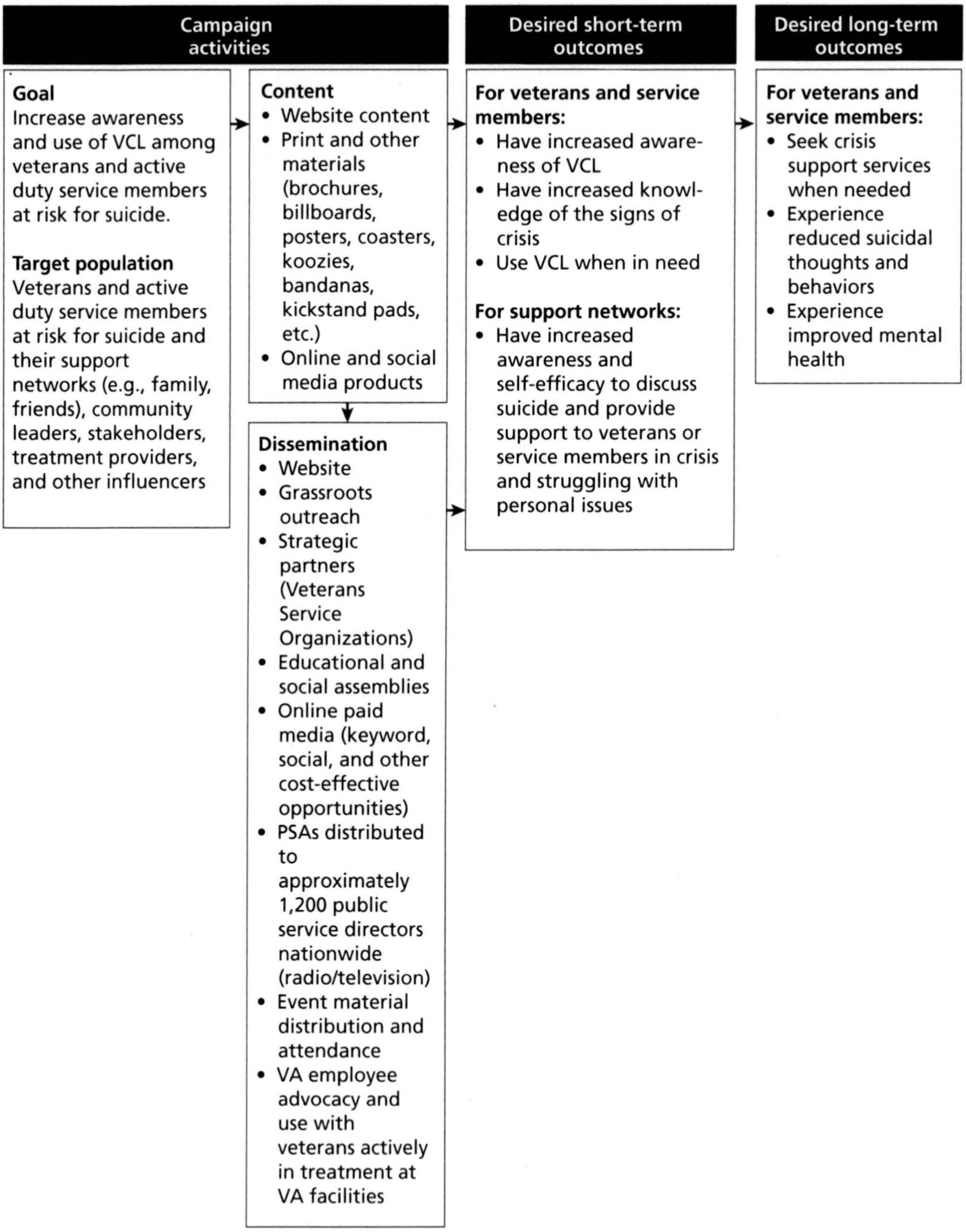

Campaign activities		Desired short-term outcomes	Desired long-term outcomes

Goal
Increase awareness and use of VCL among veterans and active duty service members at risk for suicide.

Target population
Veterans and active duty service members at risk for suicide and their support networks (e.g., family, friends), community leaders, stakeholders, treatment providers, and other influencers

Content
- Website content
- Print and other materials (brochures, billboards, posters, coasters, koozies, bandanas, kickstand pads, etc.)
- Online and social media products

Dissemination
- Website
- Grassroots outreach
- Strategic partners (Veterans Service Organizations)
- Educational and social assemblies
- Online paid media (keyword, social, and other cost-effective opportunities)
- PSAs distributed to approximately 1,200 public service directors nationwide (radio/television)
- Event material distribution and attendance
- VA employee advocacy and use with veterans actively in treatment at VA facilities

For veterans and service members:
- Have increased awareness of VCL
- Have increased knowledge of the signs of crisis
- Use VCL when in need

For support networks:
- Have increased awareness and self-efficacy to discuss suicide and provide support to veterans or service members in crisis and struggling with personal issues

For veterans and service members:
- Seek crisis support services when needed
- Experience reduced suicidal thoughts and behaviors
- Experience improved mental health

prevention coordinator (there is at least one at every VA Medical Center and large community-based outpatient clinic) is required to complete five outreach events each month, which includes dissemination of VCL campaign materials. Events vary across communities and coordinators, but examples include staffing an outreach booth at an air show, distributing brochures at a gun shop, or accepting a speaking invitation from a local veteran service organization. The VCL campaign also uses a website, service partners, celebrity endorsements, brochures, fact sheets, flyers, web banners, and newsletters to disseminate information about the signs of crisis and mental health problems and to provide clear directions on how to access VA resources for support (including resources for those in immediate crisis). Campaign materials are available for public access and use on the VCL website.

Campaign Tracking

The campaign collects implementation and dissemination metrics by tracking the distribution and use of outreach materials. VA researchers have also worked with VCL and the campaign manager to model associations between outreach efforts and changes in call volume surrounding the implementation of messaging. Currently, VA conducts a large survey of veterans (and family members) to surveil determinants (e.g., knowledge, attitudes, social norms) and help-seeking behaviors, and to further examine process metrics (e.g., exposure, reach) related to VCL campaign dissemination.

National Recovery Month

Sponsored by SAMHSA, Recovery Month is held every September and aims to educate Americans about mental health and substance use issues. Now in its 27th year, Recovery Month originally began in 1989 as "Treatment Works! Month" with a focus on recognizing the contributions of substance use treatment professionals in the field of addiction. In 1998, the observance developed into National Alcohol and Drug Addiction Recovery Month and broadened its focus to include the success of individuals in recovery from substance use disorders. In 2011, the observance evolved into Recovery Month and expanded to include mental health and substance use disorders. Though September is Recovery Month, associated events occur throughout the year. Figure 3.4 summarizes goals, target population, and desired short- and long-term outcomes of the campaign.

Goals and Target Population

Recovery Month's primary goal is to communicate to the general population that people with mental health and substance use issues can recover—by modeling the achievements and successes of individuals who have recovered—and that treatment can play a vital role in helping people lead healthy and productive lives. A secondary goal is to celebrate gains made by those in recovery and the contributions of behavioral

Figure 3.4
National Recovery Month Logic Model

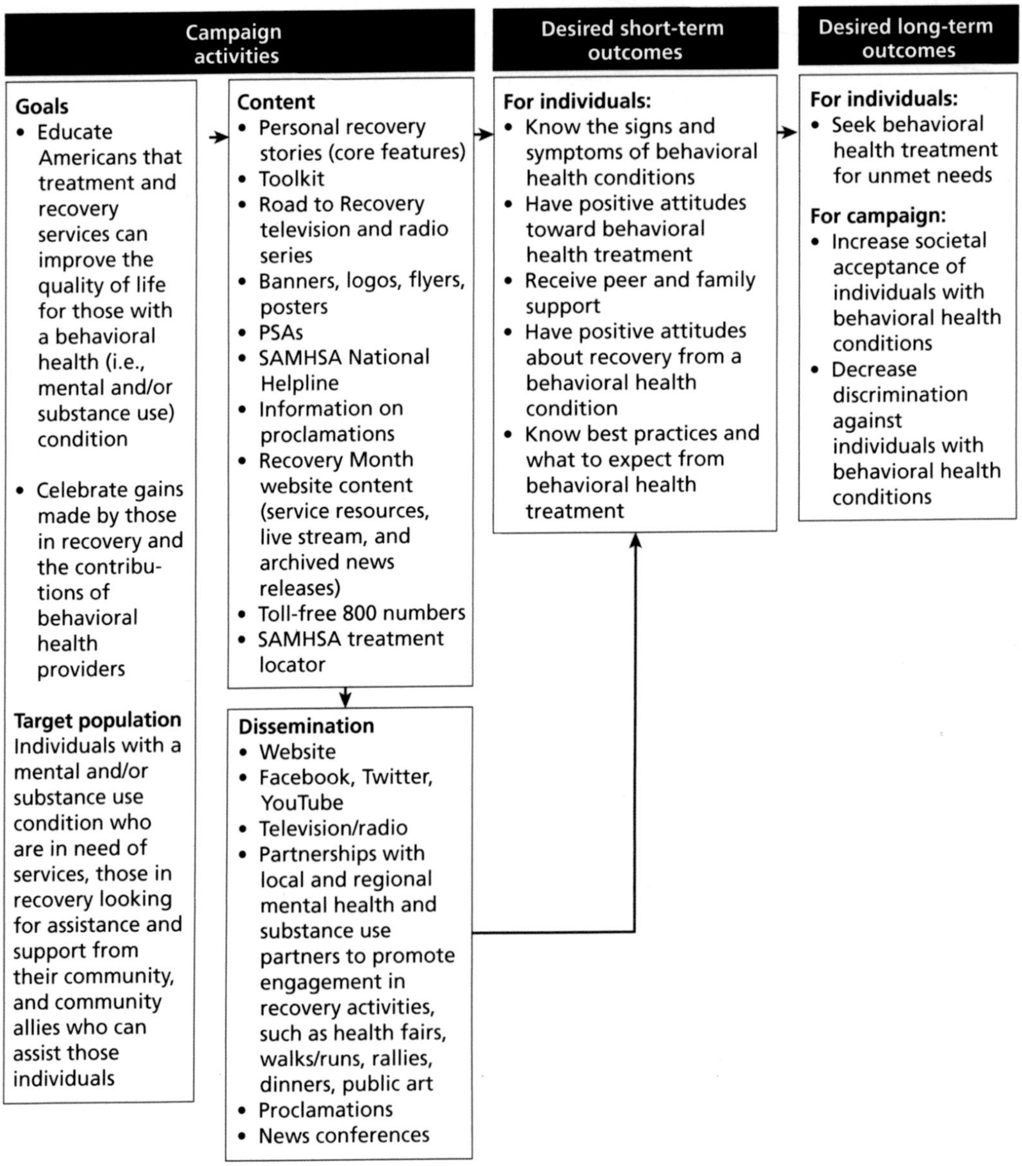

Campaign activities		Desired short-term outcomes	Desired long-term outcomes

Goals
- Educate Americans that treatment and recovery services can improve the quality of life for those with a behavioral health (i.e., mental and/or substance use) condition

- Celebrate gains made by those in recovery and the contributions of behavioral health providers

Target population
Individuals with a mental and/or substance use condition who are in need of services, those in recovery looking for assistance and support from their community, and community allies who can assist those individuals

Content
- Personal recovery stories (core features)
- Toolkit
- Road to Recovery television and radio series
- Banners, logos, flyers, posters
- PSAs
- SAMHSA National Helpline
- Information on proclamations
- Recovery Month website content (service resources, live stream, and archived news releases)
- Toll-free 800 numbers
- SAMHSA treatment locator

Dissemination
- Website
- Facebook, Twitter, YouTube
- Television/radio
- Partnerships with local and regional mental health and substance use partners to promote engagement in recovery activities, such as health fairs, walks/runs, rallies, dinners, public art
- Proclamations
- News conferences

For individuals:
- Know the signs and symptoms of behavioral health conditions
- Have positive attitudes toward behavioral health treatment
- Receive peer and family support
- Have positive attitudes about recovery from a behavioral health condition
- Know best practices and what to expect from behavioral health treatment

For individuals:
- Seek behavioral health treatment for unmet needs

For campaign:
- Increase societal acceptance of individuals with behavioral health conditions
- Decrease discrimination against individuals with behavioral health conditions

health providers. The campaign's focus on recovery has been consistent over the past 15 years, and a new theme highlighting specific aspects of recovery is developed each year in collaboration with a diverse set of more than 200 planning partners. "Join the Voices for Recovery: Visible, Vocal, Valuable!" was the theme for the 2015 Recovery Month, highlighting the importance of peer support and advocacy and of starting conversations about prevention, treatment, and recovery at earlier stages of life. SAMHSA is mandated to improve Americans' behavioral health, so Recovery Month targets the general public and many campaign-related materials are designed for a broad audience. However, several strategies are tailored to service members and veterans. Examples include featuring personal recovery stories of veterans on the Recovery Month website, addressing the role of peer and family support for military service members through episodes of the Recovery Month Road to Recovery television and radio series, and including links to SAMHSA's Veterans and Military Families website in the Recovery Month resource list. The Recovery Month site also includes links to SAMHSA's National Helpline, a referral and information service that is both free and confidential.

Key Messages

Recovery Month's overarching message is that recovery emerges from hope, is person-driven and holistic, and unfolds along diverse pathways. The tagline "Join the Voices for Recovery" has been used in all Recovery Month campaigns since 2002, followed by each year's theme or key message. For example, 2014's theme was "Join the Voices for Recovery: Speak Up, Reach Out" and 2013's was "Join the Voices for Recovery: Together on Pathways to Wellness."

Theoretical Basis

Recovery Month staff indicated that the campaign is based on the social ecological model, which

> emphasizes multiple levels of influence (such as individual, interpersonal, organizational, and community) and the idea that behaviors both shape and are shaped by the social environment. The principles of social ecological models are consistent with social cognitive theory concepts which suggest that creating an environment conducive to change is important to making it easier to adopt healthy behaviors. (Glanz, undated)

Recovery Month targets messages for individuals in recovery and those with mental health and/or substance use disorders, as well as messages for their family and friends, with the aim of creating supportive interpersonal relationships. Recovery Month also coordinates with and supports community-based organizations and works with planning partners to facilitate a supportive and engaged community. Planning partner meetings are convened to solicit input and guidance on what to focus on for each year's theme.

Dissemination Methods

Dissemination centers on National Recovery Month in September, but activities to gear up for Recovery Month (e.g., releasing PSAs and website videos) begin in the spring and events occur throughout the year. Recovery Month's dissemination methods include media outreach; community events; toolkits and collateral materials (e.g., banners, flyers with annual theme); television and radio PSAs; television and radio series (e.g., a talk-show, roundtable format that includes behavioral health experts); interactive web-based activities and information; social media content (e.g., YouTube, Facebook, and Twitter); recovery-related electronic greeting cards (where website visitors could send e-cards to support members of the online recovery community); and new media electronic newsletters that provide information about online tools, tips, and resources for leveraging new media and building an online community. SAMHSA provides a Recovery Month toolkit for local partner organizations to hold their own Recovery Month events to raise awareness about prevention, treatment, and recovery. Events can include hosting a walk, run, or rally; cookouts, dinners, or picnics; public art displays or memorials; and in-person forums, panels, and discussions. The toolkit and media resources are housed on Recovery Month's website. Many materials provide information on multiple resources, including SAMHSA's toll-free National Helpline. In addition, federal, state, and local officials actively promote the campaign by making public proclamations declaring September as National Recovery Month.

Campaign Tracking

A year-end report containing metrics on the dissemination and reach of activities is published and made available on the campaign's website. Information on community events, submitted by their hosts or sponsors, are logged on the campaign's website. The year-end report includes metrics on the number of community events held and the number of attendees. PSAs are tracked with respect to their distribution to television and radio stations, the number of times the PSAs aired, ranking within the media market, and the number of viewer or listener impressions (i.e., the number of times a PSA was viewed or heard). The television series metrics include the number of channels and cable markets that aired the shows, times aired, and views by households. Website analytics are collected on the number of text and video recovery stories submitted to the website and the number of page views (new and returning visitors). For social media, metrics are maintained for Recovery Month's Facebook page (e.g., number of likes, followers), Twitter account (e.g., number of followers, organic impressions), and YouTube account (e.g., number of subscribers, video views). The number of calls made to SAMHSA's National Helpline is also tracked. Finally, the numbers of e-cards sent and of subscribers to the new media e-newsletter are also reported.

CHAPTER FOUR

Campaign Scope

This chapter summarizes our findings from the content analysis of how campaigns align with or complement each other. First, we describe the campaigns' common target populations and desired outcomes, then we explore overlaps and gaps in campaign content, and finally we summarize the extent to which campaigns cross-reference and link to each other.

Target Populations and Desired Outcomes Common Across Campaigns

The four campaigns have distinct, yet overlapping, primary target populations that include service members and veterans. Although each campaign has several target populations, each focuses on a primary target population (Figure 4.1). RWC targets all service members and veterans, and MTC focuses on veterans and service members with unmet mental health needs. VCL targets veterans and service members in crisis and at risk for suicide. Recovery Month has a broader focus on all Americans with mental health and substance use disorders, which includes the nation's service members and veterans.

Campaigns also target support networks (e.g., family, friends) of service members and veterans. All four campaigns had a secondary emphasis on support networks of service members and veterans (or, in Recovery Month's case, the networks of any American with mental health and/or substance use problems). RWC's secondary audiences include line leaders and health professionals. MTC and VCL more broadly serve all members of support networks and those in a position to influence veterans to get care, and Recovery Month targets community allies of individuals with mental health and substance use disorders. When considering the full range of primary and secondary target populations for the campaigns (e.g., service members, veterans, and their support networks, including family, friends, and care providers), each campaign has the potential to have materials applicable to many Americans.

Campaigns share the overlapping desired short- and long-term outcomes of increasing knowledge of mental health symptoms and improving positive percep- tions of individuals with mental health conditions and of mental health treatment. Table 4.1 shows all the desired outcome areas that the campaigns aim to affect (as speci-

Figure 4.1
Overlaps Among the Campaigns' Primary Target Populations

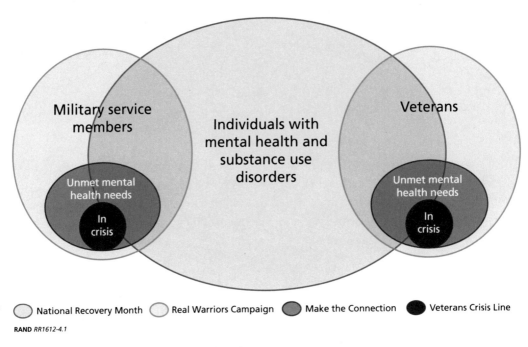

◯ National Recovery Month	◯ Real Warriors Campaign	◯ Make the Connection	● Veterans Crisis Line

RAND RR1612-4.1

fied in the prior campaign logic models and descriptions) and the specific desired outcomes they have in common. We used these desired outcomes to generate a single logic model showing shared campaign activities and desired outcomes (Figure 4.2). Aligned with the CAP-G, all campaigns aim to increase knowledge of mental health symptoms and when to seek mental health care, to improve perceptions of mental health conditions and treatment, and to build confidence to intervene and provide social support.

Campaigns offer messages to reach individuals along the mental health continuum of care. Campaigns offer resources and messages tailored to help individuals who are at risk for mental health conditions, symptomatic and considering mental health treatment, in crisis and in need of immediate support, and in recovery after completing treatment. Figure 4.3 shows a mental health continuum of care and provides example messages and materials from campaigns along the continuum. Though originally developed to conceptualize sailors' and Marines' responses to stress (U.S. Marine Corps, 2010), the continuum can also be used to conceptualize where nonmilitary individuals might fall in terms of responding to stress. For example, the most optimal state is being in the "green" (or ready) zone, optimally functioning and able to handle daily stressors easily, and the least optimal state is being in the red (ill) zone, which indicates distress and symptoms requiring professional care.

As shown in Figure 4.3, we conceptualize the campaigns in terms of this continuum. RWC and MTC focus primarily on raising awareness about mental health and providing information and resources to their target audiences (who are likely in

Table 4.1
Shared Desired Short- and Long-Term Outcomes Across Campaigns

Desired Outcome	Specific Elements of Desired Outcome	RWC	MTC	VCL	Recovery Month
Across all four campaigns					
Self-identify mental health symptoms	Awareness of symptoms	X	X	X	X
	Identified threshold needed for care	X	X	X	X
Know mental health symptoms	Symptoms of distress	X	X	X	X
	Identified thresholds for seeking care	X	X	X	X
Know mental health treatment and available resources	Crisis resources	X	X	X	X
	Treatment options	X	X	X	X
	Referral resources	X	X	X	X
Provide social support	Peer support	X	X	X	X
	Family member support	X	X	X	X
Create confidence to intervene or talk with loved one about mental health	Intervention behaviors (for family or friend)	X	X	X	X
	Efficacy to intervene	X	X	X	X
Initiate treatment-seeking	Initiated appointment[a]	X	X	X	X
	Intentions to seek care	X	X	X	X
Across three of the four campaigns					
Initiate treatment-seeking	Kept appointments	X	X	X	
	Re-initiated care	X	X		X
Improve perceptions of people with mental health conditions	Not permanently "broken"	X	X		X
	Not shameful	X	X		X
Improve perceptions of mental health treatment	Effective	X	X		X
	Easily accessed	X	X		X
	Confidential	X	X	X	
Across two of the four campaigns					
Improve perceptions of people with mental health conditions	Not weak	X	X		

[a] For VCL, "an appointment" is construed as calling VCL.

Figure 4.2
Logic Model Showing Activities and Desired Outcomes Common Across Campaigns

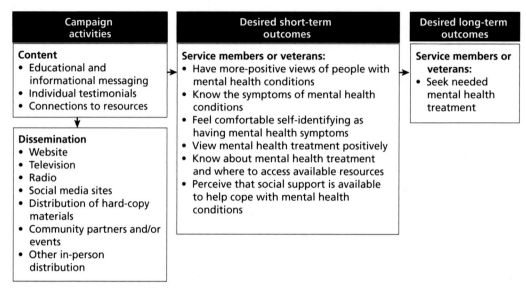

RAND RR1612-4.2

the ready, reacting, or injured zones of the continuum). VCL outreach materials drive people to its phone, text, or chat functions, which provide direct access to care for people in the United States and abroad. VCL is intended for individuals in crisis (the reacting and ill zones of the continuum), although there is a complementary campaign embedded within the VCL website called the Power of One that targets people in veterans' social networks. Despite the primary emphases of each campaign along the continuum, it is important to note that most campaigns have some materials related to each phase. For example, Recovery Month, RWC, and MTC promote or link to a call line or crisis line resource for those in the ill zone of the continuum.

How Campaigns Reference and Cross-Link with Each Other

Given that campaigns have shared desired outcomes and overlapping target populations, we also explored whether and how campaign websites referenced other campaigns and linked to their web resources. We did so by entering the terms "Real Warriors" (to capture mentions of both "Real Warriors" and "Real Warriors Campaign"), "Make the Connection," "Veterans Crisis Line," and "Recovery Month" (to capture mentions of both "National Recovery Month" and "Recovery Month") into each campaign's website search function.

Recovery Month is not linked to or cross-referenced by the DoD or VA campaign websites. The RWC, MTC, and VCL websites do not link to the Recovery

Figure 4.3
Examples of Campaign Materials and Resources Targeting Individuals Along the Mental Health Continuum of Care

	Self-care or social support		Professional care	
	Ready (green)	**Reacting (yellow)**	**Injured (orange)**	**Ill (red)**
Mental health treatment continuum	• Optimal functioning • Adaptive coping • Well trained and prepared • Fit, tough, and focused • Behaving ethically • Cohesive units, ready families	• Mild or transient distress or impairment • Anxious or irritable • Reduced self-control • Poor focus	• More severe or persistent distress or impairment • Leaves lasting evidence • Loss of control or moral values • Persistent shame, guilt, or blame	• Persistent and disabling distress or loss of function • Diagnosable clinical disorder • Symptoms and disability persist over many weeks • Symptoms and disability get worse over time
Examples of campaign materials or resources targeting individuals along the continuum	RWC offers mobile apps for staying "mission ready" and a "5 tips for staying mission ready" infographic.	MTC offers videos of veterans discussing mild symptoms and coping with life events.	MTC offers videos of (1) veterans discussing life events and experiences as well as moderate to severe symptoms and (2) self-assessments for mental health and substance use problems.	VCL offers confidential crisis line by phone, chat, and text to get help around the clock. National Recovery Month links to the National Suicide Prevention Lifeline.

RAND RR1612-4.3

Month website, and the Recovery Month site makes few references to RWC, MTC, or VCL. Specifically, the Recovery Month site featured RWC in a May 2015 Road to Recovery television and radio episode and an accompanying discussion guide. The Recovery Month site featured VCL (but not MCL) in a list of service providers in its Prevention, Treatment, and Recovery Resources document, in its 2013 Recovery Month toolkit, and in a section on health and support services for veterans.

VCL is cross-referenced or linked to by all other campaigns. RWC featured VCL in two feature stories on psychological health and suicide. Many RWC materials include information about MCL, but we tracked references only to VCL in this evaluation. MTC featured VCL in articles on a variety of topics, from jobs to specific disorders (e.g., depression) or symptoms (e.g., noise or light irritation), and on landing pages that contained a variety of content (and also made references to RWC). Recovery Month cross-referenced both RWC and VCL.

Table 4.2
Number of Cross-References or Links to Each Campaign

Campaign	Links to RWC	Links to MTC	Links to VCL	Links to Recovery Month
RWC	N/A	13	4[a]	0
MTC	4	N/A	52	0
VCL	0	23	N/A	0
Recovery Month	4	0	10	N/A

NOTE: N/A = not applicable; these cells reference a campaign linking to itself.

[a] This count only includes links and cross-references to VCL. A search was run later (in February 2017) for the alternately branded MCL and resulted in approximately 50 more cross-references and links.

VCL cross-references or links only to MTC. VCL does not cross-reference or link to RWC or Recovery Month. MTC is featured on the VCL homepage, on a landing page, and in a variety of site content (e.g., videos, frequently asked questions [FAQs], resources).

Table 4.2 shows the number of times each campaign cross-referenced or linked to each other.

Summary of Findings

This chapter summarizes our findings from the content analysis of campaign scope. These findings describe how campaigns align with or complement each other. We found that campaigns have complementary target populations, desired outcomes, and messages. Specifically, the four campaigns have distinct, yet overlapping, target populations that include service members, veterans, and their support networks (e.g., family, friends). Campaigns also share overlapping desired short- and long-term outcomes to increase knowledge of mental health symptoms and improve positive perceptions of individuals with mental health conditions and of mental health treatment. Campaigns offer a wide variety of messages for individuals who are at risk for mental health conditions, symptomatic and considering mental health treatment, in crisis and in need of immediate support, and in recovery after completing treatment.

Despite these commonalities, no shared measures are capturing these shared desired outcomes across campaigns, and not all campaigns cross-reference or link to one another. If campaigns are targeting similar populations, cross-referencing could be a low-cost way to improve the reach of each campaign because their resources would be promoted to the full range of users across all four campaigns. Recovery Month is not linked to or cross-referenced by the DoD or VA campaign websites, and VCL cross-references or links only to MTC. However, all campaigns cross-referenced or linked to VCL.

CHAPTER FIVE

Campaign Content

This chapter summarizes findings from our content analysis and expert panel. Specifically, this chapter describes whether campaign content contains information about its source, how it aligns with target populations, and how it aligns with desired outcomes common to all campaigns. This chapter also contains information about how well campaign content aligns with stated campaign messages and best practices.

Whether Campaign Content Provides Source Information

Source information for half of the campaign webpages is not clearly denoted. We determined the proportion of campaign webpages that clearly identified source information. We limited our analyses to campaign webpages, as these materials often seemed to have the goal of providing information to site visitors. Other campaign materials (e.g., an editable social media graphic) seemed to contain less informational content or were not the type of material to commonly include citations of sources.

Approximately 50 percent of campaign webpages did not clearly mark the source of the information they contained, making it difficult for users to judge the credibility of the information or seek more information on the topic (Table 5.1). RWC had sources on 82 percent of its webpages; Recovery Month had sources on only 20 percent.[1] Few, if any, MTC and VCL webpages clearly stated sources. About one-half of RWC webpages referenced scientific articles as a source, whereas the other campaigns rarely did so.

This finding is not intended to imply that the campaign websites do not rely on evidence for determining the content included in campaign materials. In fact, staff from several campaigns report relying on published research findings and internal experts to develop messages, but the staff strategically decided to minimize the provision of source information to avoid appearing overly technical, to ensure that target audiences feel that the messages are designed for them, and to appeal to target audience members who may wish to avoid being labeled as mentally ill. However, we note that

---

[1] The analysis of Recovery Month webpages included the Recovery Month Toolkit available for download from the site.

Table 5.1
Source Information Cited for Campaign Webpages

Information	RWC		MTC		VCL		Recovery Month		Across Campaigns	
	N	%	N	%	N	%	N	%	N	%
Clearly marked sources of information were used to compile the webpage										
Yes	46	33	0	0	0	0	1	20	47	20
Partially	68	49	0	0	0	0	0	0	68	30
No	25	18	65	100	21	100	4	80	115	50
Scientific journals referenced as a source										
Yes	63	45	0	0	0	0	1	20	64	28

it is recommended to provide some sources to bolster the credibility of the information presented and to allow those exposed to the campaign materials to seek out more information if they wish (Khazaal et al., 2009).

How Campaign Content Aligns with Target Populations

Campaign content aligns with the primary target populations for each campaign. Campaigns use a variety of material types to reach target populations, including web content, videos, television, radio, and print materials, such as flyers, brochures, booklets, and posters (Table 5.2). The majority of content targeting active duty, Guard and Reserve members, and family members was located on campaign websites (e.g., articles, tools). Because of MTC's emphasis on tailored video testimonials, the majority of its content targeting veterans was video.

Our analysis indicated that the content of the campaigns aligns with their primary target populations (Table 5.2). For RWC, the majority of content was tailored to active duty service members or those in the National Guard or Reserve (62 percent); for MTC, the majority was tailored to veterans (77 percent) or families of veterans (11 percent); for VCL, 14 percent of content was tailored to veterans and 75 percent to families or friends of veterans; and for Recovery Month, 93 percent of content focused on the general population. The majority of campaign content was mental health–related (71 percent). However, each campaign contained some content specific to substance use (34 percent), such as video profiles of service members and veterans who had sought treatment for alcoholism or self-assessments for alcohol abuse. Recovery Month had the most substance use–specific content (93 percent), and 62 percent was also mental health–related.

Individuals pictured in campaign materials reflect the target population for each campaign. Testimonials and visuals were used by all campaigns to communicate

Table 5.2
Campaign Material Type, Emphasis, and Target Population(s)

Characteristic	RWC		MTC		VCL		Recovery Month		Across Campaigns	
	N	%	N	%	N	%	N	%	N	%
Total records	265		745		201		209		1,420	
Material type										
Video—testimonial, recovery story, individual profile	31	11.70	601	80.67	0	0.00	13	6.22	645	45
Static webpage[a]	139	52.45	65	8.72	21	10.45	4	1.91	229	16
Print	27	10.19	27	3.62	89	44.28	55	26.32	198	14
Web ads and graphics	0	0.00	38	5.10	54	26.87	2	0.96	94	7
Video, PSA	24	9.06	11	1.48	14	6.97	40	19.14	89	6
Radio	42	15.85	0	0.00	8	3.98	16	7.66	66	5
Video, other	0	0.00	0	0.00	0	0.00	76	36.36	76	5
Social media graphics	0	0.00	2	0.27	9	4.48	0	0.00	11	1
Other[b]	2	0.75	1	0.13	6	2.99	2	0.96	11	1
Toolkit	0	0.00	0	0.00	0	0.00	1	0.48	1	0
Television, ad for campaign	0	0.00	0	0.00	0	0.00	0	0.00	0	0

Table 5.2—Continued

Characteristic	RWC N	RWC %	MTC N	MTC %	VCL N	VCL %	Recovery Month N	Recovery Month %	Across Campaigns N	Across Campaigns %
Emphasis										
Mental health	206	78.03	608	79.37	59	29.38	129	61.72	1,002	71
Substance use	51	19.32	213	27.84	22	9.95	194	92.82	480	34
Target population										
Veteran	22	5.12	596	77.40	39	14.72	6	2.74	663	47
General population (not military-specific)	3	0.70	9	1.17	1	0.38	203	92.69	216	15
Family of veterans	29	6.74	85	11.04	83	31.32	0	0.00	197	14
Active duty	156	36.28	2	0.26	7	2.64	4	1.83	169	12
National Guard or Reserve	111	25.81	50	6.49	1	0.38	0	0.00	162	11
Friends or peers of veterans	2	0.47	1	0.13	116	43.77	0	0.00	119	8
Family of service members	77	17.91	20	2.60	5	1.89	0	0.00	102	7
Other	15	3.49	0	0.00	4	1.51	6	2.74	25	2
Health professional	13	3.02	6	0.78	0	0.00	0	0.00	19	1
Friends or peers of service members	2	0.47	1	0.13	9	3.40	0	0.00	12	1

NOTE: Percentages do not always add up to 100 because materials could be coded in multiple categories.

[a] This row generally refers to static webpages containing information. However, many materials included in other categories (e.g., print, videos) are available on the websites.

[b] The "other" category includes items not easily classified as belonging to one of the "material type" categories, such as podcasts.

messages. Because perceived similarity between the communicator and target audience of communications can bolster the strength of the message being communicated (Hinyard and Kreuter, 2006; Durantini et al., 2006), we coded campaign materials to identify the demographic and military (i.e., service, component, rank, and era) characteristics of individuals appearing in the materials. Explicit mention of these characteristics[2] in testimonials and visuals thus served as a proxy for gauging how campaign users could determine whether they were similar to the individuals depicted in the testimonials or images (though these do not represent all dimensions on which a campaign user might perceive similarity with an individual depicted in a campaign material). In these visuals, all campaigns featured both men and women and members of the four services (Air Force, Army, Marine Corps, Navy) (Table 5.3). Women were featured in about half of all materials. According to a report by the Office of the Deputy Assistant Secretary of Defense (Military Community and Family Policy) (undated-b), women make up approximately 15.5 percent of the active duty force, and a recent study of U.S. Army personnel found that women have significantly elevated odds of having an internalizing disorder and several individual disorders (major depressive disorder, generalized anxiety disorder, and PTSD) (Kessler et al., 2014). Women featured could also include spouses, mothers, and other female family members. Looking at each service, Army personnel were featured most often in campaign materials. This aligns with the relative size of the services, with the Army being the largest branch (Office of the Deputy Assistant Secretary of Defense [Military Community and Family Policy], undated-b).

Only about 14 percent of all campaign materials specified rank in some way. We coded rank for these materials and found that a variety of ranks were featured from E1 to O7 or higher. The majority of RWC materials featured officers (57 percent of featured individuals were O1 or above), whereas MTC featured primarily lower ranks (52 percent of featured individuals were ranks E1–E6). Not enough materials for VCL or Recovery Month specified rank, so we are not able to describe rank of individuals in their visual images or videos.

We also coded for the featured individual's service era when it was specified on campaign materials. In 2015, census data indicated that 45 percent of veterans were 65 or older, suggesting that the majority of U.S. veterans are from the Vietnam or post–Vietnam War eras (U.S. Census Bureau, 2015b). In alignment with this population estimate, both MTC and VCL featured a larger proportion of individuals from the Vietnam War (27 and 32 percent, respectively) and post-Vietnam eras (10 and 20 percent, respectively). Eighty-five percent of featured individuals from RWC were from the Operation Enduring Freedom (OEF), Operation Iraqi Freedom (OIF), and Operation New Dawn (OND) era, which is appropriate given the focus on currently serving service members.

---

[2] Though our coders made judgments of gender based on images and videos, they were instructed to code other demographic and military characteristics only if explicitly mentioned or noted (e.g., race or ethnicity mentioned in video narrative, service and rank identified through uniform insignia or a caption).

Table 5.3
Characteristics of Individuals Pictured in Materials

Characteristic	RWC		MTC		VCL		Recovery Month		Across Campaigns	
	N	%	N	%	N	%	N	%	N	%
Gender										
Female	123	46.42	300	40.27	120	59.70	148	70.81	691	49
Service										
Air Force	31	11.15	93	13.04	3	8.11	2	18.18	129	9
Army	158	56.83	331	46.42	15	40.54	2	18.18	506	36
Coast Guard	0	0.00	6	0.84	3	8.11	0	0.00	9	1
Marine Corps	49	17.63	160	22.44	9	24.32	4	36.36	222	16
Navy	40	14.39	123	17.25	7	18.92	3	27.27	173	12
Component										
Veteran	22	9.24	596	81.20	39	66.10	6	3.43	663	47
Active duty	156	65.55	2	0.27	7	11.86	4	2.29	169	12
National Guard or Reserve	8	3.36	64	8.72	1	1.69	0	0.00	73	5
Civilian	52	21.85	72	9.81	12	20.34	165	94.29	301	21
Rank										
E1–E6	20	15.38	35	52.24	2	100.00	1	100.00	58	4
E7 and higher	36	27.69	15	22.39	0	0.00	0	0.00	51	4
O1–O6	55	42.31	17	25.37	0	0.00	0	0.00	72	5
O7 and higher	15	11.54	0	0.00	0	0.00	0	0.00	15	1
W1–W5	4	3.08	0	0.00	0	0.00	0	0.00	4	0

Table 5.3—Continued

Era	RWC		MTC		VCL		Recovery Month		Across Campaigns	
	N	*%*	*N*	*%*	*N*	*%*	*N*	*%*	*N*	*%*
OEF, OIF, OND (2001–present)	61	84.72	302	45.76	18	40.91	0	0.00	381	27
Desert Storm (1990–2000)	3	4.17	102	15.45	3	6.82	0	0.00	108	8
Post–Vietnam War (1976–1989)	0	0.00	65	9.85	9	20.45	0	0.00	74	5
Vietnam War (1960–1975)	4	5.56	177	26.82	14	31.82	1	100.00	196	14
Post–Korean War (1954–1959)	1	1.39	1	0.15	0	0.00	0	0.00	2	0
World War II through Korean War (1941–1953)	3	4.17	13	1.97	0	0.00	0	0.00	16	1

NOTE: Percentages do not always add up to 100 because materials could be coded in multiple categories.

We found that 46 percent of MTC portrayals and 41 percent of VCL portrayals featured service members and veterans of the wars in Iraq and Afghanistan (OEF, OIF, OND). The era was rarely specified in Recovery Month materials, so they were not included in this analysis.

How Campaign Content Aligns with Desired Outcomes Common Across Campaigns

We identified a series of desired short- and long-term outcomes that were common across the campaigns and then coded campaign content to determine whether it aligned with one or more of those outcomes. Because the desired outcomes were framed in terms of how an individual's behavior would change, we first identified ways in which campaign content addressed each desired outcome. For example, the logic model (Figure 4.2) shows that before service members or veterans will seek treatment, they must be able to identify that they are experiencing mental health symptoms. This being the case, we coded campaigns to see if they shared, listed, or described the symptoms of mental health conditions. Table 5.4 shows how the desired outcomes correspond to the codes we used to review campaign content, and Table 5.5 summarizes the proportion of campaign materials focusing on each desired outcome.

Table 5.4
How Desired Short- and Long-Term Outcomes Correspond with Content Codes

Desired Short- or Long-Term Outcome in Logic Model (Figure 4.2)	Corresponding Code Used in Content Analysis
Service members or veterans:	Campaign:
• Have more-positive views of people with mental health conditions and mental health treatment • Feel comfortable self-identifying as having mental health symptoms	• Positively portrays people with a mental health condition (both recognizing and accepting the condition and thriving despite it) and the benefits of treatment
• Know the symptoms of mental health conditions	• Shares, lists, or describes symptoms of mental health conditions
• Know about mental health treatment and where to access available resources	• Shares, lists, or describes treatment options and resources
• Perceive social support is available to cope with mental health conditions	• Provides an example of how friends or family can help individuals cope with a mental health condition
• Seek needed mental health treatment	• Provides the user a direct connection to mental health care (i.e., phone line or live chat line)

Table 5.5
Alignment of Content with Cross-Cutting Desired Outcomes

Content	RWC		MTC		VCL		Recovery Month[a]		Across Campaigns	
	N	%	N	%	N	%	N	%	N	%
Positively portrays people with a mental health condition (both recognizing and accepting the condition and thriving despite it) and the benefits of treatment	92	34.72	513	68.86	8	3.98	85	40.67	698	49.15
Shares, lists, or describes symptoms of mental health conditions	96	36.23	525	70.47	41	20.40	40	19.14	702	49.44
Shares, lists, or describes treatment options and resources	116	43.77	81	10.87	200	99.50	66	31.58	639	45.00
Provides an example of how friends or family can help individuals cope with a mental health condition	102	38.49	285	38.26	176	87.60	76	36.36	463	32.61
Provides the user a direct connection to mental health care (i.e., phone line or live chat line)	112	42.26	63	8.46	199	99.00	7	3.35	381	26.83
Total content that addresses at least one of the above outcomes	221	83.40	638	85.64	198	100.00	111	53.11	1,168	82.25

[a] Recovery Month has a standing navigation bar labeled "Find help or treatment" that links to SAMHSA's National Suicide Prevention Lifeline, National Helpline, Disaster Distress Helpline, and the SAMHSA Treatment Locator. However, this navigation bar functions differently in different browsers and on different devices. Sometimes, it functions as a pop-up text when you mouse over the navigation bar. Other times, it requires a click-through to see the resources. Therefore, we did not code this navigation bar as providing a direct connection to care. However, had this been coded as a direct connection to care, approximately 44 percent of Recovery Month content would offer a direct connection to care.

Most campaign content aligned with the desired outcomes shared by campaigns. The majority of content (82 percent) aligned with at least one of these outcomes, with about half of the campaign content communicating the symptoms of mental health conditions. RWC and Recovery Month's content fell evenly across desired outcomes, except that Recovery Month infrequently provided a direct connection to mental health care (3 percent of Recovery Month materials).[3] MTC had relatively more emphasis on communicating the symptoms of mental health conditions and portraying the benefits of accepting that one has a mental health condition or getting treatment. VCL was primarily focused on communicating treatment options and resources and providing examples of how friends and family can help with coping. VCL also provided a direct connection to mental health care.

Different types of content (e.g., videos, website) were used to communicate about different desired outcomes. We examined the differences in the types of content that campaigns used to communicate about desired outcomes. Video testimonials were the primary way that campaigns positively portrayed people with mental health conditions (recognizing and accepting the condition and thriving despite it) and the benefits of treatment; video was also the primary medium for providing examples of how friends and family can help with coping. Website content was the primary way campaigns shared, listed, or described treatment options and resources and provided a direct connection to mental health care. These findings are consistent with best practices for choosing a medium appropriate to the message being communicated (Dutta-Bergman, 2004).

How Campaign Messages Align with Each Other and with Their Own Stated Messages

The majority of aligned with at least one of their own stated messages. Each campaign communicates a variety of messages—for example, that reaching out is a sign of strength (RWC), treatment works (MTC), and recovery is possible (Recovery Month) (Table 5.6). Our analysis of campaign content found that the majority of each campaign's content aligned with its stated messages (Figure 5.1). Specific messages for each campaign can be found in Chapter Four.

---

[3] It should be noted that Recovery Month has a standing navigation bar labeled "Find help or treatment" that links to SAMHSA's National Suicide Prevention Lifeline, National Helpline, Disaster Distress Helpline, and the SAMHSA Treatment Locator. However, this navigation bar functions differently in different browsers and on different devices. Sometimes, it functions as a pop-up text when you mouse over the navigation bar. Other times, it requires a click-through to see the resources. Therefore, we did not code this navigation bar as providing a direct connection to care. However, had this been coded as a direct connection to care, approximately 44 percent of Recovery Month content would offer a direct connection to care.

Table 5.6
Key Campaign Messages Reported by Campaigns at the Time of Evaluation

Campaign	Message
RWC	• Experiencing psychological stress as a result of deployment is common • Unlike visible wounds, psychological wounds and brain injuries are often invisible and can go untreated if not identified • Successful treatment and positive outcomes are greatly assisted by early intervention • Service members and their families should feel comfortable reaching out to their units and chains of command for support • Reaching out is a sign of strength that benefits service members, their families, their units, and their services • Warriors are not alone in coping with mental health concerns (i.e., there is a vast network of support and resources in each service)
MTC	• Recovery is possible • Treatment works • Emphasize peer-to-peer connections among veterans • Normalize treatment-seeking
VCL	• If you are in crisis, contact VCL • One call, one text, one conversation can save a life
Recovery Month	• Recovery is possible • Recovery emerges from hope • Recovery unfolds along diverse pathways • Speak out about your mental health experiences (your voice can make a difference) • Mental health is part of overall wellness

Figure 5.1
Percentage of Campaign Content Aligned with Stated Campaign Messages

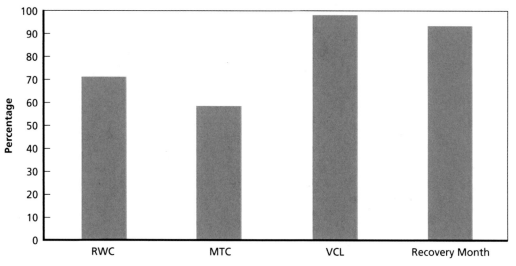

Campaigns share some overlapping messages. In addition to analyzing the messages communicated in each campaign's material, we reviewed what each campaign identified to us as being key campaign messages. These messages are not mutually exclusive (Table 5.6). Both MTC and Recovery Month communicate that recovery is possible. Recovery Month and VCL share the message that one voice can make a difference (with VCL focusing on saving a life and Recovery Month on changing public perceptions of people with mental health conditions). Both VCL and RWC communicate that service members and veterans with mental health symptoms are not alone and should reach out to sources of support.

There are several unique messages delivered by individual campaigns. Recovery Month communicates that mental health is part of overall wellness. VCL's messages are focused on marketing its call line, chat, and text. RWC has several multifaceted messages that are unique (Table 5.5; e.g., experiencing psychological stress as a result of combat is common). MTC focuses on promoting the connectedness of veterans and leveraging this to help normalize treatment-seeking.

How Campaigns Align with Best Practices in Mental Health Public Awareness Campaigns

Our 26 expert panelists identified 22 best practices in mental health public awareness campaign design and dissemination (Box 5.1). The experts were broken into four groups, and each group was asked to review a set of key materials associated with one campaign.[4] They then freely navigated the campaign's website for an additional 15 to 20 minutes. The experts then rated the extent to which the campaign aligned with a subset of these best practices related to goals and objectives, messaging and messengers, and anonymity of resources (Table 5.7).

The rating form used by expert panelists listed each checklist item (Box 5.1). Panelists were asked to rate the campaign using a seven-point Likert scale ranging from 1 ("strongly disagree") to 7 ("strongly agree"), with the midpoint being "neither agree nor disagree." The instructions specified that rating a checklist item a "1" would suggest that most or all of the campaign materials reviewed did not adhere to that checklist item and rating a checklist item a "7" would suggest that most or all of the campaign materials adhered strongly to that checklist item. For several of the checklist items (Table 5.7), panelists were asked to provide a rating specific to each target population (i.e., service members, veterans, friends and family of service members and/or veterans, or general population) based on their review of the materials for that specific target population.

---

[4] A list of these experts and their areas of expertise can be found in Appendix F, along with descriptions of the campaign materials reviewed.

Box 5.1
Checklist of Best Practices in Mental Health Public Awareness

1. The campaign has a theoretical basis. *Theoretical basis* is defined as a proposed explanation of empirical phenomena (e.g., behavior change, help-seeking).
2. The campaign's guiding theory identifies determinants of the behavior that the campaign is trying to change.
3. The campaign has clear goals and objectives.
4. The campaign's messages and activities align closely with the goals and objectives of the campaign.
5. The campaign has a logic model that guides the campaign activities and evaluation. A logic model links a goal, behaviors directly related to it, factors that influence those behaviors, and campaign activities designed to change those factors.
6. The campaign communicates messages that are targeted at determinants of the desired outcomes the campaign is trying to achieve (as specified by the campaign theory or logic models).
7. The campaign materials clearly communicate the messages of the campaign.
8. The campaign materials are simple enough to be easily understood.
9. The messages the campaign is trying to convey are simple and clear.
10. The messengers selected in pictures and videos are the types of messengers that will be seen as credible by the campaign's target audiences.
11. The campaign messages are engaging and relevant to the campaign's target audiences.
12. The campaign uses several different means of dissemination that are tailored to the campaigns' target audiences.
13. The campaign's dissemination strategy is designed to provide the campaign's target audiences with consistent exposure to messages.
14. The campaign segments audiences by one or more readily observable factors, such as age, sex, race or ethnicity, income level, occupation, area of residence, or other attributes.
15. The campaign targets relevant social network members (e.g., family members, health providers, and employers) as necessary to support campaign goal(s).
16. Some of the campaign messages use language and concepts intended to resonate with men (e.g., equating help-seeking with strength and autonomy, countering the idea that mental illness is a result of a lack of willpower).
17. The campaign involves contact (on video, in person, or through other channels) with an individual who has experienced mental health challenges.
18. The campaign shows positive role models.
19. The campaign uses one or more of the following evidence-based message recommendations:
    a. Empower those with mental health symptoms to seek care.
    b. Encourage individuals with mental illness to reduce isolation and connect with others.
    c. Build social support to increase help-seeking behavior in target audiences (e.g., family or friends encourage help-seeking).
    d. Frame messages for the general public in terms of recovery from mental illness.
    e. Provide information on the short-term benefits and consequences of behavior change (i.e., help-seeking) to individuals with mental health disorder.
    f. Dispel stereotypes that imply that individuals with mental health disorders are dangerous.
    g. Present a balanced portrayal of biological and psychosocial factors to target audiences.
    h. Communicate that suicide is everyone's issue and not the fault of the individual who attempts or completes suicide.
    i. Illustrate the prevalence of mental illness to target audiences.
    j. Increase mental health knowledge to target audiences.
20. The campaign messages convey a solution or clear course of action.
21. The campaign avoids reinforcing negative stereotypes.
22. The campaign offers options for seeking resources and support that allow for varying degrees of anonymity.

NOTE: The checklist was developed by RAND authors based on a literature review, then vetted with the expert panel.

Table 5.7
Expert Panel Ratings of Each Campaign on a Subset of the Best-Practices Checklist Items

Item (ordered from highest combined mean to lowest)	RWC	MTC	VCL	Recovery Month	Combined
The campaign involves contact (on video, in person, or through other channels) with an individual who has experienced mental health challenges.	M = 7 Md = 7 R = 7–7	M = 7 Md = 7 R = 7–7	M = 6.3 Md = 6 R = 5–7	M = 5.7 Md = 5.5 R = 5–7	M = 6.5 Md = 6.4 R = 6–7
The campaign uses one or more of the evidence-based message recommendations listed in item 19 of Box 5.1.	M = 6.8 Md = 7 R = 6–7	M = 6.5 Md = 6 R = 6–7	M = 6.4 Md = 7 R = 5–7	M = 6.2 Md = 7 R = 4–7	M = 6.5 Md = 6.8 R = 5.3–7
The campaign shows positive role models.	M = 6.5 Md = 7 R = 5–7	M = 7 Md = 7 R = 7–7	M = 5.7 Md = 6 R = 4–7	M = 6.2 Md = 6 R = 5–7	M = 6.4 Md = 6.5 R = 5.3–7
The campaign materials clearly communicate the messages of the campaign.	M = 6.3 Md = 7 R = 5–7	M = 6.3 Md = 6.5 R = 5–7	M = 6.3 Md = 6 R = 5–7	M = 6 Md = 6 R = 5–7	M = 6.2 Md = 6.4 R = 5–7
The campaign avoids reinforcing negative stereotypes.	M = 6.7 Md = 7 R = 6–7	M = 6.5 Md = 7 R = 6–7	M = 6.1 Md = 6 R = 5–7	M = 5.6 Md = 5.5 R = 4–7	M = 6.2 Md = 6.4 R = 5.3–7
The messages the campaign is trying to convey are simple and clear.	M = 6 Md = 6 R = 5–7	M = 6.5 Md = 6 R = 6–7	M = 6.4 Md = 6 R = 6–7	M = 5.7 Md = 6 R = 3–7	M = 6.2 Md = 6.0 R = 5–7
The messengers selected in pictures and videos are the types of messengers that will be seen as credible to the campaign's target audiences. *Target audience: Veterans*	M = 6.5 Md = 6.5 R = 6–7	M = 6.8 Md = 7 R = 6–7	M = 6.4 Md = 7 R = 5–7	M = 4.7 Md = 4.5 R = 3–6	M = 6.1 Md = 6.3 R = 6–6.8
The campaign has clear goals and objectives.	M = 6.3 Md = 7 R = 5–7	M = 6 Md = 5.5 R = 3–7	M = 6.4 Md = 7 R = 5–7	M = 5.2 Md = 6 R = 2–7	M = 6.0 Md = 6.4 R = 3.8–7
The campaign's messages and activities align closely with the goals and objectives of the campaign.	M = 6.2 Md = 6.5 R = 5–7	M = 6 Md = 6 R = 4–7	M = 5.6 Md = 6 R = 1–7	M = 6 Md = 6 R = 5–7	M = 6.0 Md = 6.1 R = 3.8–7
The campaign materials are simple enough to be easily understood.	M = 5.7 Md = 5.5 R = 5–7	M = 6.5 Md = 6.5 R = 6–7	M = 6.3 Md = 6 R = 5–7	M = 5.3 Md = 6 R = 2–7	M = 6.0 Md = 6.0 R = 4.5–7
The campaign messages are engaging and relevant to the campaign's target audiences. *Target audience: Veterans*	M = 5.8 Md = 6 R = 4–7	M = 6.5 Md = 7 R = 6–7	M = 6.3 Md = 6 R = 5–7	M = 5 Md = 5.5 R = 3–6	M = 5.9 Md = 6.1 R = 4.5–6.8
The campaign messages convey a solution or clear course of action.	M = 6.2 Md = 6.5 R = 5–7	M = 5.5 Md = 6 R = 4–6	M = 6 Md = 6 R = 5–7	M = 5.5 Md = 5 R = 5–7	M = 5.8 Md = 5.9 R = 4.8–6.8
The messengers selected in pictures and videos are the types of messengers that will be seen as credible by the campaign's target audiences. *Target audience: Military service members*	M = 6.5 Md = 6.5 R = 6–7	M = 6.3 Md = 7 R = 4–7	M = 5.4 Md = 6 R = 2–7	M = 4.7 Md = 4.5 R = 3–6	M = 5.7 Md = 6.0 R = 3.8–6.8

Table 5.7—Continued

Item (ordered from highest combined mean to lowest)	RWC	MTC	VCL	Recovery Month	Combined
The messengers selected in pictures and videos are the types of messengers that will be seen as credible by the campaign's target audiences. *Target audience: Friends and family of service members and/or veterans*	M = 5.8 Md = 5.5 R = 5–7	M = 6.3 Md = 6 R = 6–7	M = 5.6 Md = 6 R = 1–7	M = 5 Md = 5 R = 3–7	M = 5.7 Md = 5.6 R = 3.8–7
Some of the campaign messages use language and concepts intended to resonate with men (e.g., equating help-seeking with strength and autonomy, countering the idea that mental illness is a result of a lack of willpower).	M = 6.8 Md = 7 R = 6–7	M = 6.3 Md = 6.5 R = 5–7	M = 6 Md = 7 R = 4–7	M = 3.7 Md = 3.5 R = 2–6	M = 5.7 Md = 6.0 R = 4.3–6.8
The campaign segments audiences by one or more readily observable factors, such as age, sex, race or ethnicity, income level, occupation, area of residence, or other attributes.	M = 5.5 Md = 5.5 R = 4–7	M = 6 Md = 6 R = 5–7	M = 5.6 Md = 6 R = 4–7	M = 5.2 Md = 5 R = 4–7	M = 5.6 Md = 5.6 R = 4.3–7
The campaign offers options for seeking resources and support that allow for varying degrees of anonymity.	M = 6 Md = 6 R = 5–7	M = 5.2 Md = 5 R = 3–7	M = 5.4 Md = 5 R = 4–7	M = 5.7 Md = 6 R = 4–7	M = 5.6 Md = 5.5 R = 4–7
The campaign messages are engaging and relevant to the campaign's target audiences. *Target audience: Friends and family of service members and/or veterans*	M = 5.5 Md = 5.5 R = 4–7	M = 6 Md = 6 R = 5–7	M = 4.4 Md = 5 R = 1–6	M = 5.2 Md = 6 R = 3–6	M = 5.3 Md = 5.6 R = 3.3–6.5
The campaign targets relevant social network members (e.g., family members, health providers, and employers) as necessary to support campaign goal(s).	M = 5.5 Md = 5.5 R = 4–7	M = 6.3 Md = 6 R = 5–7	M = 4 Md = 4 R = 1–7	M = 5.2 Md = 5 R = 4–7	M = 5.3 Md = 5.1 R = 3.5–7
The campaign messages are engaging and relevant to the campaign's target audiences. *Target audience: Military service members*	M = 5.8 Md = 6 R = 4–7	M = 6 Md = 6 R = 4–7	M = 3.9 Md = 4 R = 2–6	M = 5 Md = 5.5 R = 3–6	M = 5.2 Md = 5.4 R = 3.3–6.5

NOTES: M = mean; Md = median; R = range. Response scale was a seven-point Likert scale ranging from 1 ("strongly disagree") to 7 ("strongly agree"), with the mid-point labeled as "neither agree nor disagree."

Campaigns followed best practices. Overall, campaigns followed the rated best practices; the M rating was 5.2 (out of 7) or above on all checklist items. Across campaigns, the highest rated items were *The campaign involves contact [on video, in person, or through other channels] with an individual who has experienced mental health challenges* (M = 6.5) and *The campaign uses one or more evidence-based message recommendations* (M = 6.5). The lowest rated items were *The campaign messages are engaging and relevant to the campaign's target audiences* (M = 5.2 for service members and M = 5.3 for friends and family of veterans and service members) and *The campaign targets relevant social network members [e.g., family members, health providers, and employers] as necessary to support campaign goals* (M = 5.3). The checklist items in Box 5.1 consist of affirmative statements about the characteristics of high-quality mental health public awareness campaigns derived from best practices in the literature and comments from the expert panelists.

For each campaign, we had a subset of six or seven experts provide input on the strengths of the campaign, as well as areas that could be improved (Table 5.8).

Strengths that cut across campaigns included having materials that clearly communicate the messages and having messengers who will likely serve as positive role models or will be seen as credible by target audiences.

To improve campaigns, experts suggested that campaigns offering self-assessments and/or access to direct care (e.g., MTC, VCL) clarify the extent to which participation in the assessment or service will be anonymous and/or confidential. Privacy was cited as an important issue related to mental health help-seeking, given concerns that service members or veterans may have about negative repercussions from mental health conditions becoming part of their health or mental health records. Experts felt that the degree of confidentiality (e.g., being clear about exactly what information might be shared and under what circumstances) could be made clearer.

Additionally, experts noted that campaigns target multiple audiences and consequently try to integrate multiple types of materials into their campaigns. However, the content is not equally rich across audiences; some target audiences will find a very small portion of content tailored to them (e.g., health professionals). Experts suggested campaigns carefully consider whether the benefits of creating a small amount of content for a larger number of audiences outweigh creating additional richer or deeper content for a single audience.

Summary of Findings

Through our content analysis and expert panel, we found that most of the content aligned with target populations and desired outcomes common across campaigns, as well as with stated campaign messages and best practices. Our content analysis found that individuals pictured in campaign materials reflected the target population for each campaign, which underscored the expert finding that campaigns have messengers who serve as positive role models or will be seen as credible by target audiences. About half of the campaign webpages did not clearly state the source for the content in the material (often by design), but this can potentially render it difficult for users to judge the credibility of the information or to seek out more information. Additionally, our experts indicated that campaign materials clearly communicated the messages of the campaigns and used evidence-based messaging.

The campaigns demonstrated consistency in targeting messages to certain audiences, which helped focus messages and keep them simple and clear. Evidence suggests that targeting messages to specific audiences can improve their effectiveness. Campaigns also used specific messages (e.g., ones that build social support, decrease feelings

Table 5.8
Expert Input on Campaign Strengths and Areas for Improvement

Campaign	Strengths	Areas for Improvement
RWC	• Campaign materials clearly align with campaign goals and objectives and communicate campaign messages. • Messengers in pictures and videos will be seen as credible to the campaign's target audience. • The campaign uses language and concepts intended to resonate with men. • The campaign uses contact (on video, in person, or through other channels) strategies to expose audiences to positive role models who have experienced mental health challenges.	• Make all campaign materials simple and streamlined enough to be easily understood and navigated. • Further develop content for veterans and friends and family of service members. • Organize campaign materials to make them more easily navigated based on users' gender, rank, and race. • Streamline the campaign website and update unrelated or unmoderated website content.
MTC	• Campaign materials clearly communicate messages. • Messengers in pictures and videos and campaign messages will be seen as credible to the campaign's target audiences. • The campaign portrays people with mental health challenges as positive role models.	• Allow users to schedule an appointment without leaving the website. • Clarify which supports or services are anonymous (e.g., self-assessments) and add content that talks about the challenges associated with maintaining anonymity. • Further develop the resources webpage to include more self-help resources and resource options to address some of the logistical barriers to care (e.g., transportation). • Create other unique products to drive people to the campaign website (e.g., video games, interactive tools).
VCL	• Campaign materials are easily understood, align with campaign goals and objectives, and clearly communicate campaign messages. • Messengers in pictures and videos will be seen as credible by veterans. • The campaign uses language and concepts that resonate with men. • The campaign uses evidence-based message recommendations.	• Further develop materials that highlight the role of family and friends in accessing VCL. • Clarify whether resources offered on the website can be accessed anonymously. • Consider showing users chatting, texting, or calling VCL and the associated benefits in promotional materials.
Recovery Month	• Campaign materials clearly align with campaign goals and objectives, and communicate campaign messages. • Positive role models are successfully integrated into the campaign. • The campaign uses evidence-based message recommendations.	• Tailor the campaign to a more targeted audience(s). • Clearly demarcate outreach materials from resources for individuals with substance use or mental health needs. • Remove technical language and jargon from campaign materials. • Consider whether a focused month of campaign activity is sufficient or more-sustained messaging is needed to achieve campaign goals.

of isolation, diminish beliefs that those suffering from mental illness are dangerous, empower care-seeking) to promote public awareness about mental health and potentially reduce stigmatizing attitudes and beliefs. Finally, the campaigns consistently incorporated testimonials from individuals about their own experiences with mental illness, substance use, and recovery, which can help reduce negative perceptions of people with mental illness and increase positive perceptions.

Though experts identified areas where each campaign could improve (Appendix F), several recommendations were made for all campaigns. One recommendation on privacy said that campaigns should consider clarifying the extent to which participation in any assessments or direct services offered would be anonymous and/or confidential. In some instances, campaigns may not clearly state how people's information will be collected and potentially used. This could deter people from interacting with campaign resources.

In addition, experts said campaigns must navigate the challenge of how much to focus their messaging. Segmenting audiences is beneficial when developing messages to address the concerns of specific groups by increasing the likelihood that users will find content that is relevant to them. Failing to segment content adequately may mean that in trying to reach everyone, a campaign rarely reaches any group very well. Indeed, campaigns report significant efforts to segment their target audiences. However, summarizing across campaigns, the extent to which campaigns effectively reach important secondary groups—such as family members, health providers, and employers—is still unclear. Experts said these audiences are important because of their influence on perceptions of mental health and mental health treatment and on help-seeking behavior.

CHAPTER SIX

Campaign Dissemination

Because campaigns do not collect information about whether users are part of their target audiences, we could only calculate the campaigns' *reach* (defined here as the number of exposures to campaign materials). This is the best estimate that can be generated given the data available across all four campaigns. These estimates will likely be an upper bound of the number of people reached because we are unable to account for such factors as individuals visiting a campaign website multiple times or being exposed to materials from multiple campaigns. We were also unable to identify the proportion of the target population reached across channels (e.g., website, Twitter, events) because data were not available that allowed us to determine whether those reached by the campaigns were members of one of the target populations. As a result, this chapter focuses on whether campaigns are *likely* to reach their target audiences. We assessed this by looking at their process data and Twitter data, as well as the expert panel's determination of whether the campaign is aligned with best practices in mental health public awareness campaigns. We organize these findings in three sections: campaign reach, campaign engagement, and campaign users. The key indicators used to determine reach, engagement, and user characteristics are presented in Table 6.1 and are defined more fully in Appendix D.

Campaign Reach

More than 4 million visits were made to the campaign websites in 2015. The number of website sessions (or visits) was used as an indicator of reach via each campaign's website.[1] In 2015, the four campaign websites logged more than 4.3 million sessions (Table 6.2). MTC alone contributed nearly 3 million of those sessions, and VCL more than 900,000. RWC and Recovery Month accounted for the remaining share of total visits in 2015. Of the more than 21 million veterans in the United States (National Center for Veterans Analysis and Statistics, undated), it is estimated that nearly 3 million have a current

---

[1] Google Analytics defines a session as: "A group of interactions that take place on your website within a given time frame. For example, a single session can contain multiple screen or page views, events, social interactions, and ecommerce transactions" (Google Analytics, undated).

Table 6.1
Key Indicators Used to Determine Campaign Reach, Engagement, and User Characteristics

Type of Media	Indicators of Campaign Reach	Indicators of Campaign Engagement	Indicators of Campaign User Characteristics
Website	• Number of website sessions	• Bounce rate • Page views • Average session duration • Average page views per session • Top ten pages viewed • Top ten items downloaded • Top ten videos viewed	• Top city where traffic originates
Social media sites	• Number of Facebook fans • Number of YouTube views • Number of Twitter followers	• Number of posts (Facebook) • Number of interactions (likes, comments, shares) (Facebook) • Number of impressions (Facebook) • Average view duration (YouTube) • Number of likes (YouTube) • Number of dislikes (YouTube) • Number of subscribers gained (YouTube) • Number of subscribers lost (YouTube) • Number of favorites gained (YouTube) • Number of favorites lost (YouTube) • Number of tweets (Twitter) • Number of direct messages received (Twitter) • Number of direct messages sent (Twitter)	• Gender (Facebook, YouTube) • Age (Facebook, YouTube) • Top six cities where traffic originates (Facebook) • Top six states where traffic originates (YouTube)
PSAs	• Number of radio PSA airings • Number of radio PSA listener impressions • Number of television PSA airings • Number of television PSA listener impressions	• None	• None
Outreach activities	• Number of conferences or events attended • Number of campaign materials distributed • Number of partner organizations	• None	• None

Table 6.2
Website Sessions and Percentage Change, 2012–2015

Organization	2012	2013	2014	2015	Total	Percentage Change from 2012 to 2015
RWC	258,186	331,639	290,151	315,848	1,195,824	22
MTC	1,858,207	1,683,893	2,832,269	2,955,647	9,330,016	59
VCL	368,083	727,191	838,061	930,473	2,872,808	155
Recovery Month	404,234	321,342	124,846	123,796	974,218	−69[a]
Total	2,888,710	3,064,065	4,085,327	4,325,764	14,363,866	50

[a] From 2012 to 2015, the Recovery Month website analytics program was revamped and migrated from Webtrends to Google Analytics. The systems calculate user interaction metrics differently. In addition, the site metrics changed to the standardized SAMHSA Google Analytics tracking code. In March 2015, a new Recovery Month website launched as an internal site within SAMHSA.gov. It contained 75 percent less content than the previous site and provided access to only 2014 materials and some 2015 materials—unlike the prior version, which had offered more than 15 years of content.

mental health need, and almost a half-million have considered suicide within the past year (Becerra et al., 2016). The number of website sessions represents an upper bound on the number of individuals that can be reached because the measure does not account for repeat visitors. Though we cannot identify whether website visitors were veterans, we note that the combined number of sessions on the MTC and VCL sites exceeds the estimated number of veterans with mental health needs.

RWC had 315,848 website sessions in 2015. There are more than 2 million U.S. active duty service members (Defense Manpower Data Center, 2015), and estimates derived from a representative sample indicate that approximately 300,000 service members deployed to Iraq and Afghanistan met criteria for PTSD or depression (Tanielian and Jaycox, 2008). Assuming the number of website sessions represents an upper bound on the number of individuals possibly reached, the number of website sessions exceeds the estimate for deployed service members with mental health symptoms. In contrast, Recovery Month has a much larger target population given its focus on Americans at large. More than 20 million Americans 18 or older had a substance use disorder, serious mental illness, or both in the past year (Hedden et al., 2015). Recovery Month had a total of 123,796 website sessions in 2015, indicating a relatively smaller reach, although changes to its website tracking metrics and significant reductions in content available likely contributed to this decrease.[2] Given that the number of website sessions can include

---

[2]   From 2012 to 2015, the Recovery Month website analytics program was revamped and migrated from Webtrends to Google Analytics. The systems calculate user interaction metrics differently. In addition, the site metrics changed to the standardized SAMHSA Google Analytics tracking code. In March 2015, a new Recovery Month website launched as an internal site within SAMHSA.gov. It contained 75 percent less content than the previous site and provided access to only 2014 materials and some 2015 materials—unlike the prior version, which had offered more than 15 years of content.

individuals who made repeat visits, the average monthly unique sessions are provided in Appendix D to provide the potential range of reach for each campaign. However, the number of unique sessions is also an imperfect indicator of unique individuals reached because the estimate is based on internet protocol (IP) addresses.[3] No analytic data are available that identify whether site visitors belong to a campaign target population, limiting our ability to generate more-precise estimates of reach.

The reach of all of the campaigns except Recovery Month increased from 2012 to 2015. The total number of website sessions across all of the campaigns increased by 50 percent from 2012 (2,888,710) to 2015 (4,325,764). VCL was the only campaign that showed an increase in number of website sessions each year relative to the prior year; in contrast, Recovery Month experienced a decrease in number of sessions each year relative to the prior year. As mentioned previously, the Recovery Month website analytics program was revamped and migrated during this period from Webtrends to Google Analytics, which calculates user interaction metrics differently. Additionally, in March 2015, a new Recovery Month website launched as an internal site within SAMHSA.gov, and it contained 75 percent less content than the previous site, providing access to only 2014 materials and some 2015 materials, unlike the prior version, which had offered more than 15 years of content. From 2012 to 2015, RWC's reach increased by 22 percent, MTC's by 59 percent, and VCL's by 155 percent. Recovery Month's reach decreased by 69 percent during the same time period, and there may be several reasons for this decrease. One is the aforementioned revamp and migration from Webtrends to Google Analytics, compounded by the site metrics changing to the standardized SAMHSA Google Analytics tracking code. Another possible reason is the new internal site within SAMHSA. gov. A third issue of note is that the website is not Recovery Month's primary means of dissemination: The campaign pushes out information about National Recovery Month to partner organizations that download the Recovery Month toolkit—its primary web tool—and convene local Recovery Month events, so much of its reach depends on partner organizations. Finally, the toolkit is updated each year with some additional information, but the basic components remain the same (i.e., how to promote Recovery Month, mental health and substance use information), so there may be limited value for users to revisit the website to access this somewhat static information.

More than 5.6 million people may have been reached through social media. Combined across all campaigns, reach via social media in 2015 comprised nearly 3 million Facebook fans, more than 2.5 million YouTube views, and approximately 57,000 Twitter followers (Table 6.3). MTC contributed the vast majority of the campaigns' collective social media reach, with 5,487,420 touched via Facebook or YouTube. MTC reached tar-

---

[3]   There is no way to accurately assess the number of unique site visitors because cookies, the small pieces of data stored in users' browsers to "remember" interactions with websites and that are used by Google Analytics to measure how users interact with websites, are attached to individual browsers on computers, rather than to people.

Table 6.3
Social Media Reach, 2015

Organization	Facebook Fans	YouTube Views[a]	Twitter Followers	Total
RWC	69,476	10,767	39,951	120,124
MTC	2,880,304	2,607,116	—[b]	5,487,420
Recovery Month	37,690	7,790	16,780	62,260
Total	2,987,470	2,625,673	56,731	5,669,874

NOTE: VCL is not featured in the table because it does not maintain an active Facebook page, does not have a campaign-dedicated Twitter handle, and does not have a YouTube channel.

[a] YouTube views were used as an indicator of reach because data on unique viewers were unavailable.

[b] No Twitter data are available for MTC because the campaign does not maintain a dedicated Twitter account.

geted audiences through social media (e.g., 2,880,304 Facebook fans) at rates comparable to those reached through its website (e.g., 2,955,647 website sessions).

Campaign reach via social media increased from January to December 2015. In that time, the number of Facebook fans increased by 26 percent for RWC, 7 percent for MTC, and 35 percent for Recovery Month (Appendix D). The number of Twitter followers increased by 16 percent for RWC and by 27 percent for Recovery Month. The number of monthly YouTube views fluctuated throughout the year, with a high of 1,310 views in September for RWC, 686,509 views in July for MTC, and 3,472 views in September for Recovery Month (Appendix D).

The campaigns aired more than a quarter-million radio PSAs and more than 100,000 television PSAs in 2015. In 2015, across all four campaigns, there were more than 400,000 PSAs aired on television and radio (Table 6.4). Correspondingly, there were more than 38.5 billion radio PSA listener impressions and more than 4.3 billion television PSA viewer impressions.[4] RWC was responsible for the vast majority of radio

Table 6.4
Public Service Announcement Reach, 2015

Organization	Radio PSA Airings	Radio PSA Listener Impressions	Television PSA Airings	Television PSA Viewer Impressions
RWC	36,970	37,278,207,400	15,476	3,027,994,220
MTC	11,725	110,048,000	39,135	312,560,637
VCL	128,948	619,026,200	43,616	362,261,877
Recovery Month	91,414	497,013,820	59,835	692,898,000
Total	269,057	38,504,295,420	158,062	4,395,714,734

---

[4]   Impressions reflect the estimated number of times that the PSAs were viewed or listened to during the times they were aired.

and television PSA viewer impressions, many of which came from the American Forces Radio and Television Service (AFRTS). AFRTS radio airings accounted for half of RWC's total radio airings but constituted the vast majority of total RWC radio impressions (more than 99 percent). Although AFRTS television airings made up only a small proportion of RWC's total television airings (9 percent), they constituted almost all of the total RWC television impressions (96 percent).

The timing of PSAs differed throughout the year (Figures 6.1 and 6.2). RWC and MTC primarily aired radio PSAs in the first half of the year (Figure 6.1). All of MTC's radio PSAs aired from January to March; 71 percent of RWC's were aired between January and June. In contrast, 71 percent of VCL and 89 percent of Recovery Month radio PSAs were aired in the latter part of the year, from July to December. Similar patterns were observed for radio PSA viewer impressions, except that RWC had a more even distribution of impressions throughout the year (see Appendix D for the number of monthly radio PSA airings and viewer impressions for each campaign). The combined effort across campaigns meant that radio PSAs were being disseminated continually throughout the year. However, to the extent that PSAs contained messages that were unique to a campaign, certain messages may have reached target audiences only during particular times of year.

Compared with broadcasts of radio PSAs, airings of television PSAs were more evenly distributed across the year for all campaigns (Figure 6.2). Seventy-one percent of RWC's television PSAs and 64 percent of MTC's television PSAs aired from January to June. VCL aired 55 percent of its television PSAs in the first half of the year. Two-thirds of Recovery Month's television PSAs (66 percent) aired in the latter part of

Figure 6.1
Percentage of Total Radio Public Service Announcements That Aired in 2015

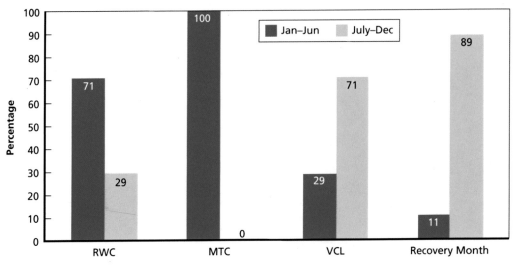

RAND RR1612-6.1

Figure 6.2
Percentage of Total Television Public Service Announcements That Aired in 2015

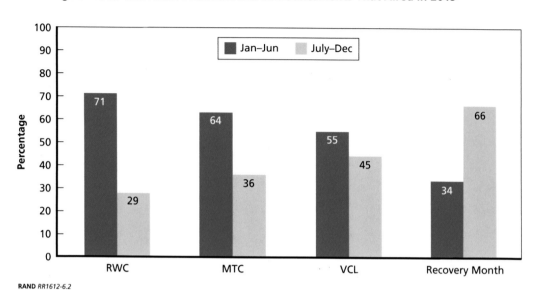

RAND *RR1612-6.2*

2015. Television PSA viewer impressions were similarly distributed for MTC and VCL, with more than two-thirds of viewer impressions occurring in the first half of the year, while 97 percent of Recovery Month's television viewer impressions occurred in the latter half (see Appendix D for the number of monthly television airings and viewer impressions for each campaign).

Campaigns distributed more than 10 million materials, attended more than 250 events, and worked with more than 1,000 partners. VCL was the biggest user of conferences or events as a vehicle for outreach, with events attended in 2015, or an average of 17 per month (Table 6.5). At events, VCL distributed more than 9 million outreach materials (e.g., brochures, key chains) to attendees in 2015. RWC and MTC utilized events to a lesser extent.

Recovery Month adopts a slightly different approach to outreach activities. Recovery Month encourages local partner organizations and groups to download a Recovery Month toolkit from its website and use it to host events in September and throughout the year. Recovery Month does not have a complete listing of events that partners have hosted because organizations voluntarily log the events on Recovery Month's website, and not all of them necessarily did so. Recovery Month provided a partial listing of Recovery Month events attended by SAMHSA officials, which totaled 26 events in 2015. The number of downloaded campaign materials from Recovery Month's website is provided in a subsequent section. (See Appendix D for a list of attendance at conferences and events submitted by MTC, VCL, and Recovery Month.)

Each of the four campaigns partnered with more than 100 organizations on outreach efforts (see Appendix D for a list of partner organizations). We compared part-

Table 6.5
Outreach Activities, 2015

Organization	Conferences or Events Attended	Campaign Materials Distributed[a]	Partner Organizations
RWC	19	242,120	126
MTC	32	419,505	403[b]
VCL	207	9,447,436	403[b]
Recovery Month	26[c]	—[d]	220
Total	258	10,109,061	716[e]

[a] Materials included brochures, infographics, toolkits, and campaign-branded merchandise (e.g., key chains, magnets).

[b] MTC and VCL partner organizations were grouped together in our assessment; 405 reflects the combined number for both campaigns.

[c] Number of Recovery Month events attended by a SAMHSA official. Does not include events independently hosted by planning partners.

[d] Recovery Month distributes campaign materials online where they can be downloaded for free from the campaign website.

[e] This number exceeds the total number of partner organizations because there was overlap among the organizations and agencies with which the four campaigns partnered.

ner lists across campaigns and identified 32 organizations that were partners of at least two of the agencies sponsoring the four campaigns. The 32 partners were American Mental Health Counselors Association; American Psychological Association; American Red Cross; Anxiety and Depression Association of America; Army Wife Network; Blue Star Families; Bob Woodruff Foundation; Catholic Charities USA; Easterseals; Elizabeth Dole Foundation; Gold Star Wives of America; Grace After Fire; Hire Heroes USA; Homes for Our Troops; Mental Health America; Mental Health America of Texas; Mental Health Association; Military Officers Association of America; MilitaryOneClick; National Alliance on Mental Illness; National Association of Social Workers; National Association of State Mental Health Program Directors; National Coalition for Homeless Veterans; National Council for Behavioral Health; National Military Family Association; Pets for Patriots; Semper Fi Fund; Student Veterans of America; Suicide Awareness Voices of Education; Team Red, White & Blue; Tragedy Assistance Program for Survivors; and United Service Organizations (USO).

Campaign Engagement

The most-viewed resources and top downloads varied across campaigns. The most-viewed RWC site page, garnering nearly 60,000 views, was a page on the military-to-civilian employment transition that is not directly related to mental health but is commonly considered a stressor that could affect the well-being of service members and their families. The most-downloaded item was an infographic with five tips to stay mission ready, which provided psychological well-being advice (finding time for yourself, breaking down obstacles, getting physical training in, avoiding alcohol and drugs, and finding someone you can count on).

For MTC, a resource locator page and a page about PTSD were viewed more than a half-million times each. The resource locator page allows visitors to find VA resources by ZIP code or state, and it links with the SAMHSA locator. The PTSD page contains video profiles of veterans who have experienced PTSD, as well as information about signs, symptoms, and treatment, and next steps for getting help. The most-downloaded MTC item was an infographic about PTSD. For VCL, the homepage was the most-viewed part of the site, at more than a half-million views. The most-downloaded item was a fact sheet about VCL.

Recovery Month's homepage was that campaign's most-visited website. The most-downloaded resource was the toolkit with resources for partners to plan and host Recovery Month events and information about mental and substance use disorders, treatment, and recovery support resources.

Looking across campaigns, we found that, for at least three of the four campaigns, the most-viewed pages focused on outreach and promotion, service, benefit and resource navigation, and testimonials. Not surprisingly, the homepage was one of the most frequently viewed pages for all campaigns. Across all four campaigns, the most-downloaded items focused on outreach and promotion. The most–frequently viewed videos differed across campaigns, but for RWC and MTC, the videos featured individual testimonies about mental illness and recovery.

More than half of all website sessions in 2015 consisted of a single page view. Table 6.6 provides the average monthly *bounce rates* (i.e., the percentage of sessions in which only one page is viewed before a user leaves the website) for campaign websites from 2012 to 2015. In 2015, the average monthly bounce rates for all campaigns exceeded 50 percent. Depending on a website's intended purpose, target bounce rates vary. Websites that mainly refer users to resources or other websites might expect higher bounce rates (e.g., 70 percent or above), whereas websites designed to provide

Table 6.6
Average Monthly Bounce Rate (%)

Organization	2012	2013	2014	2015	Percentage Change from 2012 to 2015
RWC	10.93	22.88	34.46	57.87	46.94
MTC	71.17	74.42	76.80	69.08	–2.09
VCL	60.41	64.79	66.27	65.72	5.31
Recovery Month	86.41[a]	63.43	50.68	56.39	–30.02

[a] Recovery Month bounce data were available only for July to December 2012.

information might expect bounce rates closer to 30 or 40 percent (Kaczmarek, 2014). Website industry experts consider bounce rates above 50 percent to be worrisome and an indicator of poor engagement (Clifton, 2010; Kaushik, 2007).

From 2012 to 2015, VCL and MTC had generally consistent average monthly bounce rates that hovered around 60 and 70 percent, respectively. Recovery Month had the largest average monthly bounce rate in any year examined across campaigns, at 86 percent in 2012, but ended 2015 with the lowest, at 56 percent. RWC had the lowest average monthly bounce rate at 11 percent in 2012, maintained average monthly bounce rates below 50 percent in 2013 and 2014, but ended 2015 with an average monthly bounce rate of 58 percent.

Although bounce rates serve as a useful general indicator of user engagement, other engagement metrics, such as average session duration and pages per visit, are also important and presented in the sections below (Bischoff, 2015).

Visits across all campaign websites were, on average, less than two minutes in 2015. The average time spent on a site can indicate a user's level of interest or engagement (Kaczmarek, 2014). However, sites also may be designed to contain information that is brief, to the point, and written for a low literacy level, and this content may take less time to view than larger amounts of information presented at a high literacy level. In 2015, all campaigns had an average session duration of less than two minutes (Figure 6.3), compared with an industry standard of two to three minutes (Bischoff, 2015). From 2012 to 2015, the average session length decreased by 43 percent for RWC, 12 percent for MTC,

Figure 6.3
Average Session Length, 2012–2015

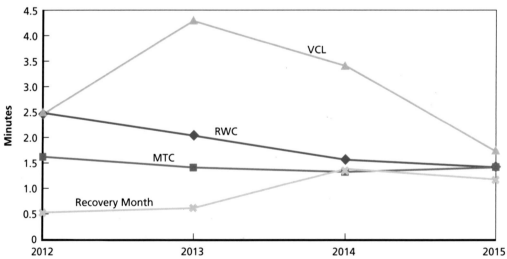

NOTE: Average session length was computed by summing yearly total session length and dividing by the yearly total number of sessions. Average session length decreased over time across all campaigns except Recovery Month.

RAND RR1612-6.3

and 30 percent for VCL. Recovery Month had the lowest average session duration of approximately 30 seconds in 2012, but by 2015 the average duration had leaped 125 percent to 1.17 minutes. It is unclear based on the data available for this evaluation whether the brevity of site visits was due to low user interest or engagement or to effective design of material that was quickly processed.

The number of pages viewed per session is another indicator of how engaging and accessible users find a site's content (Bischoff, 2015). Increasing numbers of pages viewed per session may suggest increasing satisfaction with site content (Kaczmarek, 2014) and is also considered an indicator of overall engagement.

In 2015, the average pages viewed per session ranged from less than one and a half (MTC) to three (Recovery Month). Depending on the goals of the campaigns, these rates may or may not be sufficient for users to locate and utilize needed information. If campaigns intend for most of the needed information to be obtained in a few pages, then the range of average pages viewed per session may be adequate. However, more data on user information needs upon entry to the site and whether those needs were satisfied would have to be gathered to support this interpretation.

From 2012 to 2015, the average number of pages viewed per session decreased by 62 percent for RWC and 15 percent for MTC (Figure 6.4). The average number of pages viewed per session increased by 16 percent for VCL from 2012 to 2015. Although Recovery Month had the lowest number of pages viewed per session, with an average of 1.22 pages viewed per session in 2012, it was the only campaign to make consistent

Figure 6.4
Average Number of Pages Viewed per Session, 2012–2015

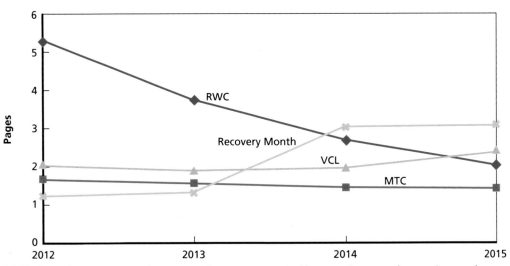

NOTE: Annual average page views per session were computed by summing annual page views and dividing by annual sessions.
RAND RR1612-6.4

gains on this metric each year. Recovery Month experienced an increase of 152 percent in the average number of pages viewed per session from 2012 to 2015.

In 2015, the campaigns facilitated more than 10 million interactions via Facebook. The number of Facebook posts, interactions (i.e., cumulative likes, comments, and shares), and impressions were used to evaluate engagement with campaigns via Facebook. Campaigns actively posted messages or materials via Facebook to engage target audiences (Table 6.7). With the exception of VCL, which does not employ Facebook, each campaign had several hundred posts in 2015, with monthly averages of 52 for RWC, 17 for MTC, and 33 for Recovery Month.

MTC contributed to the vast majority of total Facebook interactions, generating more than 9.5 million likes, comments, and shares in 2015. Levels of Facebook interactions fluctuated greatly throughout the year for MTC (Appendix D). Though MTC issued the fewest Facebook posts, it generated the highest levels of interactions and impressions. This is likely due in part to MTC having significantly more Facebook fans but may also indicate that MTC has more-engaging posts, a larger network, or more-engaged users. For example, peak engagement occurred in May with 1,716,060 likes, comments, and shares, whereas the lowest level of engagement in any year examined across campaigns occurred in September with 100,546 likes, comments, and shares (Table D.33). Recovery Month had the fewest Facebook interactions, with 48,668 likes, comments, and shares in 2015. For RWC and Recovery Month, a substantial proportion of their Facebook interactions were concentrated in their peak months (see Appendix D for monthly Facebook interactions for each campaign). RWC had a high of 398,282 interactions in September, which accounted for 63 percent of its total Facebook interactions in 2015. Recovery Month peak engagement occurred in September, which is National Recovery Month, with 25,856 likes, comments, and shares, which composed 53 percent of Recovery Month's total Facebook interactions in 2015 (Appendix D).

Campaign content was shown more than 963 million times via Facebook in 2015. Correspondingly, MTC was responsible for most of the campaigns' collective Facebook impressions (i.e., the number of times a post from a campaign's page is displayed, whether the post is clicked on or not) in 2015 (Table 6.7). Content from MTC's

Table 6.7
Facebook Engagement Indicators, 2015

Organization	Facebook Posts	Likes, Comments, and Shares	Impressions
RWC	629	633,334	19,046,756
MTC	203	9,510,703	941,786,500
Recovery Month	395	48,668	2,558,087
Total	1,227	10,192,705	963,391,343

NOTE: VCL is omitted from the table because no active campaign Facebook page is maintained. Facebook only tracks registered users.

Facebook page was exposed to other Facebook accounts nearly 942 million times. May was the peak month, with 148,393,510 Facebook impressions for MTC. As with Facebook interactions, a substantial proportion of Facebook impressions from RWC and Recovery Month was concentrated in their peak months (see Table D.34 for monthly Facebook impressions). In 2015, Recovery Month had a peak of 1,078,427 Facebook impressions in September, which made up 42 percent of its total impressions. RWC had a peak of 6,857,168 impressions in November, which constituted 36 percent of its total impressions.

YouTube was not being used consistently across campaigns. Indicators of YouTube engagement included average view duration, the number of likes and dislikes, favorites gained and lost, and subscribers gained and lost (Table 6.8). Average view duration can be considered an indicator of engagement. RWC had the longest average views at 3.6 minutes. MTC and Recovery Month averaged view durations of approximately 1 minute. This could indicate that individuals are watching mostly shorter videos or only part of longer videos.

YouTube likes or dislikes and favorites gained or lost can also be considered indicators of more-active engagement because they are reflective of viewer feedback. Similarly, subscribers generally tend to be more engaged and view content on a more regular basis. RWC and Recovery Month had fairly low levels of active engagement, according to these indicators. Though MTC had higher levels of engagement overall, this included both positive and negative responses.

Campaigns were using Twitter to communicate with users in a very limited way. Only RWC and Recovery Month actively maintain campaign-related Twitter accounts to engage their target populations (though MTC- and VCL-related information is disseminated through other VA-affiliated Twitter accounts). In 2015, the two campaigns generated 2,535 tweets. RWC had a total of 1,865 tweets, or an average of five per day, and Recovery Month had 670 tweets, or an average of two per day. Little engagement was observed with respect to direct messages (i.e., private messages sent between two or more users that are only visible to those users). For instance, RWC sent 14 direct messages and received 46, while Recovery Month sent no direct messages and received four in all of 2015.

Table 6.8
YouTube Engagement Indicators, 2015

Organization	Average View Duration (minutes)	Likes	Dislikes	Favorites Gained	Favorites Lost	Subscribers Gained	Subscribers Lost
RWC	3.6	42	1	8	0	12	0
MTC	1.3	6,269	2,565	631	74	6,918	1,586
Recovery Month	0.9	75	0	0	0	6	0

NOTE: VCL is omitted from the table because there is no dedicated VCL YouTube channel.

We studied the number of tweets posted by official channels (i.e., @RealWarriors, @DCoEPage, @MilitaryHealth for RWC; @VA_OEF_OIF, @VAVetBenefits, @DeptVetAffairs, @VA_PTSD_Info, @VeteransHealth for MTC and VCL; and @RecoveryMonth and @SAMHSA for Recovery Month). Two of these channels—@RealWarriors and @RecoveryMonth—are dedicated to a campaign. The remainder are accounts that disseminate campaign information. We also examined the number of tweets posted by nonofficial channels (i.e., other organizations' tweets that mention a campaign) to determine how well the initiatives generate interest in their messages. Figure 6.5 shows the volume of tweets posted by official channels and nonofficial channels. Figure 6.6 shows the proportion of official posts that were retweeted by nonofficial channels (furthering the messaging of the campaigns). For RWC, approximately 25 percent of its posts generated some engagement from nonofficial channels, and this volume increased over time even as the number of official tweets declined. VCL tweets resulted in high volumes of engagement, with 25 percent of messages being retweeted. For Recovery Month, 25 percent to 50 percent of its tweets were retweeted. Due to the limited number of official MTC tweets, we were unable to draw conclusions about Twitter engagement.

Figure 6.5
Tweet Volume by Month from Official and Unofficial Channels

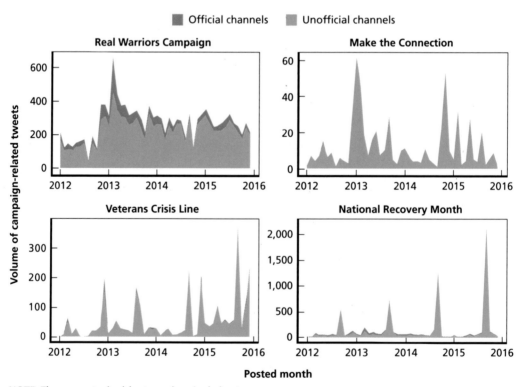

NOTE: These are stacked (not overlapping) charts.
RAND RR1612-6.5

Figure 6.6
Proportion of Official-Channel Tweets Seeking to Generate Engagement

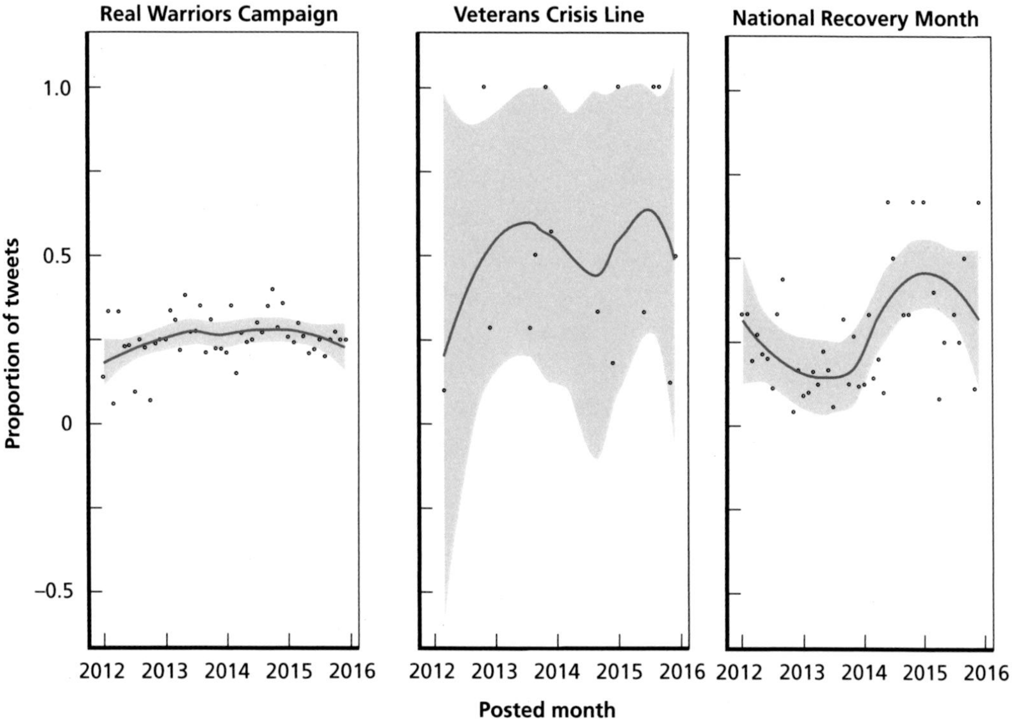

NOTE: Data are aggregated by month. The dots represent data points, the blue line is the trend line over time, and the gray area represents the confidence interval.
RAND RR1612-6.6

We could not identify a consistent pattern of Twitter activity for most campaigns (Figure 6.5). There is, however, a clear cyclical nature to the activity of Recovery Month, whose tweets peaked in volume every September (i.e., National Recovery Month). This number has increased over time, but that is largely attributable to a growth in the Twitter population.

Campaign Users

Limited demographic information is available on the users of the mental health awareness campaigns. For this evaluation, we have demographic information (i.e., age and gender) for Facebook and YouTube reach[5] and geographic location data for website (i.e., top city), Facebook (i.e., top six cities), and YouTube (i.e., top six states). We first review the demographic information available for RWC, MTC, and Recovery Month.

---

[5] RWC provided demographic data for Twitter, but because no other campaign has these data, we do not report them here. RWC's Twitter demographic data are provided in Table D.39.

VCL is omitted because it does not maintain social media accounts. Then, we review the geographic location data from all campaign websites and the Facebook and YouTube location data for RWC, MTC, and Recovery Month.

Campaign users include men and women of all ages. RWC and MTC Facebook reach was nearly evenly split between men and women (Table 6.9). In contrast, 72 percent of Recovery Month Facebook fans were women. Similar patterns were observed for YouTube reach, with RWC and MTC achieving somewhat comparable reach across gender, while Recovery Month's YouTube reach was 68 percent female.

Viewers ages 18–24 and 25–34 composed 52 percent of RWC's Facebook fans and 51 percent of its YouTube views. The majority of MTC Facebook fans (75 percent) were 45 or older, whereas 68 percent of MTC YouTube views occurred among viewers younger than 45. Recovery Month Facebook and YouTube reach was more evenly distributed across different age segments of the population (Table 6.10).

Despite limited Twitter presence, campaigns are reaching Twitter users with above-average influence on the overall group of users posting about mental health. Each campaign appears to be reaching similar populations of influential Twitter users in the area of mental health (Figure 6.7). The users who posted content related to the campaigns on Twitter were generally more influential than the average user posting mental health–related content. We defined *influence* as the centrality of a

Table 6.9
Facebook Demographics, by Percentage

| Organization | Gender | | Age | | | | | | |
	Male	Female	13–17	18–24	25–34	35–44	45–54	55–64	65+
RWC	47	52	1	29	23	14	14	10	7
MTC	46	53	<1	7	7	10	20	28	27
Recovery Month	27	72	<1	6	21	24	24	17	8

NOTE: Numbers may not add to 100 because of rounding.

Table 6.10
YouTube Demographics, by Percentage

| Organization | Gender | | Age | | | | | | |
	Male	Female	13–17	18–24	25–34	35–44	45–54	55–64	65+
RWC	45	55	1	19	32	17	16	10	5
MTC	57	43	1	22	27	18	11	10	11
Recovery Month	32	68	3	12	29	17	18	14	6

NOTE: Numbers may not add to 100 because of rounding.

Figure 6.7
Influence of Campaign-Engaged Users

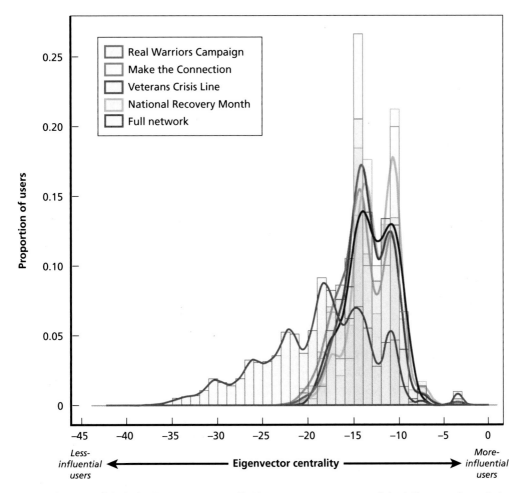

NOTE: The x-axis (labeled "eigenvector centrality") represents a measure of the influence of a node in a network. Higher values (i.e., values closer to 0) indicate that users are more influential. Eigenvector centrality has been log transformed.
RAND RR1612-6.7

user to a social network, as measured by the user's number of connections in the network and, in turn, the number of connections that those connections have. In other words, the users who posted campaign-related content were connected to more people than other users posting about mental health, suggesting that the campaign-related content could be seen by more people.

Table 6.11 lists the ten states with the highest number of active duty service members, veterans, and individuals ages 18 or older in the general population as of 2015. Each campaign's geographic reach may correspond with where its target populations are most concentrated. For instance, we might expect the campaigns with veterans as

Table 6.11
Ten States with the Largest Active Duty, Veteran, and Adult Populations

	U.S. Active Duty		U.S. Veterans		U.S. Adults	
Rank	Location	Population	Location	Population	Location	Population
1	California	155,051	California	1,851,470	California	29,526,000
2	Virginia	122,884	Texas	1,680,418	Texas	19,574,000
3	Texas	117,623	Florida	1,583,697	Florida	15,606,000
4	North Carolina	100,867	Pennsylvania	939,069	New York	15,437,000
5	Georgia	69,322	New York	892,221	Pennsylvania	9,924,000
6	Florida	60,095	Ohio	866,481	Illinois	9,833,000
7	Washington	57,926	Virginia	781,388	Ohio	8,901,000
8	Hawaii	49,519	North Carolina	775,020	Michigan	7,751,000
9	Colorado	37,731	Georgia	752,882	North Carolina	7,536,000
10	South Carolina	36,670	Illinois	721,575	Georgia	7,469,000

SOURCES: Office of the Deputy Assistant Secretary of Defense (Military Community and Family Policy), undated-a; National Center for Veterans Analysis and Statistics, 2014; U.S. Census Bureau, 2015a.

the primary target audience to have the greatest reach to California, Texas, and Florida, because these states have the highest numbers of veterans.

There was some alignment between the states with the most website sessions, Facebook activity, and YouTube activity and the locations with the most active duty and veteran populations. Table 6.12 lists the city with the most website sessions in 2015 for each campaign. We obtained data for only the top city with the greatest number of sessions because this process metric was being routinely collected and reported by campaigns. The top cities reached by MTC and VCL (Houston, Texas, and Canandaigua, New York, respectively) were in states with the largest

Table 6.12
Top City Reached by Campaign Websites, 2015

Campaign	Top City	Website Sessions
RWC	New York, New York	7,067
MTC	Houston, Texas[a]	61,488
VCL	Canandaigua, New York[a]	77,780
Recovery Month	Washington, D.C.	5,129

NOTE: Each campaign provided website geographic data in a different format. RWC provided monthly data on the single top city and number of sessions. MTC provided monthly data on the top 25 cities and VCL on the top ten cities generating the most sessions. Recovery Month provided data on the city of origin for every session each month by state. To calculate the top city from which the most sessions originated for 2015, we identified the top six cities with the greatest number of sessions each month and summed the number of sessions of the cities over the year. The table reports the top city and estimated number of sessions over the year for each of the campaigns.

[a] City is in one of the top ten states with the largest primary population targeted by the campaign.

veteran populations. In contrast, the top cities reached by RWC and Recovery Month (New York and Washington, D.C., respectively) were not in states with the largest concentrations of their target audiences.[6] The city with the most VCL website sessions, Canandaigua, New York, is where VCL is housed and where the Veterans Integrated Service Network 2 Center of Excellence for Suicide Prevention is located.

Table 6.13 provides information on the top six cities reached in 2015 by each campaign's Facebook outreach efforts. Three of the six top cities reached by RWC were outside the continental United States (i.e., Puerto Rico, United Kingdom, and Nepal). However, campaign staff report that the high number of views originating in Nepal is not representative of typical campaign reach and is due to several posts going viral, combined with an error in the Facebook algorithm for page recommendations (Duthaler, 2016). Approximately 13 percent of active duty service members reside outside the United States, with 6.7 percent in East Asia and 5.1 percent in Europe (Office of the Deputy Assistant Secretary of Defense, 2014). Moreover, DoD data (Defense Manpower Data Center, 2015) indicated that as of December 2015, less than 1 percent of active duty personnel were stationed in Puerto Rico (725 service members) or the

Table 6.13
Facebook Top Six Cities (average seven-day reach), 2015

	RWC		MTC		Recovery Month	
Rank	Location	Views	Location	Views	Location	Views
1	San Juan, Puerto Rico	2,103	Houston, Texas[a]	46,972	Philadelphia, Pennsylvania[a]	172
2	London, United Kingdom	1,785	Chicago, Illinois[a]	43,961	New York, New York[a]	166
3	Chicago, Illinois	1,503	New York, New York[a]	40,261	Los Angeles, California[a]	156
4	New York, New York	1,472	Los Angeles, California[a]	40,174	Chicago, Illinois[a]	143
5	Kathmandu, Nepal[b]	1,285	San Antonio, Texas[a]	31,054	Houston, Texas[a]	134
6	Los Angeles, California[a]	1,275	Phoenix, Arizona	29,606	Boston, Massachusetts	106

NOTE: VCL does not maintain an active Facebook page.

[a] One of the top ten states with the largest population targeted by the campaign.

[b] Campaign staff report that the high number of views originating in Nepal is not representative of typical campaign reach and is due to several posts going viral, combined with an error in the Facebook algorithm for page recommendations.

---

[6] It is possible that the high volume of Recovery Month web sessions in Washington, D.C., came from individuals who worked in the city but resided in neighboring Virginia, which was one of the top ten states in terms of veteran population. However, there is no way to test this proposition with the data available.

United Kingdom (8,397 service members). Only one of the top six cities reached by RWC—Los Angeles—was located in a state with a large active duty population. For both MTC and Recovery Month, their top five cities with the greatest Facebook reach were in states that had large numbers of their target populations.

As shown in Table 6.14, the states with the greatest YouTube reach were more closely aligned to the states with the most concentrated numbers of the targeted population across the campaigns. The top six states with the most MTC YouTube views were among the ten with the highest number of U.S. veterans. For RWC and Recovery Month, four of the top six states with the most YouTube views were among the states with some of the largest numbers of active duty service members and U.S. adults.

Across all of the media platforms, Texas and New York tied for the most frequent appearance on top ten lists (seven times each), followed by California (six times), and Illinois (four times).

Summary of Findings

Our analysis of campaigns' process data, Twitter data, and the expert panel results revealed that campaigns overall are likely reaching their target audiences, but it is unclear whether audience engagement is adequate to achieve campaign goals. Specifically, we assessed campaigns' reach, engagement, and user demographics. We found that more than 4 million visits were made to the campaign websites in 2015. We also found the following:

- More than half of all website sessions in 2015 consisted of a single page view.
- Visits across all campaign websites averaged less than two minutes in 2015.

Table 6.14
YouTube Top Six States, 2015

	RWC		MTC		Recovery Month	
Rank	Location	Views	Location	Views	Location	Views
1	Virginia[a]	1,345	California[a]	410,267	California[a]	1,502
2	California[a]	1,308	Texas[a]	282,408	Georgia[a]	1,431
3	Maryland	690	New York[a]	175,254	Maryland	1,279
4	Texas[a]	690	Florida[a]	169,243	New York[a]	997
5	New York	499	Illinois[a]	114,096	Washington, D.C.	936
6	North Carolina[a]	461	Georgia[a]	100,919	Texas[a]	849

NOTE: VCL does not maintain an active YouTube page.
[a] City is in one of the ten states with the largest population targeted by the campaign.

- Average page views per session decreased over time (2012–2015) across all campaigns except Recovery Month.

More than 5.5 million people were reached through social media (i.e., Facebook fans, YouTube views, Twitter followers). Facebook was the most consistently used social media source across campaigns. YouTube was not used consistently across campaigns, and campaigns were using Twitter in a very limited way. Despite a limited Twitter presence, campaigns were reaching Twitter users with above-average influence on the overall group of users tweeting about mental health. There was some alignment among the states with the most website sessions, Facebook activity, and YouTube activity and the U.S. locations with the largest active duty and veteran populations.

Campaigns also aired more than 400,000 radio and television PSAs in 2015, distributed more than 10.1 million materials, attended more than 250 events, and worked with more than 700 partners. We identified 32 organizations—including the American Psychological Association, American Red Cross, National Alliance on Mental Illness, Suicide Awareness Voices of Education—that were partners of at least two of the agencies, and coordinating work with this set of partners may provide a starting point for agencies to increase coordination with each other.

The reach of most campaigns increased from 2012 to 2015. We cannot draw conclusions about whether users were part of campaign target audiences because no cross-platform measures of target membership audience were being collected by campaigns or across campaigns.

CHAPTER SEVEN

Key Findings and Recommendations for Improving DoD, VA, and HHS Approaches to Mental Health Public Awareness Campaigns

This chapter presents the results of our cross-agency evaluation of the four mental health public awareness campaigns. The evaluation focuses not on the individual campaigns themselves but on the campaigns' collective reach, areas of alignment or overlap, and collective impacts. This chapter synthesizes our findings, as relevant, from the four data sources (i.e., campaign process data, Twitter data analysis, content analysis, expert panel) that contributed to our evaluation in each content area, and presents recommendations for improving the campaigns. More information about the data sources, methods used to collect and analyze the data, and the associated findings can be found in Appendixes C through F. Because this evaluation relied on existing data sources (i.e., no primary data on campaign effectiveness were collected), the recommendations focus on ways to advance efficiency and coordination across campaigns and to improve campaign content and dissemination.

Key Findings

Scope and Content: Campaigns Have Complementary Target Populations, Desired Outcomes, and Messages That Are Reflected in Their Content

When assessing the scope and content of the four campaigns, a logical question is whether these four campaigns should have overlaps or redundancies in their scope and content and whether four separate campaigns are needed (as opposed to one overarching campaign). Without conducting a large-scale needs assessment to determine which populations are most in need of a campaign, and without an outcome evaluation that takes into account the cross-media and cross-campaign effects and synergies (e.g., whether being exposed to the same message via different channels or different campaigns makes the message more salient), we are unable to answer these types of questions. We are, however, able to highlight areas of redundancy and overlap, as well as unique contributions of specific campaigns.

The four campaigns have distinct, yet overlapping, target populations, and they share overlapping desired short- and long-term outcomes to improve knowledge of mental health symptoms and increase positive perceptions of individuals with mental health conditions and of mental health treatment. There were no shared measures being used by campaigns to track these shared desired outcomes across overlapping target populations. The majority of content shared across campaigns (82 percent) aligned with desired outcomes shared across campaigns, with about half of the campaign content communicating the symptoms of mental health conditions. Campaigns vary in the desired outcomes they emphasize. Though we focus on shared desired outcomes across campaigns, we note that most individual campaign materials did align with the desired outcomes of the individual campaign. Campaigns offer a wide variety of messages for individuals who are at risk for mental health conditions, symptomatic and considering mental health treatment, in crisis and in need of immediate support, and have completed treatment and are in recovery. We also found that individuals pictured in campaign materials generally reflected the target population for each campaign. There was less alignment between rank of individuals pictured and era (for veterans); however, there was also less content with rank and era clearly identified.

All campaigns have sections of their websites providing resources for site visitors. Despite commonalities in target populations and desired outcomes, however, the campaigns did not fully cross-reference each other in their resource lists. In particular, Recovery Month is not referenced by DoD and VA campaigns (though other SAMHSA resources are referenced). In addition, about half of campaign webpages did not contain a clearly marked source of information used to compile the material, making it difficult for users to judge the credibility of the information or seek further information on the topic.

Scope and Content: Campaigns Also Cover Some Unique Scope and Content

There are several unique messages delivered by individual campaigns (Table 5.6). Recovery Month aims to communicate that mental health is part of overall wellness. VCL focuses on promoting its phone, text, and chat lines. RWC has a wide range of multifaceted messages that are unique (e.g., experiencing psychological stress as a result of combat is common). RWC's major mentioned resource is the DCoE Outreach Center. Recovery Month has a specific emphasis on substance use, although the other three campaigns have at least some substance use materials (10 to 28 percent of their content). Recovery Month is also the only campaign that targets the general population. MTC's unique contribution is a large video library of testimonials, and it is heavily focused on veterans. The Recovery Month website allows easy access to a SAMHSA Behavioral Health Treatment Locator, and the MTC and VCL websites allow easy access to a Resource Locator that allows users to find resources available through VA, the National Resource Directory, and the SAMHSA Behavioral Health Treatment Locator.

Dissemination: Campaigns Are Using Multiple Channels to Reach Their Target Audiences

All campaigns used multiple channels (e.g., websites, social media, in-person outreach) to disseminate their materials and messages to target audiences. Our analysis of campaigns' process data and Twitter data, as well as feedback from the expert panel, revealed that campaigns overall are likely to reach their target audiences. Specifically, we assessed campaigns' reach, engagement, and user demographics. Except for Recovery Month,[1] the campaigns' reach increased from 2012 to 2015. Because campaigns did not collect information showing whether users were part of their target audiences, we could not calculate the extent to which the campaigns reached their target populations.

We found that more than 4 million visits were made to the campaign websites in 2015. However, visitors often spent only a brief amount of time on the sites and interacted only minimally with them. On average, visitors remained on the sites for less than two minutes and viewed 1.5 to 3 site pages (depending on campaign). More than half of all visits were to a single webpage. Average page views per session decreased from 2012 to 2015 for all campaigns except Recovery Month.

Campaigns collectively reached as many as 5.6 million people through social media (i.e., Facebook fans, YouTube viewers, Twitter followers). MTC contributed more than 90 percent of the Facebook fans and YouTube views. Facebook was the most consistently used social media source across campaigns. YouTube was not used consistently across campaigns, and campaigns are using Twitter in a very limited way. Despite this limited Twitter presence, campaigns reached Twitter users with above-average influence on the overall group of users tweeting about mental health.

Campaigns also reached individuals through other channels. They aired 400,000 radio and television PSAs in 2015. RWC aired the most PSAs, contributing more than 90 percent of the listener and viewer impressions generated by the four campaigns combined. Campaigns also used in-person outreach (e.g., booths or tables at more than 250 events likely to reach the campaign target audiences and partnerships with more than 1,000 other organizations) to distribute more than 10.1 million materials. Campaigns also used campaign partners to distribute materials and conduct outreach to their target populations. Partners' roles vary from cross-listing the campaign on their websites to hosting campaign-related events. We identified a set of 32 national and regional partner organizations—including the American Psychological Association, American Red Cross, National Alliance on Mental Illness,

---

[1] From 2012 to 2015, the Recovery Month website analytics program was revamped and migrated from Webtrends to Google Analytics. The systems calculate user interaction metrics differently. In addition, the site metrics changed to the standardized SAMHSA Google Analytics tracking code. In March 2015, a new Recovery Month website launched as an internal site within SAMHSA.gov. It contained 75 percent less content than the previous site and provided access to only 2014 materials and some 2015 materials, whereas the prior version had offered more than 15 years of content.

and Suicide Awareness Voices of Education—that were partners of at least two of the three agencies operating public awareness campaigns.

Our findings focus only on campaign reach because campaigns did not collect information about whether users are part of their target audience, so we could not calculate the degree to which those reached were part of the target audience for any single campaign or the campaigns collectively, and no cross-platform measures of reach were being collected by campaigns or across campaigns.

Efficacy: Campaigns Followed Many Best Practices in Design and Dissemination, Which Suggests That, If They Reach Their Target Audiences, Campaigns Are Likely to Achieve Their Desired Outcomes

Overall, we found that most campaign content aligned with best practices identified by our expert panel. Specifically, our experts indicated that materials clearly communicate the messages of the campaigns, use evidence-based messaging recommendations, use messengers that will be seen as credible to the target audiences, and often incorporate positive role models.

Though experts identified individual areas for each campaign to improve (Appendix F), several recommendations applied to all campaigns. One such recommendation focused on privacy. Experts said campaigns should consider clarifying the extent to which participation in any mental health assessments or treatment would be anonymous. In some instances, campaign materials state that a service is confidential, but the materials may not clearly state exactly how people's information will be collected and potentially used. This could deter people from interacting with campaign resources.

In addition, experts said campaigns must consider how much to focus their messaging. Segmenting audiences into relevant groups helps when developing messages to address relevant concerns of the audience, increasing the likelihood that the audience will find the content relevant to their everyday lives. Failing to segment content adequately may mean that in trying to reach everyone, a campaign may not reach any one group very well. Indeed, campaigns report significant efforts to segment their target audiences. However, summarizing across campaigns, the extent to which campaigns effectively reach important secondary groups—such as family members, health providers, and employers—is still unclear. Experts said these audiences are important because of their influence on perceptions of mental health and mental health treatment and on help-seeking behavior.

Recommendations for Improving Mental Health Public Awareness Campaigns

This section presents recommendations for collectively improving DoD, VA, and HHS approaches to mental health public awareness campaigns. It is organized into four sections: (1) improving cross-agency efficiency and coordination of the campaigns, (2) improving the design and content of the campaigns, (3) improving dissemination of campaign messages, and (4) considering ways to provide direct connections to care. In each section, we begin with those recommendations that are relatively easier to implement, followed by those that will take greater effort and should be considered as part of a long-term improvement strategy or during any significant redevelopment efforts.

We direct each recommendation to the DoD, VA, and HHS campaigns (including campaign staff, contractors that work on behalf of these agencies, and leadership that guides the strategic direction and resource investments in these campaigns) or to a federal partner group (e.g., task force or working group that has cross-agency representation). When referring to a federal partner group, we presume that group includes staff from each agency in positions to influence campaign strategy. While the campaigns and the federal partner group may not be able to implement all the recommendations, we offer them for consideration because the campaigns are continually being refined. As a result of the significant delay in publishing this report, some recommendations may have already been addressed, so they should be considered with that in mind.

Recommendations for Improving Cross-Agency Efficiency and Coordination of Mental Health Messaging

Because the four campaigns are complementary in many ways (e.g., overlapping target populations and desired short- and long-term outcomes), there are many opportunities for improving efficiency and coordination across campaigns. We recommend the following changes to the campaign design, content, and cross-agency communication processes to improve efficiency and coordination.

Recommendation 1.1. Cross-Reference Other Campaigns More When Presenting Resources in Campaign Materials

Because they have some overlapping target populations and desired outcomes, campaigns could do more cross-referencing or linking to one another. Cross-referencing is an easy way to improve visibility and reach across campaigns, especially because they target similar populations. Inserting references to other campaigns is likely to be inexpensive because it requires minimal resources and no new content. While all campaigns cross-reference or link to VCL, which has the clearest purpose (i.e., promoting the crisis line, chat, and text), none mentions Recovery Month, and VCL mentions only MTC. Clearly defining areas of intentional overlap among campaigns (see more on this in Recommendation 1.3) may make it easier to identify new opportunities for appropriately cross-referencing or linking to each other.

The four campaigns could evaluate their existing materials to determine the most-appropriate places to add cross-references to the others, and then institute a process for reviewing new materials to ensure the other campaigns are mentioned where appropriate. For example, because all campaigns target service members with mental health needs, it may be important for them to reference VCL's crisis counseling. To be clear, we are recommending inserting links only when the complementary campaign or resources are appropriate for the specific overlapping target populations. **Who should take the lead: campaigns.**

Recommendation 1.2. Convene National and Regional Partners to Help Define a Strategic National Direction for Public Mental Health Education That DoD, VA, and HHS Can Use to Guide Their Efforts

All campaigns have developed partnerships to help further their outreach (e.g., partner website links to a campaign, partner hosts an event to promote a campaign). During our analysis of process data, we identified a set of 32 national and regional organizations (e.g., American Psychological Association, American Red Cross, National Alliance on Mental Illness, Suicide Awareness Voices of Education) that already partner with at least two of the three agencies. These partners are leaders in the field of mental health and could serve as valuable strategic partners. Right now, each agency conducts partnership activities with these organizations independently and focuses on campaign-specific needs (e.g., coordination of partner events). Coordinating with these partners in a more integrated way (e.g., through an advisory committee) may help provide national leadership to inform an overarching strategic direction for federal investment in mental health public awareness campaigns, as well as the specific direction of the individual campaigns. In addition, the DoD, VA, and HHS campaigns and the federal partner group could regularly convene the group of partners (plus additional organizations as appropriate) to ensure appropriate coordination is occurring across agencies (e.g., all campaign materials are being handed out at all relevant events) and to streamline or minimize the partnership burden on these organizations. **Who should take the lead: federal partner group, working with the campaigns.**

Recommendation 1.3. Clearly Define the Unique Contributions and Intentional Overlap in Messages and Target Populations Across the Campaigns

Our analysis of campaign scope and content identified both overlapping target populations and shared desired outcomes across campaigns, as well as specific unique contributions. An important next step for the campaigns and the federal partner group is to clearly define the overlaps and the rationale for the overlaps, and then ensure that each unique contribution is needed. This will help determine whether the four campaigns, as designed, are necessary or whether it is more efficient to consolidate specific messages or responsibilities into an overarching campaign. Defining unique contributions and areas of intentional overlap is also the first step to improved coordination and more-targeted messaging to shared populations across campaigns. The content analysis in this report (Appendix D) provides information that the campaigns may find useful in clearly defining and differentiating their campaigns in relation to each other. **Who should take the lead: federal partner group, working with the campaigns.**

Recommendation 1.4. Monitor Coordination of Current and New Campaign Efforts to Promote Strategic Coordination of Messaging and Dissemination

The CAP-G has provided the impetus for DoD, VA, and HHS to begin working together more closely on their mental health public awareness campaigns. Although the CAP-G Barriers to Care Working Group has dissolved, the three departments could build on the CAP-G work and create a new federal partner group tasked with strategic planning for how all federal agencies together can approach raising awareness of mental health issues and resources. In particular, MTC and RWC offer resources to active duty service members and veterans who are contemplating mental health support but are not in crisis. It may be helpful for these two campaigns to conduct a more targeted evaluation of ways to leverage each other's content, rather than each developing new content. For example, RWC has several video profiles of service members talking about their mental health experiences, but it could leverage MTC's much larger library of similar videos by using or linking to them on RWC's website. These campaigns may also want to coordinate dissemination strategies to ensure the appropriate content from each campaign reaches its target population.

The federal partner group could also be responsible for monitoring national trends related to mental health attitudes and behaviors and using the data to make coordinated decisions about the future strategic directions of campaigns. This could include using existing data from sources that track mental health stigma and barriers to care (e.g., the General Social Survey, the National Survey on Drug Use and Health) or sharing market research collected during the design of each campaign. Alternatively, the agencies may decide that a separate effort is needed to better track the mental health attitudes and behaviors that they are trying to influence, so they could jointly fund a regular needs assessment. For example, campaigns could coordinate to include a couple of items in an existing national survey to assess campaign exposure and shared desired outcomes.

Finally, the federal partner group could ensure that campaigns consider regularly sharing evaluation findings, particularly of novel or innovative campaign strategies, so that agencies can adopt the most-effective and most-appropriate cutting-edge strategies. **Who should take the lead: campaigns, working through the federal partner group.**

Recommendation 1.5. Develop a Targeted Set of Performance Measures That Cuts Across Campaigns

Persuading service members and veterans to access mental health care is a complex issue that cuts across multiple federal agencies. The Government Performance and Results Act of 1993 (GPRA) and the GPRA Modernization Act of 2010 require agencies to engage in performance measurement. However, as of June 2016, no measures existed to allow the federal government to track the performance of campaigns across DoD, VA, and HHS despite the campaigns' similar nature. A federal partner group could develop shared performance measures aligned with the campaigns' common messages and goals. For example, targets could be set for some process metrics (e.g., visits to and downloads from campaign websites, PSA airings, visits to campaign Facebook pages). Identifying targeted performance measures is likely to be challenging because of the variability in campaign goals and target audiences. Given the initial CAP-G request for a cross-agency evaluation of these efforts and the continuing visibility and importance of addressing mental health–related issues among service members and veterans, however, a federal partner group or the Government Accountability Office should consider developing some shared performance measures or targets for coordination across campaigns. **Who should take the lead: federal partner group.**

Recommendation 1.6. Explore the Development of Cross-Campaign and Cross-Platform Measures to Fully Capture Exposure and Synergy Among Campaigns

As of June 2016, the campaigns were unable to determine the degree to which those reached are part of the target audiences because they did not collect information on whether those viewing campaign websites and materials were part of their target populations. Additionally, campaigns were unable to determine whether the same user was exposed to multiple campaigns or to campaign materials across multiple platforms (e.g., website, YouTube). While the evidence base on cross-media and cross-platform measurement is nascent, these campaigns may provide an optimal setting to advance these areas of research and evaluation (given their overlapping target populations and shared desired outcomes and because they all use Google Analytics to track their web metrics). The term cross-media refers to the integration of multiple media platforms—e.g., television, online, social media (Lewis and Westlund, 2014). Ideally, an outcome evaluation would fully capture the effects of repeated exposure across campaigns and platforms. To do this, a cross-campaign and cross-media data set are required to determine the exposure of each user and to accurately understand reach among each target population. This type of data would answer such questions as: Are target audience members being exposed to the campaigns' messages targeting shared desired outcomes more frequently, and are there more impacts on shared desired outcomes as a result? Understanding this synergy would also allow campaigns to better target populations and audience segments (e.g., males ages 18–34, who are among the heaviest online video and mobile media consumers but are difficult to reach with television advertisements) and consequently approach media buys in a more integrated way. With an integrated view of campaigns and the use of multiplatform databases, campaign planners can better target outreach and associated resources (Fulgoni and Lipsman, 2015). Given the complexity and cross-agency nature of this recommendation, it may be best addressed by a federal partner group. **Who should take the lead: federal partner group.**

Recommendations for Campaign Content

We recommend changes to campaign content to streamline and focus it and clarify the level of anonymity and/or confidentiality associated with mental health self-assessments or any direct connections to care.

Recommendation 2.1. Determine Whether Source Information Should Be Clearly Marked on More Campaign Materials

Including information about the sources used to design materials allows users to better judge the credibility of campaign materials and pursue more information if they wish. During our content analysis, we found that about half of the campaign webpages (materials developed to provide informational content) did not clearly state the source for the content in the material. Campaign staff note that they rely on the evidence base to develop materials but strategically leave out source material to avoid being overly technical and to be more appealing to target audiences. However, omitting source information can render it difficult for users to judge the credibility of the information or to seek out more information. Khazaal et al. (2008) created DISCERN, a tool to help website users judge the content quality of mental health–related websites, with the goal of providing them with unbiased, evidence-based information. One criterion used by DISCERN is whether websites list a source for their information so that users can better judge credibility and pursue more information should they wish. The four campaigns should consider marking more source information on campaign materials (e.g., citing references for the effectiveness of mental health treatment). A full reference list likely does not need to be included, but providing one or two strategically selected and credible sources could help users better judge credibility and pursue more information. **Who should take the lead: campaigns.**

Recommendation 2.2. Review Campaign Content That Does Not Align with a Specific Campaign's Desired Outcome (or Shared Desired Outcome) and Consider Modification or Deletion

While our content analysis identified that most content (82 percent) was aligned with campaigns' desired outcomes (unique or shared), we still found that about 20 percent of materials did not align with a stated desired outcome for each campaign (except for VCL, whose unaligned content totaled 2 percent). It would be an easy and useful exercise for DoD, VA, and HHS campaigns to review content that does not align with campaigns' desired outcomes and determine whether to modify or delete unaligned content. This would help to ensure that users who see just one or two campaign materials (e.g., brief and minimally engaged website visitors) are still exposed to aligned messages. **Who should take the lead: campaigns.**

Recommendation 2.3. Review Content and Links to Ensure They Are All Current

During our content analysis, we identified a number of web links that were no longer working and content that had been developed prior to 2011 (i.e., more than five years old). For example, the RWC website hosts a podcast series that was last updated in May 2013. Removing outdated links and content would keep the site current and support a better user experience. If users hit a link that is no longer working or see outdated content, they may disengage and leave the site due to frustration or perceive the site as being out of date and not useful. DoD, VA, and HHS campaigns should identify outdated content and links that are no longer working on their sites and either update or delete the links and content. An easy way to identify these links is to use a service that checks for such things (e.g., generating a broken link report using the Google Analytics web package already in use for each campaign) that runs an automated and regular check to help identify any links that are not working. **Who should take the lead: campaigns.**

Recommendation 2.4. Specify the Level of Anonymity and/or Confidentiality Guaranteed by Self-Assessment and Direct Connections to Mental Health Care (e.g., Call Lines, Chat Lines)

Although we did not code for disclosures of anonymity during our content analysis, our expert panel raised concerns about the lack of explicit statements about how information collected in self-assessments would be used or saved and whether direct connections to care were anonymous. Though campaigns sometimes state that a resource is confidential, it is unclear exactly to whom information might be disclosed, for what purposes, and under what circumstances. For resources like self-assessments or direct connections to care that collect personal information from individuals, experts indicated that it was critical to specify the level of anonymity that a user could expect (e.g., all information is collected anonymously and will not be saved or reported in any way to DoD or VA). Concerns over lack of privacy of mental health information are salient in the military because there are circumstances under which service members' mental health information can be disclosed to their commanders and thus potentially affect the service members' careers (Acosta et al., 2014). Before choosing to use any of the online resources, service members will likely want to understand the level of privacy afforded to them. This will help them make more-informed choices about which resources to use, and if anonymity is guaranteed, they may be more likely to use a resource. DoD, VA, and HHS campaigns should review the self-assessment and direct connections to mental health care they offer and clearly specify the level of confidentiality or anonymity that users can expect. **Who should take the lead: campaigns.**

Recommendation 2.5. Enhance Materials Targeting Support Networks (and Other Target Audiences, as Relevant)

Campaigns have finite resources, and a key question is whether each campaign should focus less on support networks, or whether there should be a focused and well-developed independent campaign focused only on support networks. Our content analysis and expert panel ratings indicated that the campaigns' collective content for target populations other than service members and veterans was less developed (i.e., fewer materials and less clear materials). Experts recommended that the campaigns carefully consider whether the benefits of creating a small amount of content for multiple audiences outweighed creating additional richer or deeper content for a single audience. That determination was outside the scope of this evaluation, but our forthcoming outcome evaluation of the campaigns' effectiveness should reveal whether the campaigns as currently designed are changing mental health–related knowledge and perceptions among support network persons or whether a redesign is warranted. VCL has already begun to separate its materials promoting its phone line, chat, and text from its materials for veterans' support networks (e.g., the Power of One content). VCL may serve as an example to other campaigns of how to tailor content more specifically for support networks. **Who should take the lead: campaigns.**

Recommendations for Improving Dissemination and Reach of Campaign Content

We recommend changes to the campaigns' dissemination to improve their reach on social media, as well as adjustments to materials to better meet users' needs.

Recommendation 3.1. Develop Strategies to Use Twitter More Effectively

Social media is an inexpensive and potentially far-reaching outreach strategy, and a large community on Twitter engages in discourse about mental health (Appendix E). The campaigns should consider how to leverage that community to disseminate messages to extend their reach to target audiences. Our analysis of process data found that only RWC and Recovery Month actively use Twitter. Campaigns that are not already doing so could easily craft tweets for users to retweet or engage in a hashtag campaign (e.g., #StampOutStigma) to promote awareness. They could even share a hashtag to maximize reach across campaigns. Another option is for campaigns to maximize engagement with Twitter users and other campaigns focused on *military* mental health to further promote content. For more ideas, campaigns could consult experts in Twitter marketing and campaigns to expand Twitter usage. For example, Twitter has been used in public health for surveillance, such as detecting influenza epidemics through content analysis (Aramaki, Maskawa, and Morita, 2011); predicting postpartum influence on mood and behaviors of new mothers (de Choudhury, Counts, and Horvitz, 2013); modeling the spread of disease through social networks (Sadilek, Kautz, and Silenzio, 2012); and examining perceptions of emerging tobacco products (Myslín et al., 2013). **Who should take the lead: campaigns.**

Recommendation 3.2. Modify Campaign Websites to Be More Engaging and Meet the Needs of Brief Visitors

Our analysis of process data found that, although campaign websites had a large number of visits, users stayed on the sites for less than two minutes, and average page views per visit decreased for three of the four campaigns during our tracking period. Additionally, a high proportion of site visitors visited only a single webpage. To address these issues, it is important for campaigns to modify their website homepages to be as engaging as possible, given that these are typically the most visited pages. For example, homepage text should be pithy and direct, and lists should appear as bulleted items instead of long paragraphs. Because a user may visit only a single page, campaigns might consider referencing help-seeking resources on every site page (e.g., VCL putting its phone number on each page) to make sure users can find it easily. If that is not feasible, it may be worthwhile to put a help-seeking resource on typical landing pages and/or pages that are the most frequently visited or contain the most downloaded content. Additionally, campaigns may consider structuring videos so that at least some of the main messages appear at the beginning, to reach users who terminate video early. We note that brief visits to a single webpage could also mean that users' needs are being met quickly and efficiently, but support for this interpretation requires more data on user information needs upon entry to the site and whether those needs were satisfied. The campaigns could consider a study (e.g., interview users) to further understand the reasons for their short visits and limited interaction with the sites. **Who should take the lead: campaigns.**

Recommendation 3.3. Consider Whether Campaigns Should Intentionally Time Active Outreach to Overlapping Target Populations to Maximize Exposure to Key Messages Across Multiple Channels

Our findings indicated that campaigns share target populations and communicate similar messages. Research has shown that repeated exposure to campaign messages is needed to improve awareness, favorable views, behavioral intentions, and behavioral outcomes (Fulgoni and Lipsman, 2015). Similarly, using multiple platforms increases the effectiveness of a campaign because doing so supports these repeated exposures (Lewis and Westlund, 2014). Given the variety of channels used by campaigns to communicate the shared messages (video, social media, print, etc.), more-coordinated dissemination (i.e., intentionally timing their active outreach to coincide or occur during different time periods) to overlapping target populations may allow campaigns to have a greater impact collectively than independently. Identifying the most effective way to coordinate dissemination was beyond the scope of this evaluation, but DoD, VA, and HHS should conduct further research to determine whether it is more effective for their campaigns to (a) intentionally time their active outreach to occur in different months to reach their overlapping audiences at regular intervals or (b) time their active outreach at the same time of year to achieve more saturation in a shorter period. The forthcoming outcomes evaluation will help inform these decisions. Because both MTC and RWC offer resources to active duty service members and veterans contemplating mental health support, it may be especially helpful for these two campaigns to continue coordinating dissemination strategies to ensure the appropriate content from each campaign reaches its target population. **Who should take the lead: campaigns, working through the federal partner group.**

Recommendations for the Inclusion of Direct Connections to Care

Campaigns already provide some direct connections to care (i.e., crisis line or chat, a direct connection to a local medical center) on their materials, as well as other resources that provide information and referral services. The next two recommendations focus on enhancements that could allow service members, veterans, and their families to make a direct connection to some form of care as a result of viewing campaign materials. We recognize that providing direct connections to care may be a difficult task, but we provide these recommendations because a shared long-term goal of campaigns (as shown in the campaign logic models) is to encourage target audiences to seek care if they need it.

Recommendation 4.1. Ensure That a Direct Connection to Mental Health Care (i.e., Phone Line, Live Chat Line or Service That Provides a Connection to a Local Medical Center) Is Included on Relevant Campaign Materials

Given the campaigns' foci on mental health symptoms and treatment, website users may come to the campaign websites while they are in crisis and in need of immediate help. Making this type of resource clearly visible and easy to access could help better meet the needs of users during this critical period. Although almost 100 percent of VCL content provided a direct connection to care (i.e., links to connect to the VCL phone line, text, or chat), the campaigns overall provided a direct connection to care on only 27 percent of their materials. Though treatment locators and outreach lines are often provided, DoD, VA (MTC specifically), and HHS campaigns could offer more direct connections to care so that users can find a link that takes them to a phone line or chat line for immediate help. This could involve linking to existing crisis lines in more campaign materials and does not necessarily require creation of new crisis lines. **Who should take the lead: campaigns.**

Recommendation 4.2. Determine Whether a Centralized Call Line That Allows Users (Not in Immediate Crisis, But in Need of Care) to Make an Appointment for Mental Health Care Is a Resource That Should Be Offered by Campaigns

Experts suggested that a phone line that allows service members and veterans to make an appointment for mental health care (regardless of geographic location) would be a valuable resource that could be made available through these campaigns. We understand that offering such a phone service is no easy feat and would require great attention to regulatory issues and data-sharing, among other challenges. However, given the variability of timely access to care within the veteran and military mental health systems (U.S. Government Accountability Office, 2015; Hussey et al., 2015), it may be beneficial for the campaigns and those in charge of the existing care networks that provide mental health care for service members and veterans (e.g., TRICARE, the Military Health System, the Veterans Health Administration) to work together on tackling this important issue of how to provide a warm handoff of service members or veterans in need of care to the appropriate care provider in a timely fashion, especially if these campaigns are intended to be a key point of entry into the mental health systems. Given that cross-agency leadership involvement will be necessary to convene these organizations that make up the existing care networks, we suggest that federal partner group take the lead on addressing this recommendation. Though we note that this recommendation is not exclusively related to campaigns, a federal partner group may be in a position to begin consideration of this option. **Who should take the lead: federal partner group.**

Conclusions

The cross-agency evaluation of the four DoD, VA, and HHS mental health public awareness campaigns detailed in this report relied on three assumptions: (1) to align with CAP-G, the evaluation should focus on service members, veterans, and their families; (2) to be efficient, the evaluation should focus on desired outcomes shared across campaigns; and (3) to be comprehensive, the evaluation should assess the effectiveness and efficiency of campaigns. The results of the evaluation allowed us to generate a number of recommendations regarding campaign scope, content, and reach, as well as cross-agency efficiency and coordination of mental health messaging. Had we designed an evaluation under a different set of assumptions (e.g., by focusing on the most influential pieces of each campaign, rather than shared elements across campaigns), we might not have come to the same conclusions. This raises the issue of precisely which assumptions should guide a cross-agency evaluation of this type. Contemplating this issue leads to broader, overarching questions: What should each agency's role be in promoting greater access to care for service members and veterans? To what degree should efforts overlap or be unique? Continuing to take a cross-agency approach to answering these questions and understanding the success of campaigns individually and collectively will be important to improving mental health outcomes for service members, veterans, and their families. Improving mental health outcomes for these populations remains a priority, despite the fact that the CAP-G and associated interagency task force and working group that commissioned this report no longer exist.

Literature Review Methods and Recommendations for Evaluating Mental Health Public Awareness Campaigns

In the absence of strong evidence of the effects of public campaigns on key desired outcomes (e.g., help-seeking, symptoms) and best practices around outcome measurement (Coffman, 2002), we reviewed the literature to compile our own list of best practices and recommendations for evaluating mental health public awareness campaigns. This appendix describes our process and identification of best practices and recommendations for evaluating mental health public awareness campaigns. We first present the methods of two literature reviews used to derive this list. We reviewed select literature on past mental health campaign evaluations and best practices. To help guide our choices of which desired outcomes to measure as part of an evaluation, we also conducted a review of the literature linking stigma and other barriers to care with treatment and mental health–related outcomes. We focused our search strategy on this relationship because the CAP-G is closely tied to reducing stigma and other barriers to care in an effort to promote treatment-seeking. We then synthesized the two literature reviews to develop a list of best practices and recommendations for evaluating mental health public awareness campaigns.

Methods

Review of Selected Literature on Past Campaign Evaluations and Best Practices

We utilized the expertise of our team to identify evaluations of past mental health public awareness campaigns (e.g., England's Time to Change [TTC], New Zealand's Like Minds, Like Mine). Table A.1 summarizes these evaluation studies, including the intervention and survey periods, evaluation design and measures, and key findings. We also conducted an informal review of sources describing best practices for developing and evaluating public health awareness campaigns and literature recommended by experts in the course of the expert feedback process where relevant. This literature was not formally coded but served as an important source for guiding our decisions when developing an evaluation plan.

Table A.1
Mental Health Awareness Campaign Evaluations

Campaign	Intervention Period	Survey Period	Design	Measures	Findings
TTC, England					
Evans-Lacko et al., 2014	2009 Phase I: • Social marketing 2011 Phase II: • Mass media • Public relations exercises— one-day contact events • 32 small-scale antidiscrimination initiatives	• 2003 wave of UK National Attitudes to Mental Illness survey • 2007–2013 wave of UK National Attitudes to Mental Illness survey	• Representative adult population • Cross-sectional	• Mental Health Knowledge Schedule • Community Attitudes Toward the Mentally Ill • Reported and Intended Behavior Scale • Awareness of TTC (used to calculate level of regional awareness)	Phase I: • Small positive changes in public knowledge, attitudes, and intended behavior (i.e., social distance) • More positive attitudes related to prejudice and exclusion occurred after the TTC campaign but not for tolerance and support for community care (2003–2013) • Evidence of dose-effect relation between campaign awareness and regional improvement in knowledge and attitudes (tolerance and support; prejudice and exclusion) but not intended behavior
Corker et al., 2013		• 2008 wave of telephone interviews • 2011 wave of telephone interviews	• Mental health service users • Cross-sectional	• Discrimination and Stigma Scale	• Significant overall reduction in levels of experienced discrimination
Nuremberg Alliance Against Depression, Germany					
Dietrich et al., 2010	2000 4 levels • Public campaign • Interventions with community facilitators • Interventions with depressed persons, suicide attempters, and relatives • Primary care physicians	• Baseline (2-month precampaign) • 10-month follow-up • 22-month follow-up	• Nuremberg region compared with control region Wuerzburg • Cross-sectional	• Awareness of increased public discussion of depression • Awareness of campaign • General attitudes toward depression • Beliefs about causes and treatment of depression	• 24-percent decrease in number of suicidal acts (completed suicides and suicide attempts) • Many changes in general population declined in second year of campaign when there was lower intensity of activities (e.g., attributions to lack of self-control, acceptability of treatment) • Among subset who were aware of the campaign, attitudes

Campaign	Intervention Period	Survey Period	Design	Measures	Findings
Open the Doors, Germany					
Gaebel et al., 2008	• Lectures at adult education centers, art exhibitions, cinema events, readings, theatre events, and charity events; most included panel discussion with mental health professionals and people who have experienced mental health problems • Prior to events, press conferences held and/or press mailings distributed; press workshops about schizophrenia and misconceptions in the public to improve media reporting	• 2001 (before start of a number of antistigma interventions) • 2004 follow-up	Six cities • 2 antistigma • 2 awareness • 2 no programs Longitudinal 64 percent follow-up rate	• Schizophrenia-specific items • Social distance • Stereotype scale • Beliefs about causes • Treatment • Recovery • Awareness of antistigma campaigns	• 6.7 percent knew at least one of the antistigma projects • Cities where antistigma initiatives were conducted correlated with decreasing social distance, as well as knowledge of at least one antistigma program • When taking into account the differences of social distance changes between the survey cities, a significant reduction is only found in those cities where antistigma projects have taken place
beyondblue, Australia					
Jorm, Christensen, and Griffiths, 2005	2000 • Public community awareness and destigmatization campaign • Consumer and carer support • Prevention and early intervention • Primary care training	• 1995 (before campaign) • 2003–2004 (3 years after)	• Compared high-exposure states with low-exposure states (based on funding for activities) • Cross-sectional	• Depression vignette–based measures • Recognition of depression • Help-seeking • Discrimination • Beliefs about positive and negative outcomes	• High-exposure states had greater changes in beliefs about treatments (i.e., benefits of counseling, medication, and help-seeking in general); recognition of depression improved greatly at a national level but slightly more so in the high-exposure states • High-exposure states saw an increase in anticipated discrimination • No differences in percentage endorsing treatment or services for person described in depression vignette

Table A.1—Continued

Campaign	Intervention Period	Survey Period	Design	Measures	Findings
Like Minds, Like Mine, New Zealand					
Thornicroft et al., 2014	1997 (ongoing) • Mass media campaign • Community workers • Policy initiatives • Involvement of and leadership by people with mental illness experience, particularly in community-level initiatives	• 2010–2011	• Stratified sample of mental health service users	• Discrimination and Stigma Scale (self-administered version) • Perceived change in discrimination	• 54 percent reported some improvement in stigma and discrimination over the previous five years, 16 percent reported that this had become worse over this period, and 19 percent thought there had been no change • 40 percent felt they had been treated more positively by their family because of their mental health problems
Wyllie and Lauder, 2012	• Phase 5 of campaign focused on persons who had a member of family or friend who had experience of mental illness	• Annual surveys since 2000 • Survey 10 (2010) • Survey 12 (2012) (20-month follow-up)	• Random sample of 15–44-year-olds • Cross-sectional	• Awareness of mental illness • Attitudes, perceptions, and opinions relating to mental illness, stigma, and discrimination • Acceptance of mental illness • Awareness of supportive behaviors • Changes in behavior • Response to advertising	Improvements in six attitudes: • Know how I could be supportive (60–67 percent) • People are more accepting of people with mental illness than they used to be (61–67 percent) • Providing support to someone living with a mental illness would be difficult (disagree 15–20 percent) • People with mental illness need to stop feeling sorry for themselves (disagree 62–67 percent) • If I got a mental illness, some of my friends would reject me (disagree 39–44 percent)

Table A.1—Continued

Campaign	Intervention Period	Survey Period	Design	Measures	Findings
See Me, Scotland					
Mehta et al., 2009	2002 (ongoing) • Specific messages to Scottish population by using all forms of media, including cinema advertising; outdoor posters; and supporting leaflets in general practitioner surgeries, libraries, prisons, schools, and youth groups • Detailed website containing interactive resources; impact regularly monitored and progress reported in public domain	• 1994–1997, 2000, and 2003 waves of annual Research Surveys of Great Britain Omnibus	• Representative sample of adults using random location sampling method • Compared Scotland with England • Cross-sectional	• Community Attitudes Toward the Mentally Ill	• No interactions between country and year were significant in the regression models for each of the items, so the evidence for overall trend differences between England and Scotland over the whole period was weak • Between 2000 and 2003, 17 out of 25 items shifted negatively in England vs. 4 out of 25 in Scotland (e.g., burden of people with mental illness to society); none of the items shifted positively during this time period for either country

Table A.1—Continued

Campaign	Intervention Period	Survey Period	Design	Measures	Findings
One Voice, Canada					
Livingston et al., 2014	January 2012 to March 2012 • Social media intervention of a two-minute PSA featuring a popular male professional Canadian hockey team speaking about mental health issues and promoting a youth-focused educational website • Posted on Vancouver Canucks' Facebook and Twitter pages	• Baseline (before) • 2-month follow-up (T2) • 1-year follow-up (T3)	• Market research company administered online survey to panel of residents ages 13–25 • Cross-sectional	• Awareness of campaign, mindcheck.ca website, and other youth-focused mental health websites • Self-rated ability to help friend experiencing mental health issues • Personal stigma • Social distance • Behaviors targeted by campaign (e.g., talking about mental health issues with others, effort to learn about mental health symptoms, effort to learn about mental health information and services, helping someone with mental health issues)	• 25 percent heard or saw campaign at T2; increased to 49 percent at T3 • 16 percent visited mindcheck.ca website in T2; increased to 18 percent in T3; increased activity at T2 and T3 (i.e., number of visits, unique visits, page views) • At T3, 72.9 percent of respondents felt "equipped to assist a friend who is feeling really down all the time," which was significantly fewer than T1 (79.5 percent) and T2 (80.4 percent) • Decreases in personal stigma at T3 compared with T1 (i.e., sign of personal weakness, could snap out of it if they wanted, dangerousness) • Among those exposed, more positive attitudes toward mental health issues at T3 than those unexposed • Social distance improved at T3 compared with T1 but not with T2 • No significant increases for talking about mental health issues, effort to learn about mental health symptoms, or helping someone with mental health issues

Table A.1—Continued

Campaign	Intervention Period	Survey Period	Design	Measures	Findings
Each Mind Matters, United States					
Collins et al., 2015	• Social media campaign, stigma and discrimination reduction programs	• 2013 baseline (after start of campaign) • 1-year follow-up	• California statewide representative sample • Longitudinal	• Social distance • Recovery beliefs • Treatment attitudes • Support intentions • Concealment of mental health problem	• Improvements in social distance, support toward individuals with mental illness, awareness of stigma encountered by individuals with mental health problems

Review of the Literature Linking Stigma and Barriers to Care to Treatment and Mental Health–Related Outcomes

The goal of this literature review was to help guide our choices of which desired outcomes to measure as part of an evaluation. Because the CAP-G is closely tied to reducing stigma and other barriers to care in an effort to promote treatment-seeking, we focused our literature review on this relationship. Because much research on the outcomes related to reducing stigma and barriers to care is cross-sectional and primarily focuses on nonbehavioral outcomes (e.g., attitudes, intentions), we focused on identified longitudinal research with a focus on such behavioral outcomes as treatment initiation. To ensure that we captured literature on other outcomes related to stigma, we also included mental health outcomes, such as symptom severity. In addition to identifying research conducted among the general populations of the United States or other countries, we aimed to capture research on military and veteran populations. Because of the small number of studies meeting these criteria and a lack of standardization across such studies, a meta-analytic approach to this literature is not justified. We conducted a qualitative assessment of the association between barriers to care and treatment and mental health outcomes.

Search Method

To identify articles discussing a direct impact of stigma, we conducted a search of the following ten databases, focusing on substantive areas pertaining to health, defense, and the social sciences:

1. PsycINFO (psychology)
2. PubMed (medicine)
3. MEDLINE (medicine)
4. CINAHL (health care)
5. EconLit (economics)
6. Social Sciences Abstracts (social sciences)
7. ProQuest Military Collection (defense)
8. Sociological Abstracts (ProQuest) (social sciences)
9. Published International Literature on Traumatic Stress (PILOTS) (mental health)
10. Web of Science (general).

We report the result of two sets of search queries, each focusing on a research question about how stigma or another barrier to care affects an outcome of interest (Table A.2). The first set of queries (round 1) was conducted prior to the initiation of this evaluation and focused specifically on stigma as a barrier to care. The second set of queries (round 2) was conducted for this evaluation and focused on identifying

Table A.2
Details on Specific Searches

Query	Research Question	Search Terms	Search Limits
1	How are mental health stigma and other barriers to care related to help- and treatment-seeking? (This query is intended to capture any literature that occurred after the prior review detailed in Acosta et al. [2014] was completed.)	Concept 1: ("mental health" OR "mental illness" OR "behavioral health" OR "mental disorder" OR "psychiatric disorder") AND Concept 2: (stigma OR "self-stigma" OR barrier* OR discriminat* OR blame* OR blaming OR shame* OR worthlessness OR family pressure* OR family stress* OR "social distance" OR attitud*[ti] OR perception* OR literacy OR illitera* OR misinform* OR religious OR disclos* OR non-disclos* OR self-esteem OR "self esteem" OR stereotyp*) AND Concept 3: (literac* OR "barriers to care" OR resilienc* OR "help seeking" OR "help-seeking" OR "treatment seeking" OR "treatment-seeking" OR "care utilization" OR "treatment utilization" OR discriminat* OR stereotyp* OR career*)	Round 1: December 2012–June 2014 Round 2: May 2014–July 2015
2	How are mental health stigma and other barriers to care related to other treatment-related outcomes, such as treatment adherence?	Concept 1: ("mental health" OR "mental illness" OR "behavioral health" OR "mental disorder" OR "psychiatric disorder") AND Concept 2: (stigma OR "self-stigma" OR barrier* OR discriminat* OR blame* OR blaming OR shame* OR worthlessness OR family pressure* OR family stress* OR "social distance" OR attitud*[ti] OR perception* OR literacy OR illitera* OR misinform* OR religious OR disclos* OR non-disclos* OR self-esteem OR "self esteem" OR stereotyp*) AND Concept 3: (outcomes OR "treatment outcomes" OR "treatment adherence" OR "retention" OR "retention (psychology)" OR "productivity" OR "medication adherence") OR (adherence[Title] AND (treatment* OR therap* OR medication* OR prescription* OR therapeutics[MeSH])) OR ([Treatment[Title/Abstract]) AND ("starting" OR "stopping" OR "continuing" OR "quitting" OR "abandoning" OR "dropout" OR "dropping out"))	Round 1: January 2004–June 2014 Round 2: May 2014–July 2015
3	How are mental health stigma and other barriers to care related to recovery?	Concept 1: ("mental health" OR "mental illness" OR "behavioral health" OR "mental disorder" OR "psychiatric disorder") AND Concept 2: (stigma OR "self-stigma" OR barrier* OR discriminat* OR blame* OR blaming OR shame* OR worthlessness OR family pressure* OR family stress* OR "social distance" OR attitud*[ti] OR perception* OR literacy OR illitera* OR misinform* OR religious OR disclos* OR non-disclos* OR self-esteem OR "self esteem" OR stereotyp*) AND Concept 3: (Recovery OR "symptom severity" OR impairment OR "randomized controlled trial" OR "randomized controlled trial" [Publication Type] OR RCT OR "controlled trial" OR "comparison trial" OR "controlled clinical trial" OR "clinical trials as topic" OR "randomized controlled trials as topic" OR "clinical trial")	Round 1: January 2004–June 2014 Round 2: May 2014–July 2015

NOTE: Italicized search terms are those that were added for the Round 2 search.

recent literature focusing on barriers to care (in addition to stigma) that may be amenable to change as a result of a public campaign. We worked with a librarian to create search queries that would capture both military- and nonmilitary-specific literature. In general, query 1 addressed barriers to care and treatment-seeking behavior. Query 2 searched for effects of barriers to care on treatment-related outcomes, such as adherence and retention. Query 3 searched for literature on the effects of barriers to care on recovery. The searches were restricted to articles in English and published in peer-reviewed journals since 2004, with the exception of Query 1 (treatment-seeking), which was limited to the period of time following a different report on this topic (Acosta et al., 2014) to minimize redundancy.

Title, Abstract, and Full-Text Review

Each query was reviewed independently to identify articles that illustrated a direct impact of a barrier to care on treatment-related outcomes. Because of the focus on the direct impact of barriers to care, we discarded articles that used cross-sectional study designs or that reported only correlations. We also focused on identifying articles in which treatment-related outcomes were assessed using standard instruments of treatment-related outcomes or other data (e.g., medical record data), and thus we discarded articles that used other types of measures (e.g., qualitative interview data) or that measured precursors to treatment utilization (e.g., measures of intentions to seek treatment). The inclusion and exclusion criteria applied to the review are summarized in Table A.3.

The titles and abstracts for each item were first reviewed, and articles that did not focus on the research questions of interest or that did not meet the criteria described were removed from consideration. If an article's title and abstract did not contain sufficient information on which to judge article content, we obtained the full text for the

Table A.3
Inclusion and Exclusion Criteria

Criterion	Consideration
Inclusion	Content: • Articles that discuss effects of barriers to care on treatment-related outcomes of interest General: • Articles focused on civilian or military populations • Articles written or published outside the United States
Exclusion	Content: • Articles that use cross-sectional methods only • Articles that do not use standard instruments or objective measures (e.g., medical records) to assess treatment and mental health–related outcomes General: • Articles published in a language other than English • Nonempirical articles (e.g., conceptual or theoretical papers, commentaries) • Dissertation papers and master's theses

article and reviewed it according to the abstraction process described. At this stage, we also reviewed the reference lists of review articles that resulted from our search.

Round 1 yielded 17 articles for full-text review, and round 2 yielded five, for a total of 22 articles. Figure A.1 depicts the literature search process, and Table A.4 summarizes all articles reviewed.

Figure A.1
Search Process for Literature Focusing on Stigma as a Barrier to Care

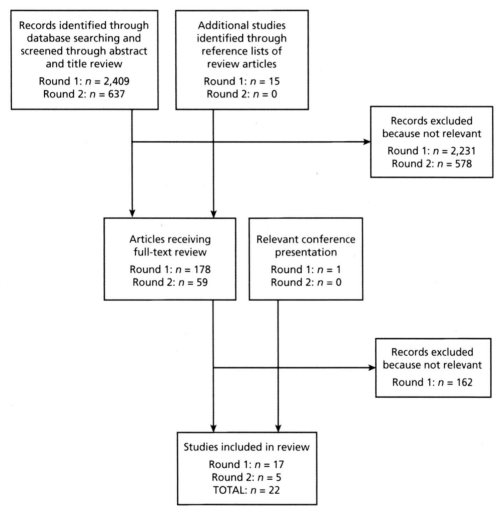

Table A.4
Summary of Reviewed Literature Linking Stigma and Other Barriers to Care to Outcomes

Study	Population (civilian vs. military)	Sample (general vs. symptomatic or diagnosed)	Mental Health Condition	Barrier to Care Assessed[a]	Treatment-Related Outcome Assessed	Controlled for Treatment Need, Diagnosis, Symptom Severity, Functioning, or Quality of Life	Direction of Association Between Barrier to Care and Treatment-Related Outcome	Direction of Association Between Barrier to Care and Mental Health–Related Outcome
Drake et al., 2015	Civilian	Outpatient	Schizophreniform disorder, schizophrenia, schizoaffective, delusional disorders, and "psychosis not otherwise specified"	Insight into illness, attitudes to medication	Readmission, relapse (2-week exacerbation of symptoms) (reversed)	Yes	+	NA
Spoont et al., 2015	Military (VA)	Outpatient	PTSD	Perceived need for care, beliefs about medication, psychotherapy beliefs	Treatment retention (at least 8 sessions of psychotherapy, 120 days of guideline-recommended medication)	Yes	+/–	NA
Campbell et al., 2014; Campbell et al., 2016	Military (VA)	Outpatient	Depression	Self-stigma[a] (label avoidance)	Treatment initiation (visits; receipt of care)	Yes	–	NA
Harpaz-Rotem et al., 2014	Military (VA)	Outpatient (screened)	Depression, PTSD	Perceived stigma about mental health services	Treatment retention (12+ visits)	Yes	+	NA
Ilic et al., 2014	Civilian	Inpatient and outpatient	Psychosis, bipolar, substance use, depression, anxiety	Experienced stigma	NA	NA	NA	–
Kelley et al., 2014	Military (active duty)	General	PTSD	Perceived stigma	NA	NA	NA	–

Table A.4—Continued

Study	Population (civilian vs. military)	Sample (general vs. symptomatic or diagnosed)	Mental Health Condition	Barrier to Care Assessed[a]	Treatment-Related Outcome Assessed	Controlled for Treatment Need, Diagnosis, Symptom Severity, Functioning, or Quality of Life	Direction of Association Between Barrier to Care and Treatment-Related Outcome	Direction of Association Between Barrier to Care and Mental Health–Related Outcome
Luoma et al., 2014	Civilian	Inpatient	Substance use	Self-stigma	Length of stay in treatment	Yes	+	NA
Rüsch et al., 2014	Civilian	Outpatient	At risk for schizophrenia	Stigma stress	NA	Yes	NA	–
Spoont et al., 2014	Military (VA)	Outpatient	PTSD	Treatment beliefs (perceived need, self-efficacy, beliefs about psychotherapy and anti-depressants)	Receipt of guideline-recommended antidepressant medication, Receipt of psychotherapy	Yes	+	NA
Wright, Britt, and Moore, 2014	Military (active duty)	General	Depression, PTSD	Stigma, practical barriers to care, and negative treatment attitudes	NA	Yes	NA	–
Arbisi et al., 2013	Military (National Guard)	Outpatient	Anxiety, depression, or substance use or dependence	Self-stigma	Utilization of psychotherapy or psycho-pharmacology	Yes	NS	NA
Bowersox, Saunders, and Berger, 2013	Military (VA)	Inpatient	Substance use, psychosis, mood, anxiety, personality disorder	Expected self-stigma	Treatment attrition (reversed)	Yes	–	NA
Ben-Zeev et al., 2012	Civilian	Medical	Schizophrenia	Self-stigma	NA	NA	NA	NS

Table A.4—Continued

Study	Population (civilian vs. military)	Sample (general vs. symptomatic or diagnosed)	Mental Health Condition	Barrier to Care Assessed[a]	Treatment-Related Outcome Assessed	Controlled for Treatment Need, Diagnosis, Symptom Severity, Functioning, or Quality of Life	Direction of Association Between Barrier to Care and Treatment-Related Outcome	Direction of Association Between Barrier to Care and Mental Health–Related Outcome
Lysaker et al., 2012	Military (VA)	Outpatient	Schizophrenia or schizoaffective disorder diagnoses	Self-stigma, experienced stigma	NA	NA	NA	NS
Yanos et al., 2012	Military (VA) and civilian	Outpatient	Schizophrenia-spectrum	Self-stigma	NA	NA	NA	–
Rosen et al., 2011	Military (VA)	Outpatient	PTSD	Stigma concerns	Therapy visits	Yes	+	NA
Yanos, Lysaker, and Roe, 2010	Military (VA) and civilian	Outpatient	Schizophrenia and schizoaffective	Self-stigma (stereotype endorsement)	NA	NA	NA	–
Edlund et al., 2008	Military (VA)	Outpatient	Depression	Perceived stigma for seeking treatment	NA	Yes	+	NA
Yen et al., 2009	Civilian	Outpatient	Depression	Self-stigma	NA	Yes	NA	NS
Lysaker et al., 2007	Military (VA)	Outpatient	Schizophrenia	Self-stigma about illness	NA	NA	NA	–
Ritsher and Phelan, 2004	Military (VA)	Outpatient	Psychosis, schizophrenia, depression	Self-stigma	NA	NA	NA	–
Total (–)							3	8
Total (+)							7	0
Total (NS)							1	3

NOTE: This table includes barriers to care likely to be influenced by public campaigns (e.g., stigma, attitudes toward treatment) and excludes barriers unlikely to be influenced by such campaigns (e.g., distance from clinic). NA = not available, NS = not statistically significant at the $p < 0.05$ level.

Abstracting Information from Each Source

For each full-text article we reviewed, we abstracted the following types of information where possible:

- general information: citation information, population described (military, veteran, or nonmilitary), study location (United States [US] or non-US), type of study (e.g., cross-sectional, longitudinal, prospective)
- barrier to care measurement: detail on how barrier to care was assessed
- outcome measurement: detail on what treatment-related outcome was assessed and how
- other variables included: brief summary of other constructs assessed in the study
- effects of the barrier to care: effects on treatment or mental health–related outcomes described in detail.

Upon reviewing this information, we excluded 162 articles in round 1 and 54 articles in round 2 (Figure A.1) that were not relevant (e.g., the study design was cross-sectional, no direct effect of a barrier to care on treatment-related outcomes was measured).

Final Number of Articles Included in Review

Ultimately, 22 items were included in the review (Table A.4). Twenty-one were articles identified through the literature search. We also opted to include one study that was not published at the time of review (Campbell et al., 2014; Campbell et al., 2016) that an author encountered at a conference and that was directly relevant to the question of the direct effect of stigma on treatment-related outcomes. Note, the next section focuses on best practices and recommendations related to evaluation design. For a discussion of the literature itself and its implications for the design of help-seeking strategies (e.g., how to determine best direction given the contradictory evidence that says stigma can both negatively affect and positively affect the design of help-seeking strategies), see Acosta et al. (2014).

Best Practices and Recommendations for Evaluating Mental Health–Related Public Awareness Campaigns

We reviewed the studies identified through both literature reviews and team discussion and then developed a list of best practices for evaluating mental health public awareness campaigns.

Administer Repeated Assessments over Time in the Target Population

Many evaluations of large mental health campaigns include a baseline assessment preceding the launch of the campaign and follow-up assessments after the start of the campaign (Table A.1). Repeated assessments can not only capture changes occurring before and after the implementation of campaigns but also minimize biases related to social desirability and data-collection methods, particularly when the same methods are employed at each assessment period (e.g., telephone interviews). The most commonly employed time frame for follow-up assessments is one year following the implementation of a campaign, with some evaluations conducting follow-up assessments annually (Table A.1). Allowing such a time frame is especially appropriate in the case of mental health campaigns that seek to change social norms because an evaluation of such a campaign needs to allow time to observe small incremental changes in norms (Hornik, 2002).

If Feasible, Incorporate a Control or Comparison Population into the Evaluation Design

A number of evaluations have also employed controls by administering assessments in regions not exposed to the campaign. Control comparisons can be vital to linking changes in desired outcomes to the effects of a campaign, especially if similar efforts are occurring during the same period of time. For example, Australia saw multiple overlapping mental health campaign efforts during the same period of time; these campaigns included the Compass campaign to improve mental health literacy among youth, the beyondblue national depression initiative, the MindMatters school-based initiative, and the SANE initiative targeted at those affected by mental illness (Wright et al., 2006). The ability to attribute improvements in desired outcomes to the Compass campaign was strengthened through the use of regional controls. In addition, without regional controls, it can be difficult to know whether any observed changes in desired outcomes would have occurred irrespective of the campaign (Jorm, Christensen, and Griffiths, 2005).

It is not always possible to identify a control population or to assess baseline measurements (Hornik, 2002)—if, for example, a campaign is already in the field (as in the case of RWC or MTC). In these cases, employing a strong quasi-experimental design, such as an interrupted time series design,[1] is most desirable (Hornik, 2002). This approach is in line with those taken in evaluating other public health awareness campaigns, such as those targeting HIV/AIDS (human immunodeficiency virus, acquired immunodeficiency syndrome) prevention and testing (Noar et al., 2009; Wright et al., 2006).

---

[1] A *time series design* is where a participant is observed multiple times over a period of time, including before and after an intervention or treatment period, to determine an intervention or treatment effect (Marczyk, DeMatteo, and Festinger, 2005).

Employ Rigorous Sampling Procedures

Most large-scale mental health campaigns are directed at the general population, but some target specific groups (e.g., youth, physicians). To assess the impact of a mental health campaign, rigorous sampling methods should be used to ensure that changes in desired outcomes are tracked for the population of interest with minimal bias. Employing random sampling to obtain representative population-based samples is one of the most rigorous sampling strategies and is characteristic of most large-scale mental health campaign evaluations (Table A.1). Most commonly, postal addresses or telephone listings are used to randomly select households for participation in the evaluation.

Assess Campaign Reach by Incorporating Measures of Message Exposure Among Target Audiences

Campaign effectiveness is dependent on successfully reaching the intended target audience (Weiss and Tschirhart, 1994). Thus, many evaluations of large-scale mental health campaigns include measures of exposure and/or whether those exposed to campaign messages are part of the target audience. Exposure is often assessed by asking participants whether they have heard of or seen ads for the mental health campaign (Table A.1). Campaign exposure has been associated with improved attitudes toward people who are experiencing mental health challenges, taking medication, and living at reduced social distance (an indicator of mental illness stigma) (Livingston et al., 2014; Dietrich et al., 2010; Gaebel et al., 2008). The TTC campaign also assessed the frequency of participants' exposure to the campaign, which was then used to estimate the degree to which the campaign was reaching target audiences across various regions of England and to test whether this was related to outcomes (Evans-Lacko, Henderson, and Thornicroft, 2013). Without a measure of exposure or a control and comparison group, any shifts observed over the course of a campaign may simply reflect secular trends—that is, what would have happened over time with or without a campaign. Moreover, for evaluations that employ comparison control regions, measures of exposure among target audiences can be used to verify greater campaign exposure in intervention regions (Dietrich et al., 2010; Jorm, Christensen, and Griffiths, 2005; Wright et al., 2006).

For campaigns conducted online, several web metrics are available that are akin to measures of exposure and reach among members of target audiences (Sponder, 2012). For instance, one construct known as *user engagement* can be measured using either self-report questions (e.g., "Have you ever referred a friend to this site?" [see Paek et al., 2013]) or behavioral measures (e.g., the rate at which visitors navigate away from the site after viewing just one page ["bounce rate'] or the reach of a posting in a social media network). Constructs such as user engagement enable analysts to draw inferences about users' motivational attitudes and behaviors associated with the campaign goals. A growth in online tools offer researchers many options for estimating the efficiency of web ad campaigns (e.g., Harvard Business School Publishing, 2007).

Examine the Impact of Mental Health Campaigns on Individuals with Unmet Mental Health Needs

Although most studies have investigated the effects of mental health campaigns on the general population, a number of studies have also included a focus on specific targeted populations. For instance, some evaluations have examined the potential influence of campaigns on the lives of mental health service users (Evans-Lacko, Henderson, and Thornicroft, 2013; Thornicroft et al., 2014). The TTC campaign surveyed current mental health service users in the National Health System in England and found reductions in experienced discrimination in this group in the one year following the campaign (Evans-Lacko, Henderson, and Thornicroft, 2013). Similarly, the Like Minds, Like Mine campaign in New Zealand found that among a random sample of mental health service users, more than half reported some improvement in stigma and discrimination over the previous five years (Thornicroft et al., 2014). Such studies provide important information about outcomes that are integral to creating a supportive environment for individuals recovering from mental health challenges. However, surveys with mental health service users do not provide information on whether a campaign is positively influencing those with mental health needs but who have not yet obtained treatment (i.e., individuals with unmet mental health needs) (Wong et al., 2015). Select measures have been shown to detect changes in desired outcomes, most commonly for social distance or social inclusion, treatment attitudes (e.g., acceptability of treatment), and support provision.

Evaluate the Impact of Mental Health Public Awareness Campaigns on Initiation of Treatment-Seeking (i.e., the Desired Target Behavior)

A common goal across most mental health campaigns is to increase the recognition of mental health problems and to facilitate the use of needed treatment. However, the majority of mental health campaigns track changes in attitudes or intentions toward mental health service use rather than actual treatment utilization. For example, the beyondblue campaign found that Australian states with high campaign exposure had more-positive attitudes toward counseling, medication, and general help-seeking than low-exposure states, but the campaign evaluation did not show that those exposed actually sought treatment more than those unexposed (Jorm, Christensen, and Griffiths, 2005). The Compass Strategy is one of the few campaigns that assessed mental health service use rates and showed an overall increase in mental health service use over time (from baseline to follow-up assessment) among youths ages 12 to 25 in the intervention regions (Wright et al., 2006). However, the effects were no longer significant when mental health service utilization rates were examined among respondents who self-reported having a mental health problem.

These studies highlight the notion that because attitudes do not predict behavior in all cases, it is important to assess relevant behavior (e.g., treatment initiation) among the campaign's target population (e.g., individuals with mental health symptoms) if possible. We note, however, that measures of mental health service utilization do not need to be self-reported. Validated mental health service utilization measures can be drawn from existing and ongoing population surveys. For example, the National Household Survey of Drug Use and Health tracks mental health and substance use treatment utilization annually among a representative sample of individuals in the United States ages 12 or older (SAMHSA, 2014).

Include Assessments of Barriers to Care and Outcomes for Which There Are Documented Causal Relationships

Though many cross-sectional studies show an association between stigma and other barriers to care and such outcomes as treatment-seeking–related attitudes, beliefs, intentions, and behavior (Clement et al., 2015), little empirical evidence rigorously assesses causal relationships between stigma (and other barriers to care) and such outcomes. What evidence does exist is mixed and utilizes different measures of barriers to care and mental health–related and treatment-related outcomes across studies. Because of this, we recommend assessing a variety of outcomes for which there are documented causal relationships. These outcomes may include attitudes, beliefs, perceptions, intentions, and behavior related to barriers to care, mental health, and mental health treatment. Measuring a wide variety of outcomes ensures that campaign-related changes will be captured.

Evaluations of Public Awareness Campaigns Targeting Substance Use Stigma Should Assess the Stigma Specific to Substance Use

A review of the literature on efforts to reduce substance use stigma (Livingston et al., 2012) revealed only two studies that evaluated public awareness campaigns aimed at reducing substance use stigma. Both campaigns focused on reducing the stigma of substance use among the general public. The evaluations of these campaigns used the Attitudes to Mental Illness Questionnaire (Luty et al., 2006) as the outcome of interest (Luty et al., 2007; Luty et al., 2008). Of the two evaluations of these campaigns, one found that a positively framed educational leaflet was associated with reductions in negative attitudes toward people with substance use disorders (Luty et al., 2008). The other found that educational fact sheets had no effect on attitudes toward people with substance use disorders (Luty et al., 2007). Given the dearth of studies on substance use stigma campaign evaluation, we recommend following the earlier identified best practices in evaluating mental illness stigma reduction campaigns. We also recommend that researchers continue to develop and validate measures that capture substance use–specific stigma.

Methods to Elicit Expert Feedback on Evaluation Design and Recommendations

To inform the evaluation plan, we sought recommendations from recognized national and international experts in barriers to mental health treatment and evaluation of public awareness campaigns. To elicit feedback, we used two primary strategies. First, for experts internal to RAND, we organized a video conference with ten attendees joining from the three main RAND offices and other sites. The two-hour panel discussion was moderated, and a semistructured interview guide was used to stimulate conversation about gold standards in public awareness campaign evaluation, advantages and disadvantages of identified evaluation methods, appropriate intermediate and long-term outcome variables, and recommendations for assessing cross-agency desired outcomes. Second, we conducted semistructured telephone interviews lasting 30–60 minutes with eight experts external to RAND. Experts were selected because they had expertise on stigma and barriers to mental health care or on evaluation of public awareness campaigns or they were knowledgeable about existing data sources (or running a large-scale evaluation or survey related to stigma or barriers to mental health care). We initially invited 16 experts to participate in the interviews, but only 11 were available to participate in the interviews during the three weeks we had to conduct interviews (Table B.1). These interviews covered the same topics already described. Notes were taken by a research team member during the video conference and the semistructured telephone interviews. A separate research team member then read through all the notes to identify common themes, lessons learned, and recommendations to inform the evaluation design. The recommendations that follow are insights shared by all participating experts.

We tailored our interview questions to experts based on their area of expertise. Table B.2 contains the questions we asked each type of expert.

Table B.1
Experts Interviewed for Input on the Evaluation Design

Area of Expertise	Name and Affiliation
Existing data and evaluation methods	• Michael Schoenbaum, senior adviser for mental health services, National Institute of Mental Health; also part of the Army Study to Assess Risk and Resilience in Service Members • Mark A. Zamorski, head of research and analysis, Directorate of Mental Health, Canadian Forces Health Services Group Headquarters
Stigma and barriers to mental health care	• Patty Barron, director of family programs, Association of the United States Army • Thomas Britt, professor of social and organizational psychology, Clemson University • Patrick Corrigan, professor of psychology, Illinois Institute of Psychology • John Roberts, executive vice president of warrior relations, Wounded Warrior Project • Tracy Stecker, assistant professor of community and family medicine, Dartmouth Psychiatric Research Center
Evaluation of public education campaigns	• Julia Coffman, director, Center for Evaluation Innovation • Sara Evans-Lacko, research associate, Institute of Psychiatry, London School of Economics and Political Science • Tony Foleno, senior vice president of research, Ad Council • Rebecca Collins, senior behavioral scientist, RAND Corporation

Recommendations on Evaluation Design

Match the Evaluation Sample to the Campaign Target Population

Expert panelists noted that there is variability in the targeted population across campaigns, and they also highlighted the need to consider carefully who should be included in the evaluation. Some experts saw value in a population sample to understand how Americans in general perceive mental health conditions and treatment for those conditions. The experts noted that the general population represents general social norms related to mental health. However, it was more common for experts to caution against overly broad evaluation samples and instead recommend that the sample be matched to the group targeted by the campaigns. For example, several experts recommended that the evaluation should assess service members and veterans who need mental health care but are not currently receiving it. Others noted that some campaigns target those who hold social or occupational influence over service members and veterans with mental health conditions (e.g., spouses, military leaders) and that an evaluation might also include these groups.

Some experts noted the difficulty of identifying an appropriate comparison group (by which to determine the effect of the campaign on the population of interest). Some offered that if the campaign is rolled out to one geographic area, then people living in other regions can serve as a comparison group. Others indicated that campaign evaluators often compare the outcomes among those who self-report that they saw or inter-

Table B.2
Interview Questions, by Type of Expertise

Area of Expertise	Interview Questions

Existing data and evaluation methods	1. One option for evaluating these campaigns is to use existing secondary data that capture the need for and utilization of mental health care, as well as care-related desired outcomes, such as improved quality of life. It would be important for these data sources to cover service members, veterans, or the general U.S. population—which are all possible target populations for the campaigns we are evaluating. Given your expertise in this area, do you know of any data sources that you think capture the need for mental health care for these populations? Barriers to mental health care? Utilization of mental health care (including initiation of care and retention in care)? Other care-related outcomes (e.g., quality of life, productivity)?
	  a. Population covered: What is the sample surveyed for this data source (e.g., service members)?
	  b. Strengths and weaknesses: In your experience, what are the strengths and weaknesses of X data source?
	  c. Permissions needed to access the data source: What are the regulatory hurdles to using these data for research purposes?
	2. As we shared in the background information, we have been asked to conduct a cross-agency evaluation to look at effectiveness of the campaigns and to help identify areas for efficiency across agencies (e.g., where messages could align for greater impacts, where costs could be shared). If you had unlimited funds, what are some of the design and measurement approaches you might consider for an evaluation like this?
	  a. What time period should the evaluation cover (e.g., a single wave of the campaign or multiple waves)?
	  b. What types of data would you want on each campaign (i.e., process data, such as exposure)?
	  c. What kinds of cross-campaign desired outcomes would you want to capture the effectiveness of campaigns? How about to capture cross-agency efficiency?
	3. In our reviews of past campaign evaluations, we have noticed a number of potential pitfalls that could undermine the rigor of the evaluation and credibility of evaluation findings. In your experience, what are the common pitfalls we should avoid? Any suggestions you have for how best to avoid these pitfalls are also appreciated.
	  a. If we were looking at campaign impacts over the past five years, what confounds should we account for? For example, major policy changes, other campaigns not funded by DOD, VA, HHS, etc.

Table B.2—Continued

Area of Expertise	Interview Questions
Stigma and barriers to mental health care	1. As part of our evaluation design, we want to provide some recommendations for cross-agency desired outcomes in both the short and long terms that should be tracked to help understand the potential impacts of the campaigns. These can include perceived barriers and indicators of access (e.g., number of initial appointments) or utilization (e.g., number of appointments kept). These could also include longer-term desired outcomes, such as improved quality of life or productivity. In your opinion, what desired short- and long-term outcomes would you recommend as important indicators to track? a. Any suggestions for ways to capture the need for mental health care for these populations? Barriers to mental health care? Utilization of mental health care (including initiation of care and retention in care)? Other care-related outcomes (e.g., quality of life, productivity)? b. It would be useful to ensure that any shorter-term indicators we recommend are empirically linked with desired longer-term outcomes—meaning that there's research supporting that the shorter-term changes (e.g., reductions in certain barriers) will contribute to longer-term outcomes (e.g., improvements in quality of life). Which of the indicators (i.e., shorter-term) have research linking them to the longer-term outcomes? 2. In our reviews of past campaign evaluations, we have noticed a number of potential pitfalls that could undermine the rigor of the evaluation and credibility of evaluation findings. In your experience, what are the common pitfalls we should avoid? Any suggestions you have for how best to avoid these pitfalls are also appreciated. a. If we were looking at campaign impacts over the past five years, what confounds should we account for? For example, major policy changes, other campaigns not funded by DOD, VA, HHS, etc. 3. As we shared in the background information, we have been asked to conduct a cross-agency evaluation to look at effectiveness of the campaigns and to help identify areas for efficiency across agencies (e.g., where messages could align for greater impacts, where costs could be shared). If you had unlimited funds, what are some of the design and measurement approaches you might consider for an evaluation like this? a. What time period should the evaluation cover (e.g., a single wave of the campaign or multiple waves)? b. What types of data would you want on each campaign (i.e., process data, such as exposure)? c. What kinds of cross-campaign desired outcomes would you want to capture the effectiveness of campaigns? How about to capture cross-agency efficiency?

Table B.2—Continued

Area of Expertise	Interview Questions
Evaluation of public education campaigns	1. To help inform our thinking about the evaluation design, we have been reviewing articles that describe evaluations of other public awareness campaigns, such as beyondblue and Time to Change. In your opinion, which evaluation articles represent the best or gold-standard approaches to evaluating public awareness campaigns? These can include evaluations of mental health or suicide prevention public awareness campaigns or campaigns in allied areas that could be relevant to the research team (e.g., evaluations of public awareness campaigns to reduce HIV/AIDS stigma, increase treatment-seeking for other medical conditions). a. Why do you consider this evaluation a gold-standard approach? b. Do you think it would be helpful for us to use any similar approaches in our evaluation of DoD, VA, and HHS public awareness campaigns? 1. As we shared in the background information, we have been asked to conduct a cross-agency evaluation to look at effectiveness of the campaigns and to help identify areas for efficiency across agencies (e.g., where messages could align for greater impacts, where costs could be shared). If you had unlimited funds, what are some of the design and measurement approaches you might consider for an evaluation like this? a. What time period should the evaluation cover (e.g., a single wave of the campaign or multiple waves)? b. What types of data would you want on each campaign (i.e., process data, such as exposure)? c. What kinds of cross-campaign desired outcomes would you want to capture the effectiveness of campaigns? How about to capture cross-agency efficiency? 1. In our reviews of past campaign evaluations, we have noticed a number of potential pitfalls that could undermine the rigor of the evaluation and credibility of evaluation findings. In your experience, what are the common pitfalls we should avoid? Any suggestions you have for how best to avoid these pitfalls are also appreciated. a. If we were looking at campaign impacts over the past five years, what confounds should we account for? For example, major policy changes, other campaigns not funded by DOD, VA, HHS, etc.

acted with campaign materials with those who do not remember seeing or interacting with campaign materials.

Consider Efficacy Trials, Which Can Provide Useful Information but Test Artificial Conditions

Efficacy trials are tightly controlled, experimental studies that assess the effect of campaign materials on study participants. For example, an efficacy trial could involve exposing one group of service members with a mental health condition to a video from the campaign and another group of service members to an unrelated video. By asking participants to fill out questionnaires before and after they watch the campaign video, researchers can track whether service members who view the campaign materials develop more-positive attitudes toward mental health conditions or treatment for mental health conditions than the service members who viewed unrelated materials. This type of research can be helpful in documenting whether the campaign materials operate as expected, determining the magnitude of attitude change that could arise from campaign exposure, and identifying any unforeseen negative impact of campaign materials on attitudes.

Some experts were in favor of such an approach and noted instances in the past where public awareness campaign materials were found to be ineffective because the message they had intended to convey had not been heard or processed by the intended audience. Had campaign officials conducted an efficacy trial early in the process, they might have learned that the message was poorly communicated *before* investing resources in disseminating the faulty message. Other experts believed that efficacy trials are too artificial and fail to capture dynamic influences of the campaign that happen as an individual is exposed to the campaign multiple times or as the people around the individual are exposed and change their own attitudes and behaviors.

Consider Process Evaluations, Which Provide Explanatory Power to Outcome Evaluations

Rather than assessing the ultimate outcome of an evaluation, process evaluations assess whether the campaign was rolled out and disseminated as planned, in a theory-consistent way, and in a manner most likely to achieve the aims of the program. Experts suggested that the campaign evaluations include process measures that assess whether the target population was exposed to the campaign and interacted with materials as intended. A process evaluation might also include a comparison of campaign strategies and techniques with known best practices as outlined in the research literature.

Incorporate Social Media into the Evaluation, Given the Role Social Media Plays in Dissemination

We received two recommendations that social media be leveraged to evaluate the influence of the campaigns. In recent years, data-mining programs have allowed researchers to track how the "chatter" around a given topic changes over time or changes in response to a national event. Experts suggested that we consider measuring the valence or content of social media posts, tweets, etc., that reference mental health and service status in proximity. If the evaluated campaign has a distinct kickoff date or a distinct period during which a group is targeted, then the social media chatter can be examined retrospectively to assess changes in the valence or content after the campaign was active.

Consider Cost Analyses, Which Can More Accurately Represent the Contributions of Campaigns

One expert noted that public awareness campaigns, particularly those that do not rely on traditional media (such as television PSAs), may be relatively inexpensive programs to implement. When a program is not costly and reaches a large population, even a very small effect size may be cost-effective. That is, even if it successfully sparks treatment engagement and recovery for only a handful of veterans or service members, the cost savings associated with their recovery may be greater than the cost associated with disseminating the message to a large population. When this is true, it raises a problem with evaluation design. Most evaluations lack the power to detect very small effect sizes. Therefore, even if the program has a meaningful but small positive effect, the evaluation may fail to "see" that effect and conclude instead that the program is not effective. An alternative in this situation is to calculate how large the effect would need to be (e.g., how many individuals recovered; how many service members retained in the active component) for the expenditure associated with the campaign to be cost-effective. If the number of recoveries or service members retained is small and a logically reasonable outcome to expect, it may be appropriate to conclude that the campaign is valuable even if an evaluation capable of observing the calculated effect size is infeasible.

Consider Using Longitudinal Designs, Which Are Preferred

A longitudinal design would track the expected outcomes associated with a campaign over more than one assessment point. Our experts recommended that a longitudinal design track desired outcomes before the campaign is implemented, after it rolls out, and then over subsequent assessment points to determine whether the impact of the campaign grows as more people are exposed and some people are exposed repeatedly. Alternatively, the effect of the campaign might be sizable initially but then fade as the target population habituates to the message. Most of the campaigns included in this evaluation have already been implemented and therefore an assessment before rollout is not possible. However, this approach may be appropriate for those campaigns that target new or unique populations during each year's campaign, or for those campaigns that implement new messaging over small time periods (e.g., National Recovery Month). Even if the campaign is in the middle of implementation, using a longitudinal design still may be preferred as the only design that would allow a campaign to attribute changes in outcomes to campaign exposure.

Recommendations for Evaluation Measures

Assess Campaign Exposure Using Measures That Guard Against False Memories

Process measures assess whether a campaign was implemented as intended. For example, a web-hosted campaign can assess whether it is reaching an audience via web metrics, such as page hits, page views, or time on the website. Experts did not discuss process measures at length, but they did discuss the challenges associated with assessing exposure to a campaign. Although it is common to assess exposure by self-report, they cautioned that people are not always able to reliably and accurately report whether they saw campaign materials. For example, remembering exposure to a specific campaign can be linked to characteristics associated with that campaign (e.g., preexisting positive attitudes toward the campaign message), which may also bias the evaluation toward positive results. Experts recognized that self-reported exposure to a campaign may be the only strategy by which to measure campaign effects in some cases; however, they suggested that strategies to guard against biased memory be implemented. For example, one expert suggested that a more robust measure of exposure could involve assessing whether the respondent remembers more than one element of the campaign and does not remember elements that were not present in the campaign. It is important to note that, in cross-sectional designs, any changes in outcome detected may be attributable to differences between the exposed and unexposed groups and not to campaign exposure.

Positive Attitudes Toward Individuals with Mental Health Conditions and Mental Health Treatment Are Important to Measure but Are Not Necessarily Linked to Help-Seeking

Although it is common for mental health public awareness campaigns to target negative perceptions of mental health conditions (or "stigma"), the experts we interviewed voiced concern about this target. Several cited research literature that does not provide strong support to link mental health stigma to reduced treatment-seeking. Others noted counterexamples, such as research in Europe indicating that higher negative perceptions of those with mental health conditions are associated with more treatment-seeking and utilization. One researcher made the observation that highly stigmatized medical conditions, such as herpes, do not seem to be associated with lower treatment-seeking. In general, they cautioned against use of stigma-related measures as important outcomes, given that the literature linking mental health stigma to the primary goal of treatment initiation is limited and mixed (see the literature review in Appendix A). Some researchers felt that measuring negative perceptions of mental health conditions could be useful as an indicator of whether campaigns produced the same attitude changes as other successful campaigns; they suggested considering social distance measures and global mental health stigma scales.

Several experts indicated that military-specific attitudes may limit treatment-seeking among service members and veterans. For example, some experts averred that many midlevel military leaders believe that mental health conditions are incompatible with serving in the military. Other experts highlighted beliefs that people with mental health conditions degrade the unit and present a security threat and noted that successful campaigns would change leaders' perceptions of those with mental health conditions so that leaders can be role models and communicate with the troops. Experts also encouraged increasing concurrence with the beliefs that (1) mental health conditions are a "war wound" rather than a personal failing, (2) people with some mental health conditions can perform military roles, and (3) mental health treatment will help them recover and return to those roles.

Finally, other attitude variables that experts raised for consideration were measures of "label avoidance," perception of the VA system, and hope for recovery. *Label avoidance* was described as an explicit or implicit desire to avoid being categorized as a having a mental health condition. By rejecting mental health labels, the individual effectively blocks most routes to treatment. Someone who does believe that he or she has mental health symptoms will perceive mental health services as neither personally relevant nor potentially useful. Perception of the VA system was deemed an important variable for veterans: While VA is a central resource for veterans, many have negative views about the quality and availability of VA services, which may serve as a barrier to accessing care. Finally, several experts suggested that positive perceptions of mental health treatment and beliefs that recovery is possible are attitudinal measures that should be considered for inclusion in a comprehensive evaluation.

Knowledge of Mental Health Signs and Symptoms and Available Resources May Be a Prerequisite to Help-Seeking

There were mixed recommendations about the utility of knowledge measures when assessing the effect of a public awareness campaign on treatment-seeking. Some researchers pointed to health and HIV/AIDS literature that document campaigns that improved knowledge about a condition but also showed that increases in knowledge do not subsequently predict the likelihood that individuals engage in the targeted health behavior. However, other experts pointed to specific topics within the knowledge domain that they considered relevant to mental health treatment–seeking, including

- awareness of symptoms that are linked to mental health conditions
- understanding the etiology of mental illness (e.g., awareness of genetic influences on mental illness increases the belief that people with mental health conditions should seek care)

- accurate expectations about the likelihood of recovery (with and without treatment)
- accurate expectations about the content of treatment (e.g., behavioral interventions are available for those who prefer to avoid medications)
- accurate expectations about the trajectory of care (e.g., treatment will not begin on the first visit, symptom improvement may not begin for four to six weeks)
- understanding the likelihood that the content of mental health visits will be held in confidence (e.g., not shared with a commander).

Finally, expert panelists generally agreed that knowledge about the availability of services and the information necessary to make contact with a mental health provider was a necessary final link to accessing care for mental health conditions. Knowledge of local resources could include the location, name, and phone number of a local clinic but could also be satisfied by accurate knowledge about where or how to find that information. For example, a veteran may not know whether his or her local community-based outpatient clinic has an embedded mental health clinician but would have adequate knowledge of local resources if he or she was aware of resource search tools embedded in the MTC website and the procedural knowledge to access the website and navigate to the search tool.

Social Norms May Be Linked with Help-Seeking and Should Be Measured

Experts in barriers to mental health care pointed out that if the goal is to encourage people with mental health conditions to seek treatment, then the social environment surrounding them also must be conducive to treatment-seeking. If people with mental health conditions understand that acknowledging their symptoms and asking for help will lead to rejection by their social network, discrimination at work, and social isolation, then they are unlikely to seek help. Experts noted that, in such an environment, the personal attitudes and knowledge of the individual may be irrelevant relative to the power of social norms to make treatment-seeking an undesirable choice. Thus, they recommended that research participants' beliefs about the social norms in their environment be measured. This could include assessment of how members of the respondents' social network and broader work and social communities would perceive them if they admitted to having a mental health condition or entered treatment for a mental health condition. One expert noted that subjective norms (respondent perception of social norms) are sometimes better predictors of treatment-seeking than objective social norms. Another suggested that social norms among friends and family can sometimes be less predictive of treatment-seeking than the social norms in one's occupational setting.

Measures of Behavioral Intentions and Self-Efficacy May Serve as Helpful Intermediate Outcomes

Although not discussed at length, several experts brought up intentions to seek care as a potential intermediate outcome. When it is challenging to detect campaign effects on an ultimate outcome (e.g., scheduling and attending a mental health intake session), measuring the steps that lead up to that behavior can provide greater clarity around the impact of the program. They suggested considering interim outcomes, such as whether people have looked for information about mental health, made the decision to seek care, searched for or inquired about local mental health resources, or felt confident that they had the skills to find and schedule an appointment for appropriate treatment (self-efficacy).

Treatment Initiation Should Be Measured

There was relatively broad consensus across experts that treatment initiation (e.g., attending a mental health intake appointment, calling a mental health crisis line) would be an appropriate and measurable outcome across campaigns. They cautioned that treatment initiation is only an appropriate campaign outcome among those in the audience who have unmet mental health needs. One expert also recommended that treatment initiation be measured broadly to include a variety of mental health resources (e.g., faith-based counseling via a religious organization).

Short-Term Length of Campaign Evaluations May Limit Ability to Measure Treatment Engagement, Mental Health, and Quality of Life

Although many campaigns focus on treatment initiation as the primary goal, presumably the purpose of treatment initiation is to open the door to longer-term positive outcomes. Experts noted that the positive ends that could follow from treatment initiation are

- treatment engagement (i.e., continuation of care)
- receipt of a clinically significant dose of treatment (e.g., six weeks of antidepressants)
- mental health symptom improvement or amelioration
- reduced suicide ideation, attempts, and deaths
- recovery from a mental health condition
- improved quality of life
- increased work productivity, retention in the service or civilian workforce
- improved social functioning, marital satisfaction, and parenting.

At the same time, although campaigns encourage treatment-seeking as a route to these ultimate desired outcomes, our experts cautioned that it may not be appropriate or fair to evaluate public awareness campaigns on the basis of their capacity to achieve these long-term outcomes. Once a veteran or service member initiates treatment, the probability that they remain engaged and recover from their condition likely depends far more on the quality of care they receive, their comfort with their providers, and other variables related to the mental health care system than on campaign messaging. While a public awareness campaign can encourage service members and veterans to enter the mental health care system and, to some extent, prepare them for the care they are likely to receive, our experts did not believe it was appropriate to hold the campaign itself accountable for whether the mental health care system is effective. That said, one expert did note that public awareness campaigns should be certain that the message they are communicating (e.g., that the treatment the individual will receive is effective) is an accurate claim for the population they target and the mental health resources they endorse.

Evaluation Pitfalls to Avoid

Over the course of the panel discussion and phone interviews, experts in barriers to mental health care and evaluation designs for public awareness campaigns offered their observations of fatal or damaging flaws that can make the findings of an evaluation uninterpretable and offered advice on how to avoid them.

- A campaign that has a very small positive effect on important desired outcomes (e.g., suicide prevention, recovery from mental health) can still be a good use of resources if the cost of the program is low. An evaluation design that lacks the power to detect a very small positive effect associated with a widely disseminated campaign could erroneously conclude that the campaign is ineffective—which, in turn, could lead to discontinuation of a campaign that is actually having a positive impact.
- Good evaluation must always include a comparison group by which to determine whether any positive effects observed in the group exposed to the campaign are larger than improvements that might be observed in a nonexposed group. For widely disseminated campaigns, it can be difficult to access a well-matched, nonexposed comparison group.
- Public awareness campaigns have influences beyond the individual. For example, if a campaign message diffuses through the social network surrounding a veteran, that veteran may benefit from improved social norms that destigmatize mental illness and support care-seeking. In fact, the veteran may benefit from the campaign even if he or she never sees the messages. Most conventional evaluation designs fail to take into account such paths toward campaign impacts.
- Campaign messages may be particularly salient and notable to those who already have positive attitudes toward mental health conditions and believe that treatment-seeking is appropriate. In other words, campaigns may "preach to the choir." If these people are more likely to notice and attend to campaign messages, they will also be more likely to be included in an "exposed group" during campaign evalu-

ation. This will bias the evaluation toward finding that campaign exposure is associated with positive attitudes toward mental health conditions and treatment-seeking. Although researchers and/or decisionmakers may believe that campaign exposure caused the improved attitudes, it may be instead that the preexisting positive attitudes caused improved memory for campaign exposure. This is part of why longitudinal designs are important; prior beliefs can be statistically controlled.

- Evaluations should attend to and, to the extent possible, control for historical confounds and secular trends. For example, if a high-salience event, such as a celebrity death by suicide, co-occurs with the campaign launch, the evaluation team must acknowledge that they cannot untangle the effect of the campaign from the effect of the cultural or policy event that could drive similar outcomes. Experts noted that use of experimental efficacy trials can be useful adjuncts to correlational survey data, as these methods are not sensitive to historical confounds. Additionally, if there is a shift in societal attitudes without a direct link to campaign exposure, these trends should not be interpreted as a campaign effect.
- Close attention must be paid to selecting intermediate desired outcomes that have evidence to support an empirical link to the ultimate goal of the campaign. For example, measures of mental health stigma may not be appropriate evaluation targets given limited evidence linking mental health stigma to care-seeking.

Conclusion

Eighteen national and international experts in barriers to mental health treatment and evaluation of public awareness campaigns shared their suggestions for designing a strong evaluation of DoD, VA, and HHS public awareness campaigns to improve mental health care–seeking among veterans and service members. The experts' guidance and suggestions were wide-ranging and included advice on evaluation design options, selection of appropriate desired intermediate and long-term outcomes, and reminders about common pitfalls in evaluation designs for public awareness campaigns. The RAND research team has carefully considered all their suggestions, and expert insights were positive contributors to the evaluation design options outlined in this report.

Content Analysis Methods and Findings

To assess the content of the campaigns, we conducted a systematic review of each campaign's materials, including all content posted on the campaign website, campaign dissemination materials, and video and audio content.

Content Analysis Methods

Between November 2015 and January 2016, members of the RAND research team reviewed and catalogued the content of each of the evaluated campaigns to gain a better understanding of the types of materials available. Materials were reviewed to identify the information listed below.

Coders were instructed to code an item as being present or addressing a desired outcome only if the item explicitly did so. If any inference was required, an item would not be coded as being present or addressing a desired outcome. For example, we conceptualized positive depictions of those with mental health conditions or of mental health treatment (see the bulleted item on "desired short-term outcomes addressed" in the next section) as materials that positively portray people with mental health conditions (e.g., both recognizing a condition and thriving despite it) or treatment. Coders were instructed to code only materials that explicitly showed or stated positive characteristics or strengths.

Coding Categories

- *Name or title of the material.*
- *Type of material.* Common material types included news releases; online chat features; print materials, such as brochures, fliers, posters, and campaign ads; testimonials, recovery stories, or individual profiles; radio or video campaign ads or PSAs; toolkits; and webpages. Coders could also select "other" and write in a material type.
- *Location of material.* Because most materials were available online, this field was typically used to record the URL for the material.

- *Clarity of when information in material was produced.* Coders indicated whether no dates were given, whether some publication dates or dates of sources cited in the material were given, or whether dates for the material and all sources contained in it were given.
- *Date material was last updated.*
- *Clarity of what sources of information were used to compile the publication.* Coders indicated whether no sources of evidence were mentioned, whether some sources of evidence were clear, or whether all sources of evidence were very clear.
- *Reference to scientific journal articles.* Coders indicated whether scientific journal articles were referenced as a source or not.
- *Focus on mental health and/or substance use.* Coders indicated whether the material focused on mental health, substance use, or both topics.
- *Target population.* Coders indicated the target population for each material, selecting all that applied from a list containing the following possible populations: active duty service members, service members in the National Guard or Reserve, veterans, family of service members, family of veterans, health professional, or general population (i.e., not military specific). An "other" option allowed coders to write in additional target populations.
- *Characteristics of individuals pictured in material.* Coders indicated the characteristics of individuals who appeared in the material, including gender, race or ethnicity, age (under 35 years, 35–64 years, 65 years or older), service branch (Air Force, Army, Coast Guard, Marine Corps, Navy, or civilian), service component (active duty, National Guard or Reserve, veteran, civilian), rank, and era (e.g., Vietnam War [1960–1975]). Coders inferred gender from visual depictions, but all other characteristics were coded as "unknown" unless explicitly stated in the material.
- *Target population.* Coders indicated which of the following target audiences the materials were tailored to: active duty service members, National Guard or Reserve service members, veterans, family of service members, family of veterans, health professionals, the general population (i.e., not military specific), or other groups. More than one group could be selected.
- *Communication of campaign-specific messages.* Coders indicated whether materials corresponding with each campaign communicated the campaign-specific messages listed here. These campaign-specific messages were identified by the campaigns prior to the coding process.
  - RWC
    - Experiencing psychological stress as a result of deployment is common.
    - Unlike visible wounds, psychological wounds and brain injuries are often invisible and can go untreated if not identified.
    - Successful treatment and positive outcomes are greatly assisted by early intervention.

- Service members and their families should feel comfortable reaching out to their units and chain of command for support.
- Reaching out is a sign of strength that benefits service members, their families, their units, and their services.
- Warriors are not alone in coping with mental health concerns (i.e., there is a vast network of support and resources throughout each of the services).
  - MTC
    - Recovery is possible.
    - Treatment works.
  - VCL
    - If you are in crisis, contact VCL.
    - One call, one text, one conversation can save a life.
  - Recovery Month
    - Recovery is possible.
    - Speak out about your mental health experiences (your voice can make a difference).
    - Mental health is part of overall wellness.
- *Desired short-term outcomes addressed.* Coders indicated whether the material was likely to address one of the desired short-term outcomes of interest for the study. Each material was coded for the set of cross-agency desired short-term outcomes listed here, as well as the listed campaign-specific desired short-term outcomes.
  - Cross-agency desired outcomes
    - People with mental health conditions and mental health treatment are portrayed positively.[1]
    - Symptoms of mental health conditions are shared, listed, or described.
    - Treatment options and resources are shared, listed, or described.
    - Examples are provided of how friends or family can help individuals cope with a mental health condition.
  - RWC
    - Users are urged to seek mental health treatment.
  - MTC
    - Users are urged to seek mental health treatment.
  - VCL
    - The purpose of VCL is described.
    - Individuals are encouraged to use VCL.

---

[1] This category was originally coded as two separate items—"depicts people with mental health conditions as having positive characteristics or strengths and portrays benefits associated with recognizing and accepting that one has a mental health condition" and "provides information on the benefits of treatment"—but on further consideration, these codes were combined into a single category.

   ◦ Examples are provided of the ways friends or family can discuss suicide or concerns about an individual in crisis.
   – Recovery Month
   ◦ People with substance use conditions are depicted as having positive characteristics or strengths.
   ◦ Symptoms of substance use conditions are shared, listed, or described.
   ◦ Information on the benefits of substance use treatment is provided.
   ◦ Examples are provided of how friends or family can help individuals cope with a substance use condition.
   ◦ Examples are provided of how individuals with mental health or substance use conditions have recovered successfully.
   ◦ Substance use treatment options and resources are shared, listed, or described.
• *Direct connection to care.* Coders indicated whether the material provided a direct connection to mental health care. For the purposes of this report, we defined direct connection to care as providing information for a crisis line or live chat for professional counseling or connecting a user directly to a phone line for a specific medical center local to the user. Resource materials that included general information on where mental health services were provided, treatment locators (e.g., where users must enter their location and receive a list of places to possibly get care), and outreach phone lines with no mental health care provided were not coded as including a direct connection to care.

Reviews of Content Analysis

Three reviewers participated in the content analysis process. One reviewer was assigned to each campaign to visit the campaign website, identify all content, and review additional campaign materials supplied by the points of contact from each campaign. This reviewer read or viewed each material from beginning to end and then coded the content in terms of the characteristics listed previously. To ensure that the content analysis was consistently conducted by this single reviewer, a second reviewer also coded 5 percent of the content. Upon completing this process, the points of contact for each campaign were provided with a list of the content catalogued and asked to verify that it was complete. Any additional materials supplied by the campaigns were then coded.

Overall, reviewers had reasonably high agreement when coding materials, agreeing on 78 to 92 percent of the materials for each campaign (Table C.1). We also analyzed interrater reliability using a kappa statistic. The kappa statistic provides a normalized measure of agreement, adjusted for the agreement expected by chance. The kappa rating ranges from –1 to 1, where –1 is complete disagreement, 0 is agreement expected by chance, and 1 is complete agreement. Content analysis reviews for three of the four campaigns yielded kappa ratings greater than 0.80 (Table C.1), which is considered indicative of almost perfect agreement (Landis and Koch, 1977). For one

Table C.1
Interrater Agreement and Reliability for Campaign Content Coding

Characteristic	RWC	MTC	VCL	Recovery Month
Percent agreement	83.3%	92.2%	77.9%	91.0%
Kappa (reliability)	0.83	0.86	0.60	0.82

campaign, the kappa rating was slightly lower, but still high enough to indicate moderate agreement (Landis and Koch, 1977). This may have been because of the wide variety of campaign content for VCL—this included materials marketing VCL to service members and family members and materials that were more broadly focused on messages of support to veterans and services members (i.e., the Power of One materials). A greater challenge was determining how these broadly focused messages (e.g., it only takes 1 minute to stand by our nation's veterans) aligned with the narrower goals of the campaign to get veterans support during a time of crisis through VCL.

Findings from the Campaign Content Analysis

The following tables are intended to complement the tables in Chapter Five. These tables evaluate the sources used to compile campaign materials (Table C.2) and each campaign's alignment with campaign-specific goals and unique desired outcomes (Tables C.3 to C.6).

How Campaigns Cross-Reference Each Other

We also cataloged the ways in which campaigns cross-referenced or linked to one another. The specific link and a brief description of the context for the cross-reference or link were cataloged.

Real Warriors Campaign

We searched the RWC website (Real Warriors, undated-b) for references to other campaigns and related resources (Table C.7). The search yielded 13 links to MTC, four links to VCL, 46 links to MCL,[2] and no links to Recovery Month. Cross-references to MCL were also included in the template of every page. Also, some links were available via the search bar and included cross-references to other campaigns, but were not easily discovered through typical browsing of the website. These types of links included one link to MTC, three to VCL, and seven to MCL.

---

[2] As explained in Chapter Three, VCL is co-branded as MCL for active duty service members. This evaluation focused on the public awareness campaign for promoting awareness and use of VCL, not the actual operations of the crisis line. Further, we focused only on the public awareness campaign that intends to increase awareness and use of VCL among veterans and their families (not of MCL among active duty service members).

Table C.2
Evaluation of Sources Used to Compile Campaign Materials

Source Characteristic	RWC		MTC		VCL		Recovery Month	
	N	%	N	%	N	%	N	%
Information used or reported on the webpage was clearly marked with a date								
Yes	25	17.99	0	0.00	0	0.00	4	80.00
Partially	0	0.00	0	0.00	0	0.00	1	20.00
No	114	82.01	65	100.00	21	100.00	0	0.00
Sources of information used to compile the webpage were clearly marked								
Yes	46	33.09	0	0.00	0	0.00	1	20.00
Partially	68	48.92	0	0.00	0	0.00	0	0.00
No	25	17.99	65	100.00	21	100.00	4	80.00
Scientific journals referenced as a source	63	45.32	0	0.00	0	0.00	1	20.00

Table C.3
Real Warriors Campaign: Alignment of Content with Campaign Messages and Unique Desired Outcomes

Characteristic	N (total = 265)	%
Campaign messages		
Experiencing psychological stress as a result of deployment is common	67	25.28
Unlike visible wounds, psychological wounds and brain injuries are often invisible and can go untreated if not identified	36	13.58
Successful treatment and positive outcomes are greatly assisted by early intervention	35	13.21
Service members and their families should feel comfortable reaching out to their units and chains of command for support	73	27.66
Reaching out is a sign of strength that benefits service members, their families, their units, and their services	121	45.66
Warriors are not alone in coping with mental health concerns (i.e., there is a vast network of support and resources throughout each of the services)	115	43.40
Any campaign message	189	71.32
Unique desired outcome		
Tell users to seek mental health treatment	82	30.94

Table C.4
Make the Connection: Alignment of Content with Campaign Messages and Unique Desired Outcomes

Characteristic	N (total = 745)	%
Campaign messages		
Recovery is possible	147	19.73
Treatment works	412	55.38
Any campaign message	437	58.66
Unique desired outcome		
Tell users to seek mental health treatment	230	30.87

Table C.5
Veterans Crisis Line: Alignment of Content with Campaign Messages and Unique Desired Outcomes

Characteristic	N (total = 201)	%
Campaign messages		
Message about support	191	95.02
If you are in crisis, contact VCL	55	27.40
One call, one text, one conversation can save a life	8	3.98
Any campaign message	197	98.01
Unique desired outcomes		
Describe the purpose of VLC	110	54.73
Encourage individuals to use VCL	49	24.40
Provide examples of the ways that friends or family can discuss suicide or concerns that an individual is in crisis	3	1.49
Any unique desired outcome	121	60.20

Table C.6
National Recovery Month: Alignment of Content with Campaign Messages and Unique Desired Outcomes

Characteristic	N (total = 209)	%
Campaign messages		
Recovery is possible	193	92.34
Speak out about your mental health experiences (your voice can make a difference)	30	14.35
Mental health is part of overall wellness	27	12.92
Any campaign message	196	93.78
Unique desired outcome		
Depict people with substance use conditions as having positive characteristics or strengths	92	44.02
Share, list, or describe symptoms of substance use conditions	67	32.06
Provide information on the benefits of substance use treatment	104	49.76
Provide an example of how friends or family can help individuals cope with a substance use condition	105	50.24
Provide examples of how individuals with mental health or substance use conditions have recovered successfully	110	52.63
Share, list, or describe substance use treatment options and resources	83	39.71
Any desired outcome	180	86.12

Make the Connection

We searched the MTC website (Make the Connection, undated) for references to other campaigns and related resources (Table C.8). The search yielded four links to RWC, 52 links to VCL, and no links to MCL or Recovery Month.

Veterans Crisis Line

We searched the VCL website (VCL, undated-b) for references to other campaigns and related resources (Table C.9). The search yielded no links to RWC or Recovery Month, 24 links to MTC, and two links to MCL. Also, some links were available via searching and included cross-references to other campaigns, but were not easily discovered through typical browsing of the website. These types of links included one to MTC.

National Recovery Month

We searched the Recovery Month website (National Recovery Month, undated) for references to other campaigns and related resources (Table C.10). The search yielded four links to RWC, no links to MTC or MCL, and ten links to VCL. Also, some links were available via the search bar and included cross-references to other campaigns, but were not easily discovered through typical browsing of the website. These types of links included two links to RWC and four to VCL.

Table C.7
Real Warriors Campaign: Cross-Referencing and Linking to Other Campaigns (as of July 21, 2016)

Webpage Name or Description	URL	Campaign(s) Referenced	Description of How Other Campaign Is Referenced	Notes
"Resources for Military Veterans"	http://www.realwarriors.net/veterans/resources.php	MTC	This webpage, which provides a list of resources for military veterans, includes a hyperlink to the MTC website. This webpage also includes a feature box, which provides a hyperlink to the MTC website and a description of the campaign's purpose.	
"Veterans"	http://www.realwarriors.net/veterans	MTC	This webpage, which provides a brief description of information available for veterans, includes a feature box with a hyperlink to the MTC website and a description of the campaign's purpose.	
"Mind over Mood: Six Ways to Think Positively"	http://www.realwarriors.net/veterans/treatment/positivethinking.php	MTC	This article, which provides tips for thinking positively, includes a hyperlink to the MTC website under the "Additional Resources" section.	
"Alcohol Abuse: Signs and Symptoms"	http://www.realwarriors.net/active/treatment/alcoholabuse.php	MTC	This article, which discusses the signs and symptoms of alcohol abuse, includes a hyperlink to the MTC website under a section providing resources for National Guard and Reserve members. The article suggests visiting MTC's "resource database to find substance abuse care in your community."	
"Your Post-Military Career: Tips for Finding a Job and Achieving Success in the Civilian Workplace"	http://www.realwarriors.net/veterans/treatment/career.php	MTC	This webpage, which provides tips and resources for finding a job after serving in the military, includes a feature box with a hyperlink to the MTC website and a description of the campaign's purpose.	
"Peer Support Resources for Members of the National Guard, Reserve and Individual Augmentees"	http://www.realwarriors.net/guardreserve/treatment/peersupport.php	MTC	This article, which discusses peer support resources for members of the National Guard, reserve, and individual augmentees, includes hyperlinks to sections of the MTC website that provide support resources for these component types. The article states: "Make the Connection has a section just for members of the National Guard and reserve to connect with support resources and help manage military life challenges. If you are an individual augmentee, visit their Active Duty section for support resources."	

Table C.7—Continued

Webpage Name or Description	URL	Campaign(s) Referenced	Description of How Other Campaign Is Referenced	Notes
"Building Resilience to Cope with Difficult Situations"	http://www.realwarriors.net/veterans/treatment/postdeploymentstress.php	MTC	This article, which discusses building resilience to cope with difficult situations, includes a feature box with a hyperlink to the MTC website and a description of the campaign's purpose.	
"Veterans Affairs in the Digital Age"	http://www.realwarriors.net/veterans/discharge/VAsocialmedia.php	MTC	This article, which discusses how VA is embracing social media and technology in serving veterans, describes MTC as a service for reaching transitioning veterans. A positive quote from the VA Secretary calling MTC "an approachable online resource that links veterans to personal stories from their peers, to VA resources and support and to reliable information about mental health and resilience" and a hyperlink to MTC's website are included. This article also includes a feature box with a hyperlink to the MTC website and a description of the campaign's purpose.	
"Five Resources for Returning to School"	http://www.realwarriors.net/veterans/treatment/studentveterans.php	MTC	This article, which discusses resources for returning to school after serving in the military, includes a feature box with a hyperlink to the MTC website and a description of the campaign's purpose.	
"How to Develop Healthy Sleep Habits"	http://www.realwarriors.net/active/deployment/sleep.php	MTC	This article, which discusses how to develop healthy sleep habits, includes a hyperlink to the MTC website under the "Additional Resources" section.	
"Five Steps Veterans Can Take to Support PTSD Treatment"	http://www.realwarriors.net/veterans/treatment/ptsdtreatment.php	MTC	This article, which discusses steps that veterans can take to support recovery from PTSD, includes a feature box with a hyperlink to the MTC website and a description of the campaign's purpose.	

Table C.7—Continued

Webpage Name or Description	URL	Campaign(s) Referenced	Description of How Other Campaign Is Referenced	Notes
"Your Civilian Life and Psychological Health: Episode 032—Transcript"	http://www.realwarriors.net/podcasts/episode032-transcript	MTC, MCL	This transcript of a podcast episode focused on transitioning to civilian life describes the MTC website as an important resource "for information about reintegration, maintaining resilience throughout your transition and how to access available tools and resources to address psychological health concerns." A hyperlink to the MTC website is not provided. Additionally, the transcript describes MCL as a resource to access "if you or someone you love is contemplating suicide or experiencing a psychological health crisis." The MCL phone number is provided.	
"PTSD Help Guide"	http://www.realwarriors.net/node/2137	MTC	This webpage, which provides a record of the news article "PTSD Help Guide," published by the *Dayton Daily News*, describes MTC as "a website for veterans where you can hear others' stories of survival and strength, symptoms of PTSD and other conditions, find more information on the conditions that affect veterans or more resources." A hyperlink to the MTC website is not provided.	Not easily discovered
"The Veterans Crisis Line Offers Support 24/7"	http://www.realwarriors.net/node/3238	VCL	This webpage provides a record of a news article published by Veterans of Foreign Wars, titled "The Veterans Crisis Line Offers Support 24/7" (24 hours a day, seven days a week). A hyperlink to the VCL website or other contact information is not provided.	Not easily discovered
"Seven Tools That Reinforce Psychological Health for Veterans"	http://www.realwarriors.net/materials/brochure_veterans.php	VCL, MCL	This HTML version of a brochure, which describes resources available for veterans, provides the VCL phone number under a list of resources. The brochure also includes a section focused on MCL, which discusses the purpose of MCL and provides a phone number, the number to text, and the hyperlink to the MCL website. The MCL logo is also included in this section.	
"Defeating Military Suicides with Listening, Caring, Responding"	http://www.realwarriors.net/content/defeating-military-suicides-listening-caring-responding	VCL	This webpage, which provides a record of the news article "Defeating Military Suicides with Listening, Caring, Responding," published by the Marine Corps, states: "Trained Professionals at the Veterans Crisis Line, headquartered in Canandaigua, New York, respond every day to provide help and guidance to Service members and veterans who are thinking of taking their lives." A hyperlink to the VCL website or other contact information is not provided.	Not easily discovered

Table C.7—Continued

Webpage Name or Description	URL	Campaign(s) Referenced	Description of How Other Campaign Is Referenced	Notes
"Help Prevent Vet Suicide"	http://www.realwarriors.net/node/3305	VCL	This webpage, which provides a record of the news article "Help Prevent Vet Suicide," published by The Hill, states: "The Veterans Crisis Line is a place for vets to go, confidentially and privately, for help and support. If you are a vet facing great hardship and stress, you can call these people who know a lot about the subject and have many ways they can help." A hyperlink to the VCL website or other contact information is not provided.	Not easily discovered
"Reintegrating into Family Life After Deployment"	http://www.realwarriors.net/active/afterdeployment/familylife.php	MCL	This article, which provides tips for reintegrating into family life after deployment, describes MCL as a resource to access for 24/7 confidential support if one is feeling stressed. The MCL phone number is provided.	
"Understanding the Types of Psychological Health Care"	http://www.realwarriors.net/active/treatment/types-of-psychological-health-care.php	MCL	This article, which discusses types of psychological health care within the military health system, describes MCL as a resource to access in case of an immediate crisis. The MCL phone number and a hyperlink to the MCL website are provided.	
"Seek Help 24/7"	http://www.realwarriors.net/seek-help.php	MCL	This webpage, which provides an overview of psychological health sources, includes a feature box with hyperlinks to the MCL website and location to chat online, as well as the MCL phone number. In the box, MCL is described as a resource for access to free, 24/7 confidential support.	
"Recognizing and Seeking Help for Substance Misuse"	http://www.realwarriors.net/active/treatment/substancemisuse.php	MCL	This article, which focuses on identifying substance misuse and options for care, describes MCL as a resource to access "if you or someone you know is in crisis." The MCL phone number and a hyperlink to the MCL website are provided.	

Table C.7—Continued

Webpage Name or Description	URL	Campaign(s) Referenced	Description of How Other Campaign Is Referenced	Notes
"Know the Facts: Psychological Health Booklet"	http://www.realwarriors.net/materials/booklet-know-the-facts.php	MCL	This HTML version of a booklet provides psychological health information and resources. In a quiz to test knowledge about psychological health, the booklet includes MCL as an answer choice to a question focused on resources for seeking help. The answer key describes the purpose of MCL and includes the phone number to access it. MCL is also included in a list of various resources, and the phone number, hyperlink to access the online chat, and description of MCL as a resource for immediate assistance, offering 24/7, free, confidential support are provided.	
"5 Apps for Staying Mission Ready"	http://www.realwarriors.net/materials/booklet_apps.php	MCL	This HTML version of a brochure, which features five apps for staying mission ready, includes MCL under a list of resources to reach out to for help. The MCL phone number and the hyperlink to access the online chat are provided. MCL is described as a resource to call "if you or someone you know is in a crisis."	
"5 Questions to Ask Your Psychological Health Provider"	http://www.realwarriors.net/materials/booklet-5-questions.php	MCL	This HTML version of a booklet, which focuses on preparing to meet with a health care provider, includes MCL under a list of resources if one is in need of immediate care between appointments. The reader is instructed to "Call/text/chat if you or someone you know is in a crisis," and the MCL phone number, the number to text, and the hyperlink to access the online chat are provided.	
"You Are Not Alone: Suicide Prevention Tools for Warriors"	http://www.realwarriors.net/active/treatment/suicidesigns.php	MCL	This article, which discusses suicidal warning signs and related resources, cites MCL throughout as a resource to access if one is in crisis or experiencing thoughts of suicide. Hyperlinks to the MCL website and location to chat online, as well as the MCL phone number, are provided. The MCL logo and phone number are also provided on the page.	
"Understanding Posttraumatic Stress with PTSD Coach"	http://www.realwarriors.net/active/treatment/ptsdcoach.php	MCL	This article, which discusses the PTSD coach mobile app for service members and veterans, provides a hyperlink to the MCL website, explaining that the app can link individuals in need of immediate help to MCL. A feature box with the hyperlink to the MCL website and an explanation that the app can connect the user to MCL for immediate assistance is also included.	

Table C.7—Continued

Webpage Name or Description	URL	Campaign(s) Referenced	Description of How Other Campaign Is Referenced	Notes
"Suicide Prevention Resources for Military Families"	http://www.realwarriors.net/family/support/preventsuicide.php	MCL	This article, which discusses suicide prevention resources available for military families, cites MCL throughout the text and in a feature box as a resource to access for immediate help if one is in crisis or experiencing thoughts of suicide. Hyperlinks to the MCL website and location to chat online are provided, as well as the MCL phone number. The MCL logo and phone number are also provided in the feature box.	
"Do Something Meaningful This Veterans Day: Episode 028—Transcript"	http://www.realwarriors.net/podcasts/episode028-transcript	MCL	This transcript of a podcast episode focused on showing appreciation for service members, veterans, and their families on Veterans Day describes MCL as a resource to access "if you or someone you love is contemplating suicide or experiencing a psychological health crisis." The MCL phone number is provided.	
"Understanding and Managing Anxiety Disorders"	http://www.realwarriors.net/active/treatment/anxietydisorders.php	MCL	This article, which discusses anxiety disorders, describes MCL as a resource to access "if you or someone you know is in crisis." The MCL phone number and a hyperlink to the MCL website are provided.	
"Resiliency Programs for Military Families"	http://www.realwarriors.net/family/change/MFLC.php	MCL	This article, which discusses resiliency programs for military families, includes a feature box with free resources that can be called 24/7 to speak with trained professionals. A hyperlink to access MCL's online chat and the MCL phone number are provided.	
"Using Social Media to Stay Connected"	http://www.realwarriors.net/active/treatment/socialmedia.php	MCL	This article, which discusses how social media can be used to stay connected with family, friends, and other service members, describes MCL as a resource to access "if you or someone you know is in crisis and needs immediate help." The MCL phone number is provided.	
"Taking the First Steps to Get Help for Psychological Health Concerns"	http://www.realwarriors.net/active/treatment/gettinghelp.php	MCL	This article, which discusses steps to take to seek care for psychological health concerns, describes MCL as a resource to access "if you or someone you know is in crisis and needs immediate help." The MCL phone number is provided.	

Table C.7—Continued

Webpage Name or Description	URL	Campaign(s) Referenced	Description of How Other Campaign Is Referenced	Notes
"Security Clearances and Psychological Health Care"	http://www.realwarriors.net/active/treatment/clearance.php	MCL	This article, which discusses security clearances and psychological health care, lists MCL as a resource under a section focused on reaching out for help. The article states that MCL should be contacted "if you or someone you love needs help coping with psychological health concerns" and the MCL phone number is provided.	
"Dealing with Depression: Symptoms and Treatment"	http://www.realwarriors.net/active/treatment/depression.php	MCL	This article, which discusses depression symptoms and treatment, includes a feature box with a hyperlink to the MLC website and the MCL phone number. The reader is told to dial the number "if you or someone you know is thinking about suicide" and is instructed to visit the website "for more information on support, warning signs and what to do in a crisis."	
"Seven Tools That Reinforce Warrior Resilience"	http://www.realwarriors.net/materials/brochure_activeduty.php	MCL	This HTML version of a brochure, which describes resources available for active duty service members, includes a section focused on MCL, which discusses the purpose of MCL and features the phone number, the number to text, and the hyperlink to the MCL website. The MCL logo and phone number are also included in this section. Additionally, MCL is included under a list of resources to reach out to for help and the MCL phone number is provided. MCL is described as a resource to call "if you are in a crisis."	
"Accessing Care at Military Treatment Facilities"	http://www.realwarriors.net/active/afterdeployment/treatmentfacilities.php	MCL	This article, which focuses on accessing care at military treatment facilities, lists MCL as a resource under a section on reaching out for help. The article states that MCL should be contacted "if you or someone you know is in crisis," and the MCL phone number and a hyperlink to the MCL website are provided.	
"7 Tools to Reinforce Military Family Resilience"	http://www.realwarriors.net/materials/brochure_families.php	MCL	This HTML version of a brochure, which describes resources available for military families, includes a section focused on MCL, which discusses the purpose of MCL and features the phone number, the number to text, and the hyperlink to the MCL website. The MCL logo and phone number are also included in this section.	
"Understanding Moral Injury"	http://www.realwarriors.net/active/treatment/moralinjury.php	MCL	This article, which focuses on moral injury, includes a hyperlink under the "Additional Resources" section to access the MCL online chat on the MTC website.	

Table C.7—Continued

Webpage Name or Description	URL	Campaign(s) Referenced	Description of How Other Campaign Is Referenced	Notes
"Suicide Prevention Training for Line Leaders"	http://www.realwarriors. net/active/leaders/ suicideprevention.php	MCL	This article, which focuses on suicide prevention for line leaders, includes MCL contact information in two separate feature boxes. In one box, the MCL phone number and a hyperlink to access the online chat are provided. MCL is described as a resource to access "for crisis intervention for service members, veterans and families." In the other box, the MCL phone number and chat link are also provided, and the reader is instructed to contact MCL "if you or someone you love is contemplating suicide or experiencing a psychological health crisis."	
"Military Crisis Line Saves Lives"	http://www.realwarriors. net/node/2878	MCL	This webpage provides a record of the news article "Military Crisis Line Saves Lives," published by DCMilitary.com. It states: "When someone is in crisis and feeling despondent, reaching out for help is a stronger step to take than doing nothing, which can lead to a worsening state, a Military Crisis Line responder told American Forces Press Service Sept. 10." A hyperlink to the MCL website or other contact information is not provided.	Not easily discovered
"Supporting Your Service Member with Psychological Health Concerns"	http://www.realwarriors. net/family/support/ psychhealth.php	MCL	This article, which discusses supporting service members with psychological health concerns, includes the MCL phone number and a hyperlink to the MCL website next to the area of the article focused on suicidal thoughts. MCL is described as a resource to access "if you think your family member may be feeling suicidal." MCL is also included in a list of resources with a hyperlink to the MCL website and the phone number.	
"You Are Your Friend's Biggest Support"	http://www.realwarriors. net/ active/treatment/ suicideprevention.php	MCL	This article, which focuses on supporting fellow service members at risk of suicide, includes the MCL phone number and the hyperlinks to access the MCL website and online chat under a list of resources for immediate assistance. This article also includes a feature box, which provides the MCL phone number and a hyperlink to the website, and MCL is described as a resource to access "if you or someone you love is contemplating suicide or experiencing a psychological health crisis." The MCL logo and phone number are also included in this box.	

Table C.7—Continued

Webpage Name or Description	URL	Campaign(s) Referenced	Description of How Other Campaign Is Referenced	Notes
"For Military and Families Coping with Psychological Health Concerns, the Real Warriors Campaign Offers Resources, Support"	http://www.realwarriors.net/pressroom/printfeatures/warriorsupport.php	MCL	This article, which provides an overview of RWC, mentions MCL as a resource to access for additional materials. A hyperlink to the MCL website and the MCL phone number are provided.	Not easily discovered
"Veterans Affairs Health Benefits Overview"	http://www.realwarriors.net/veterans/discharge/VAhealthbenefits.php	MCL	This article, which provides an overview of benefits available through VA, includes the MCL phone number under a section providing resources for those affected by invisible wounds. The article suggests calling MCL if one is in crisis.	
"Tips for National Guard and Reserve Members to Manage Stress"	http://www.realwarriors.net/guardreserve/treatment/copewithstress.php	MCL	This article, which provides tips for National Guard and reserve members to manage stress, includes MCL under a list of resources to reach out to for help coping with stress. The MCL phone number and a hyperlink to access the online chat are provided. MCL is described as a resource to contact "for 24/7 confidential support."	
"Crisis Hot Line Saves Suicidal War Veterans"	http://www.realwarriors.net/node/1907	MCL	This webpage provides a record of the news article "Crisis Hot Line Saves Suicidal War Veterans," published by CNN. It states: "The men and women who answer the Military Crisis Line phones are on the front lines of an all-out war on suicide. Each speaks to the caller with a very clear purpose: keep the person on the phone long enough to get help." A hyperlink to the MCL website or other contact information is not provided.	Not easily discovered
"Battlefield Skills That Make Reintegration Challenging: Episode 027—Transcript"	http://www.realwarriors.net/podcasts/episode027-transcript	MCL	This transcript of a podcast episode focuses on the challenges of transitioning to civilian life based on experiences during combat. The transcript describes MCL as a resource to access "if you or someone you love is contemplating suicide or experiencing a psychological health crisis." The MCL phone number is provided.	
"FAQs"	http://www.realwarriors.net/faq	MCL	This is the FAQ section of the RWC website. The MCL phone number and a hyperlink to access the online chat are provided under the FAQ focused on where relatives can call to get assistance. MCL is described as a resource to contact "for 24/7 confidential support."	

Table C.7—Continued

Webpage Name or Description	URL	Campaign(s) Referenced	Description of How Other Campaign Is Referenced	Notes
"Maintaining Psychological Strength While Deployed"	http://www.realwarriors.net/active/treatment/maintainstrength.php	MCL	This article, which discusses maintaining psychological strength during deployment, includes MCL under a list of resources to access to talk to someone 24/7. The MCL phone number is provided.	
"You Are Not Alone: Suicide Prevention Resources for Warriors: Episode 026—Transcript"	http://www.realwarriors.net/podcasts/episode026-transcript	MCL	This transcript of a podcast episode focused on experiencing traumatic events and suicide prevention resources describes MCL as a resource to access "if you or someone you love is contemplating suicide or experiencing a psychological health crisis." The MCL phone number is provided.	
"Coping with Survivor Guilt and Grief"	http://www.realwarriors.net/active/treatment/survivorguilt.php	MCL	This article, which discusses coping with survivor guilt and grief, describes MCL as a resource that is "available 24 hours a day, 7 days a week for those who need immediate care and support." A hyperlink to the MCL website is provided.	
"Resilience: There's an App for That: Episode 034—Transcript"	http://www.realwarriors.net/podcasts/episode034-transcript	MCL	This transcript of a podcast episode focused on building resilience describes MCL as a resource to access "if you or someone you love is having thoughts of suicide or experiencing a psychological health crisis." The MCL phone number is provided.	
"Veterans in Crisis Can Now Text for Help"	http://www.realwarriors.net/node/1998	MCL	This webpage provides a record of the news article "Veterans in Crisis Can Now Text for Help," published by the *Air Force Times*, formerly the *Air Force Times*. It states: "Veterans and service members contemplating suicide can now text for help through the Military Crisis Line, formerly the national Veterans Suicide Prevention Hotline." A hyperlink to the MCL website or other contact information is not provided.	Not easily discovered
"Kids Serve Too: Helping Children Cope: Episode 033—Transcript"	http://www.realwarriors.net/podcasts/episode033-transcript	MCL	This transcript of a podcast episode focused on helping children cope with deployment describes MCL as a resource to access "if you or someone you love is having thoughts of suicide or experiencing a psychological health crisis." The MCL phone number is provided.	
"Staying Connected Can Build Resilience: Episode 031—Transcript"	http://www.realwarriors.net/podcasts/episode031-transcript	MCL	This transcript of a podcast episode focused on building resilience through maintaining close ties with others describes MCL as a resource to access "if you or someone you love is contemplating suicide or experiencing a psychological health crisis." The MCL phone number is provided.	

Table C.7—Continued

Webpage Name or Description	URL	Campaign(s) Referenced	Description of How Other Campaign Is Referenced	Notes
"The Importance of Total Fitness: Episode 030—Transcript"	http://www.realwarriors.net/podcasts/episode030-transcript	MCL	This transcript of a podcast episode focused on the importance of total fitness describes MCL as a resource to access "if you or someone you love is contemplating suicide or experiencing a psychological health crisis." The MCL phone number is provided.	
"Tips for Coping with Stress During the Holidays: Episode 029—Transcript"	http://www.realwarriors.net/podcasts/episode029-transcript	MCL	This transcript of a podcast episode providing tips to cope with stress during the holidays describes MCL as a resource to access "if you or someone you love is contemplating suicide or experiencing a psychological health crisis." The MCL phone number is provided.	
"Captain America Lends 'A Little Help' to Raise Suicide Prevention Awareness"	http://www.realwarriors.net/node/1403	MCL	This webpage provides a record of the news article "Captain America Lends 'A Little Help' to Raise Suicide Prevention Awareness," published by comicsalliance.com. It states that the comic "Captain America: A Little Help" was created to "raise awareness of suicide prevention and to direct those in need to the Military Crisis Line." A hyperlink to the MCL website or other contact information is not provided.	Not easily discovered
"Family Matters Blog: Families Can Support Suicide Standdown"	http://www.realwarriors.net/node/2326	MCL	This webpage provides a record of the news article "Family Matters Blog: Families Can Support Suicide Standdown," published by DoD. It suggests that family members can enter contact information for MCL into their smart phones to support the Army's standdown for suicide prevention. The MCL phone number, URL, and number to text are provided.	Not easily discovered
"VA Expands Suicide Prevention Tools"	http://www.realwarriors.net/node/2011	MCL	This webpage provides a record of the news article "VA Expands Suicide Prevention Tools," published by Military.com. It states: "The Department of Veterans Affairs (VA) has expanded its efforts to prevent suicide by introducing text messaging to its Military Crisis Line toolbox." A hyperlink to the MCL website or other contact information is not provided.	Not easily discovered
All webpages	All	MCL	The MCL phone number and a hyperlink to the MCL website are provided on every page, along with contact information for the DCoE Outreach Center.	

Table C.8
Make the Connection: Webpage Cross-Referencing and Linking to Other Campaigns (as of July 21, 2016)

Webpage Name or Description	URL	Campaign(s) Referenced	Description of How Other Campaign Is Referenced	Notes
"Transitioning from Service"	https://maketheconnection.net/events/transitioning-from-service	RWC, VCL	This article, which discusses challenges with transitioning from military service, provides a hyperlink to the RWC website under a list of related resources. The purpose of RWC, to "promote the processes of building resilience, facilitating recovery, and supporting reintegration of returning Service members, Veterans, and their families," is noted. The VCL logo and phone number with a built-in hyperlink to the VCL website are also provided on the page.	
"Preparing for Deployment"	https://maketheconnection.net/events/preparing-for-deployment	RWC, VCL	This article, which discusses preparing for deployment, provides a hyperlink to the RWC website under a list of resources, along with a description of the campaign's purpose. The VCL logo and phone number with a built-in hyperlink to the VCL website are also provided on the page.	
"Student Veterans/ Higher Education"	https://maketheconnection.net/events/students-higher-education	RWC, VCL	This article focuses on school-related challenges among veterans. It provides a hyperlink to an RWC article that discusses resources for returning to school after serving in the military. The VCL logo and phone number with a built-in hyperlink to the VCL website are also provided on the page.	
"Social Withdrawal/ Isolation"	https://maketheconnection.net/symptoms/social-withdrawal	RWC, VCL	This article discusses social withdrawal and social isolation among veterans. It provides a hyperlink to an RWC article focused on PTSD treatment under a list of resources for more information about veterans experiencing social withdrawal and isolation. The article describes the connection between PTSD and social isolation. The VCL logo and phone number with a built-in hyperlink to the VCL website are also provided on the page.	
"Suicide"	https://maketheconnection.net/conditions/suicide	VCL	This article focuses on suicide among veterans. Throughout the article, VCL is cited as a resource to access immediate support if one is in crisis or has suicidal thoughts and behaviors. The VCL phone number, the number to text, and the hyperlinks to the website and online chat are provided. VCL is mentioned as offering "free, confidential support 24 hours a day, 7 days a week, 365 days a year." The VCL logo and phone number with a built-in hyperlink to the VCL website are also provided on the page. VCL is mentioned in the description of a video testimonial as a resource that some veterans accessed for recovery.	

Table C.8—Continued

Webpage Name or Description	URL	Campaign(s) Referenced	Description of How Other Campaign Is Referenced	Notes
"Self-Assessments"	https://maketheconnection.net/resources/self-assessments	VCL	This webpage provides a list of self-assessments that can be filled out to gauge whether one's feelings and behaviors may be symptoms of conditions, including depression, PTSD, alcohol use, substance use, and crisis. In the list, a hyperlink to the VCL self-check quiz and a description that the quiz can be taken to "better understand what you're going through, learn if it may be a good idea to seek professional help, and see how you might benefit from VA or community-based services" are provided. Hyperlinks to the VCL website and online chat are provided, as are the VCL phone number and number to text. VCL is noted as offering "free, confidential support 24 hours a day, 7 days a week, 365 days a year."	
"Feelings of Hopelessness"	https://maketheconnection.net/symptoms/feelings-of-hopelessness	VCL	This article focuses on thoughts of hopelessness among veterans. Throughout the article, VCL is cited as a resource for access to immediate support if one is having thoughts of death or suicide or is thinking of harming oneself. The VCL phone number, the number to text, and the hyperlinks to the website and online chat are provided. VCL is mentioned as offering "free, confidential support 24 hours a day, 7 days a week, 365 days a year." The VCL logo and phone number with a built-in hyperlink to the VCL website are also provided on the page. VCL is mentioned in the description of a video testimonial as a resource that some veterans accessed for recovery.	
"Jobs and Employment"	https://maketheconnection.net/events/jobs-employment	VCL	This article discusses work-related issues among veterans. Under the section focused on reaching out for support, VCL is mentioned as a resource to speak to someone "if your work situation is leading to a bigger crisis in your life." The VCL phone number, the number to text, and the hyperlinks to the website and online chat are provided. VCL is mentioned as offering "free, confidential support 24 hours a day, 7 days a week, 365 days a year." The VCL logo and phone number with a built-in hyperlink to the VCL website are also provided on the page.	
"Schizophrenia"	https://maketheconnection.net/conditions/schizophrenia	VCL	This article, which discusses schizophrenia among veterans, cites VCL as a resource to contact for immediate support if one has thoughts of death or suicide. The VCL phone number, the number to text, and the hyperlinks to the website and online chat are provided. VCL is mentioned as offering "free, confidential support 24 hours a day, 7 days a week, 365 days a year." The VCL logo and phone number with a built-in hyperlink to the VCL website are also provided on the page.	

Table C.8—Continued

Webpage Name or Description	URL	Campaign(s) Referenced	Description of How Other Campaign Is Referenced	Notes
"Depression"	https://maketheconnection.net/conditions/depression	VCL	This article, which discusses depression among veterans, cites VCL as a resource to contact for immediate support if one has thoughts of death or suicide. The VCL phone number, the number to text, and the hyperlinks to the website and online chat are provided. VCL is mentioned as offering "free, confidential support, 24 hours a day, 7 days a week, 365 days a year." The VCL logo and phone number with a built-in hyperlink to the VCL website are also provided on the page.	
"Adjustment Disorder"	https://maketheconnection.net/conditions/adjustment-disorder	VCL	This article, which discusses adjustment disorder among veterans, cites VCL as a resource to contact for immediate support if one has thoughts of death or suicide. The VCL phone number, the number to text, and the hyperlinks to the website and online chat are provided. VCL is mentioned as offering "free, confidential support, 24 hours a day, 7 days a week, 365 days a year." The VCL logo and phone number with a built-in hyperlink to the VCL website are also provided on the page.	
"VA Information and Resources"	https://maketheconnection.net/resources/va-information	VCL	This webpage, which provides a list of VA resources, services, and benefits, includes hyperlinks to the VCL website and online chat, as well as the VCL phone number and number to text. VCL is mentioned as offering "free, confidential support, 24 hours a day, seven days a week."	
"Bipolar Disorder"	https://maketheconnection.net/conditions/bipolar	VCL	This article, which discusses bipolar disorder among veterans, cites VCL as a resource to contact for immediate support if one has thoughts of death or suicide. The VCL phone number, the number to text, and the hyperlinks to the website and online chat are provided. VCL is mentioned as offering "free, confidential support 24 hours a day, 7 days a week, 365 days a year." The VCL logo and phone number with a built-in hyperlink to the VCL website are also provided on the page.	
"Military Sexual Trauma"	https://maketheconnection.net/conditions/military-sexual-trauma	VCL	This article, which discusses military sexual trauma, cites VCL as a resource to contact for immediate support if one has thoughts of death or suicide. The VCL phone number, the number to text, and the hyperlinks to the website and online chat are provided. VCL is mentioned as offering "free, confidential support, 24 hours a day, 7 days a week, 365 days a year." The VCL logo and phone number with a built-in hyperlink to the VCL website are also provided on the page.	

Table C.8—Continued

Webpage Name or Description	URL	Campaign(s) Referenced	Description of How Other Campaign Is Referenced	Notes
"Effects of Traumatic Brain Injury"	https://maketheconnection.net/conditions/traumatic-brain-injury	VCL	This article, which discusses effects of traumatic brain injury, cites VCL as a resource to contact for immediate support if one has thoughts of death or suicide. The VCL phone number, the number to text, and the hyperlinks to the website and online chat are provided. VCL is mentioned as offering "free, confidential support 24 hours a day, 7 days a week, 365 days a year." The VCL logo and phone number with a built-in hyperlink to the VCL website are also provided on the page.	
"Confusion"	https://maketheconnection.net/symptoms/confusion	VCL	This article focuses on the experience of confusion among veterans. VCL is mentioned in the description of a video testimonial as the resource that a veteran's wife called when he was having thoughts about death. The veteran was helped by receiving treatment for his traumatic brain injury and PTSD. Contact information for VCL is not provided in the video. The VCL logo and phone number with a built-in hyperlink to the VCL website are provided on the page.	
"Stories/Compilation"	https://maketheconnection.net/stories/635	VCL	This webpage includes a series of videos. The video that is showcased is focused on veterans regaining hope after losing interest in life and feeling hopeless. VCL is mentioned in the description of the video testimonial as a resource that some veterans accessed for recovery. Contact information for VCL is not provided.	
"Loss of Interest or Pleasure"	https://maketheconnection.net/symptoms/loss-of-interest	VCL	This article is focused on loss of interest or pleasure among veterans. The video that is showcased is focused on veterans regaining hope after losing interest in life and feeling hopeless. VCL is mentioned in the description of the video testimonial as a resource that some veterans accessed for recovery. Contact information for VCL is not provided in the description, but the VCL logo and phone number with a built-in hyperlink to the VCL website are provided on the page.	
"Information for Veterans"	http://maketheconnection.net/veterans?exp_id = 5,7,9,11,8,2,48&expblurb_id = 6,8,10&sym_id = 10,24,16,8,17&symblurb_id = 8&con_id = 1,2,5,6,7&conblurb_id = 28&story_id = 269	VCL	This webpage provides links to information focused on challenges that veterans are facing. The VCL logo and phone number with a built-in hyperlink to the VCL website are provided on the page.	

Table C.8—Continued

Webpage Name or Description	URL	Campaign(s) Referenced	Description of How Other Campaign Is Referenced	Notes
"Spirituality"	http://maketheconnection.net/events/spirituality?experience_id = 10&story_id = 301	VCL	This article focuses on spirituality-related issues among veterans. The VCL logo and phone number with a built-in hyperlink to the VCL website are provided on the page.	
"Anxiety Disorders"	http://maketheconnection.net/conditions/anxiety-disorder?condition_id = 3&story_id = 252	VCL	This article focuses on anxiety disorders among veterans. The VCL logo and phone number with a built-in hyperlink to the VCL website are provided on the page.	
"Stories/Scott's Story"	http://maketheconnection.net/stories/332	VCL	This webpage includes a series of videos. The video that is showcased is focused on a veteran who experienced suicidal thoughts after returning from service and how receiving help positively changed his life. VCL is mentioned in the description of the video testimonial as the resource that a veteran's wife called when he was having thoughts about death. The veteran was helped by receiving treatment for his traumatic brain injury and PTSD. Contact information for VCL is not provided.	
"Problems with Drugs"	http://maketheconnection.net/conditions/problems-with-drugs?condition_id = 6&story_id = 7	VCL	This article focuses on drug problems among veterans. The VCL logo and phone number with a built-in hyperlink to the VCL website are provided on the page.	
"Gambling"	https://maketheconnection.net/symptoms/gambling	VCL	This article focuses on gambling problems among veterans. The VCL logo and phone number with a built-in hyperlink to the VCL website are provided on the page.	
"Guilt"	http://maketheconnection.net/symptoms/guilt?symptom_id = 3&story_id = 31	VCL	This article focuses on feelings of guilt among veterans. The VCL logo and phone number with a built-in hyperlink to the VCL website are provided on the page.	
"Trouble Sleeping"	http://maketheconnection.net/symptoms/trouble-sleeping?symptom_id = 9&story_id = 138	VCL	This article focuses on sleep problems among veterans. The VCL logo and phone number with a built-in hyperlink to the VCL website are provided on the page.	
"Financial and Legal Issues"	http://maketheconnection.net/events/financial-legal-issues?experience_id = 6&story_id = 9	VCL	This article focuses on financial and legal issues among veterans. The VCL logo and phone number with a built-in hyperlink to the VCL website are provided on the page.	

Table C.8—Continued

Webpage Name or Description	URL	Campaign(s) Referenced	Description of How Other Campaign Is Referenced	Notes
"Retirement and Aging"	http://maketheconnection.net/events/retirement-aging?experience_id = 7&story_id = 72	VCL	This article focuses on aging and retirement issues among veterans. The VCL logo and phone number with a built-in hyperlink to the VCL website are provided on the page.	
"PTSD"	https://maketheconnection.net/conditions/ptsd	VCL	This article focuses on PTSD among veterans. The VCL logo and phone number with a built-in hyperlink to the VCL website are provided on the page.	
"Relationship Problems"	https://maketheconnection.net/symptoms/relationship-problems	VCL	This article focuses on relationship problems among veterans. The VCL logo and phone number with a built-in hyperlink to the VCL website are provided on the page.	
"Problems with Alcohol"	https://maketheconnection.net/conditions/problems-with-alcohol	VCL	This article focuses on alcohol problems among veterans. The VCL logo and phone number with a built-in hyperlink to the VCL website are provided on the page.	
"Physical Injury"	https://maketheconnection.net/events/injury	VCL	This article focuses on physical injuries among veterans. The VCL logo and phone number with a built-in hyperlink to the VCL website are provided on the page.	
"Family and Relationships"	https://maketheconnection.net/events/family-relationships	VCL	This article focuses on family- and relationship-related issues among veterans. The VCL logo and phone number with a built-in hyperlink to the VCL website are provided on the page.	
"Information for National Guard and Reserve"	https://maketheconnection.net/national-guard-reserve	VCL	This webpage provides links to information focused on challenges that National Guard members and Reservists are facing. The VCL logo and phone number with a built-in hyperlink to the VCL website are provided on the page.	
"Stress and Anxiety"	http://maketheconnection.net/symptoms/stress-anxiety?symptom_id = 7&story_id = 12	VCL	This article focuses on stress and anxiety among veterans. The VCL logo and phone number with a built-in hyperlink to the VCL website are provided on the page.	
"Information for Family and Friends"	https://maketheconnection.net/family-friends	VCL	This webpage provides links to information focused on challenges that veterans and their family members and friends are facing. The VCL logo and phone number with a built-in hyperlink to the VCL website are provided on the page.	

Table C.8—Continued

Webpage Name or Description	URL	Campaign(s) Referenced	Description of How Other Campaign Is Referenced	Notes
"Information for Clinicians"	https://maketheconnection.net/clinicians	VCL	This webpage provides videos and resources for clinicians working with veterans. The VCL logo and phone number with a built-in hyperlink to the VCL website are provided on the page.	
"Information for Active Duty"	https://maketheconnection.net/active-duty	VCL	This webpage provides links to information focused on challenges that active duty service members are facing. The VCL logo and phone number with a built-in hyperlink to the VCL website are provided on the page.	
"Death of Family or Friends"	https://maketheconnection.net/events/death-family-friends	VCL	This article focuses on veterans experiencing loss of family members or friends. The VCL logo and phone number with a built-in hyperlink to the VCL website are provided on the page.	
"Homelessness"	https://maketheconnection.net/events/homelessness	VCL	This article focuses on homelessness among veterans. The VCL logo and phone number with a built-in hyperlink to the VCL website are provided on the page.	
"Alcohol or Drug Problems"	https://maketheconnection.net/symptoms/alcohol-drug-problems	VCL	This article focuses on alcohol or drug problems among veterans. The VCL logo and phone number with a built-in hyperlink to the VCL website are provided on the page.	
"Anger and Irritability"	https://maketheconnection.net/symptoms/anger-irritability	VCL	This article focuses on anger and irritability among veterans. The VCL logo and phone number with a built-in hyperlink to the VCL website are provided on the page.	
"Chronic Pain"	https://maketheconnection.net/symptoms/chronic-pain	VCL	This article focuses on chronic pain among veterans. The VCL logo and phone number with a built-in hyperlink to the VCL website are provided on the page.	
"Difficulty Concentrating"	https://maketheconnection.net/symptoms/difficulty-concentrating	VCL	This article focuses on concentration difficulties among veterans. The VCL logo and phone number with a built-in hyperlink to the VCL website are provided on the page.	
"Eating Problems"	https://maketheconnection.net/symptoms/eating-problems	VCL	This article focuses on eating problems among veterans. The VCL logo and phone number with a built-in hyperlink to the VCL website are provided on the page.	

Table C.8—Continued

Webpage Name or Description	URL	Campaign(s) Referenced	Description of How Other Campaign Is Referenced	Notes
"Feeling on Edge"	https://maketheconnection.net/symptoms/hypervigilance	VCL	This article focuses on hypervigilance among veterans. The VCL logo and phone number with a built-in hyperlink to the VCL website are provided on the page.	
"Flashbacks"	https://maketheconnection.net/symptoms/flashbacks	VCL	This article focuses on flashbacks among veterans. The VCL logo and phone number with a built-in hyperlink to the VCL website are provided on the page.	
"Headaches"	https://maketheconnection.net/symptoms/headaches	VCL	This article focuses on headaches among veterans. The VCL logo and phone number with a built-in hyperlink to the VCL website are provided on the page.	
"Nightmares"	https://maketheconnection.net/symptoms/nightmares	VCL	This article focuses on nightmares among veterans. The VCL logo and phone number with a built-in hyperlink to the VCL website are provided on the page.	
"Noise or Light Irritation"	http://maketheconnection.net/symptoms/noise-light-irritation	VCL	This article focuses on noise and light sensitivity among veterans. The VCL logo and phone number with a built-in hyperlink to the VCL website are provided on the page.	
"Reckless Behavior"	http://maketheconnection.net/symptoms/reckless-behavior	VCL	This article focuses on reckless behavior among veterans. The VCL logo and phone number with a built-in hyperlink to the VCL website are provided on the page.	
"Treatment and Recovery"	http://maketheconnection.net/resources/treatment-recovery	VCL	This article focuses on treatment and recovery for veterans, including types of treatment, when to get treatment, and factors that can affect treatment. The VCL logo and phone number with a built-in hyperlink to the VCL website are provided on the page.	

Table C.9
Veterans Crisis Line: Cross-Referencing and Linking to Other Campaigns (as of July 21, 2016)

Webpage Name or Description	URL	Campaign(s) Referenced	Description of How Other Campaign is Referenced	Notes
VCL Homepage	https://www.veteranscrisisline.net/	MTC	The homepage to the VCL website provides a hyperlink to the MTC website in the blue section at the bottom of the page, under "Resources." A hyperlink to the MTC website is also included under the "Resources" tab.	
"Videos"	https://www.veteranscrisisline.net/Resources/Videos.aspx	MTC	This webpage, with videos from VA and other organizations, provides a hyperlink to the MTC website in the blue section at the bottom of the page, under "Resources." A hyperlink to the website is also provided at the top of the page in blue text (under the "Get Help" tab). In addition, an image and MTC logo on the right side of the page also includes a built-in hyperlink to the MTC website.	
"Veterans Text"	https://www.veteranscrisisline.net/TextTermsOfService.aspx	MTC	This webpage, with information about the VCL text-messaging service, provides a hyperlink to the MTC website in the blue section at the bottom of the page, under "Resources."	
"About the Veterans Crisis Line"	https://www.veteranscrisisline.net/About/AboutVeteransCrisisLine.aspx	MTC	This webpage, which contains an overview of VCL, provides a hyperlink to the MTC website in the blue section at the bottom of the page, under "Resources." In addition, an image and MTC logo on the right of the page also includes a built-in hyperlink to the MTC website.	
"Veteran Suicide"	https://www.veteranscrisisline.net/About/VeteranSuicide.aspx	MTC	This webpage, which discusses VA's resources and initiatives to address veteran suicide, provides a hyperlink to the MTC website in the blue section at the bottom of the page, under "Resources." In addition, an image and MTC logo on the right side of the page also includes a built-in hyperlink to the MTC website.	
"Veterans Chat"	https://www.veteranscrisisline.net/ChatTermsOfService.aspx	MTC	This webpage, with information about the VCL online chat, provides a hyperlink to the MTC website in the blue section at the bottom of the page, under "Resources."	
"FAQs"	https://www.veteranscrisisline.net/About/FAQs.aspx	MTC	This is the FAQ section of the VCL website. A hyperlink to the MTC website is provided under the FAQ focused on mental health sources. MTC is described as a resource to access "for information about mental health and VA services and benefits pertaining to mental health." A hyperlink to the MTC website is also provided in the blue section at the bottom of the page, under "Resources." In addition, an image and MTC logo on the right side of the page also includes a built-in hyperlink to the MTC website.	

Table C.9—Continued

Webpage Name or Description	URL	Campaign(s) Referenced	Description of How Other Campaign is Referenced	Notes
"Resources"	https://www.veteranscrisisline.net/Resources/	MTC	This webpage, which provides a list of resources for veterans and their family and friends, includes a hyperlink to the MTC website and a description of the campaign's purpose to "[connect] Veterans and their friends and family members with information, resources, and solutions to issues affecting their health, well-being, and everyday lives." A hyperlink to the MTC website is also provided in the blue section at the bottom of the page, under "Resources." In addition, an image and MTC logo on the right side of the page also includes a built-in hyperlink to the MTC website. Lastly, a hyperlink to the MTC website is provided at the top of the page in blue text (under the "Get Help" tab).	
"About"	https://www.veteranscrisisline.net/About/	MTC	This webpage, which briefly describes the purpose of VCL, provides a hyperlink to the MTC website in the blue section at the bottom of the page, under "Resources." In addition, an image and MTC logo on the right side of the page also includes a built-in hyperlink to the MTC website.	
"Contact Us"	https://www.veteranscrisisline.net/GetHelp/ContactUs.aspx	MTC	This webpage, which includes a "contact us" form, provides a hyperlink to the MTC website in the blue section at the bottom of the page, under "Resources." In addition, an image and MTC logo on the right side of the page also includes a built-in hyperlink to the MTC website.	
"I Am Family/Friend"	https://www.veteranscrisisline.net/ForFamilyAndFriends.aspx	MTC	This webpage, which describes how family and friends can support veterans in need, provides a hyperlink to the MTC website in the blue section at the bottom of the page, under "Resources."	
"Support for Deaf/Hard of Hearing"	https://www.veteranscrisisline.net/GetHelp/Accessibility.aspx	MTC	This webpage, which describes services available for individuals who are deaf or hard of hearing, provides a hyperlink to the MTC website in the blue section at the bottom of the page, under "Resources." In addition, an image and MTC logo on the right side of the page also includes a built-in hyperlink to the MTC website.	
"I Am Active Duty/Reserve and Guard"	https://www.veteranscrisisline.net/ActiveDuty.aspx	MTC, MCL	This webpage, which describes resources available for service members and their families, provides a hyperlink to the MTC website in the blue section at the bottom of the page, under "Resources." In addition, this webpage provides a hyperlink to the MCL online chat, the MCL phone number, and the number to text, as well as the MCL logo in the first half of the page. MCL is described as a free, 24/7, confidential service that is available to all service members and veterans and that is "staffed by caring, qualified responders from VA—some of whom have served in the military themselves." At the bottom of the page, the MCL phone number, a hyperlink to the online chat, and the number to text are also listed.	

Table C.9—Continued

Webpage Name or Description	URL	Campaign(s) Referenced	Description of How Other Campaign is Referenced	Notes
"Military Crisis Line Chat"	https://www.veteranscrisisline.net/MilitaryChatTermsOfService.aspx?account = Military%20Chat	MTC, MCL	This webpage, with information about the MCL online chat, provides a hyperlink to the MTC website in the blue section at the bottom of the page, under "Resources." A link to the MCL chat is also provided on the page.	
"Additional Information"	https://www.veteranscrisisline.net/Resources/AdditionalInformation.aspx	MTC	This webpage, which features links "for additional information about VA and other organizations' suicide prevention resources and other Veterans' issues," lists MTC under the "Resources and Programs" section. A hyperlink to the MTC website is provided and MTC is described as "helping Veterans recognize they are not alone and resources and solutions are available." Readers are told they can "watch hundreds of video testimonials of Veterans and their loved ones overcoming challenges, reaching positive outcomes for treatment and recovery, and finding paths to fulfilling lives." A hyperlink to the MTC website is also provided in the blue section at the bottom of the page, under "Resources." In addition, an image and MTC logo on the right side of the page also includes a built-in hyperlink to the MTC website. Lastly, a hyperlink to the MTC website is provided at the top of the page in blue text (under the "Get Help" tab).	
"Support Our Nation's Veterans"	https://www.veteranscrisisline.net/ThePowerof1/ShareTarget.aspx?share_image = msg_7-bg_14	MTC	This webpage shows a graphic with a supportive quote and message (1 small act shows you care) for the Power of 1 campaign. A hyperlink to the MTC website is provided in the blue section at the bottom of the page, under "Resources."	Not easily discovered
"Resource Locator"	https://www.veteranscrisisline.net/GetHelp/ResourceLocator.aspx	MTC	This webpage, which provides a resource locator tool to identify resources for veterans, includes a hyperlink to the MTC website in the blue section at the bottom of the page, under "Resources." In addition, an image and MTC logo on the right side of the page also includes a built-in hyperlink to the MTC website.	
"Get Help"	https://www.veteranscrisisline.net/GetHelp/	MTC	This webpage, which lists links to resources and mentions that help is available for veterans in crisis or those who know them, includes a hyperlink to the MTC website in the blue section at the bottom of the page, under "Resources." In addition, an image and MTC logo on the right side of the page also includes a built-in hyperlink to the MTC website.	

Table C.9—Continued

Webpage Name or Description	URL	Campaign(s) Referenced	Description of How Other Campaign is Referenced	Notes
"I Am a Veteran"	https://www.veteranscrisisline.net/ForVeterans.aspx	MTC	This webpage, which describes resources available for veterans and their families, provides a hyperlink to the MTC website in the blue section at the bottom of the page, under "Resources."	
"Signs of Crisis"	https://www.veteranscrisisline.net/SignsOfCrisis/	MTC	This webpage, which describes signs of crisis for veterans, includes a hyperlink to the MTC website in the blue section at the bottom of the page, under "Resources." In addition, an image and MTC logo on the right side of the page also includes a built-in hyperlink to the MTC website.	
"Homeless Resources"	https://www.veteranscrisisline.net/Resources/HomelessResources.aspx	MTC	This webpage, which describes resources available for homeless veterans, provides a hyperlink to the MTC website in the blue section at the bottom of the page, under "Resources." A hyperlink to the website is also provided at the top of the page in blue text (under the "Get Help" tab). In addition, an image and MTC logo on the right side of the page also includes a built-in hyperlink to the MTC website.	
"Identifying: Learn to Recognize the Signs"	https://www.veteranscrisisline.net/SignsOfCrisis/Identifying.aspx	MTC	This webpage, which describes signs of crisis for veterans, includes a hyperlink to the MTC website in the blue section at the bottom of the page, under "Resources." In addition, an image and MTC logo on the right side of the page also includes a built-in hyperlink to the MTC website.	
"Homeless Veterans Chat"	https://www.veteranscrisisline.net/ChatTermsOfService.aspx?account = Homeless Veterans Chat	MTC	This webpage, with information about the VCL online chat, provides a hyperlink to the MTC website in the blue section at the bottom of the page, under "Resources."	
"Join #ThePower-Of1Movement"	https://www.veteranscrisisline.net/ThePowerof1.aspx	MCL	This webpage, which introduces the Power of 1 movement, includes the MCL logo at the top of the page.	

Table C.10
National Recovery Month: Cross-Referencing and Linking to Other Campaigns (as of July 21, 2016)

Webpage Name or Description	URL	Campaign(s) Referenced	Description of How Other Campaign Is Referenced	Notes
"May 2015 Radio Episode: Healing and Empowerment: Families on the Road to Recovery"	http://www.recoverymonth.gov/sites/default/files/roadtorecovery/may-2015-road-to-recovery-radio-transcript.pdf	RWC	This transcript of a May 2015 radio episode, which focuses on recovery for families, mentions that RWC has resources "more for the active duty side but has a number of great resources for the family members and for adolescents and how to re-gear the family when the service member returns home." Contact information for RWC is not provided.	
"May 2015 Television Episode: Healing and Empowerment: Families on the Road to Recovery"	http://www.recoverymonth.gov/sites/default/files/roadtorecovery/may-2015-road-to-recovery-television-show-transcript.pdf	RWC	This transcript of a May 2015 television episode, which focuses on recovery for families, mentions RWC as having resources "more for the active duty side but [that it also] has a number of great resources for the family members and for adolescents and how to re-gear the family when the service member returns home." Contact information for RWC is not provided.	
"The Road to Recovery 2011: Military Families: Access to Care for Active Duty, National Guard, Reserve, Veterans, Their Families, and Those Close to Them: Discussion Guide"	http://ec2-96-127-46-6.us-gov-west-1.compute.amazonaws.com/~/media/Images/Files/Webcast%20Transcript/Rev_508_Military2011.ashx	RWC	This is the discussion guide for a Road to Recovery episode focused on access to care for active duty, National Guard, reserve, veterans, and their families. The Panel 3 section focused on strategies and programs to address behavioral health needs includes a hyperlink to a news article posted on the RWC website. The article describes how "the Veterans Inpatient Priority (VIP) project at the Rosecrance Harrison campus offers priority admission to veterans with co-occurring substance use and mental health disorders." Additionally, under the final section, "Resources for Behavioral Health Needs of Military Families," a hyperlink to the RWC website and descriptions of the campaign's purpose and its resources are provided.	Not easily discovered
"Coming Home: Supporting Military Service Members, Veterans, and Their Families: Discussion Guide"	http://ec2-96-127-46-6.us-gov-west-1.compute.amazonaws.com/~/media/Images/Files/Webcast%20Transcript/R2R2012_Military_Families_Discussion_Guide_508.ashx	RWC, VCL	This is the discussion guide for a Road to Recovery episode focused on supporting military service members, veterans, and their families. The Panel 3 section focused on strategies and programs for supporting military families includes a hyperlink to a news article posted on the RWC website. The article describes how "the Veterans Inpatient Priority project at the Rosecrance Harrison campus offers priority admission to veterans with co-occurring substance use and mental disorders." Additionally, under the final section, "Resources for Military Families," a hyperlink to the RWC website and descriptions of the campaign's purpose and its resources are provided. In this resources section, a hyperlink to the VCL website and a description of VCL's availability in multiple countries and role in saving 17,000 veterans' lives are mentioned as well.	Not easily discovered

Table C.10—Continued

Webpage Name or Description	URL	Campaign(s) Referenced	Description of How Other Campaign Is Referenced	Notes
"VA," Veterans Crisis Line"	http://www. recoverymonth.gov/ organizations-programs/ va-veterans-crisis-line	VCL	This entry page, part of a list of organizations and resources that provide services or information pertaining to substance use and/or mental health disorders, provides the URL for the VCL website, a description of the purpose of the campaign, and the VCL phone number.	
"Military/Veterans"	http://www. recoverymonth.gov/ resource-category/ militaryveterans?page = 1	VCL	This webpage, which is a compilation of organizations that "offer support services to active military, veterans, and their families," lists "VA, Veterans Crisis Line." Contact information for VCL is not provided on this webpage, but it is included when the specific entry is accessed (see row above).	
"Health Care"	http://www. recoverymonth.gov/ resource-category/ health-care?page = 4	VCL	This webpage, which is a compilation of organizations that "work to increase access to health care services and provide support to provider organizations," lists "VA, Veterans Crisis Line." Contact information for VCL is not provided on this webpage, but it is included when the specific entry is accessed (see row above).	
"Organizations and Program Resources"	http://www. recoverymonth.gov/ events/plan-events/ organizations-programs?field_ resource_category_tid = All&combine = &field_ resource_us_state_value = All&field_resource_ fed_yesno_value = All&page = 68	VCL	This webpage features a list of organizations and resources that provide services or information pertaining to substance use and/or mental health disorders. An entry for "VA, Veterans Crisis Line" is provided, with a description of the purpose of the campaign, a hyperlink to the VCL website, and the VCL phone number.	
"Ask the Expert: Military Families: Access to Care for Active Duty, National Guard, Reserve, Veterans, Their Families, and Those Close to Them"	http://ec2-96-127-46-6. us-gov-west-1.compute. amazonaws.com/ Resources-Catalog/2011/ Ask-the-Expert/May-Military-Families.aspx	VCL	This is a webpage spotlight of a participant in the Road to Recovery episode focused on access to care for active duty, National Guard, reserve, veterans, and their families. The webpage mentions that VCL has one of VA's suicide prevention initiatives. The purpose and use of the crisis line, as well as the VCL phone number and a hyperlink to the VCL website, are provided. The webpage also describes VCL as being developed through a partnership between VA and SAMHSA and includes the VCL phone number again.	Not easily discovered

Table C.10—Continued

Webpage Name or Description	URL	Campaign(s) Referenced	Description of How Other Campaign Is Referenced	Notes
"2012 Recovery Month Toolkit"	http://www. recoverymonth.gov/sites/ default/files/toolkit/ 2012-recovery-month-toolkit.pdf	VCL	This 2012 Recovery Month toolkit includes VCL in the "Additional Recovery Resources" sections, along with the VCL phone number, a hyperlink to the VCL website, and a description of the purpose of the campaign. VCL (with a hyperlink to the VCL website) is also mentioned as a resource targeted to veterans that can be used to access substance use and/or mental health care. In addition, under the section "Understanding Substance Use Disorders in the Military," a hyperlink to the VCL website, the VCL phone number, and a description of VCL providing an anonymous chat service are provided.	
"2013 Recovery Month Toolkit"	http://www. recoverymonth.gov/sites/ default/files/toolkit/ 2013-recovery-month-toolkit.pdf	VCL	This 2013 Recovery Month toolkit includes VCL in the list of agencies that "offer mental and substance use disorder resources to active military and veterans, and their families." The VCL phone number, the number to text, a hyperlink to the VCL website, and a description of the campaign's purpose are provided.	
"Recursos de Información acerca de la Prevención, Tratamiento, y Recuperación"	http://ec2-96-127-46-6.us-gov-west-1. compute.amazonaws. com/Recovery-Month-Kit/Resources/~/ media/Images/Files/1_ Spanish%20Toolkit%20 2014%20Docs/ PreventionTreatmentand RecoveryResources_ Spanish_ FINAL508.ashx	VCL	This Prevention, Treatment, and Recovery Resources document (in Spanish) includes VCL in the list of agencies that "offer mental and substance use disorder resources to active military and veterans, and their families." The VCL phone number and a hyperlink to the VCL website are provided.	Not easily discovered
"Prevention, Treatment, and Recovery Resources"	http://ec2-96-127-46-6.us-gov-west-1. compute.amazonaws. com/Recovery-Month-Kit/~/media/Images/ Files/1_%202014%20 Toolkit%20Docs/RM2014 PreventionTreatment andRecoveryResources FINAL508.ashx	VCL	This Prevention, Treatment, and Recovery Resources document (in English) includes VCL in the list of agencies that "offer mental and substance use disorder resources to active military and veterans, and their families." The VCL phone number, the number to text, a hyperlink to the VCL website, and a description of the campaign's purpose are provided.	Not easily discovered

Methods Used to Analyze Campaign Process Evaluation Data and Findings

To evaluate the reach of campaigns among target audiences, we conducted secondary analyses of existing campaign process data.

Methods for Analyzing Process Metrics

All of the agencies routinely collect a range of metrics to track the dissemination and reach of their mental health awareness campaigns. At the start of the evaluation (June–July 2015), we reviewed existing campaign materials (e.g., items posted on the website) and extracted information related to the campaigns' main objectives, key messages, target populations, core dissemination vehicles and process metrics. We followed up with campaign staff to review the accuracy of the extracted information and to retrieve any missing information that could not be gleaned from existing materials. During this process, we obtained information regarding the types of process metrics maintained by campaigns, how frequently the process metrics are collected (e.g., monthly, quarterly, annually), and how the data are stored. Based on this information, we identified and requested a limited set of process metrics that appeared to be commonly and routinely tracked by all of the campaigns to better capture the collective and differential dissemination of campaign efforts.

Requested process metrics covered campaigns' main vehicles of dissemination, which included websites, social media (i.e., Facebook, YouTube, Twitter), media relations (i.e., radio and television PSAs), and outreach activities (i.e., attendance at conferences or events, distribution of campaign materials, and collaborations with partner organizations) (Table D.1). Although the campaigns mostly used the same vehicles for dissemination, certain types of social media were not uniformly employed across campaigns. For instance, VCL did not actively use Facebook, YouTube, or Twitter as part of its arsenal for dissemination efforts.

In Table D.1, we also list the time frame and intervals for the process metrics that we requested. Given that campaign websites serve as the central hub where information is stored and disseminated, we obtained monthly data for multiple years (from 2011 to 2015). This allowed for the exploration of longitudinal trends. For all other

Table D.1
Campaign Process Data Sources

Venue	Time Period	Interval	RWC	MTC	VCL	Recovery Month
Website	2011–2015	Monthly	x	x	x	x
Facebook	2015	Monthly	x	x		x
YouTube	2015	Monthly	x	x		x
Twitter	2015	Monthly	x			x
Radio PSAs	2015	Monthly	x	x	x	x
Television PSAs	2015	Monthly	x	x	x	x
Conferences or events	2015	Monthly	x	x	x	x
Campaign materials	2015	Monthly	x	x	x	x
Partner organizations	2015	Monthly	x	x	x	x

NOTE: Website data from 2011 were dropped from the analyses because Recovery Month used a different web analytic tool (Webtrends) than the other campaigns. Google Analytics was employed by all campaigns from 2012 to 2015 except for the period from January to June 2012 in which Recovery Month was still using Webtrends.

vehicles of dissemination, we requested monthly data for 2015 only. Campaigns provided the process data to the research team either in Microsoft Excel or Word files. The process data files were transferred to the team either through email or links to a password-protected site that housed the data. There was one exception with respect to the method for obtaining Facebook data from Recovery Month. In this case, we were provided access to Recovery Month's Facebook account for a restricted period of time to download requested process metrics.

The process data files varied across years and campaigns in terms of content, structure, and the length of time covered. All files were initially cleaned, formatted, and saved in machine-readable format for analysis in R software. The necessary data elements were extracted from each file series and metrics were tabulated on a monthly or annual basis as needed, with results from the various campaigns output in a common format. Statistics were generally descriptive, most often involving the calculation of monthly or annual counts, sums, and means from daily or monthly raw data. For "Top Ten" calculations, data were collapsed by material or geography and time period to obtain the most prevalent values for a given period.

The secondary process data and analyses were used to examine three main aspects of the mental health awareness campaigns: reach, user engagement, and characteristics of users. We detail the process metrics used to assess each of these domains.

Table D.2 describes the metrics used to evaluate the reach of the mental health awareness campaigns. For websites, the number of sessions or visits made to campaign websites was used as an indicator of reach.

Table D.2
Reach Metrics

Reach Metric	Definition
Website	
Website sessions	*Session* refers to the group of interactions that take place on a website within a given time frame
Social media	
Facebook fans	Number of Facebook accounts that like a Facebook page
YouTube views	Number of times videos were viewed
Twitter followers	Number of accounts that follow a campaign's account
PSAs	
Radio airings	Number of radio PSAs aired
Radio listener impressions	Number of times a specific radio PSA was listened to when aired
Television airings	Number of television PSAs aired
Television viewer impressions	Number of times a specific television PSA was viewed when aired
Outreach activities	
Conferences or events attended	Number of conferences or events attended by campaign staff
Campaign materials distributed	Number of campaign materials distributed
Partner organizations	Number of organizations with which campaign collaborates

Table D.3 details the metrics used to assess user engagement with campaign websites and social media platforms.

Limited data on campaign user characteristics were available (Table D.4). For website and Facebook metrics, the geographic location data were provided at the city level. YouTube, on the other hand, provided geographic location data at the state level. Demographic data regarding gender and age were provided for Facebook and YouTube. Only RWC provided demographic data for Twitter.

Findings from the Process Data Evaluation

Findings with respect to campaign reach, user engagement, and characteristics of users reached by campaigns are presented in the subsequent sections.

Table D.3
Engagement Metrics

Engagement Metrics	Definition
Website	
Bounce rate	Percentage of total sessions that are single-page visits
Page views	Counted every time a website page loads
Average session duration	Total duration of all sessions divided by number of sessions
Average page views per session	Average number of pages viewed on website by all visitors over set amount of time
Top ten pages viewed	Website pages with top ten greatest number of views
Top ten downloads	Materials hosted on the website (e.g., pdf, video, audio files) with top ten greatest number of downloads
Top ten videos	Videos hosted on the website with top ten greatest number of views
Facebook	
Posts	Number of posts by campaign page
Interactions (likes, comments, shares)	Number of comments, likes, and shares of campaign page's posts
Impressions	Number of times any content associated with page was shown to Facebook accounts
YouTube	
Average view duration	Average of all view durations for given time frame
Likes and dislikes	Number of video likes and number of dislikes in a given time frame
Subscribers gained and lost	Number of times people subscribed and number of times people unsubscribed to channel in given time frame
Favorites gained and lost	Number of times people added and number of times people removed favorites from channel in given time frame
Twitter	
Number of tweets	Number of tweets posted by account
Direct messages received	Number of direct messages received
Direct messages sent	Number of direct messages sent

Table D.4
User Characteristics

User Characteristics	Definition
Website	
Top city	U.S. city with the greatest number of website sessions based on IP address of the hit
Facebook	
Gender	Percentage of people who saw any campaign page content that were male or female based on the information users entered in their personal profiles
Age	Percentage of people who saw any campaign page content who fall within the following age categories: 13–17, 18–24, 25–34, 35–44, 45–54, 55–64, and 65 or older
Top six cities	Six cities with the greatest number of people who saw any campaign page content based on IP address
YouTube	
Gender	Percentage of views composed of male or female viewers based on logged-in user accounts
Age	Percentage of views composed of the following age categories: 13–17, 18–24, 25–34, 35–44, 45–54, 55–64, and 65 or older. Information is based on logged-in user accounts
Top six states	Six states with the greatest number of YouTube views based on logged-in user accounts

Campaign Reach

Website Reach

From 2012 to 2015, more than 14 million sessions were logged across the four campaign websites (Table D.5). The total number of sessions in 2015 (4,325,764) was a 50-percent increase from sessions made in 2012 (2,888,710). As shown in Table D.6, VCL was the only campaign that garnered consistent increases in the number of sessions each year. In contrast, Recovery Month experienced consistent annual decreases in number of sessions. However, we do note that from 2012 to 2015, the Recovery Month website analytics program was revamped and migrated from Webtrends to Google Analytics. The systems calculate user interaction metrics differently. In addition, the site metrics

Table D.5
Number of Website Sessions, 2012–2015

Campaign	2012	2013	2014	2015	Campaign Total
RWC	258,186	331,639	290,151	315,848	1,195,824
MTC	1,858,207	1,683,893	2,832,269	2,955,647	9,330,016
VCL	368,083	727,191	838,061	939,473	2,863,808
Recovery Month[a]	404,234	321,342	124,846	123,796	974,218
Total	2,888,710	3,064,065	4,085,327	4,325,764	14,363,866

[a] From 2012 to 2015, the Recovery Month website analytics program was revamped and migrated from Webtrends to Google Analytics. The systems calculate user interaction metrics differently. In addition, the site metrics changed to the standardized SAMHSA Google Analytics tracking code. In March 2015, a new Recovery Month website launched as an internal site within SAMHSA.gov. It contained 75 percent less content than the previous site and provided access to only 2014 materials and some 2015 materials, compared with the prior version, which had offered more than 15 years of content.

Table D.6
Percentage Change in Website Sessions, 2012–2015

Campaign	2012	2013	2014	2015	2012–2015
RWC	—	28	–13	9	22
MTC	—	–9	68	4	59
VCL	—	98	15	11	155
Recovery Month[a]	—	–21	–61	–1	–69
Total	—	6	33	6	50

[a] From 2012 to 2015, the Recovery Month website analytics program was revamped and migrated from Webtrends to Google Analytics. The systems calculate user interaction metrics differently. In addition, the site metrics changed to the standardized SAMHSA Google Analytics tracking code. In March 2015, a new Recovery Month website launched as an internal site within SAMHSA.gov. It contained 75 percent less content than the previous site and provided access to only 2014 materials and some 2015 materials, whereas the prior version had offered more than 15 years of content.

changed to the standardized SAMHSA Google Analytics tracking code. In March 2015, a new Recovery Month website launched as an internal site within SAMHSA. gov. It contained 75 percent less content than the previous site and provided access to only 2014 materials and some 2015 materials—unlike the prior version, which had offered more than 15 years of content. This change likely affected trends in metrics being tracked over time. Even though MTC website reach decreased in 2013, MTC maintained the greatest number of sessions each year, with a total cumulative number of visits from 2012 to 2015 that was three times more than VCL, nearly eight times more than RWC, and nearly ten times more than Recovery Month. Table D.7 provides the average monthly unique sessions from 2012 to 2015 for each campaign. The same general patterns hold as found with the number of website sessions.

Social Media Reach

The potential maximum reach achieved across all campaign social media platforms totaled more than 5.6 million in 2015 (Table D.8). Nearly 3 million were reached by Facebook and approximately 57,000 via Twitter. Under the condition that the number of YouTube views represented individual unique users, more than 2.5 million may have been maximally reached by YouTube. For each of the campaigns, Facebook yielded the greatest reach compared with the other social media platforms. MTC accounted for 97 percent of the total reach achieved via social media. MTC also reached targeted audiences through social media (e.g., 2,880,304 Facebook fans) at rates comparable to those reached through its website (e.g., 2,955,647 website sessions). Even though Recovery Month is intended to reach a much broader target audience than RWC, its reach via social media was half that of RWC.

Table D.9 describes the monthly cumulative reach and percentage change in reach attained by Facebook for each campaign. Both RWC and MTC experienced a drop in the number of Facebook fans in the month of April (–5 and –2 percent, respectively).

Table D.7
Average Monthly Unique Sessions, 2012–2015

Campaign	2012	2013	2014	2015
RWC	17,727	23,579	21,106	22,908
MTC	135,576	120,157	201,367	211,237
VCL	25,406	51,227	58,900	61,972
Recovery Month[a]	32,505	26,779	10,404	10,316

[a] From 2012 to 2015, the Recovery Month website analytics program was revamped and migrated from Webtrends to Google Analytics. The systems calculate user interaction metrics differently. In addition, the site metrics changed to the standardized SAMHSA Google Analytics tracking code. In March 2015, a new Recovery Month website launched as an internal site within SAMHSA.gov. It contained 75 percent less content than the previous site and provided access to only 2014 materials and some 2015 materials, whereas the prior version had offered more than 15 years of content.

Table D.8
Social Media Reach, 2015

Campaign	Facebook Fans	YouTube Views[a]	Twitter Followers	Campaign Total
RWC	69,476	10,767	39,951	120,124
MTC	2,880,304	2,607,116	—	5,487,420
Recovery Month	37,690	7,790	16,780	62,260
Total	2,987,470	2,625,673	56,731	5,669,874

[a] YouTube views were used as an indicator of reach because data on unique viewers was unavailable.

NOTE: VCL is not featured in the table because it does not actively employ Facebook, YouTube, or Twitter to disseminate campaign resources.

Table D.9
Facebook Monthly Cumulative Reach and Percentage Change, 2015

Month	RWC		MTC		Recovery Month	
	Fans	Percentage Change	Fans	Percentage Change	Fans	Percentage Change
January	55,094	—	2,701,466	—	27,941	—
February	55,442	1	2,769,585	3	28,580	2
March	55,431	<1	2,823,979	2	28,556	<1
April	52,576	−5	2,779,736	−2	28,993	2
May	53,010	1	2,796,987	1	29,635	2
June	53,470	1	2,824,845	1	30,162	2
July	54,617	2	2,845,708	1	30,977	3
August	56,102	3	2,877,414	1	32,011	3
September	59,056	5	2,877,222	<1	36,122	13
October	60,275	2	2,876,472	<1	36,756	2
November	65,508	9	2,878,069	<1	37,204	1
December	69,476	6	2,878,589	<1	37,690	1
January to December	+14,382	26	+177,123	7	+9,749	35

Recovery Month lost Facebook fans in March (<1 percent). The greatest percentage increase in the number of Facebook fans occurred in November for RWC (+9 percent) and in September for Recovery Month (+13 percent), which is when National Recovery Month is observed (though events occur throughout the year). Over the course of 2015, the overall number of Facebook fans increased by 26 percent for RWC, 7 percent for MTC, and 35 percent for Recovery Month.

As shown in Table D.10, the number of monthly YouTube views fluctuated throughout the year, with a high of 1,310 views in September for RWC, 686,509 views in July for MTC, and 3,472 views in September for Recovery Month. The majority of YouTube views for Recovery Month were isolated to the summer months and September. Recovery Month experienced its greatest reach during the time when National Recovery Month is observed. The lowest reach occurred in July for RWC (595 views), in September for MTC (17,780 views), and in April for Recovery Month (0 views).

As shown in Table D.11, the number of Twitter followers steadily increased throughout 2015 with no notable highs or lows. Neither campaign experienced any loss in Twitter followers. From January to December 2015, the total number of Twitter followers increased by 16 percent for RWC and by 24 percent for Recovery Month.

Public Service Announcements

In 2015, across all four campaigns, more than a quarter-million radio PSAs and more than 100,000 television PSAs aired (Table D.12). Correspondingly, the number of radio PSA viewer impressions totaled 38,504,295,420, and the number of television PSA viewer impressions totaled 4,395,714,734. RWC was responsible for the vast majority of radio and television PSA viewer impressions, many of which came from the American Forces Radio and Television Service.

Campaigns differed in their levels of PSA reach throughout the 2015 year. For radio PSA airings, RWC and MTC reach occurred primarily during the first half of the year. MTC aired radio PSAs only during the period between January and March,

Table D.10
YouTube Monthly Views and Percentage Change, 2015

	RWC		MTC		Recovery Month	
Month	Views	Percentage Change	Views	Percentage Change	Views	Percentage Change
January	786	—	271,793	—	55	—
February	916	17	270,121	−1	71	29
March	1,303	42	121,987	−55	14	−80
April	966	−26	228,526	87	0	−100
May	769	−20	280,472	23	115	—
June	640	−17	342,066	22	1,199	943
July	595	−7	686,509	101	992	−17
August	670	13	26,758	−96	1,491	50
September	1,310	96	17,780	−34	3,472	133
October	861	−34	148,385	735	241	−93
November	1,097	27	129,753	−13	2	−99
December	854	−22	82,966	<1	138	6,800

Table D.11
Twitter Monthly Cumulative Reach and Percentage Change, 2015

Month	RWC		Recovery Month	
	Followers	Percentage Change	Followers	Percentage Change
January	34,441	—	13,098	—
February	35,128	2	13,478	3
March	35,879	2	13,842	3
April	36,502	2	14,291	3
May	37,067	2	14,676	3
June	37,536	1	14,936	2
July	37,878	1	15,139	1
August	38,173	1	15,326	1
September	38,483	1	15,585	2
October	38,935	1	16,089	3
November	39,568	2	16,365	2
December	39,943	1	16,581	1
January to December	+5,502	16	+3,483	24

Table D.12
Public Service Announcement Reach, 2015

Campaign	Radio PSA Airings	Radio PSA Listener Impressions	Television PSA Airings	Television PSA Viewer Impressions
RWC	36,970	37,278,207,400	15,476	3,027,994,220
MTC	11,725	110,048,000	39,135	312,560,637
VCL	128,948	619,026,200	43,616	362,261,877
Recovery Month	91,414	497,013,820	59,835	692,898,000
Total	269,057	38,504,295,420	158,062	4,395,714,734

with no other airings the rest the year, and 71 percent of RWC's radio PSAs were aired between January and June. In contrast, 71 percent of VCL's and 89 percent of Recovery Month's radio PSAs were aired in the latter part of the year, between July and December. Similar patterns were observed for radio PSA viewer impressions, with the exception of RWC having a more even distribution of impressions throughout the year (see Tables D.13 and D.14 for number of monthly radio PSA airings and viewer impressions for each campaign).

Table D.13
Monthly Radio Public Service Announcement Reach, 2015

Month	RWC	MTC	VCL	Recovery Month	Total
January	3,957	2,368	3,819	0	10,144
February	5,651	2,963	3,584	0	12,198
March	4,881	6,394	100	0	11,375
April	5,086	0	16,064	0	21,150
May	3,811	0	3,255	0	7,066
June	2,790	0	10,715	6,835	20,340
July	2,087	0	12,573	7,524	22,184
August	1,759	0	34,065	10,132	45,956
September	1,616	0	20,663	13,328	35,607
October	1,581	0	21,673	16,103	39,357
November	2,170	0	2,437	17,287	21,894
December	1,581	0	0	15,454	17,035

Table D.14
Monthly Radio Impressions, 2015

Month	RWC	MTC	VCL	Recovery Month	Total
January	3,164,494,100	15,889,600	6,368,600	0	3,186,752,300
February	2,876,177,500	33,810,700	60,872,500	0	2,970,860,700
March	3,173,550,400	60,347,700	20,000	0	3,233,918,100
April	3,064,545,200	0	32,394,000	0	3,096,939,200
May	3,164,371,200	0	5,691,800	0	3,170,063,000
June	3,065,681,600	0	91,019,500	11,602,500	3,168,303,600
July	3,163,003,000	0	119,007,600	53,227,400	3,335,238,000
August	3,162,051,200	0	110,747,300	53,666,500	3,326,465,000
September	3,060,017,200	0	152,603,000	69,054,600	3,281,674,800
October	3,162,000,000	0	34,140,800	70,586,900	3,266,727,700
November	3,060,316,000	0	6,161,100	122,651,400	3,189,128,500
December	3,162,000,000	0	0	76,059,400	3,238,059,400

Relative to radio PSAs, airings for television PSAs were more evenly distributed across the year for all of the campaigns. Seventy-one percent of RWC's and 64 percent of MTC's television PSAs were aired between January and June. VCL aired 55 percent of its television PSAs during the first half of the year. Two-thirds (66 percent) of Recovery Month's television PSAs aired in the latter part of 2015. Television PSA viewer impressions were similarly distributed for MTC and VCL, with more than two-thirds of viewer impressions occurring in the first half of the year, whereas 97 percent of Recovery Month's television viewer impressions occurred in the latter half of the year (see Tables D.15 and D.16 for number of monthly television airings and viewer impressions for each campaign).

Outreach Activities

Conferences or events were most highly utilized by VCL as a vehicle for outreach, with a total of 207 events attended in 2015—or the equivalent of an average of 17 events per month (Table D.17). VCL often distributed outreach materials as part of attending events and distributed more than 9 million campaign materials in 2015. Attendance at events was utilized to a lesser extent by RWC and MTC. Recovery Month adopts a slightly different approach to its outreach activities: It encourages local partner organizations and groups to host Recovery Month events and makes campaign materials available for download on its website. Recovery Month does not have a complete listing of events that have been hosted; organizations voluntarily post events on the campaign website. Recovery Month provided a partial listing of events attended by a representative from their organization, which totaled 26 in 2015. The number of campaign material downloads from Recovery Month's website are provided in a subsequent section. See Tables D.18–D.21 for a list of attendance at conferences and events submitted by MTC, VCL, and Recovery Month. RWC provided a written description of its outreach activities at conferences and events (Table D.21).

Each of the campaigns partnered with more than 100 organizations as part of its outreach efforts (see Table D.22 for list of partner organizations). With respect to partner organizations shared across agencies, there was very little overlap. There were no partner organizations shared across all three agencies. Of the total partner organizations, only 4 percent, or 32 partner organizations, were shared across two or more agencies.

User Engagement and Interaction with Campaigns

Using secondary data obtained from agencies, we examined users' engagement and interaction with campaign websites and social media platforms.

Table D.15
Monthly Television Public Service Announcement Reach, 2015

Month	RWC	MTC	VCL	Recovery Month	Total
January	3,208	4,003	4,160	0	11,371
February	1,798	4,973	4,718	0	11,489
March	1,863	5,430	1,779	0	9,072
April	1,603	2,549	5,687	0	9,839
May	1,402	3,400	3,618	0	8,420
June	1,191	4,549	4,196	714	10,650
July	1,559	4,735	6,611	3,919	16,824
August	926	3,102	5,953	3,978	13,959
September	874	3,236	3,573	4,439	12,122
October	770	3,158	1,831	4,985	10,744
November	120	0	1,490	4,999	6,609
December	162	0	0	4,672	4,834

Table D.16
Monthly Television Impressions, 2015

Month	RWC	MTC	VCL	Recovery Month	Total
January	273,792,385	36,339,579	45,419,809	0	355,551,773
February	235,041,864	30,109,614	54,047,648	0	319,199,126
March	267,259,520	46,895,548	11,720,292	0	325,875,360
April	251,878,085	25,016,414	53,904,254	0	330,798,753
May	259,453,417	32,018,471	31,081,168	0	322,553,056
June	246,996,781	44,932,039	44,876,311	7,980,500	344,785,631
July	255,263,818	30,356,532	40,214,446	42,468,500	368,303,296
August	251,523,812	32,137,229	38,138,059	31,436,500	353,235,600
September	244,282,204	18,641,936	19,881,060	33,945,500	316,750,700
October	251,855,334	16,113,275	11,947,910	38,243,000	318,159,519
November	240,000,000	0	11,030,920	36,569,500	287,600,420
December	250,647,000	0	0	36,657,000	287,304,000

Table D.17
Outreach Activities, 2015

Organization	Conferences or Events Attended	Campaign Materials Distributed[a]	Partner Organizations
RWC	19	242,120	126
MTC	32	419,505	403[b]
VCL	207	9,447,436	403[b]
Recovery Month	26[c]	—[d]	220
Total	258	10,109,061	716[e]

[a] Materials included brochures, infographics, toolkits, and campaign-branded merchandise (e.g., key chains, magnets).

[b] MTC and VCL partner organizations were grouped together in our assessment; 403 reflects the combined number for both campaigns.

[c] Number of Recovery Month events attended by a SAMHSA official. Does not include events independently hosted by planning partners.

[d] Recovery Month distributes campaign materials online where they can be downloaded for free from the campaign website.

[e] This number exceeds the total number of partner organizations because there was overlap among the organizations and agencies with which the four campaigns partnered.

Table D.18
Make the Connection: Conferences and Events, 2015

Event Information	Location	Date	Nature of Participation in the Event (e.g., delivered presentation, distributed materials)
April 2015			
U.S. Department of Veterans Affairs Capitol Hill Showcase	Washington, D.C.	April 7	Secured exhibitor space
Wounded Warrior Prosperity Fair	Bethesda, Md.	April 8	Provided outreach materials for distribution
American Association of Suicidology Annual Conference	Atlanta, Ga.	April 15–18	Coordinated speaking engagement and secured exhibitor space
Gold Star Wives of America Southeast Regional Conference	Columbia, S.C.	April 17–18	Provided outreach materials for distribution
May 2015			
American Psychiatric Association Annual Meeting	Toronto, Canada	May 16–20	Provided outreach materials for distribution
Rolling Thunder—Memorial Day Weekend on the National Mall	Washington, D.C.	May 23–24	Secured exhibitor space
Baltimore Orioles—baseball game	Baltimore, Md.	May 26	Secured exhibitor space
National Coalition for Homeless Veterans Annual Conference	Washington, D.C.	May 27–29	Provided outreach materials for distribution

Table D.18—Continued

Event Information	Location	Date	Nature of Participation in the Event (e.g., delivered presentation, distributed materials)
June 2015			
National Association of County Veterans Service Officers Annual Training Conference	Appleton, Wisc.	May 30–June 6	Secured exhibitor space
Mental Health America Annual Conference	Alexandria, Va.	June 3–5	Secured exhibitor space
American Military University Student and Alumni Organization Meeting	National Harbor, Md.	June 12	Provided outreach materials for distribution
RecruitMilitary—Washington, D.C., All Veterans Job Fair	Greater Landover, Md.	June 18	Secured exhibitor space
Mission Complete Open House	Alexandria, Va.	June 22	Provided outreach materials for distribution
July 2015			
Benevolent and Protective Order of Elks National Convention	Indianapolis, Ind.	July 5–9	Secured exhibitor space
National Alliance on Mental Illness National Convention	San Francisco, Calif.	July 6–9	Secured exhibitor space
American Mental Health Counselors Association Annual Conference	Philadelphia, Pa.	July 9–11	Secured exhibitor space
Veterans of Foreign Wars National Convention	Pittsburgh, Pa.	July 18–22	Secured exhibitor space
Vietnam Veterans of America National Convention	Springfield, Ill.	July 21–25	Provided outreach materials for distribution
National Association of State Workforce Agencies Veteran Services Conference	Washington, D.C.	July 22–23	Secured exhibitor space
August 2015			
American Psychological Association Annual Convention	Toronto, Canada	August 6–9	Provided outreach materials for distribution
Disabled American Veterans National Convention	Denver, Colo.	August 8–11	Secured exhibitor space
National Alliance on Mental Illness (NAMI) California Annual Conference	Newport Beach, Calif.	August 21–22	Provided outreach materials for distribution
American Legion National Convention	Baltimore, Md.	August 28–September 3	Secured exhibitor space

Table D.18—Continued

Event Information	Location	Date	Nature of Participation in the Event (e.g., delivered presentation, distributed materials)
September 2015			
National Association of State Directors of Veterans Affairs Annual Conference	Orlando, Fla.	August 30–September 2	Secured exhibitor space
National Guard Association of the United States General Conference and Exhibition	Nashville, Tenn.	September 10–13	Secured exhibitor space
Joint Base Andrews—air show	Joint Base Andrews, Md.	September 18–19	Secured exhibitor space
Depression and Bipolar Support Alliance—I to We Weekend	Chicagoland, Ill.	September 24–27	Provided outreach materials for distribution
October 2015			
National Association of Veterans' Program Administrators Annual Training and Conference	Nashville, Tenn.	October 5–9	Provided outreach materials for distribution
Military Officers Association of America Annual Meeting	Orlando, Fla.	October 26–28	Provided outreach materials for distribution
Military Chaplains Association of America National Meeting	Orlando, Fla.	October 28–31	Provided outreach materials for distribution
Navy Wounded Warrior Safe Harbor—Naval District Washington Wounded Warrior Family Symposium and Resource Fair	Bethesda, Md.	October 30	Secured exhibitor space
November 2015			
Washington, D.C., VA Medical Center—Welcome Home 2015	Washington, D.C.	November 17	Provided outreach materials for distribution

Table D.19
Veterans Crisis Line: Conferences and Events, 2015

Event Information	Location	Date	Nature of Participation in the Event (e.g., Delivered presentation, distributed materials)
January 2015			
Boston Celtics—basketball game	Boston, Mass.	January 5	Secured exhibitor space
Arizona Coyotes—hockey game	Phoenix, Ariz.	January 8	Secured exhibitor space
Student Veterans of America National Conference	San Antonio, Tex.	January 8–11	Provided outreach materials for distribution
Rock 'n' Roll Marathon Health and Fitness Expo	Phoenix, Ariz.	January 16–17	Secured exhibitor space
Hiring Our Heroes job fair	Wilmington, Del.	January 22	Secured exhibitor space
Progressive International Motorcycle Show	Dallas, Tex.	January 23–25	Secured exhibitor space
Waste Management Open Military Career Event and Job Fair	Scottsdale, Ariz.	January 26	Secured exhibitor space
Progressive International Motorcycle Show	Cleveland, Ohio	January 30–February 1	Secured exhibitor space
February 2015			
Oklahoma City Thunder—basketball game	Oklahoma City, Okla.	February 2	Secured exhibitor space
American Foundation for Suicide Prevention (AFSP) Out of the Darkness Walk	Orlando, Fla.	February 7	Secured exhibitor space
NASPA—Student Affairs Administrators in Higher Education Veterans Conference	Louisville, Ky.	February 8–10	Secured exhibitor space
Disabled American Veterans (DAV) Mid-Winter Conference	Arlington, Va.	February 15–22	Coordinated speaking engagement during past conference
Each Mind Matters 7th International Together Against Stigma Conference	San Francisco, Calif.	February 17–20	Secured exhibitor space
AFSP Out of the Darkness Walk	Stuart, Fla.	February 21	Secured exhibitor space
American Legion Mid-Winter Conference	Washington, D.C.	February 23	Provided outreach materials for distribution

Table D.19—Continued

Event Information	Location	Date	Nature of Participation in the Event (e.g., delivered presentation, distributed materials)
March 2015			
Detroit Red Wings—hockey game	Detroit, Mich.	March 6	Secured exhibitor space
Carolina Hurricanes—hockey game	Raleigh, N.C.	March 8	Secured exhibitor space
Hiring Our Heroes job fair	Louisville, Ky.	March 11	Secured exhibitor space
Southeastern Psychological Association—annual meeting	Hilton Head, S.C.	March 18–21	Provided outreach materials for distribution
Rock 'n' Roll Marathon Health and Fitness Expo	Dallas, Tex.	March 20–21	Secured exhibitor space
AFSP Out of the Darkness Walk	Las Vegas, Nev.	March 21	Provided outreach materials for distribution
American Legion Veterans Affairs & Rehabilitation Town Hall	Los Angeles, Calif.	March 23	Provided outreach materials for distribution
Hiring Our Heroes job fair	Dallas, Tex.	March 25	Secured exhibitor space
Hiring Our Heroes job fair	Indianapolis, Ind.	March 27	Secured exhibitor space
April 2015			
Hiring Our Heroes job fair	Norman, Okla.	April 7	Secured exhibitor space
Charlotte Hornets—basketball game	Charlotte, N.C.	April 8	Secured exhibitor space
National Association of Broadcasters Convention	Las Vegas, Nev.	April 12–16	Provided outreach materials for distribution
American Association of Suicidology Annual Conference	Atlanta, Ga.	April 15–18	Secured exhibitor space
National Association of Social Workers West Virginia Chapter 2015 Spring Continuing Education Conference for Social Workers	Charleston, W. Va.	April 15–17	Provided outreach materials for distribution
Hiring Our Heroes job fair	Tampa, Fla.	April 17	Secured exhibitor space
41st Toyota Grand Prix of Long Beach	Long Beach, Calif.	April 17–19	Secured exhibitor space
Thunder over Louisville	Louisville, Ky.	April 18	Secured exhibitor space
Mental Health First Aid National Council for Behavioral Health National Conference	Orlando, Fla.	April 20–22	Secured exhibitor space
Arizona Coalition for Military Families 2015 Statewide Symposium	Phoenix, Ariz.	April 22–23	Secured exhibitor space
Norman Music Festival	Norman, Okla.	April 23–25	Secured exhibitor space
AFSP Out of the Darkness Walk	State College, Pa.	April 26	Secured exhibitor space
Birmingham Automobile Dealers Association Alabama Auto Show	Birmingham, Ala.	April 30–May 3	Provided outreach materials for distribution

Table D.19—Continued

Event Information	Location	Date	Nature of Participation in the Event (e.g., delivered presentation, distributed materials)
May 2015			
Baptist Health South Florida 14th Annual Pediatric Symposium	Miami, Fla.	May 2	Provided outreach materials for distribution
Hiring Our Heroes job fair	Glen Allen, Va.	May 7	Secured exhibitor space
Senior Synergy Expo	Fort Worth, Tex.	May 7	Secured exhibitor space
Hiring Our Heroes job fair	Austin, Tex.	May 11	Secured exhibitor space
12 May: Military Officers Association of America career fair	Washington, D.C.	May 12	Provided outreach materials for distribution
Arizona Diamondbacks—baseball game	Phoenix, Ariz.	May 13	Secured exhibitor space
Guadalupe Cultural Arts Center Tejano Conjunto Festival	San Antonio, Tex.	May 13–17	Secured exhibitor space
AFSP Out of the Darkness Walk	Anchorage, Alaska	May 16	Secured exhibitor space
Hire Heroes USA 5K Race for Heroes	Alpharetta, Ga.	May 16	Secured exhibitor space
Nashville Sounds—baseball game	Nashville, Tenn.	May 17	Secured exhibitor space
Hiring Our Heroes job fair	Boston, Mass.	May 20	Secured exhibitor space
Abbey Road on the River	Louisville, Ky.	May 21–25	Secured exhibitor space
Tragedy Assistance Program for Survivors–National Military Survivor Seminar and Good Grief Camp for Young Survivors	Arlington, Va.	May 21–25	Provided outreach materials for distribution
Rolling Thunder	Washington, D.C.	May 23–24	Secured exhibitor space
National Coalition for Homeless Veterans Annual Conference–Bridging the Gap	Washington, D.C.	May 27–29	Provided outreach materials for distribution
AFSP Out of the Darkness Walk	Palmer, Alaska	May 30	Secured exhibitor space
National Association of County Veterans Service Officers Annual Conference	Appleton, Wisc.	May 30–June 6	Provided outreach materials for distribution

Table D.19—Continued

Event Information	Location	Date	Nature of Participation in the Event (e.g., Delivered presentation, distributed materials)
June 2015			
West Virginia University Summer Institute on Aging	Morgantown, W. Va.	June 2–4	Secured exhibitor space
Mental Health America 2015 Annual Conference	Alexandria, Va.	June 3–5	Provided outreach materials for distribution
Arizona Diamondbacks—baseball game	Phoenix, Ariz.	June 5	Secured exhibitor space
San Antonio Summer Art & Jazz Festival	San Antonio, Tex.	June 5–7	Secured exhibitor space
Grand Old Day	St. Paul, Minn.	June 7	Secured exhibitor space
American Military Retirees Association National Convention 2015	Cincinnati, Ohio	June 12–13	Provided outreach materials for distribution
American Military University speaking engagement	Washington, D.C.	June 15	Provided outreach materials for distribution
Hiring Our Heroes job fair	Columbia, S.C.	June 16	Secured exhibitor space
Arizona Diamondbacks—baseball game	Phoenix, Ariz.	June 18	Secured exhibitor space
Hiring Our Heroes job fair	Nashville, Tenn.	June 18	Secured exhibitor space
Eastern Foundry 2015 Foundry Cup	Arlington, Va.	June 20	Provided outreach materials for distribution
Vectren Dayton Air Show	Dayton, Ohio	June 20–21	Secured exhibitor space
American Gold Star Mothers Annual Convention	Kansas City, Mo.	June 25–27	Provided outreach materials for distribution
Hearing Loss Association of America Convention 2015	St. Louis, Mo.	June 25–28	Provided outreach materials for distribution
Medal of Honor Rockstar Energy Drink Mayhem Festival	Chula Vista, Calif.	June 26	Provided outreach materials for distribution
Hiring Our Heroes job fair	East Rutherford, N.J.	June 27	Secured exhibitor space
NBC 4 New York and New York Giants Health & Fitness Expo	East Rutherford, N.J.	June 27–28	Secured exhibitor space
St. Pete Pride 2015 Festival	St. Petersburg, Fla.	June 28	Secured exhibitor space

Table D.19—Continued

Event Information	Location	Date	Nature of Participation in the Event (e.g., delivered presentation, distributed materials)
July 2015			
Elks National Convention	Indianapolis, Ind.	July 5–9	Provided outreach materials for distribution
San Francisco Giants—baseball game	San Francisco, Calif.	July 6	Secured exhibitor space
League of United Latin American Citizens National Convention & Exposition	Salt Lake City, Utah	July 7–11	Secured exhibitor space
2015 American Mental Health Counselors Association Annual Conference	Philadelphia, Pa.	July 9–11	Provided outreach materials for distribution
National Association for the Advancement of Colored People (NAACP) 106th Annual Convention	Philadelphia, Pa.	July 11–15	Secured exhibitor space
Hiring Our Heroes job fair	Montgomery, Ala.	July 14	Secured exhibitor space
Veterans of Foreign Wars 116th National Convention	Pittsburgh, Pa.	July 18–22	Secured exhibitor space
Vietnam Veterans of America Leadership and Education Conference	Springfield, Ill.	July 20–25	Secured exhibitor space
Kansas Suicide Prevention Resource Center Midwest Regional Suicide Prevention Conference	Kansas City, Mo.	July 21–23	Secured exhibitor space
National Association of State Workforce Agencies Veteran Services Conference	Washington, D.C.	July 22–23	Provided outreach materials for distribution
Country Jam USA—music festival	Eau Claire, Wisc.	July 23–26	Secured exhibitor space
National Association for Rural Mental Health Annual Conference	Honolulu, Hawaii	July 20–August 2	Provided outreach materials for distribution

Table D.19—Continued

Event Information	Location	Date	Nature of Participation in the Event (e.g., delivered presentation, distributed materials)
August 2015			
Jewish War Veterans of the USA Annual National Convention	Tampa, Fla.	August 2–9	Secured exhibitor space
Military Order of the World Wars National Convention	Tampa, Fla.	August 4–8	Provided outreach materials for distribution
American Psychological Association Annual Convention	Toronto, Canada	August 6–9	Provided outreach materials for distribution
DAV National Convention	Denver, Colo.	August 8–11	Secured exhibitor space
Catholic War Veterans & Auxiliary National Convention	Las Vegas, Nev.	August 9–16	Provided outreach materials for distribution
Greenwood Lake Air Show	West Milford, N.J.	August 14–16	Secured exhibitor space
Atlanta Braves—baseball game	Atlanta, Ga.	August 15	Secured exhibitor space
Blinded Veterans Association National Convention	Louisville, Ky.	August 17–21	Secured exhibitor space
American Veterans (AMVETS) National Convention	Birmingham, Ala.	August 19–21	Secured exhibitor space
Air Force Sergeants Association Professional Airmen's Conference	San Antonio, Tex.	August 22–26	Secured exhibitor space
Thunder Over the Valley air show	Santa Maria, Calif.	August 22	Provided outreach materials for distribution
Wings Over Camarillo air show	Camarillo, Calif.	August 22–23	Provided outreach materials for distribution
Hiring Our Heroes job fair	Tucson, Ariz.	August 27	Secured exhibitor space
New Mexico Veterans Annual Business Expo and Job Fair	Albuquerque, N.M.	August 27	Secured exhibitor space
American Legion National Convention	Baltimore, Md.	August 28–September 3	Secured exhibitor space
AFSP Out of the Darkness Walk	Fort Wayne, Ind.	August 29	Secured exhibitor space
AFSP Out of the Darkness Walk	Pittsburgh, Pa.	August 29	Secured exhibitor space
Commemorative Air Force AIRSHO	Midland, Tex.	August 29–30	Secured exhibitor space
Thunder Over Michigan air show	Ypsilanti, Mich.	August 29–30	Secured exhibitor space
National Association of State Directors of Veterans Affairs Fall Conference	Lake Buena Vista, Fla.	August 30–September 2	Secured exhibitor space

Table D.19—Continued

Event Information	Location	Date	Nature of Participation in the Event (e.g., delivered presentation, distributed materials)
September 2015			
Akron RubberDucks—baseball game	Akron, Ohio	September 3	Secured exhibitor space
American Music Festival	Virginia Beach, Va.	September 4–6	Secured exhibitor space
AFSP Out of the Darkness Walk	Greenwich, R.I.	September 5	Secured exhibitor space
Mackinac Bridge Walk	Mackinaw, Mich.	September 7	Secured exhibitor space
The Clifford Beers Foundation and the University of South Carolina 2015 Ninth World Congress on the Promotion of Mental Health	Columbia, S.C.	September 9–11	Provided outreach materials for distribution
National Guard Association of the United States General Conference & Exhibition	Nashville, Tenn.	September 10–13	Provided outreach materials for distribution
AFSP Out of the Darkness Walk	Gulfport, Miss.	September 12	Secured exhibitor space
AFSP Out of the Darkness Walk	Oklahoma City, Okla.	September 12	Secured exhibitor space
Boulder Crest Retreat Healing Heroes Ride—100 Mile Poker Run	Bluemont, Va.	September 12	Secured exhibitor space
AFSP Out of the Darkness Walk	Fargo, N.D.	September 13	Secured exhibitor space
AFSP Out of the Darkness Walk	Omaha, Neb.	September 13	Secured exhibitor space
Hiring Our Heroes job fair	Pittsburgh, Pa.	September 16	Secured exhibitor space
Hiring Our Heroes job fair	Philadelphia, Pa.	September 17	Secured exhibitor space
Mental Health Association Oklahoma Zarrow Mental Health Symposium	Tulsa, Okla.	September 17–18	Provided outreach materials for distribution
U.S. Air Force Marathon Sports and Fitness Expo	Dayton, Ohio	September 17–18	Provided outreach materials for distribution
Joint Base Andrews Air Show	Joint Base Andrews, Md.	September 17–19	Secured exhibitor space
Indigo Consortium Bull City Stand Down	Durham, N.C.	September 18	Secured exhibitor space
AFSP Out of the Darkness Walk	Richmond, Va.	September 19	Secured exhibitor space

Table D.19—Continued

Event Information	Location	Date	Nature of Participation in the Event (e.g., delivered presentation, distributed materials)
Rotary Club of Dougherty Valley and San Ramon V3 Hopfest	San Ramon, Calif.	September 19	Secured exhibitor space
Sister II Sister Women's Expo	Mobile, Ala.	September 19	Secured exhibitor space
Naval Air Station Oceana Air Show	Virginia Beach, Va.	September 19–20	Secured exhibitor space
Bikes, Blues, and BBQ Motorcycle Rally	Fayetteville, Ark.	September 23–26	Secured exhibitor space
AFSP Out of the Darkness Walk	Radford, Va.	September 26	Secured exhibitor space
AFSP Out of the Darkness Walk	Sugar Land, Tex.	September 26	Secured exhibitor space
Broward National Recovery Month Walk	Deerfield Beach, Va.	September 26	Secured exhibitor space
AFSP Out of the Darkness Walk	Augusta, Ga.	September 27	Secured exhibitor space
AFSP Out of the Darkness Walk	Rochester, N.Y.	September 27	Provided outreach materials for distribution
AFSP Out of the Darkness Walk	San Francisco, Calif.	September 27	Provided outreach materials for distribution
AFSP Out of the Darkness Walk	Springfield, Mass.	September 27	Provided outreach materials for distribution
AFSP Out of the Darkness Walk	Twin Cities, Minn.	September 27	Secured exhibitor space
Baltimore Orioles—baseball game	Baltimore, Md.	September 30	Secured exhibitor space
Emergency Nurses Association Annual Conference	Orlando, Fla.	September 29– October 3	Secured exhibitor space
National Association of Broadcasters Radio Show	Atlanta, Ga.	September 30– October 2	Secured exhibitor space

Table D.19—Continued

Event Information	Location	Date	Nature of Participation in the Event (e.g., delivered presentation, distributed materials)
October 2015			
Arizona Diamondbacks—baseball game	Phoenix, Ariz.	October 1	Secured exhibitor space
Portland Marathon Sports & Fitness Expo	Portland, Oreg.	October 2–3	Secured exhibitor space
AFSP Out of the Darkness Walk	Chittenango, N.Y.	October 3	Secured exhibitor space
AFSP Out of the Darkness Walk	Portland, Oreg.	October 3	Secured exhibitor space
AFSP Out of the Darkness Walk	Bronx, N.Y.	October 4	Secured exhibitor space
AFSP Out of the Darkness Walk	Hamden, Conn.	October 4	Secured exhibitor space
AFSP Out of the Darkness Walk	Tuscaloosa, Ala.	October 4	Secured exhibitor space
American Psychiatric Association's IPS: The Mental Health Services Conference	New York City	October 8–11	Secured exhibitor space
AFSP Out of the Darkness Walk	Montclair, N.J.	October 10	Secured exhibitor space
AFSP Out of the Darkness Walk	Westland, Mich.	October 10	Secured exhibitor space
AFSP Out of the Darkness Walk	Columbus, Ohio	October 11	Provided outreach materials for distribution
AFSP Out of the Darkness Walk	Miami, Fla.	October 11	Secured exhibitor space
AFSP Out of the Darkness Walk	Cleveland, Ohio	October 17	Provided outreach materials for distribution
AFSP Out of the Darkness Walk	Fresno, Calif.	October 17	Secured exhibitor space
AFSP Out of the Darkness Walk	Memphis, Tenn.	October 17	Secured exhibitor space
San Antonio Coalition for Veterans and Families—Bridging the Gap	San Antonio, Tex.	October 17	Provided outreach materials for distribution
AFSP Out of the Darkness Walk	Charleston, S.C.	October 18	Secured exhibitor space
AFSP Out of the Darkness Walk	Cincinnati, Ohio	October 18	Secured exhibitor space
Alabama Tactical Officers Association Tactical Operations Conference	Columbiana, Ala.	October 19–22	Secured exhibitor space
Hiring Our Heroes job fair	Warwick, R.I.	October 20	Secured exhibitor space
Nevada Office of Suicide Prevention Conference	Las Vegas, Nev.	October 22–23	Provided outreach materials for distribution

Table D.19—Continued

Event Information	Location	Date	Nature of Participation in the Event (e.g., delivered presentation, distributed materials)
NAMI North Carolina Annual Conference	Raleigh, N.C.	October 23–24	Provided outreach materials for distribution
AFSP Out of the Darkness Walk	Kernersville, N.C.	October 24	Secured exhibitor space
AFSP Out of the Darkness Walk	San Diego, Calif.	October 24	Secured exhibitor space
International Association of Chiefs of Police Annual Conference and Exposition	Chicago, Ill.	October 24–27	Secured exhibitor space
AFSP Out of the Darkness Walk	Asheville, N.C.	October 25	Secured exhibitor space
AFSP Out of the Darkness Walk	Columbia, Mo.	October 25	Secured exhibitor space
AFSP Out of the Darkness Walk	Seattle, Wash.	October 25	Secured exhibitor space
American Psychiatric Nurses Association 29th Annual Conference	Lake Buena Vista, Fla.	October 28–31	Secured exhibitor space
Progressive International Motorcycle Show	Portland, Oreg.	October 31–November 1	Secured exhibitor space

Table D.19—Continued

Event Information	Location	Date	Nature of Participation in the Event (e.g., delivered presentation, distributed materials)
November 2015			
American Public Health Association Annual Meeting & Exposition	Chicago, Ill.	October 31– November 4	Secured exhibitor space
AFSP Out of the Darkness Walk	Ann Arbor, Mich.	November 1	Secured exhibitor space
AFSP Out of the Darkness Walk	Atlanta, Ga.	November 1	Secured exhibitor space
AFSP Out of the Darkness Walk	Birmingham, Ala.	November 1	Secured exhibitor space
AFSP Out of the Darkness Walk	Lakeland, Fla.	November 1	Secured exhibitor space
AFSP Out of the Darkness Walk	Little Rock, Ark.	November 1	Secured exhibitor space
Hiring Our Heroes job fair	Des Moines, Iowa	November 3	Secured exhibitor space
International Society for Traumatic Stress Studies 31st Annual Meeting	New Orleans, La.	November 5–7	Provided outreach materials for distribution
Pensacola Blue Angels Homecoming Air Show	Pensacola, Fla.	November 6–7	Secured exhibitor space
Progressive International Motorcycle Show	Sacramento, Calif.	November 6–8	Secured exhibitor space
AFSP Out of the Darkness Walk	Louisville, Ky.	November 7	Secured exhibitor space
AFSP Out of the Darkness Walk	New Port Richey, Fla.	November 7	Provided outreach materials for distribution
Color Run 5K	Little Rock, Ark.	November 7	
DAV 5K—Run to Honor Veterans	San Diego, Calif.	November 7	Provided outreach materials for distribution
NAMI Minnesota's 2015 State Conference	St. Paul, Minn.	November 7	Provided outreach materials for distribution
AFSP Out of the Darkness Walk	Aiken, S.C.	November 8	Secured exhibitor space
Iraq and Afghanistan Veterans of America (IAVA) Veterans Day parade	New York, N.Y.	November 11	Secured exhibitor space
Boston Celtics—basketball game	Boston, Mass.	November 11	Secured exhibitor space
2015 Neuroscience Education Institute Psychopharmacology Congress	Orlando, Fla.	November 12–15	Provided outreach materials for distribution
Active Minds National Mental Health on Campus Conference	Irvine, Calif.	November 13–15	Secured exhibitor space
AFSP Out of the Darkness Walk	Knightdale, N.C.	November 14	Secured exhibitor space

Table D.19—Continued

Event Information	Location	Date	Nature of Participation in the Event (e.g., delivered presentation, distributed materials)
AFSP Out of the Darkness Walk	Montgomery, Ala.	November 14	Secured exhibitor space
AFSP Out of the Darkness Walk	Wrightsville Beach, N.C.	November 15	Secured exhibitor space
Color Run 5K	San Francisco, Calif.	November 15	Provided outreach materials for distribution
Washington, D.C., VA Medical Center DC and Walter Reed National Military Medical Center Welcome Home 2015	Washington, D.C.	November 17	Provided outreach materials for distribution
Philadelphia Marathon and Comcast Health and Fitness Expo	Philadelphia, Pa.	November 20–21	Provided outreach materials for distribution
Progressive International Motorcycle Show	Long Beach, Calif.	November 20–22	Secured exhibitor space
AFSP Out of the Darkness Walk	Pearl, Miss.	November 21	Secured exhibitor space
American Foundation for Suicide Prevention International Survivors of Suicide Loss Day	Anchorage, Alaska	November 21	Coordinated speaking engagement during past conference
March for 22 Corpus Christi	Corpus Christi, Tex.	November 21	Provided outreach materials for distribution
December 2015			
Mount Sinai Hospital 6th Annual National Update on Behavioral Emergencies Conference	Las Vegas, Nev.	December 2–4	Provided outreach materials for distribution
AFSP Out of the Darkness Walk	Tampa, Fla.	December 5	Secured exhibitor space
AFSP Out of the Darkness Walk	Tempe, Ariz.	December 5	Secured exhibitor space
Color Run 5K	Clearwater, Fla.	December 5	Secured exhibitor space
Rock 'n' Roll Marathon Health & Fitness Expo	San Antonio, Tex.	December 5–6	Secured exhibitor space
Special Operations Medical Association Scientific Assembly & Exhibition	San Marcos, Tex.	December 14–16	Secured exhibitor space
Quick Lane Bowl game	Detroit, Mich.	December 28	Secured exhibitor space
Military Bowl game	Annapolis, Md.	December 28	Secured exhibitor space
Lockheed Martin Armed Forces Bowl game	Fort Worth, Tex.	December 28	Secured exhibitor space
Birmingham Bowl game	Birmingham, Ala.	December 30	Secured exhibitor space

Table D.20
National Recovery Month: Conferences and Events, 2015

Event Information	Location
Rally for Recovery—Treatment Works in Cincinnati	Cincinnati, Ohio
"Run 4 Recovery" Run, walk 5K or 1-mile Fun Run	Ft. Worth, Tex.
David Lewis 5K—A Celebration of Recovery	Falmouth, Mass.
9th Annual Recovery Run, Walk & Rally	Baltimore, Md.
2015 Run for Recovery	Watertown, N.Y.
Michigan Celebrate Recovery Walk & Rally	Detroit, Mich.
2015 4th Annual Ride for Recovery	Red House, W. Va.
McShin's 11th Annual Recovery Fest	Richmond, Va.
National Recovery Night at the Ballpark	Philadelphia, Pa.
National Recovery Month Partnership Breakfast	Lynchburg, Va.
Recovery Month event	Scottsburg and Austin, Ind.
Pennsylvania Recovery Organization–Achieving Community Together (PRO-ACT) Recovery Walks!	Philadelphia, Pa.
Rockin' Recovery Rally	Madison, Wisc.
New Jersey Celebrates Recovery	Asbury Park, N.J.
New York State Social Security Administration	New York, N.Y.
University of North Texas–Dallas; Young People's Conference Presentation	Dallas, Tex.
National Recovery Month Exhibit	Asheville, N.C.
New Jersey Statewide Recovery Walk & Rally	Jersey City, N.J.
2015 Recovery Jam	Little Rock, Ark.
Kentucky School Banquet	Louisville, Ky.
Recovery Month Press Conference	Washington, D.C.
Fire Walk and Rally	Providence, R.I.
Recovery Month Event	Manchester, N.H.
Office of National Drug Control Policy (ONDCP) Reception for National Recovery Month	Washington, D.C.
Unite to Face Addiction Rally	Washington, D.C.

Table D.21
Real Warriors Campaign: Conferences and Events, 2015

Conferences and Events	
2015 number of events attended	19
Cumulative number of events attended, 2009–2015	168
2015 number of events hosted	none
Cumulative number of events hosted, 2009–2015	17
Nature of events (e.g., national or local, meeting goals)	Local, regional or state, and national events are held to engage with all campaign target audiences, including and especially audiences that may not have ready access to campaign or other support materials to support health literacy, such as Guardsmen and reservists not based near installations, military treatment facilities, or military communities. Examples include: • Local: USO Operation Community Connection events, Department of Housing and Urban Development and VA Health Education Fair, Joint Base Andrews Open House Air Show • Regional or State: National Guard and Reserve Yellow Ribbon Reintegration Program events • National: Association of the United States Army (AUSA) Annual Meeting and Expo; AMSUS Annual Society of Federal Health Professionals Continuing Education Meeting, National Guard Association of the United States General Conference and Exhibition At the beginning of each fiscal year, the campaign contributes to a DCoE organizationwide conference and event tracker. All events attended by the campaign are conferences or events that further the goals of the campaign to educate and reduce misperception, foster a culture of support for psychological health, restore faith in the Military Health System, improve support systems, and empower behavior change.
Nature of participation in the event (e.g., delivered presentation, distributed materials)	At minimum for all conferences and events, the campaign engages participants through exhibiting at the booth with materials, videos, and displays; discussing resources available through RWC; encouraging material orders; and signing up attendees to the campaign listserv. In 2015, the campaign engaged with 1,708 attendees, disseminated 8,982 materials, and received orders for more than 52,427 materials at 19 events. Cumulatively, the campaign has engaged with 22,445 event attendees, disseminated 16,050 materials, and received orders for more than 302,920 materials at 168 events. Additionally, the campaign actively seeks opportunities to present or speak at events to better educate and reduce misperceptions and to engage audiences on ways the campaign can empower self-efficacy. In 2015, the campaign presented at 12 events, engaging more than 1,291 individuals, including serving as the keynote (along with the DCoE Outreach team) at a Louisiana National Guard Yellow Ribbon Reintegration Program event. Cumulatively, the campaign has presented at 64 events, engaging more than 13,011 individuals to foster a culture of support for psychological health.

Table D.22
Campaign Partners

Partners (N = 716)	RWC	VCL and MTC	Recovery Month
Partners shared across 3 agencies: <1% (N = 1)			
Team Red, White & Blue	x	x	x
Partners shared across at least 2 agencies: 4% (N = 31)			
American Mental Health Counselors Association		x	x
American Psychological Association		x	x
American Red Cross	x	x	
Anxiety and Depression Association of America	x	x	
Army Wife Network	x	x	
Blue Star Families	x	x	
Bob Woodruff Foundation	x	x	
Catholic Charities		x	x
Easter Seals	x	x	
Elizabeth Dole Foundation	x	x	
Gold Star Wives of America	x	x	
Grace After Fire	x	x	
Hire Heroes USA	x	x	
Homes for Our Troops	x	x	
Mental Health America	x	x	
Mental Health America of Texas	x	x	
Mental Health Association		x	x
Military Officers Association of America	x	x	
MilitaryOneClick	x	x	
National Alliance on Mental Illness	x	x	
National Association of Social Workers		x	x
National Association of State Mental Health Program Directors	x	x	
National Coalition for Homeless Veterans	x	x	
National Council for Behavioral Health		x	x
National Military Family Association	x	x	
Pets for Patriots	x	x	
Semper Fi Fund	x	x	
Student Veterans of America	x	x	
Suicide Awareness Voices of Education	x	x	
Tragedy Assistance Program for Survivors	x	x	
USO	x	x	

Table D.22—Continued

Partners (N = 716)	RWC	VCL and MTC	Recovery Month
Partners not shared across campaigns: 96% (N = 684)			
1, 2 Many: Veteran Suicide		x	
1200 Miles		x	
A&E Television Networks			x
AARP		x	
AARP–Maryland		x	
Abbey Road on the River		x	
Academy for Addiction Professionals			x
AcademyWomen		x	
Active Minds		x	
Adaptive Adventures	x		
AdCare Hospital AdCare Outpatient Clinic			x
Addiction Survivors			x
Addiction Treatment Services			x
Administration for Children and Families (ACF) Family and Youth Services Bureau (FYSB)			x
AdoptaPlatoon		x	
Adult Children of Alcoholics World Service Organization			x
Advocacy Unlimited		x	
Advocates for Recovery Through Medicine, D.C. Chapter			x
Agency for Health Care Administration		x	
Air Force Reserve Command Psychological Health Advocacy Program	x		
Air Force Sergeants Association		x	
Airman2Mom		x	
Akron RubberDucks		x	
Al-Anon Family Group Headquarters			x
Alcoholics Anonymous General Services Organization			x
Alcoholics Anonymous World Services			x
Alcoholism and Substance Providers of New York State			x
Alexandria Department of Community and Human Services		x	
Alliance for Children and Families, D.C.			x
Alliance for Retired Americans		x	
ALS Association		x	
American Academy of Physician Assistants	x		
American Association for Marriage and Family Therapy			x

Table D.22—Continued

Partners (*N* = 716)	RWC	VCL and MTC	Recovery Month
American Association of Pastoral Counselors			x
American Association of Suicidology		x	
American Bar Association			x
American College of Mental Health Administration, College of Behavioral Health Leadership			x
American Council for Drug Education and Children of Alcoholics Foundation			x
American Counseling Association		x	
American Dental Association			x
American Foundation for Suicide Prevention		x	
American GI Forum—National Veterans Outreach		x	
American Gold Star Mothers		x	
American Indian Community House			x
American Legion		x	
American Legion Auxiliary		x	
American Legion Department of California		x	
American Legion Riders (Post 537)		x	
American Library Association		x	
American Medical Informatics Association		x	
American Military Partner Association		x	
American Military Retirees Association		x	
American Military University		x	
American Nurses Association—California		x	
American Psychiatric Association		x	
American Public Health Association		x	
American Public Human Services Administration			x
American Society of Addiction Medicine			x
American Veterans (AMVETS)		x	
American Veterans Center		x	
American Veterans for Equal Rights		x	
Amy Paffrath		x	
Anaheim Ducks		x	
Anchor Recovery Community Centers Manager			x
Arab American and Chaldean Council			x
Arizona Coalition for Military Families		x	
Arizona Diamondbacks		x	
Arizona Rattlers		x	
Armed Forces Foundation	x		
Armed Forces Motorsports, Vets on Track Foundation		x	

Table D.22—Continued

Partners (*N* = 716)	RWC	VCL and MTC	Recovery Month
Armed Services YMCA	x		
Army National Guard Health Promotion	x		
Army Women's Foundation		x	
Aspen Institute: Forum for Community Solutions			x
Associate Director of Recovery Support Services			x
Association for Addiction Professionals			x
Association for Psychological Science		x	
Association of Persons Affected by Addiction			x
Association of Professional Chaplains		x	
Association of Recovery Schools			x
A Star in My Own Universe		x	
Atlanta Braves		x	
Atlanta Hawks		x	
Auburn University		x	
Augsburg College			x
Aurora Foundation	x		
Back on Land		x	
Baltimore Clubhouse		x	
Baltimore Orioles		x	
Baptist Health		x	
Behavioral Health Services			x
Beit T'Shuvah			x
Benevolent and Protective Order of Elks		x	
Benevolent and Protective Order of Elks of the USA			x
Berkeley College		x	
BestCompaniesAZ		x	
Birdies for the Brave	x		
Birmingham Automobile Dealers Association		x	
Blinded Veterans Association		x	
Boston Bruins		x	
Boston Celtics		x	
Boston Red Sox		x	
Boston University		x	
Boulder Crest Retreat		x	
Bradley Cooper		x	
BrainLine Military	x		
BraveHeart: Welcome Back Veterans Southeast Initiative	x		
Brent Budowsky		x	

Table D.22—Continued

Partners (N = 716)	RWC	VCL and MTC	Recovery Month
Brooklyn College		x	
Bureau of Drug and Alcohol Programs, Pennsylvania Department of Health			x
C4 Recovery			x
California Association for Addiction Recovery Resources			x
California Association of County Veterans Service Officers		x	
California Department of Veterans Affairs		x	
Cammo Style Love		x	
Campbell Center			x
Campbell Outreach Group			x
Candypolooza		x	
Capitol Decisions			x
Captain Sully Sullenberger		x	
Care Coalition (Team Room)		x	
Carolina Hurricanes		x	
Caron NY			x
CASAColumbia			x
Catholic War Veterans of the USA		x	
CEASe of Scott County			x
Center for Alcohol and Drug Research and Education			x
Center for BrainHealth	x		
Center for Neuroscience and Regenerative Medicine	x		
Center for Veterans Issues	x		
Center for Young Adult Addiction and Recovery State Coordinator: GA NETWORK President Association of Recovery in Higher Education, Kennesaw State University			x
Champagne Living		x	
Change Matrix—Young People in Recovery			x
Charlotte Hornets		x	
Chicago Blackhawks		x	
Chicago Cubs		x	
Chicago Fire		x	
Chicago Hispanic Health Coalition			x
Chicago School of Professional Psychology			x
Children of Fallen Patriots Foundation		x	
Cincinnati Reds		x	
City College of New York		x	

Table D.22—Continued

Partners (*N* = 716)	RWC	VCL and MTC	Recovery Month
City of Albuquerque Mayor's Office Veteran Liaison Office		x	
City of New York Mayor's Office of Veterans Affairs		x	
Civic Entertainment Group			x
Clearinghouse for Military Family Readiness	x		
Cleveland Browns		x	
Cleveland Cavaliers		x	
Cleveland National Air Show		x	
Coaching into Care	x		
Coalition to Salute America's Heroes		x	
Coast Guard All Hands		x	
Code of Support Foundation		x	
Collaborative Support Programs of New Jersey, Institute for Wellness and Recovery Initiatives			x
Colorado Avalanche		x	
Columbus Blue Jackets		x	
Communities of Tomorrow's Economic Redevelopment			x
Community Anti-Drug Coalitions of America			x
Comprehensive Soldier Fitness	x		
Concert for Valor		x	
Connecticut Counseling Association		x	
Connecticut Turning to Youth and Families			x
Convenience Kits International		x	
Corporation for Supportive Housing			x
Council of State Governments			x
Country Jam USA		x	
Craig Morgan		x	
CRC Health Group			x
Danbury Hospital		x	
DC Bar			x
Defense Media Activity		x	
Deployment Health Assessment Program	x		
Depression and Bipolar Support Alliance		x	
Detroit Red Wings		x	
Dina Farmer		x	
Direction Diva		x	
Disabled American Veterans		x	
Disabled Sports USA		x	

Table D.22—Continued

Partners (*N* = 716)	RWC	VCL and MTC	Recovery Month
DIY Adulation		x	
DoD Hearing Center of Excellence	x		
Dover Downs		x	
Dream Center for Recovery			x
Drug Free America Foundation			x
DSTRESS Line	x		
Each Mind Matters		x	
Eastern Foundry		x	
Easy Does It			x
Eaton County Recovery Month Coalition			x
Edelman			x
Education & Outreach Services, Center for Health & Wellbeing			x
El Paso Alliance			x
Emergency Nurses Association		x	
Employee Assistance Professionals Association			x
Employer Support of the Guard and Reserve	x		
Entertainment Industries Council			x
Esposas Militares Hispanas USA		x	
Executive Office of the President			x
Face It TOGETHER			x
Faces & Voices of Recovery			x
Faces of America's Brave	x		
Fair Haven Community Health Center		x	
Faith Partners			x
Family and Youth Service Bureau			x
Fayetteville State University		x	
FED UP! Coalition			x
Fellowship Hall			x
Fellowship of Catholic University Students	x		
Final Salute Inc.	x		
Finding Joy		x	
First Advantage			x
Firstline Creative and Media			x
Fisher House Foundation		x	
Florida Council for Community Mental Health		x	
Florida Department of Veterans' Affairs		x	
Florida Mental Health Counselors Association		x	
Florida Panthers		x	

Table D.22—Continued

Partners (*N* = 716)	RWC	VCL and MTC	Recovery Month
Florida Psychological Association		x	
Fort Bragg Army Community Service: Spouse Resiliency Academy		x	
Foundation for Recovery			x
Foundation NuestraMente			x
Foundations Associates			x
Fraternal Order of Police		x	
Friends of Recovery–New York		x	
Friends of SAMHSA			x
Gaudenzia			x
Gay Military Signal		x	
General Board of Church and Society—United Methodist Church			x
General Electric		x	
George Washington University—Collegiate Recovery Program			x
George Washington University—Office of Military and Veteran Student Services		x	
Georgetown University, Health Policy Institute			x
Georgetown University, McCourt School of Public Policy, Center for Juvenile Justice Reform			x
Georgetown University, Veterans Services		x	
Georgia Department of Behavioral Health and Developmental Disabilities		x	
Georgia Hospital Association		x	
Georgia Veterans Day Parade Association of Atlanta		x	
Good Girl Gone Redneck		x	
Got Your 6		x	
Grand Prix of Long Beach		x	
Green Bay Packers		x	
Growing Veterans		x	
Guadalupe Cultural Arts Center		x	
Habitat for Humanity of Georgia		x	
Habitat for Humanity of Ventura County		x	
Happy Fit Navy Wife		x	
Healing Heroes Ride		x	
Health Matrix			x
Health Net Federal Services (TRICARE North Region)		x	
Health Resources and Services Administration			x

Table D.22—Continued

Partners (*N* = 716)	RWC	VCL and MTC	Recovery Month
HealthCare Chaplaincy Network		x	
Hearing Loss Association of America		x	
Heart Songs for Veterans		x	
Hearts and Ears		x	
Hero Dogs	x		
Heroes on the Water	x		
HHS, SAMHSA, Center for Substance Abuse Treatment			x
Hidden Heroes Campaign		x	
Hidden Wounds	x		
High Heels & Combat Boots		x	
Higher Grounds Sun Valley	x		
Hire a Patriot		x	
Hiring Our Heroes		x	
Hogs for Heroes		x	
Homefront United Network		x	
Honor for ALL	x		
HopeNGriffin		x	
Horses 4 Heroes	x		
Houston Astros		x	
Houston Rockets		x	
Howie the Harp Advocacy Center Community Access			x
IAVA		x	
If the Saddle Fits		x	
Illinois Patriot Education Fund	x		
Indian Health Services—Albuquerque Area		x	
INFINITY Signature Solutions			x
Institute for Veterans and Military Families	x		
International Association of Chiefs of Police		x	
International Nurses Society on Addictions			x
inTransition	x		
Invicta Challenge		x	
Iraq Star	x		
J&A Racing		x	
Jason's Box	x		
Jewish Alcoholics, Chemically Dependent Persons, and Significant Others, a Program of the Jewish Board of Family and Children Services			x
Jewish War Veterans of the United States of America		x	

Table D.22—Continued

Partners (*N* = 716)	RWC	VCL and MTC	Recovery Month
Jo, My Gosh!		x	
Joe Mantegna		x	
John Oliver		x	
Johns Hopkins University		x	
Joint Base Andrews		x	
Just a Splash of Diva		x	
Just Wandering		x	
Justice for Vets		x	
K9s for Warriors	x		
Kansas Consumer Advisory Council for Adult Mental Health			x
Keep Kids Drug Free			x
Kentucky Derby Festival		x	
Knights of Columbus—Southern Illinois		x	
Ladies Auxiliary to Veterans of Foreign Wars Post 6873		x	
LaGuardia Community College		x	
Lake Erie Crushers		x	
Leadership Council of Aging Organizations		x	
League of Women Voters		x	
Legal Action Center			x
Lehman College		x	
Lest We Forget PTSD Family & Military Support	x		
Licensed Clinical Professional Counselors of Maryland		x	
Life of Creed		x	
Lions Club International			x
Live Nation Entertainment		x	
LivingThruCrisis.com		x	
Lone Survivor Foundation	x		
Louisiana State University—Veteran and Military Student Services		x	
Maine Military & Community Network	x		
Many Kind Regards		x	
Marine Corps Community Services Henderson Hall	x		
Marine Corps League—Department of Pennsylvania		x	
Maryland Department of Health and Mental Hygiene Maryland's Commitment to Veterans		x	
Maryland Department of Veterans Affairs		x	
Massachusetts Organization for Addiction Recovery c/o Boston ASAP			x

Table D.22—Continued

Partners (N = 716)	RWC	VCL and MTC	Recovery Month
McShin Foundation			x
Mental Health America of Colorado	x		
Mental Health Connecticut		x	
Mental Health First Aid		x	
Metropolitan State University			x
Military Chaplains Association of the USA		x	
Military Family Advisory Network Board of Directors		x	
Military Order of the Purple Heart		x	
Military Order of the World Wars		x	
Military Partners and Families Coalition		x	
Military Spouse		x	
Military Spouse Advocacy Network		x	
Military Spouse Behavioral Health Clinicians		x	
Military Spouses of Strength		x	
Military Wife and Mom		x	
Military.com		x	
Milwaukee Brewers		x	
Minnesota Recovery Connection			x
Minnesota Twins		x	
Mission Complete		x	
MISSION: Milpreneur		x	
MODDHA International Foundation			x
Mom Muggle Princess		x	
Mount Sinai Hospital		x	
MSB New Media		x	
MyActiveChild.com		x	
NAMI STAR (Support, Technical Assistance, and Resources) Center			x
Nar-Anon			x
Narconon Arrowhead			x
Narcotics Anonymous World Services			x
Nashville Sounds		x	
NASPA: Student Affairs Administrators in Higher Education		x	
National Action Alliance for Suicide Prevention		x	
National Affordable Housing Management Association		x	
National Alliance for Drug Endangered Children			x
National Alliance for Medication Assisted Recovery			x
National Alliance of Advocates for Buprenorphine Treatment			x

Table D.22—Continued

Partners (*N* = 716)	RWC	VCL and MTC	Recovery Month
National Alliance to End Homelessness			x
National Association for Black Veterans		x	
National Association for Children of Alcoholics			x
National Association for Rural Mental Health		x	
National Association of Addiction Treatment Providers			x
National Association of Black Military Women		x	
National Association of Broadcasters		x	
National Association of County and City Health Officials		x	
National Association of County Behavioral Health and Developmental Disability Directors			x
National Association of County Veteran Service Officers		x	
National Association of Drug Court Professionals			x
National Association of Jewish Chaplains		x	
National Association of Lesbian and Gay Addiction Professionals			x
National Association of State Alcohol and Drug Abuse Directors			x
National Association of State Directors of Veterans Affairs		x	
National Association of State Veterans Homes		x	
National Association of State Workforce Agencies		x	
National Association of Veterans' Program Administrators		x	
National Center for Veterans Studies—University of Utah	x		
National Center on Addiction and Substance Abuse at Columbia University			x
National Coalition for Mental Health Recovery			x
National Council for Community Behavioral Health Care			x
National Council of State Legislatures			x
National Council on Alcoholism and Drug Dependence			x
National Council on Patient Information and Education			x
National Football League Corporate		x	
National Football League Players Association		x	
National Governors Association			x

Table D.22—Continued

Partners (N = 716)	RWC	VCL and MTC	Recovery Month
National Guard Association of the United States		x	
National Highway Traffic Safety Administration			x
National Hispanic Medical Association			x
National Institute of Mental Health		x	
National Institute on Alcohol Abuse and Alcoholism			x
National Institute on Drug Abuse			x
National Latino Behavioral Health Association			x
National Network of Depression Centers	x		
National Organization of Veterans' Advocates		x	
National Organization on Fetal Alcohol Syndrome			x
National Resource Directory	x		
National Rural Health Association		x	
National Safety Council			x
Navy Exchange		x	
Navy Marine Corps Health Promotion & Wellness	x		
Navy Operational Stress Control Program (OPNAV N171)	x		
Navy Wounded Warrior Safe Harbor		x	
NBC 6 South Florida		x	
Network for the Improvement of Addiction Treatment (NIATx)			x
New Directions for Veterans	x		
New England Center for Homeless Veterans	x		
New Vision House of Hope—Supportive Services for Veteran Families		x	
New York City Department of Health and Mental Hygiene			x
New York Islanders		x	
New York State Office on Alcoholism and Substance Abuse Services			x
New York State Office of Mental Health		x	
Newport Academy and Recovery Living			x
NextGen MilSpouse		x	
Non Commissioned Officers Association		x	
Norman Music Festival		x	
North Carolina Mental Health Consumers' Organization		x	

Table D.22—Continued

Partners (*N* = 716)	RWC	VCL and MTC	Recovery Month
North Carolina Psychiatric Association		x	
North Dakota Suicide Prevention Program	x		
Northern Ohio Recovery Association			x
Not a Supermom		x	
NY MetroVets		x	
Oakland Athletics		x	
Office of National Drug Control Policy			x
Office of Science Policy and Communications (NIDA)			x
Ohio Department of Mental Health and Addiction Services		x	
Oklahoma Citizen Advocates for Recovery and Treatment Association			x
Oklahoma City Thunder		x	
Old Dominion University—Military Connection Center		x	
One Vet One Voice		x	
Only Passionate Curiosity		x	
Operation Climb On	x		
Operation College Promise	x		
Operation Gratitude	x		
Operation Live Well	x		
Operation Revamp	x		
Operation Second Chance	x		
Operation UNITE			x
Orchard Recovery			x
Oregon International Air Show		x	
Organized 31		x	
Outreach and Program Development, Two Dreams Outer Banks			x
Oxford House			x
Pace University		x	
Panama City Beach Motorcycle Rally		x	
Paralyzed Veterans of America		x	
Partners in Care		x	
Partnership at Drugfree.org			x
Pat Tillman Foundation		x	
Patriot PAWS Service Dogs	x		
Patriot Rovers		x	
Pawsitive Perspectives Assistance Dogs	x		
Peak Military Care Network	x		

Table D.22—Continued

Partners (N = 716)	RWC	VCL and MTC	Recovery Month
Peerlink National Technical Assistance Center Mental Health America of Oregon			x
PenFed Foundation		x	
Peninsula Health Concepts, Door to Hope			x
Pennsylvania Coalition Against Domestic Violence		x	
Pennsylvania Department of Health			x
Pennsylvania Department of Military and Veterans Affairs		x	
Pennsylvania Mental Health Consumers' Association		x	
Pennsylvania Psychiatric Society		x	
Pennsylvania Psychological Association		x	
Pennsylvania Society for Clinical Social Work		x	
Pepsi Gulf Coast Jam		x	
Pets for Vets	x		
Philadelphia Eagles		x	
Philadelphia Flyers		x	
Phoenix Coyotes		x	
Phoenix House		x	
Pin-Ups for Vets		x	
Pittsburgh Penguins		x	
Pittsburgh Pirates		x	
Poison Control Program			x
Portland State University, Graduate School of Social Work			x
Prevention Partnership International, Celebrating Families!			x
PRO-ACT, Bucks County Council on Alcoholism and Drug Dependence			x
Program for Anxiety and Traumatic Stress	x		
Project Lips		x	
Project New Hope Massachusetts	x		
Project Welcome Home Troops	x		
Psychology Today			x
Puerto Rico Addiction Research Foundation			x
Queens College		x	
R4 Alliance	x		
Ramble Jam		x	
Ramblings of a Marine Wife		x	
Randerson Cares: Senior Care Management and Consulting Services			x

Table D.22—Continued

Partners (*N* = 716)	RWC	VCL and MTC	Recovery Month
RASE (Recovery, Advocacy, Service, Empowerment) Project			x
Reach Out Recovery, Rehabilitation Productions			x
Real Jei		x	
Reality House			x
Reasons to HOPE Foundation, DC Peer Support Association			x
Reclaiming Futures			x
Recovering Your Body			x
Recovery Alliance			x
Recovery Connection			x
Recovery Consultants of Atlanta			x
Recovery Is Happening			x
Recovery People			x
Recovery People, SoberHood			x
Recovery Redefined			x
Recovery Resources Consulting			x
RecoveryNC & Oxford House			x
RecruitMilitary		x	
Reese's Senior Bowl		x	
Renew Media			x
Reserve Officers Association of the United States	x		
ReserveAid	x		
Resource Training Center Recovery & Life Coaching Academy DYSO (Do You See Opportunity?)			x
ReStart Human Services			x
Restart			x
Returning Veterans Project	x		
Rhode Island Communities for Addiction Recovery Efforts Inc.			x
Richmond Flying Squirrels		x	
Ride 2 Recovery		x	
Rio Rancho Family Healthcare Center		x	
Rob Riggle		x	
Rock 'n' Roll Expo		x	
Rockland Independent Living Center			x
Rockstar Superstar Project			x
Rolling Thunder		x	
Ryan Pitts		x	

Table D.22—Continued

Partners (N = 716)	RWC	VCL and MTC	Recovery Month
Sagebrush			x
Salvation Army		x	
SAMHSA	x		
SAMHSA, Center for Mental Health Services			x
SAMHSA, Center for Substance Abuse Treatment			x
SAMHSA Office of the Administrator			x
San Diego Padres		x	
San Francisco Giants		x	
San Francisco Suicide Prevention		x	
San Jose Earthquakes		x	
Saratoga WarHorse	x		
Seattle Mariners		x	
Second Road			x
Senior Synergy Expo, Tarrant County Texas		x	
Serving Together	x		
SHARE! the Self-Help and Recovery Exchange			x
Shoulder 2 Shoulder		x	
Sierra Club—Military Families and Veterans Initiative	x		
SimplyEJ		x	
Sir Charles Cary			x
Slick Housewives		x	
SMART Recovery			x
Snowball Express		x	
Sobriety TV			x
Soldier's Wife, Crazy Life		x	
Southern Methodist University MilVets		x	
Special Operations Medical Association		x	
Spokane Shock		x	
Spouse Deployed	x		
SpouseBox		x	
Spring Reins of Life	x		
Sprint		x	
St. Louis Blues		x	
St. Louis Cardinals		x	
St. Louis Rams		x	
Star Behavioral Health Providers	x		
Stars, Stripes, & Hearts	x		
State of Connecticut Department of Mental Health and Addiction Services		x	

Table D.22—Continued

Partners (N = 716)	RWC	VCL and MTC	Recovery Month
State of New Mexico Department of Cultural Affairs—New Mexico Arts Veterans' Program		x	
State of New Mexico Department of Veterans' Services		x	
State of New Mexico Human Services Department—Behavioral Health Services Division		x	
Step Up for Soldiers	x		
Steppin' Out Radio, Powerful Radio Productions			x
Stepping Stones			x
Stewart-Marchman-Act Behavioral Healthcare			x
Still Serving Veterans	x		
Stop Soldier Suicide	x		
Student Veterans Association at University of Louisville		x	
Student Veterans Association at University of Minnesota		x	
Substance Use Disorders, OptumHealth Behavioral Solutions			x
Suicide Prevention Resource Center	x		
Suicide Prevention Resource Center, Education Development Center			x
Support for Addictions Prevention and Treatment in Africa			x
Supportive Services for Veteran Families		x	
Swords to Plowshares	x		
Synergies, National Inhalant Prevention Coalition			x
Synergy Enterprises			x
Talk Therapy Television			x
Tampa Bay Rays		x	
Task & Purpose		x	
Team River Runner—Atlanta	x		
Team Rubicon		x	
Team Rubicon–Region III		x	
Technical Assistance Center of Doors to Wellbeing, Copeland Center of Wellness and Recovery			x
TechnoTherapy.org			x
Tee It Up for the Troops	x		
Teen Challenge International USA			x
TeenCentral.net	x		
Texas A&M University—Veteran Resource and Support Center		x	
Texas Recovers!			x

Table D.22—Continued

Partners (N = 716)	RWC	VCL and MTC	Recovery Month
Texas Suicide Prevention		x	
Thunder over Louisville		x	
TogetherWeServed		x	
Total Administrative Services Corporation			x
Towson University—Student Veterans Center		x	
Toyota Grand Prix of Long Beach		x	
Traitmarker Publishing		x	
Trans Lifeline		x	
Transforming Youth Recovery			x
Transgender American Veterans Association		x	
Trauma and Resiliency Resources	x		
Treatment Communities of America			x
Turning Point			x
Twin County Recovery Services			x
Ty Herndon		x	
Under Armour		x	
United Advocates for Children and Families			x
United Services Automobile Association		x	
United Through Reading	x		
United Way		x	
United Way of Northwest Connecticut		x	
UnitedHealthcare		x	
University of Baltimore, School of Law			x
University of California, Irvine—Veteran Services		x	
University of Colorado, Denver—Veteran Student Services		x	
University of Delaware—Blue Hen Veterans		x	
University of Missouri—Kansas City			x
University of New Mexico—Veterans Resource Center and Student Veterans of America Chapter		x	
University of Tennessee—Knoxville		x	
U.S. Agency for International Development, Office of HIV/AIDS			x
U.S. Chamber of Commerce Foundation		x	
U.S. Department of Transportation			x
U.S. Drug Enforcement Administration			x
U.S. Psychiatric and Mental Health Congress		x	
USMC Life		x	
Utah Jazz		x	

Table D.22—Continued

Partners (N = 716)	RWC	VCL and MTC	Recovery Month
VA National Center for PTSD	x		
VA OEF, OIF Outreach Teams	x		
Vanderbilt University Athletics		x	
Vectren Dayton Air Show		x	
Velvet-Rose.net		x	
Verizon Communications		x	
Veteran Artist Program	x		
Veteran eMentor Program		x	
Veterans Helping Veterans Now	x		
Veterans in Film & Television		x	
Veterans Moving Forward		x	
Veterans Multi-Service Center		x	
Veterans of Foreign Wars		x	
Veterans of Foreign Wars—Department of New York		x	
Veterans Victory Velo		x	
Veterans Yoga Project	x		
VeteransPlus	x		
VetJobs, VetEagle		x	
Vets 360	x		
Via Hope Texas Mental Health		x	
Vietnam Veterans of America		x	
Virginia Department of Veterans Services		x	
Voices of Recovery San Mateo County			x
Volunteers of America			x
Walgreens		x	
Walla Walla Sweets		x	
Walmart		x	
Warrior 360		x	
Warrior Care Policy	x		
Warrior Family Community Partnership	x		
Warrior Salute	x		
Warrior Transition Command	x		
Warriors for Freedom Foundation	x		
Washington Nationals		x	
Washington Redskins Fit Fest		x	
Waste Management Phoenix Open		x	
Welcome Home Program		x	
Wells Fargo		x	

Table D.22—Continued

Partners (N = 716)	RWC	VCL and MTC	Recovery Month
Wendy Davis		x	
Westmoreland County Air Show		x	
White Bison			x
White Bison in Wellbriety			x
Whole Health Peer Workforce Development, Georgia Mental Health Consumer Network			x
Wildlight Productions			x
Window on the World		x	
Wings over North Georgia		x	
Women Veterans of New Mexico		x	
Work First Foundation	x		
Wounded Warrior Project		x	
Wounded Warrior Prosperity Fair		x	
WSMV Channel 4 Nashville		x	
Yellow Ribbon Registry Network	x		
You Matter	x		
Young People in Recovery			x
Young Professionals in Foreign Policy—Connect Veterans	x		
Youth Move National			x
Zero to Three	x		

NOTE: The total number of partner organizations listed here and the total number listed in the outreach activities table (Table D.17) may be slightly different because we counted only unique organizations in the outreach table (e.g., NAMI California and NAMI Texas were listed only once as NAMI in the outreach table).

Website Engagement

To better understand the types of resources and materials that users interacted with most, we looked at the top ten pages viewed, downloads, and videos watched in 2015, as already detailed in Table D.3. To assess user engagement with campaign websites, we analyzed the following metrics: bounce rate, page views, average session duration, and average page views per session.

Top Ten Page Views, Downloads, and Video Views

Real Warriors Campaign

The most-visited RWC pages contained a mix of mental health and non-mental health–related content. The RWC site page with the most page views (nearly 60,000), was a page on the military-to-civilian employment transition (Figure D.1). Although this page is not directly related to mental health, this transition can serve as a stressor that may be associated with mental health problems. The second most-viewed page was the RWC homepage, containing links to many resources throughout the site. Several other pages in the top ten are directly related to mental health

Figure D.1
Real Warriors Campaign: Top Ten Pages Viewed, 2015

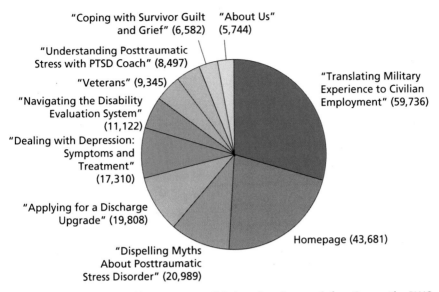

"Coping with Survivor Guilt and Grief" (6,582)

"About Us" (5,744)

"Understanding Posttraumatic Stress with PTSD Coach" (8,497)

"Veterans" (9,345)

"Navigating the Disability Evaluation System" (11,122)

"Dealing with Depression: Symptoms and Treatment" (17,310)

"Applying for a Discharge Upgrade" (19,808)

"Dispelling Myths About Posttraumatic Stress Disorder" (20,989)

"Translating Military Experience to Civilian Employment" (59,736)

Homepage (43,681)

NOTE: All webpages listed here are accessible by using the search function on the RWC homepage (Real Warriors, undated-b).
RAND RR1612-D.1

(e.g., dispelling myths about PTSD, dealing with depression, understanding posttraumatic stress, coping with survivor guilt and grief). Two other pages do not make extensive mention of mental health but may be of interest to service members who have experienced mental health conditions. Although the page does not specifically highlight information relevant to those with mental health diagnoses (relative to other diagnoses), "Navigating the Disability Evaluation System" (Real Warriors, undated-c) may be of interest to those with service-related psychological health problems. "Applying for a Discharge Upgrade" (Real Warriors, undated-a) may be of interest to those seeking mental health care despite having received an other-than-honorable discharge from the military.[1] The page contains one brief mention of a mental health–related topic, stating that

> In cases where the veteran believes post-traumatic stress disorder or another psychological health issue led to conduct resulting in the less than honorable discharge, it is important that the argument is supported with a properly worded medical opinion (Real Warriors, undated-a).

---

[1] In recent years, discussion has arisen around the issue of whether behavior that is symptomatic of mental health or substance use disorders leads to other-than-honorable discharges (also known as being discharged with "bad paper"). The American Public Health Association (2014) cites bad paper as a barrier to mental health care, and recent research indicates that those with bad paper have greater suicide risk (Reger et al., 2015).

The most-popular RWC downloads were brochures and infographics providing tools for finding resources and information. The RWC site had fewer than 2,000 file downloads of the top ten most-downloaded items in 2015 (Table D.23). The top nine downloads from the RWC site were brochures and infographics housed on the RWC campaign materials site (http://www.realwarriors.net/materials). Clicking on materials on that page redirects site visitors to the item location on www.scribd.com. These items are also available in HTML versions (though views of the HTML versions are not accounted for in the count of downloads in Table D.23). The top download is an infographic providing five steps to stay mission ready: (1) Find time for yourself, (2) break down obstacles, (3) get your physical training in, (4) avoid alcohol and substance misuse, and (5) identify people you can turn to. Many of the other top downloads are brochures highlighting tools for different target audiences. All brochures contain the following five tools: calling the DCoE Outreach Center, logging on to the RWC live chat, watching others tell their stories through the RWC multimedia page, sharing personal stories on the RWC forums, and receiving education by reading articles on the RWC site. The remaining tools varied by audience. For example, veterans were told to use their local Vet Center as a resource and to call MCL if needed. Other commonly downloaded items included background information about RWC and an app promotion kit targeted toward individuals aiming to promote apps available through DCoE that included sample tweets and blog posts for promoting awareness. At the time of writing, the app promotion kit could be located on the site only by searching for it specifically. RWC staff reported that the kit is available by request and is shared with program managers, partner organizations, and media looking for more information on how to discuss the app.

Table D.23
Real Warriors Campaign: Top Ten Downloads, 2015

Title	Type of Material	Number of Downloads
"5 Tips to Stay Mission Ready"	Infographic	672
"5 Tools That Reinforce Psychological Strength"	Brochure	209
"7 Tools That Reinforce Psychological Health" (for veterans)	Brochure	184
"7 Tools That Reinforce Psychological Strength" (for National Guard and reserve)	Brochure	160
"7 Tools to Reinforce Military Family Resilience"	Brochure	160
"Military Health Resources"	Infographic	160
"Real Warriors Campaign Overview"	Fact sheet	101
"Real Warriors Campaign Backgrounder"	Fact sheet	92
"7 Tools That Reinforce Warrior Resilience" (for active duty)	Brochure	76
"Real Warriors App Promo Kit"	Handout	65
Total downloads for top ten most downloaded		**1,879**

The most-popular RWC videos were profiles of service members, veterans, and their families. More than 10,000 views were tallied for the top ten most-viewed videos on the RWC site (Table D.24). Nine of the ten videos were profiles of service members, veterans, and family members discussing their experiences of mental health and substance use disorders, as well as challenges with reintegration after deployment or upon separation from service. These videos ranged in length from a few minutes to nearly half an hour. These videos are all available on the RWC video profiles page (Real Warriors, undated-e). Additionally, a video PSA about downloading the Real Warriors mobile app received more than 400 views. It is unclear whether videos were viewed in their entirety.

Make the Connection

The top ten most-viewed MTC pages were diverse in focus, featuring video profiles and pages providing information and resources. As illustrated earlier, the MTC site was viewed very often, and the top ten most-viewed pages were seen more than 2.5 million times (Figure D.2). Of the top ten pages viewed, two—a resources page and a page about PTSD—were viewed more than half a million times each (Figure D.2). Other items viewed frequently included pages featuring video profiles of individual veterans' experiences (e.g., "Brent's story"), information about anxiety and chronic pain, a video PSA encouraging Vietnam veterans to seek support, the MTC "Connect with Stories" page (a page that provides users with ways to promote positive conversations about mental health), and the MTC homepage.

The most-downloaded MTC materials were infographics and mental health awareness posters. About 1,800 file downloads of the top ten most-downloaded items occurred in 2015 (Table D.25). This is perhaps not surprising, given that the main focus of the MTC campaign was the video gallery, which is intended to be viewed and not downloaded. Most of the top downloaded items were infographics about PTSD,

Table D.24
Real Warriors Campaign: Top Ten Video Views, 2015

Video	Number of Views
Staff Sgt. Stacy Pearsall Profile	2,361
Sgt. Maj. Raymond Chandler Profile	2,039
First Sgt. Simon Sandoval Profile	1,589
Real Warriors and Psychological Health Profile	1,516
Real Warriors and Reintegration Profile	927
Download the Real Warriors App	442
First Sgt. Aaron Tippett Profile	426
Real Warriors and Families Profile	347
Maj. Ed Pulido Profile	303
Sgt. Josh Hopper Profile	265
Total views for top ten most-viewed	**10,215**

Figure D.2
Make the Connection: Top Ten Pages Viewed, 2015

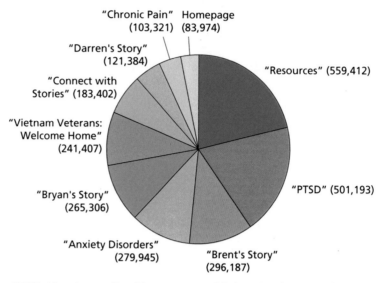

NOTE: All webpages listed here are accessible by using the search function on the MTC homepage (Make the Connection, undated).
RAND RR1612-D.2

Table D.25
Make the Connection: Top Ten Downloads, 2015

Title	Type of Material	Number of Downloads
"PTSD"	Infographic	624
"Depression"	Infographic	390
"Facebook Cover Photo Graphic 2"	Photo graphic	194
"Military Sexual Trauma"	Infographic	165
"Mental Health Awareness"	Poster	116
"Mental Health Awareness 1"	Poster	72
"Mental Health Awareness 2"	Poster	68
"Make the Connection"	e-book	67
"Information Card"	Handout	47
"Mental Health Awareness 4"	Poster	44
Total downloads of top ten most downloaded items		**1,787**

depression, and military sexual trauma or mental health awareness cards. The other items were various outreach materials, including a Facebook cover photo, an e-book, and an information card.

The most-viewed MTC videos were veteran profiles and PSAs. The top ten most-viewed MTC videos garnered more than 1.4 million views (Table D.26). Given

Table D.26
Make the Connection: Top Ten Video Views, 2015

Video	Number of Views
"There Was a Time When There Was Just No Laughing"	394,969
"When the Welcome Home Fades 30 Second"	239,867
"We Are All in This Together"	191,650
"Leading and Living Strong After Facing Adversity"	182,203
"Vietnam Veterans: Welcome Home 60 Second"	121,133
"When the Welcome Home Fades 60 Second"	96,400
"Righting the Course After Money and Legal Trouble"	63,960
"Veteran Strength and Connection Public Service Announcement 60 Second"	53,966
"It Has Motivated Me to Keep My Head High"	46,909
"Veteran Strength and Connection Public Service Announcement 30 Second"	37,644
Total views of top ten most-viewed items	**1,428,701**

the focus of MTC on developing a video gallery, the high number of views is expected. Half of the top ten videos are video profiles of individual veterans' experiences that range in length from about three to seven minutes. The other half of the top ten videos are briefer PSAs that range from 30 to 60 seconds in length.

Veterans Crisis Line
The most-viewed VCL pages were the homepage, a resource locator, Power of 1 materials, and pages related to the confidential chat. The top ten most-viewed VCL pages garnered more than 1.3 million views (Figure D.3). The most-viewed pages fell largely into three categories. The first was the VCL homepage. The second category included pages related to the Power of 1, a set of campaign materials aiming to promote support of veterans and the message that "One click, one call, one text—one life. One small act can make a big difference in the life of a Veteran or Service member in crisis." The third category included pages related to the confidential veterans chat, a chat function that is available around the clock to help veterans in crisis. Additional pages in the top ten included a resource location that helps site visitors find resources near them and a landing page for site visitors who are veterans.

  Outreach items were the most popular downloads from the VCL site. The top ten items were downloaded more than 7,000 times (Table D.27). These items were mostly outreach materials, such as fact sheets, wallet cards, graphics, newsletters, and guidelines for partners around messaging. In addition, graphics containing customized messages of support and intended for use on social media were downloaded 1,685 times. These graphics were created using the VCL Graphic Generator tool (Veterans Crisis Line, undated-a).

Figure D.3
Veterans Crisis Line: Top Ten Pages Viewed, 2015

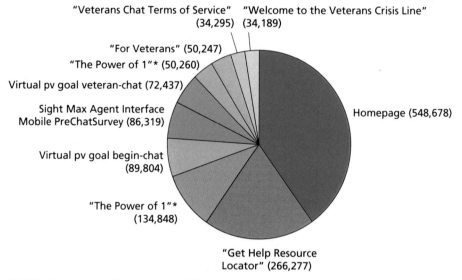

SOURCE: Data provided to authors by VCL via spreadsheet.
* The URLs corresponding to these items differed only by letter case and were tracked separately by Google Analytics. Content at these URLs was likely very similar.
RAND RR1612-D.3

Table D.27
Veterans Crisis Line: Top Ten Downloads, 2015

Title or Type of Material	Number of Downloads
"Veterans Crisis Line Public Fact Sheet"	1,497
Graphic Generator Square	1,250
"VCL Spread the Word"	919
VCL partner messaging guidelines	867
VCL wallet card 2	572
VCL social media graphic	461
Graphic Generator Wide	435
VCL wallet card 1	429
Suicide Prevention Month Outreach Newsletter	409
Power of 1 newsletter content	374
Total downloads of top ten items	**7,213**

The VCL site contains embedded videos (Veterans Crisis Line, undated-c). However, because the videos are hosted by other entities, such as the Veterans Health Administration, Medal of Honor, and Blue Star Families, no viewing data were provided.

National Recovery Month

The most-viewed Recovery Month pages and most downloaded items focused on promotion of Recovery Month. The top ten most-viewed pages on the Recovery Month site garnered approximately 140,000 views. The most-viewed page was the homepage (Figure D.4). Many of the other most-viewed materials (e.g., banners, logos, flyers; toolkit; event calendars; PSAs) were pages intended to promote Recovery Month, many of which target organizers of Recovery Month events in their area. Other items in the top ten include information about Recovery Month and personal stories of recovery.

The Recovery Month site makes resources available to individuals organizing Recovery Month events in their area. The top ten most downloaded items all met this purpose (see Table D.28). Of the 17,520 downloads of the top ten most downloaded items, 10,219 of these were of the Recovery Month Toolkit (the full kit or sections of it). Other top ten downloads included web banners, logos, posters, and flyers for promoting Recovery Month.

The streaming media on the Recovery Month site was not viewed very frequently. The top ten videos were viewed 1,231 times in 2015 (see Table D.29). Although the URLs were inactive at the time of writing, the top ten most-viewed videos appeared to be episodes of the Road to Recovery series from prior years.

Figure D.4
National Recovery Month: Top Ten Pages Viewed, 2015

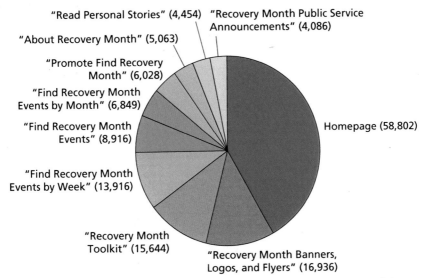

NOTE: All webpages listed here are accessible from the National Recovery Month homepage (National Recovery Month, undated).

RAND RR1612-D.4

Table D.28
National Recovery Month: Top Ten Downloads, 2015

Title or Type of Material	Downloads
Recovery Month toolkit	4,527
Recovery Month web banners	2,097
Recovery Month logos	1,861
Recovery Month poster	1,687
Recovery Month flyer	1,656
Recovery Month toolkit data visualizations	1,655
Recovery Month toolkit section fast facts	1,470
Recovery Month toolkit section media outreach	1,175
Recovery Month toolkit section targeted outreach	744
Recovery Month toolkit section voices for recovery	648
Total downloads of top ten items	17,520

Table D.29
National Recovery Month: Top Ten Video Views (as of July 21, 2016)

URL	Views
http://www.recoverymonth.gov/ASF1/Web/RecoveryMonth/2011/April/11-0403_R2R_PrevEarlyIntervFINAL.wmv	443
http://www.recoverymonth.gov/asf1/Web/RecoveryMonth/2012/June/R2R2012_FamilyShow.wmv	424
http://www.recoverymonth.gov/ASF1/3CSAT/R2R-06/06-0705Justiceshow.wmv	127
http://www.recoverymonth.gov/asf1/Web/RecoveryMonth/2012/April/R2R_ResearchShow_Final.wmv	54
http://www.recoverymonth.gov/ASF1/Web/RecoveryMonth/2011/April/11-0428_PreventionShow_FINAL_ApprovedRevision.wmv	51
http://www.recoverymonth.gov/ASF1/Web/RecoveryMonth/2011/June/RecoverySupportShow.wmv	30
http://www.recoverymonth.gov/asf1/Web/RecoveryMonth/2012/May/R2R2012_YouthShow.wmv	30
http://www.recoverymonth.gov/ASF1/Web/RecoveryMonth/2011/September/11-0901_R2R_TraumaShow.wmv	27
http://www.recoverymonth.gov/ASF1/Web/RecoveryMonth/2007/07-0404R2Ralcoholshow SP.wmv	26
http://www.recoverymonth.gov/asf1/Web/RecoveryMonth/2010/R2R2010_ResiliencyShow_FINALexp.wmv	19

Cross-Agency Commonalities in Top Ten Page Views, Downloads, and Video Views

Looking across the items that were most frequently viewed and downloaded yields some insight into the types of information with which site users are likely to engage (Table D.30).

At least three campaigns' most-viewed pages focused on outreach, navigation to resources, and testimonials. As would be expected, the homepage for all campaigns was one of the most frequently viewed pages. Three of the four campaigns' most-viewed pages included ones focused on outreach and the provision of promotional information; information about navigating services, benefits, or resources; and testimonials or recovery stories. Two campaigns' most-viewed pages included information about mental health and/or substance use disorders.

Across campaigns, the most-downloaded items focused on outreach and promotion. The majority of all four campaigns' top downloads were for these materials. Infographics were also some of the top downloaded items for RWC and MTC.

Table D.30
Cross-Campaign Comparison of Most-Frequent Page Views, Downloads, and Video Views

Interaction	RWC	MTC	VCL	Recovery Month	Across Campaigns
Page views					
Outreach or promotional	1	0	2	8	11
Service, benefit, resource navigation	3	1	5	0	9
Mental health or substance use info	4	2	0	0	6
Homepage	1	1	2	1	5
Testimonial or recovery story	1	2	1	0	4
Other page	0	4	0	1	5
Downloads					
Outreach or promotional	8	7	10	10	35
Infographic	2	3	0	0	5
Video views					
Testimonial or recovery story	6	5	—[a]	0	11
PSA	0	5	—[a]	0	5
Other video	4	0	—[a]	10	14

[a] Because videos on the VCL site were hosted on other organizations' websites, no viewing data were provided.

We note that downloads represent only one way in which individuals can obtain campaign-related materials and that others may have been distributed through other channels (e.g., in-person engagement, ordering printed materials directly from campaigns rather than downloading and printing them).

Testimonial videos were some of the most-viewed items on the RWC and MTC sites. Video content varied across the three campaigns that provided viewing data (RWC, MTC, and Recovery Month). Many of the most-viewed videos for RWC and MTC were testimonials or stories of recovery from metal health or substance use problems. Recovery Month's most-viewed videos were from its Road to Recovery series—but because these videos were not available for viewing at the time of writing, we are unsure of their content.

Facebook Engagement

As outlined in Table D.31, the number of Facebook posts, interactions (i.e., cumulative likes, comments, and shares), and impressions were used to evaluate engagement with campaigns via Facebook. Campaigns actively posted messages or materials via Facebook to engage target audiences. MTC contributed the vast majority of total Facebook interactions, generating more than 9.5 million likes, comments, and shares in 2015. Of note, even though MTC issued the least number of Facebook posts, it generated the highest levels of interactions and impressions. This is likely due to MTC having a significantly larger number of Facebook fans but may also be an indication of MTC having more-engaging posts, a larger network, or more-engaged users.

With the exception of VCL, which does not employ Facebook, each campaign made several hundred posts in 2015, with an average number of 52 monthly posts for RWC, 17 for MTC, and 33 for Recovery Month (Table D.32).

Levels of Facebook interactions fluctuated greatly throughout the year for MTC (Table D.33). For example, peak engagement occurred in May with 1,716,060 likes, comments, and shares, whereas the lowest level of engagement occurred in September with 100,546 likes, comments, and shares. Recovery Month had the lowest number

Table D.31
Facebook Engagement Indicators, 2015

Campaign	Facebook Posts	Likes, Comments, and Shares	Impressions
RWC	629	633,334	19,046,756
MTC	203	9,510,703	941,786,500
VCL	—	—	—
Recovery Month	395	48,668	2,558,087
Total	1,227	10,192,705	963,391,343

Table D.32
Monthly Facebook Posts, 2015

Month	RWC	MTC	Recovery Month
January	44	16	16
February	45	15	25
March	49	18	39
April	52	17	38
May	52	26	31
June	55	14	40
July	53	15	31
August	52	15	32
September	77	15	38
October	44	17	37
November	48	19	31
December	58	16	37
Monthly mean	**52.42**	**16.92**	**32.92**

Table D.33
Monthly Facebook Likes, Comments, and Shares, 2015

Month	RWC	MTC	Recovery Month
January	19,193	949,305	965
February	21,094	954,672	1,383
March	14,748	555,010	2,721
April	21,694	994,445	3,774
May	19,889	1,716,060	2,305
June	11,710	1,292,384	2,010
July	20,573	1,724,338	1,836
August	16,094	186,910	2,623
September	27,108	100,546	25,856
October	31,260	290,380	2,648
November	398,282	431,141	910
December	31,689	315,512	1,637

of Facebook interactions, with a total of 48,668 likes, comments, and shares in 2015. For RWC and Recovery Month, a substantial proportion of its total Facebook interactions was concentrated within their peak months (Table D.33). RWC had a high of 398,282 interactions in November, which accounted for 63 percent of its total Facebook interactions in 2015. Recovery Month peak engagement occurred in September, with 25,856 likes, comments, and shares, which made up 53 percent of Recovery Month's total Facebook interactions in 2015 (Table D.33).

Correspondingly, MTC was responsible for most of the total Facebook impressions generated by campaigns in 2015 (Table D.34). MTC was recorded as having content from its Facebook page shown nearly 942 million times to other Facebook accounts. May was the peak month, with the greatest number of Facebook impressions for MTC (148,393,510 impressions). As found with Facebook interactions, RWC and Recovery Month had a substantial proportion of their total Facebook impressions concentrated within its peak months (Table D.34). In 2015, Recovery Month had a peak of 1,078,427 Facebook impressions in September, which composed 42 percent of its total impressions. RWC had a peak of 6,857,168 impressions in November, which constituted 36 percent of its total impressions.

YouTube Engagement

Indicators of YouTube engagement included average view duration, the number of likes and dislikes, favorites gained and lost, and subscribers gained and lost (Table D.35). Average view duration can be considered an indicator of level of engagement with

Table D.34
Monthly Facebook Impressions, 2015

Month	RWC	MTC	Recovery Month
January	515,458	129,861,160	90,871
February	747,599	123,898,970	135,578
March	488,144	70,767,080	180,097
April	642,034	103,092,890	172,582
May	1,570,989	148,393,510	125,700
June	1,141,969	89,598,310	120,410
July	833,296	106,763,860	112,776
August	1,327,602	58,752,250	161,911
September	1,268,477	39,990,070	1,078,427
October	791,546	20,159,900	174,843
November	6,857,168	26,591,200	77,985
December	2,862,474	23,917,300	126,907

Table D.35
YouTube Engagement Indicators, 2015

Campaign	Average View Duration (minutes)	Likes	Dislikes	Favorites Gained	Favorites Lost	Subscribers Gained	Subscribers Lost
RWC	3.6	42	1	8	0	12	0
MTC	1.3	6,269	2,565	631	74	6,918	1,586
Recovery Month	0.9	75	0	0	0	6	0

NOTE: VCL does not have a dedicated YouTube account and so is not included in the table.

videos. RWC had the longest average view duration, with 3.6 minutes. MTC and Recovery Month had average view durations of approximately 1 minute. This could be an indication that individuals were watching mostly videos that are of shorter duration or that individuals were only partially watching longer videos.

Likes or dislikes and favorites gained or lost can be considered indicators of more-active engagement, given that they are reflective of viewer feedback. Similarly, subscribers generally tend to be viewers who are more engaged and view content on a more regular basis. RWC and Recovery Month had fairly low levels of active engagement according to these indicators. Although MTC had higher levels of engagement overall, this included both positive and negative responses. Of those who responded to the respective engagement indicators, 29 percent expressed dislikes, 10 percent had removed a favorite video, and 19 percent had retracted their subscription.

Twitter Engagement

Only RWC and Recovery Month actively use official Twitter accounts to engage their target populations. In 2015, a total of 2,535 tweets were posted across the two campaigns (Table D.36). RWC had a total of 1,865 tweets, which amounts to an average of five tweets per day over the year, and Recovery Month had a total of 670 tweets, amounting to an average of two tweets daily. Little engagement was observed with respect to direct messages sent and received. For instance, RWC sent 14 direct mes-

Table D.36
Twitter Engagement Indicators, 2015

Campaign	Tweets	Direct Messages Sent	Direct Messages Received
RWC	1,865	14	46
Recovery Month	670	0	4

NOTE: MTC and VCL are not featured in the table because they do not actively employ Twitter to disseminate campaign resources.

sages and received 46 messages, while Recovery Month had no direct messages sent and only four direct messages received in all of 2015.

Campaign Users

Limited demographic information is available on the users of the mental health awareness campaigns. For this evaluation, we have demographic information (i.e., age and gender) for Facebook and YouTube reach and geographic location data for website (i.e., top city), Facebook (i.e., top six cities), and YouTube (i.e., top six states). Only RWC provided demographic data for Twitter.

Demographic Reach
Gender
RWC and MTC Facebook reach was nearly evenly split between males and females (Table D.37). In contrast, 72 percent of Recovery Month Facebook fans were female. Recovery Month has a higher proportion of female Facebook users compared with the overall Facebook user base, which is estimated to be 64 percent female (Fitzgerald, 2012); RWC and MTC have lower proportions. Similar patterns were observed for YouTube reach (Table D.38), with RWC and MTC achieving somewhat comparable reach across gender, while Recovery Month's YouTube reach included 68 percent female viewers. RWC and Recovery Month appear to have a greater proportion of female YouTube viewers relative to YouTube viewers overall, which is 46 percent female (Rashtchy et al., 2007). With respect to Twitter (Table D.39), approximately 36 percent of RWC users were female, lower than the 64 percent of overall Twitter users who are female (Fitzgerald, 2012).

Age
Viewers ages 18–24 years and 25–34 years composed 52 percent of RWC's total Facebook fans and 51 percent of total YouTube views. The majority of MTC Facebook fans (75 percent) were 45 or older, whereas 68 percent of MTC YouTube viewers were younger than 45. Recovery Month Facebook and YouTube reach was more evenly distributed across different age segments of the population.

The age distribution of adult U.S. Facebook users is as follows: 18–24 years, 16 percent; 25–34 years, 22 percent; 35–44 years, 19 percent; 45–54 years, 18 percent; 55–64 years, 15 percent; and 65 years or older, 10 percent (Hoelzel, 2015). A greater proportion of MTC Facebook users are in the upper age brackets of 45 years or older compared with this baseline distribution.

RWC, MTC, and Recovery Month have a significantly smaller proportion of YouTube viewers who are younger than 18 and a larger proportion of 18–34-year-olds compared with overall YouTube viewers—18 percent and 21 percent, respectively (Rashtchy et al., 2007).

Table D.37
Facebook Demographics, by Percentage

Organization	Gender		Age						
	Male	Female	13–17	18–24	25–34	35–44	45–54	55–64	65+
RWC	47	52	1	29	23	14	14	10	7
MTC	46	53	<1	7	7	10	20	28	27
Recovery Month	27	72	<1	6	21	24	24	17	8

NOTE: Numbers may not add to 100 because of rounding.

Table D.38
YouTube Demographics, by Percentage

Organization	Gender		Age						
	Male	Female	13–17	18–24	25–34	35–44	45–54	55–64	65+
RWC	45	55	1	19	32	17	16	10	5
MTC	57	43	1	22	27	18	11	10	11
Recovery Month	32	68	3	12	29	17	18	14	6

NOTE: Numbers may not add to 100 because of rounding.

Table D.39
Twitter Demographics, by Percentage

Campaign	Gender		Age						
	Male	Female	13–17	18–24	25–34	35–44	45–54	55–64	65+
RWC	64	36	1	4	22	30	25	14	4

Derived from monthly average estimates, the following is a breakdown of the percentage of RWC Twitter users by age group: 13–17 years, 1 percent; 18–24 years, 4 percent; 25–34 years, 22 percent; 35–44 years, 30 percent; 45–54 years, 25 percent; 55–64 years, 14 percent; and 65 years or older, 4 percent. A smaller proportion of RWC Twitter users were younger than 18 and a higher proportion were in the 35–44 range, compared with Twitter users overall (18 percent and 20 percent, respectively; Table D.39) (Statista, 2016).

Geographic Reach

Table D.40 lists the top ten states with the highest number of U.S. active duty service members, veterans, and general population individuals ages 18 or older. The geographic reach of each of the campaigns may correspond with where its target popula-

Table D.40
Ten States with the Largest Active Duty, Veteran, and Adult Populations, 2015

Rank	U.S. Active Duty		U.S. Veterans		U.S. Adults	
	Location	Population	Location	Population	Location	Population
1	California	155,051	California	1,851,470	California	29,526,000
2	Virginia	122,884	Texas	1,680,418	Texas	19,574,000
3	Texas	117,623	Florida	1,583,697	Florida	15,606,000
4	North Carolina	100,867	Pennsylvania	939,069	New York	15,437,000
5	Georgia	69,322	New York	892,221	Pennsylvania	9,924,000
6	Florida	60,095	Ohio	866,481	Illinois	9,833,000
7	Washington	57,926	Virginia	781,388	Ohio	8,901,000
8	Hawaii	49,519	North Carolina	775,020	Michigan	7,751,000
9	Colorado	37,731	Georgia	752,882	North Carolina	7,536,000
10	South Carolina	36,670	Illinois	721,575	Georgia	7,469,000

SOURCES: Office of the Deputy Assistant Secretary of Defense (Military Community and Family Policy), undated-a; National Center for Veterans Analysis and Statistics, 2014; U.S. Census Bureau, 2015a.

tion is most highly concentrated. For instance, we might expect the campaigns to have the greatest reach in California and Texas because these states have some of the highest numbers of each of the campaigns' target populations.

Table D.41 lists the cities with the most website sessions in 2015 for each campaign. We obtained data for only the top city with the greatest number of sessions because this was the process metric routinely collected and reported by campaigns. The top cities reached by MTC and VCL were located in states with the most-populous veteran populations. In contrast, the top cities reached by RWC and Recovery Month (New York and Washington, D.C., respectively) were not in the states that had the largest concentrations of their target audiences. Note that the city with the most VCL website sessions, Canadaigua, New York, is where the Veterans Integrated Service Network 2 Center of Excellence for Suicide Prevention is located, which houses VCL and its online chat.

Table D.42 provides information on the top six cities reached in 2015 by each of the campaigns' Facebook outreach efforts. Interestingly, three of the six top cities reached by RWC were outside of the continental United States (i.e., Puerto Rico, United Kingdom, and Nepal). However, campaign staff report that the high number of views originating in Nepal is not representative of typical campaign reach and is due to several posts going viral, combined with an error in the Facebook algorithm for page recommendations (Duthaler, 2016). Approximately 13 percent of active duty service members reside outside of the United States, with 6.7 percent in East Asia and 5.1 percent in Europe (Office of the Deputy Assistant Secretary of Defense, 2014). Moreover, data from the DoD Defense Manpower Data Center (undated-b) indicated that as of December 2015, less than 1 percent of active duty military

Table D.41
Top City Website Reach, 2015

Campaign	Top City	Website Sessions
RWC	New York, New York	7,067
MTC	Houston, Texas[a]	61,488
VCL	Canandaigua, New York[a]	77,780
Recovery Month	Washington, D.C.	5,129

NOTE: Each campaign provided website geographic data in a different format. RWC provided monthly data on the single top city and number of sessions. MTC provided monthly data on the top 25 cities and VCL on the top ten cities generating the most sessions. Recovery Month provided data on the city of origin for every session each month by state. To calculate the top city from which the most sessions originated for 2015, we identified the top six cities with the greatest number of sessions each month and summed the number of sessions of the cities over the year. The table reports the top city and estimated number of sessions over the year for each of the campaigns.

[a] City is in one of the ten states with the largest population targeted by the campaign.

Table D.42
Facebook Top Six Cities (average seven-day reach), 2015

Rank	RWC Location	Views	MTC Location	Views	Recovery Month Location	Views
1	San Juan, Puerto Rico	2,103	Houston, Texas[a]	46,972	Philadelphia, Pennsylvania[a]	172
2	London, United Kingdom	1,785	Chicago, Illinois[a]	43,961	New York, New York[a]	166
3	Chicago, Illinois	1,503	New York, New York[a]	40,261	Los Angeles, California[a]	156
4	New York, New York	1,472	Los Angeles, California[a]	40,174	Chicago, Illinois[a]	143
5	Kathmandu, Nepal[b]	1,285	San Antonio, Texas[a]	31,054	Houston, Texas[a]	134
6	Los Angeles, California[a]	1,275	Phoenix, Arizona	29,606	Boston, Massachusetts	106

NOTE: VCL does not maintain an active Facebook page.

[a] City is in one of the ten states with the largest population targeted by the campaign.

[b] Campaign staff report that the high number of views originating in Nepal is not representative of typical campaign reach and is due to several posts going viral, combined with an error in the Facebook algorithm for page recommendations.

were stationed in Puerto Rico (725 service members) and the United Kingdom (8,397 service members). Only one of the top six cities reached by RWC (i.e., Los Angeles) was located within a state with a large active duty population. For both

MTC and Recovery Month, the top five cities with the greatest Facebook reach were in states that had large numbers of their target populations.

As shown in Table D.43, the states with the greatest YouTube reach were more closely aligned to the states with the most-concentrated numbers of the targeted population across the campaigns. The top six states with the most MTC YouTube views were among the ten states with the highest number of U.S. veterans. For RWC and Recovery Month, four of the top six states with the most YouTube views were ones that had some of the largest numbers of active duty service members and U.S. adults.

Across all of the media platforms, Texas and New York tied for the most-frequent appearance on top ten lists (seven times each), followed by California (six times), and Illinois (four times).

Table D.43
YouTube Top Six States, 2015

	RWC		MTC		Recovery Month	
Rank	Location	Views	Location	Views	Location	Views
1	Virginia[a]	1,345	California[a]	410,267	California[a]	1,502
2	California[a]	1,308	Texas[a]	282,408	Georgia[a]	1,431
3	Maryland	690	New York[a]	175,254	Maryland	1,279
4	Texas[a]	690	Florida[a]	169,243	New York[a]	997
5	New York	499	Illinois[a]	114,096	Washington, D.C.	936
6	North Carolina[a]	461	Georgia[a]	100,919	Texas[a]	849

NOTE: VCL does not maintain an active YouTube page.

[a] City is in one of the ten states with the largest population targeted by the campaign.

Twitter Data Analysis Methods and Findings

We conducted an analysis of Twitter data to understand how people discuss mental health in social media contexts and how the campaigns are utilizing social media. Twitter provides a vast source of data on what people express outside of a research setting and one that covers a broad cross-section of American internet users (Duggan, 2015). The research questions that we seek to answer are as follows:

- Which mental health topics are characterized by positive and supportive discourse, and which are discussed in a stigmatizing way?
- What are the longitudinal trends in content and sentiment of Twitter conversation around mental health and mental health treatment?
- Do sentiment and topic changes correlate with Twitter activities of the campaigns being evaluated?

We analyzed Twitter data by developing a qualitative coding scheme for tweets that human researchers implemented for a sample of the data. We then used a machine-learning approach to extend this coding strategy to a large volume of Twitter data. Finally, we analyzed the large volume of machine-coded data to identify the structure of social ties between users and the communities to which they belong. This allowed us to understand what topics are being discussed, how much stigma is present, and who is speaking to whom about these issues.

Overview of Social Media Analysis Methods

The social media analysis work follows two parallel streams of analysis (Figure E.1). To analyze general mental health discourse on Twitter, we developed a search strategy of mental health–related keywords, sampled approximately 100 days between January 2009 and January 2016, and collected 13.4 million tweets. We then developed a qualitative coding scheme to describe the content of the general mental health tweets. A sample of tweets was coded by members of the research team. Then we applied machine-learning algorithms to allow a computer to code the remainder of the tweets. This allowed us to

Figure E.1
Twitter Data Analysis Process

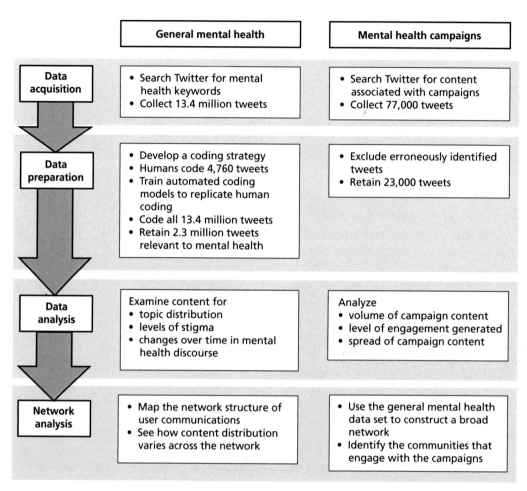

RAND RR1612-E.1

classify the categories of content that are shared online, how stigmatizing the content is, and how the relative volumes of these categories shift over time. Finally, we used our machine learning–filtered data to perform network analysis to identify "communities" using instances of Twitter users communicating directly with each other.

In parallel, we developed a search strategy to collect campaign-related tweets. The campaign search covered January 2012 through January 2016 and sampled 200 days. The timeline for the campaign search was selected because MTC became active in late 2011 and we wanted our sample of tweets to capture the period of time in which all campaigns were active. We then filtered and cleaned the campaign data and answered questions about volumes of campaign content and the level of popular engagement with the campaigns on Twitter. Finally, we used the resulting data set of general mental health tweets to identify which communities the campaigns are reaching.

Data Acquisition

Gathering Tweets About Mental Health

To understand Twitter discourse about mental health and the campaigns, we first developed a set of search terms to identify tweets related to mental health. We then used this search strategy to sample 200,000 tweets per day for 100 time points, approximately one day per month from January 2009 to February 2016. We sampled one random day per month, and two days for May and September. The additional days were selected to correspond to Mental Health Month in May and National Recovery Month in September. In 2009, we sampled three days per month because the data volumes were low at the start of the year and gradually grew to where we could reduce sampling to a single day. We also identified campaign-related terms and accounts and sampled 200 days of tweets by and about the campaigns. We sampled four days a month from January 2012 through January 2016. For the majority of our analyses, we focus on the text content of tweets, but date information is retained and used for longitudinal analysis. Twitter data were gathered using Gnip, a commercial data gathering tool. The details on how these steps were performed follow.

To collect data on the overall mental health discourse, we created search strings designed to capture tweets with mental health–relevant content. These strings were developed based on the expertise of the research team and a review of literature and other sources that discuss language used to describe mental health and illness. The initial set of search terms (Box E.1) included common terms for general mental illness, as well as disorder-specific language.

Box E.1
Initial Twitter Search Strategy

Hashtags Included in Search	Strings Included in Search
#mentalhealth	mental health
#depression	depression
#worldmentalhealthday	stigma
#WMHD2015	eating disorder
#nostigma	mental illness
#nostigmas	suicide
#eatingdisorders	ptsd
#suicide	addiction
#ptsd	bipolar
#mentalhealthawareness	
#mentalillness	
#stopsuicide	
#IAmStigmaFree	
#suicideprevention	
#MH	
#addiction	
#bipolar	
#stigma	

NOTE: MH = mental health

Using the initial set of search terms, we drew a sample of 400,000 tweets from three days of activity. We cleaned the content of the tweets by removing non–roman letter characters and combining variants of words to a single root (e.g., reducing "sandy" to "sand"). Using the cleaned sample, we computed the relative frequencies of individual words and used the R package *qdap* to compare those frequencies with the distribution found in a reference collection of 1 million tweets (Sanders Analytics, 2011). By comparing the two sets of frequencies, we identified the words that appeared 70 times more frequently in the sample of tweets than in Standard English. These words were reviewed by a member of the research team and, if deemed relevant to mental health, were retained as search terms in the final search strategy. If it was unclear whether the word was relevant to mental health, it was retained in the final set of search terms. After this review, we also added recovery-focused language to disorder-focused language. The literature we reviewed included negative terms used by teenagers to describe individuals with mental illness (Rose et al., 2007), as well as several phrases recommended by advocacy groups to describe individuals with mental illness (Disability Rights California, 2014). Using this updated search strategy, we collected another sample of tweets and identified problem terms. We found a number of terms that returned very large volumes of tweets that were not actually relevant to mental health. From these, we chose to remove the search terms "crazy," "stressed," "stress," and "freak." The final search strategy is presented in Boxes E.2 and E.3.

Gathering Campaign-Relevant Tweets

In order to identify tweets related to the campaigns being evaluated, we searched for the Twitter handles of all campaign accounts, the campaign names, and campaign-associated hashtags (Table E.1). MTC and VCL do not have campaign-associated Twitter handles and rely on the accounts of various government entities (such as VA) to disseminate their messages. We identified the key accounts intended to disseminate the content of those two campaigns, but we did not actively sample the data of those accounts because the majority of the content shared on those accounts was not focused on the campaigns being evaluated. We sampled four days per month from January 2012 to January 2016 for a total of 200 days.

Search Results and Working Data Sets

We collected a working data set of 13.4 million tweets possibly related to mental health by applying our search strategy across 128 days, from January 2009 through February 2016. We intended to sample 100 days but the lower data volumes in 2009 (when Twitter was still primarily an early adopter network) meant that we sampled time periods greater than a single day to get needed volumes of tweets. Once we used the machine-learning methods developed in the analytic step of this work to code every tweet for every variable of interest, we were able to filter the data to 2.3 million tweets relevant to mental health.

Box E.2
Final Twitter Search Strategy: Strings

abusive
addict
addiction
Alzheimer's
asylum
autism
bipolar
bonkers
brain damage
brain dead
breakdown
coping
demented
depressed
depression
deranged
difficulty learning
dignity
disabled
distressed
distressing
disturbed
disturbing
eating disorder
escaped from an
   asylum
few sandwiches short
   of a picnic basket

gone in the head
halfwit
hallucinating
hallucinations
hand fed
handicapped
head case
hurting yourself
in recovery
insane
intellectually
   challenged
learning difficulties
lived experience
living with addiction
living with alcoholism
living with depression
living with PTSD
loony
loony bin
lunatic
madness
manic depression
mass murderers
mental
mental health
mental health
   challenges

mental hospital
mental illness
mental institution
mentally challenged
mentally
   handicapped
mentally ill
no-one upstairs
not all there
not quite there
not the sharpest knife
   in the drawer
numscull
nutcase
nuts
nutter
nutty as a fruitcake
OCD
off their rocker
operational stress
out of it
padded cells
paranoid
pedophile
perverted
psychiatric
psychiatric health
psychiatrist

psycho
psychopath
PTSD
recovery
retard
schizo
schizophrenia
schizophrenic
screw loose
screwed
self-control
self-determination
self-harm
shock syndrome
sick in the head
simpleton
split personality
stigma
strait jackets
stress
suicide
therapist
therapy
wheelchair jockey
window licker
you belong in a home

NOTE: OCD = obsessive compulsive disorder.

Box E.3
Final Twitter Search Strategy: Hashtags

#1SmallAct
#AA
#abuse
#addiction
#adhd
#alcoholism
#alzheimers
#anxiety
#bipolar
#bpd
#depressed
#depression
#eatingdisorders
#endthestigma
#IAmStigmaFree

#mentalhealth
#mentalhealthawareness
#mentalhealthmatters
#mentalillness
#MH
#mhchat
#mhsm
#nostigma
#nostigmas
#ocd
#Operationalstress
#presspause
#psychology
#pts
#ptsd

#schizophrenia
#shellshock
#spsm
#stigma
#stopsuicide
#stress
#suicide
#suicideprevention
#therapy
#trauma
#wellbeing
#WMHD2015
#worldmentalhealthday

NOTE: AA = Alcoholics Anonymous; adhd = attention deficit hyperactivity disorder; bpd = bipolar disorder; mhsm = mental health and social media; spsm = suicide prevention via social media.

Table E.1
Campaign-Related Twitter Search Strategy

Campaign	Account	Hashtags
RWC	@realwarriors	
MTC		#ConnectWith
VCL		#VeteransCrisisLine, #ThePowerof1
Recovery Month	@RecoveryMonth	#RecoveryMonth

For the campaign-relevant tweet data set, we collected 77,000 tweets across 200 days between 2012 and 2016. After manual examination of the data set, we realized that the phrase "make the connection" is not only the name of one of the campaigns of interest but also a common colloquial phrase. This resulted in more than 50,000 tweets that were identified as campaign-related but were, in fact, parts of unrelated conversations. To address this, we excluded all tweets that were selected into the data set based on the "make the connection" string that did not also include the roots "vet" or "mil" in the tweet. The resulting body of 23,000 campaign-relevant tweets came from 196 days sampled from January 2012 through December 2015. Among the campaign-related tweets, 2,800 originated from official government-affiliated accounts that publicize campaign content, and 20,800 from users who were not identified as having an affiliation with campaign-related channels.

Development of Coding Scheme

Having used our string-based search strategy to establish a working data set of 13.4 million tweets likely to be relevant to mental health, we wanted to filter the data into what was actually relevant and what was erroneously identified, as well as to characterize the content. We first developed a hand-coding scheme for categorizing the content of the tweets. Building a hand-coded example data set is how large volumes are typically classified with the use of supervised machine learning.[1] We identified the kind of tweet characteristics that were of interest, developed a guideline to identify said characteristics, and then had a team of three coders apply the qualitative coding guidelines to a subset of tweets ($n = 4,760$). We refer to this set of tweets as our training data set because once coded, this data set was used as an input to train our algorithm to automatically code the full data set of tweets (a process described in more detail later). We worked with the coding team iteratively, clarifying and refining the coding guidelines while working to maximize interrater reliability. Table E.2 contains the guidelines and examples of coding for mental health relevance, type of content, mental health stigma, and topic.

---

[1]   For a definition of supervised learning, see Kohavi and Provost (1998). For a classic example of supervised learning for spam message identification and the need for training data, see Benevenuto et al. (2010).

Coders first coded the tweets in the training data set for mental health relevance, and if a tweet was identified as not relevant to mental health, no further coding was conducted for that tweet. Tweets coded as somewhat or highly relevant were coded for all subsequent categories. Tweets were then coded for their type of content and the topic of the tweet (Table E.2). The type of content and topic categories were not mutually exclusive, and a tweet could be coded as a 1 for multiple categories. The type-of-content codes focused on capturing the nature of the content of the tweet (e.g., whether it described self-relevant information or provided information of general interest). The topic codes were designed to capture whether tweets discussed a wide variety of conditions and disorders. Several topics that were of interest (ADHD, domestic and child abuse, traumatic brain injury) were initially included in the coding scheme but did not appear in the training data set. In the early phases of coding, we

Table E.2
Tweet Coding Scheme

Category	Description	Binary Code	Example
Mental health–relevant			
Relevance	• Ambiguous, colloquial mental health–related language (somewhat relevant) • Explicit, clinically appropriate mental health–related language (highly relevant)	Not relevant = 0 Relevant = 1	• RT @[username][a]: Talking to your BEST FRIEND is sometimes all the therapy you need • RT @[username]: Another bright light snuffed out by the deadly disease of addiction . . . There is help! #RipCoryMonteith #GoneTooSoon
Type of content (only applied for tweets coded as mental health–relevant)			
Appropriation	• Misuse of mental health language—describing states not related to mental health, describing concepts or things	Absent = 0 Present = 1	I am becoming a tums addict again
Information	• Information, data, opinion, advocacy info on mental health • Impartial and factual information related to mental health	Absent = 0 Present = 1	We need #PeerSupport workers in all MH team who are the voice that speaks positively of hope and recovery, regardless of what has gone before
Mental health resources	• References to resources that are useful to individuals suffering mental health conditions	Absent = 0 Present = 1	RT @[username]: Suicide Hotline: 1-800-273-8255 a simple reTweet, might save someone's life.
Other-focused	• Tweets that are discussing a specific person or persons other than the author • A general abstract "other" is not coded in this category	Absent = 0 Present = 1	Even Though Jordan Is Like 3 Days From Insane, She's The Best Girl I Know.
Self-focused	• Tweets that discuss the author	Absent = 0 Present = 1	Still #depressed. Can't bring myself to do anything #bipolar

Table E.2—Continued

Category	Description	Binary Code	Example
Topic (only applied for tweets coded as mental health–relevant)			
Addiction	General discussion of addiction states	Absent = 0 Present = 1	Addiction is a serious disease; it will end with jail, mental institutions, or death if you do not get professional help.
Anxiety	Anxiety as mental health status or anxiety as descriptor	Absent = 0 Present = 1	RT @[username]: Who struggles with depression or anxiety? I feel like more people do than we all realize.
Autism	Autism disorder or autism as descriptor	Absent = 0 Present = 1	RT @[username]: Fantastic pulls-no-punches article from Mayada Elsabbagh on A Global Vision for Autism Research https://t.co/UUgxv0NjdQ
Bipolar disorder	Bipolar disorder or bipolar disorder as descriptor	Absent = 0 Present = 1	@[username] yeh..ppl are bipolar with their opinions of her
Depression	Depression as disorder or depression as descriptor of emotional state	Absent = 0 Present = 1	The only problem is that staying in leads to making me all depressed and shizz.
Developmental disability	Mental or learning disability or mental or learning disability as descriptor	Absent = 0 Present = 1	Have you ever been discriminated against at Wilson for your mental illness, learning disability, or physical disability?
General mental health	No explicit condition, focus on mental health in general	Absent = 0 Present = 1	RT @[username]: BACA fights again racism in mental health services at the grassroots and the new DSM.
Military- or veteran-related mental health concerns	Any mental health topic related to military service members or veterans	Absent = 0 Present = 1	RT @[username]: MoD confirms more British soldiers commit suicide than are killed in battle http://t.co/1ElLDKrg83
OCD	Obsessive-compulsive disorder or use of as descriptor	Absent = 0 Present = 1	My boss has OCD. Lord..
PTSD	Posttraumatic stress disorder used as descriptor	Absent = 0 Present = 1	@[username]: PTSD effects all the family, please support @[username], supporting Veterans, vital work being done http://t.co/YVa50lCVcB
Recovery	Focus on a return to health after mental illness or addiction disorder	Absent = 0 Present = 1	We need #[username] workers in all MH team who are the voice that speaks positively of hope and recovery, regardless of what has gone before
Substance use (alcohol)	Use and misuse of alcohol	Absent = 0 Present = 1	Survey of 663 published in J Addict Dis April 2012: Great Recession begun in 2010 linked w/problematic drinking from no job & bad job woes.

Table E.2—Continued

Category	Description	Binary Code	Example
Substance use (illicit drugs)	Use and misuse of illicit drugs	Absent = 0 Present = 1	RT @[username]: RT @[username]: Cory Monteith tapped into his troubled past to play a drug addict in his final role--watch a clip here: http:/
Suicide	Discussion of suicide, clinical or colloquial	Absent = 0 Present = 1	This broke my heart RT @[username]: Bullied NM gay teen posts suicide note before taking his life http://t.co/v6lfwmHby9
Stigma (only applied for tweets coded as mental health–relevant, coded by expert)			
Mental illness stigma	Derogatory use of mental health language or negative reference to mental health treatment	Absent = 0 Present = 1	Pointless closing the borders. It's like having a house party and you let the complete mental, twitching nutter in then say nobody else in.

[a] Any specific usernames have been replaced with "[username]."

included a "write-in" category for topics to allow us to iterate on the coding strategy with our team. As a result of this, we added a general "addiction" code to the coding scheme. The coders did not identify any other topics that occurred with a high enough frequency to be added to the list.

The stigma code was designed to capture whether a tweet contained stigmatizing content about mental health. In early rounds of coding, we observed that the coding team had difficulty reaching sufficient levels of interrater reliability on this code. As a result, we opted to identify an expert (one of the principal investigators on the project) and have her code 500 tweets from the training data set that were identified as mental health–relevant.

Reliability of Coders

Approximately 10 percent of the tweets were coded by all three coders, allowing us to compute the mean of pairwise Cohen's kappas to assess interrater reliability for each binary presence-or-absence score (Table E.3). Cohen's kappa can range from –1 to 1, with higher scores indicating better agreement among raters. We interpreted the kappa values using labels of "poor" for kappa ≤0.40, "fair" for 0.41–0.60, "good" for 0.61–0.80, and "excellent" for 0.81–1.00 (Hallgren, 2012). Mean pairwise Cohen's kappa indicated fair to excellent agreement across most codes. There was poor agreement among coders for only three codes (mental health resources, recovery, and traumatic brain injury). These codes also correspond with categories for which few tweets were identified by coders (as indicated by lower figures in the column listing average number of observations in Table E.3). We did not eliminate codes from the coding scheme based on interrater reliability because our later strategy of using automated coding allows for the elimination of variables that cannot be effectively modeled.

Table E.3
Interrater Reliability for 500 Tweets Coded by Three Coders

Code	Mean Cohen's Kappa	Average Number of Times Feature Was Coded as "Present"[a]
Mental health–relevant		
Relevance	0.77	185.00
Type of content		
Appropriation	0.55	61.33
Information	0.60	58.00
Mental health resources	0.23	5.67
Other-focused	0.51	33.00
Self-focused	0.72	79.00
Topic		
Abuse[b]	0.33	0.67
Addiction	0.81	28.33
ADHD[b]	N/A	0.00
Anxiety	0.61	5.67
Autism	0.87	7.67
Bipolar disorder	0.94	12.00
Depression	0.92	43.33
Developmental disability	0.41	6.00
General mental health	0.48	48.67
Military- or veteran-related mental health concerns	0.90	3.67
OCD	0.50	0.67
PTSD	1.00	1.00
Recovery	0.22	1.00
Substance use (alcohol)	0.77	1.33
Substance use (illicit drugs)	0.80	6.67
Suicide	0.85	14.00
Traumatic brain injury[b]	0.00	0.33

NOTE: N/A = not applicable. Could not be calculated because no tweets were present.

[a] The numbers in the last column are the mean number of instances in which each of the three coders coded a tweet as having the feature in question.

[b] Code later removed from the coding scheme due to low volume of tweets.

Automated Coding

Our goal was to classify the 13.4 million tweets in the working data set. This volume of tweets would require more than a decade of labor time to code manually. Instead, we developed an automated system of classification. We used the 4,760 human-coded tweets in the training data set to build an automated coding model that could replicate human hand-coding on a large scale. To create an automated coding model, we developed models for each characteristic of interest so that we could use the model to predict the presence or absence of each of these characteristics for any tweet.[2]

We first transformed the coded training data set of tweets into a spreadsheet known as a *document matrix*. In the matrix, every tweet is represented as a single row, and every column represents a possible word. The number of columns is equal to the total number of different words in the entire sample of human-coded tweets. The cells of the spreadsheet are populated with zeroes and ones representing the presence or absence of the word corresponding with a given column. To simplify the matrix, we first cleaned our documents to eliminate nonstandard characters and reduce multiple versions of a word to a common spelling—for example, turning "go" and "going" into a single word. There are also many words that appear very rarely in the data set. For example, a particular misspelling may occur only in a single tweet. Such a word would create a column that was all zeros except for one row. Words that appear less frequently than once in 1,000 tweets were not included in the matrix.[3] The resulting matrix had 1,297 columns representing 1,297 distinct words present in the training data set and served as the input for our automated coding models.

We highlight two key features of the automated coding models. First, the output of each automated coding model is binary and indicates the presence or absence of the tweet characteristic of interest analyzed in that model (e.g., mental health relevance, PTSD, stigma). Second, each model predicts a single tweet characteristic, so we built a separate predictive model for each tweet characteristic of interest. Note that our coding scheme called for a primary evaluation of whether the tweet was, in fact, relevant to mental health; if it was not, no further categories were coded. This means that we used all 4,760 tweets in the training data set to build a model predicting whether a tweet is mental health–relevant and the 500 tweets in the training data set coded for stigma by an expert to build a model predicting whether a tweet contains stigmatizing content or not. Only the 1,618 mental health–relevant tweets in the training data set were used to construct models for all other characteristics.

We compared two possible analysis strategies for use in our automated coding models—logistic regression and support vector machine (SVM). Logistic regression is a common statistical approach and has the advantage of providing information on how variables contribute to outcomes. In our case, each word represented in the document matrix served as a variable that predicted whether a tweet would have the characteristic of interest being tested in that model. SVM is a machine–learning method designed

---

[2] For an example of such classification for topic relevant study, see Aphinyanaphongs et al. (2014). For another example of such classification for topic relevant study using the same underlying mathematical model as this work, see Cole-Lewis et al. (2015).

[3] There is no standard to assess the level of frequency that is too low to be meaningful. In our case, the level was selected to reduce the number of words in our matrix while also maintaining more than 1,000 words to be used in our predictive model.

to separate observations into similar groups based on their quantifiable properties. In our case, this means separating tweets that have a characteristic from those that do not based on the presence or absence of specific words in the tweet. In our testing, SVM produced more accurate prediction as determined by comparing several statistics that serve as indicators of model performance (area under the curve, true positives, and true negatives) that are described in detail in the next section. As a result, we elected to use SVM for our automated coding models, and we present the results and performance below. Interested readers may find more details and theory on automated coding model approaches in Bishop (2006).

Model Performance and Selection

In this section, we review the quality of performance of our SVM-based automated coding models in predicting from the training data set whether a tweet has a characteristic that is relevant to our research question. When considering model performance, we review the following statistics, presented in Table E.4 for each automated coding model:

- **area under the curve (AUC)**—a summary statistic of the number of accurate predictions that a model makes. In other words, it is a summary metric of the number of times the automated coding model codes a tweet in the same way that a human coder coded it. An AUC of 1 indicates perfect agreement between the value predicted by the model and the human-assigned value, and an AUC of 0.5 indicates that the model predictions are no better than chance (Huang and Ling, 2005).[4]
- **true positives**—the number of tweets that were predicted to contain the code of interest by the automated coding models and were coded as such by human coders.
- **false positives**—the number of tweets that were predicted to not contain the code of interest by the automated coding models but were identified as having said code by the human coders.
- **true negatives**—the number of tweets that were predicted to not contain the code of interest by the automated coding models and were coded as not having that coded by the human coders.
- **false negatives**—the number of tweets that were predicted to contain the code of interest by the automated coding models but were identified as not having the code of interest by human coders.
- **total actual positives**—the number of tweets that were identified by the human coders as having the code of interest. Total actual positives are always the sum of true positives and false negatives.

---

[4]   For a discussion of the challenges of AUC and the need to report the types of errors and not simply overall error, see Lobo, Jiménez-Valverde, and Real (2008).

- **total actual negatives**—the number of tweets that were identified by the human coders as not having the code of interest. Total actual negatives are always the sum of true negatives and false positives.

Although no formal procedure exists for determining the quality of model performance, we developed several rules of thumb for examining Table E.4. We examined AUC to identify models that had lower values relative to other models. While there is no standard for an acceptable AUC level for a model, values below 0.700 appear to represent models that are low performing relative to the rest of our models.[5] Also, we tried to examine models to determine where there might be a high number of false negatives relative to true negatives or a high number of false positives relative to true positives.

A review of Table E.4 indicates that the automated coding models performed well for most categories, including mental health relevance, many of the topic codes, and stigma. For these categories, AUCs were sufficiently high, and examination of false positives compared with true positives and of false negatives compared with true negatives did not yield an indication of poor performance. We elected to apply these models (i.e., those with a black circle in the model retention column) to the larger Twitter data set.

We identified several models that performed too poorly to consider using (those with white circles in the model retention column). We also examined models for the following characteristics for potential poor performance but ultimately decided to retain them: type-of-content codes for information and self-focused, as well as the topic code for military- and veteran-related mental health concerns. Examining the model performance revealed that many of the poorly performing models were those for which that topic of interest occurred infrequently in the training data set. Specifically, many of the models that failed have between five and 22 occurrences. This makes it unlikely that an accurate model can be developed to predict such a rare event.

The type-of-content codes were among those that performed somewhat poorly. The presence of appropriation, information, and self-focused content was difficult to predict, and these models had an AUC of 0.750. Because these categories were deemed by the research team to be critical to understanding tweet content and the AUCs for these categories were at threshold, we retained these models. Another type-of-content code capturing whether tweet content is other-focused was not retained because the AUC was below 0.700 and because it yielded more false positives than true positives.

We note that modeling type of content is likely more challenging than modeling, for example, topic, due to the nature of the category. While there are likely keywords for identifying mental health topics that clearly indicate whether a feature is present or absent (e.g., most tweets about depression will have some version of the

---

[5] We note that the baseline model for topic classification for Twitter's internal researchers has an AUC of 0.720, so we elected to use 0.700 as a baseline for which to judge our models (Yang et al., 2014).

Table E.4
SVM-Based Automated Coding Model Performance for Each Tweet Characteristic

Characteristic	Model Retention ● = retained ○ = not retained	AUC	True Positives	False Positives	True Negatives	False Negatives	Total Actual Positives	Total Actual Negatives
Mental health relevance								
Relevance	●	0.864	1,026	331	2,811	592	1,618	3,142
Type of content								
Appropriation	●	0.785	305	143	916	241	546	1,059
Information	●	0.750	400	263	726	217	617	989
Mental health resources	●	0.869	20	0	1,574	23	43	1,574
Other-focused	○	0.668	72	106	1,213	219	291	1,319
Self-focused	●	0.734	393	272	721	226	619	993
Topic								
Abuse	○	1.000	1	0	1,610	6	7	1,610
Addiction	●	0.972	207	19	1,368	20	227	1,387
ADHD	○	0.940	0	0	1,608	9	9	1,608
Anxiety	●	0.913	23	11	1,556	26	49	1,567
Autism	●	0.927	51	1	1,540	25	76	1,541
Bipolar disorder	●	0.983	109	3	1,499	6	115	1,502
Depression	●	0.997	418	4	1,190	5	423	1,194
Developmental disability	●	0.972	36	2	1,565	14	50	1,567
General mental health	●	0.907	184	60	1,256	110	294	1,316

Table E.4—Continued

Characteristic	Model retention ● = retained ○ = not retained	AUC	True Positives	False Positives	True Negatives	False Negatives	Total Actual Positives	Total Actual Negatives
Military- or veteran-related mental health concerns	●	0.947	5	1	1,593	17	22	1,594
OCD	●	1.000	20	1	1,592	4	24	1,593
PTSD	●	0.968	20	0	1,586	11	31	1,586
Recovery	○	0.589	0	0	1,610	5	5	1,610
Substance use (alcohol)	○	0.953	3	1	1,604	9	12	1,605
Substance use (illicit drugs)	●	0.930	14	4	1,570	29	43	1,574
Suicide	●	0.991	176	5	1,430	6	182	1,435
Traumatic brain injury	○	0.977	5	0	1,608	4	9	1,608
Stigma								
Mental illness stigma	●	0.804	42	9	384	68	110	393

NOTE: The total actual positives and total actual negatives columns contain the counts of presence or absence of a code in the training data set that was used to train the automated coded models.

word "depression"), there may not be equivalent keywords for considering type of content. For example, if trying to identify whether a tweet is self- or other-focused, words like "I" and "you" are too common to be unique keywords. Thus, the models for predicting type of content rely on patterns of co-occurrence among words to make predictions.

Applying each model yielded a prediction of the number of tweets in the working data set of 13.4 million tweets that would have that characteristic (Table E.5).

Table E.5
Volumes of Tweet Predictions in Working Data Set

Characteristic	Predicted Count in Working Data Set
Mental health relevance	
Relevant	2,277,092
Type of content	
Appropriation	681,514
Information	697,206
Mental health resources	16,837
Self-focused	924,806
Topic	
Addiction	151,059
Anxiety	3,404
Autism	41,672
Bipolar disorder	141,817
Depression	249,397
Development disability	13,579
General mental health	321,477
Military- or veteran-related mental health concerns	473
OCD	26,128
PTSD	9,468
Substance use (illicit drugs)	11,687
Suicide	111,318
Stigma	
Mental illness stigma	220,991

NOTE: Working data set, N = 13,432,321.

Network Analysis

To better understand how Twitter users communicate with each other about mental health and the campaigns being evaluated, we conducted a network analysis to understand the connections among users. To conduct this analysis, we focused on directed tweets in which one user addresses another (as opposed to undirected tweets, which are posts meant to be read by anyone on Twitter, or retweets, which involve reposting other users' tweets). We used the directed tweets to identify instances of users communicating with others and used these connections as inputs into the *igraph* package for R to construct a social network of how users are linked by communication about mental health (Csardi and Nepusz, 2006).

Social networks often give rise to groups of people, known as *communities*, that are connected more densely inside the group than to individuals outside of the group. Constructing a social network based on directed tweets allows us to understand whether organically occurring communities of users communicate about mental health in ways that are distinct from overall patterns observed in the 2.3 million mental health–relevant tweets in the working data set. Doing so also allows us to determine whether these communities are distinct from each other in meaningful ways. We can also understand who campaign-related Twitter content reaches, how far campaign messages are spreading, and if there are groups of people that converse about topics that are relevant to the campaigns.[6]

Understanding how the conversation about mental health may vary for individuals based on who they communicate with and understanding how the campaigns are spreading online required two different methods of network construction. To understand the variation in the overall conversation about mental health on Twitter, we had to reduce the volumes of observation that did not have meaningful mental health information. The general mental health conversation includes data from spam accounts (which post in ways intended to avoid detection by Twitter's automated detection methods) and very influential users (e.g., celebrities) who may not actually be central to mental health discourse. As a result, we focused on mental health–relevant tweets from our working data set that were directed tweets. Undirected tweets were not included because they do not mention other users, making such tweets irrelevant for the goal of our social network analyses—to identify connections among users. Retweets were omitted because often the audience for the retweet is unclear, and retweets are often associated with spam accounts. After omitting undirected tweets and retweets, a large volume of tweets was available to construct a network (534,000 connections among 777,000 users).

Understanding how campaigns spread online requires examination of a smaller network than the one associated with general mental health discourse. So, for the

---

[6]   For an early discussion of community structure on Twitter and the insights that community analysis offers, see Java et al. (2007).

purposes of understanding the network of users who engaged with the campaigns—either by sending messages to the campaigns, retweeting the campaigns, or mentioning the campaigns by name—we used both directed tweets and retweets in our analysis. To understand the network of campaign-engaged users, we created a network from our total data set of 2.3 million mental health–relevant tweets, located the campaign-engaged users within that network, and identified which communities they belonged to. Our data set of campaign-related tweets contained a small volume of users (n = 10,134) who engaged with the campaigns. Of those 10,134 users, we identified 9,123 users within our data set of 2.3 million mental health–relevant tweets. We found that a network constructed of only directed tweets did not allow us to identify communities focused on military or veteran mental health issues to which the campaign-engaged users belonged. We opted to use both directed messages and retweets because communities became apparent when using both types of tweets. Furthermore, in the case of engaged users, we focused on a targeted subset of the overall social network. That way, such issues as scam accounts and popular users skewing networks had less of a negative effect in this analysis because those users lie outside our communities of interest.

Having constructed these two networks, we focused on detecting communities within the networks. Community detection involves identifying clusters of users that are densely interconnected but separate from users outside of the group. To identify clusters, we used the *walktrap method* because it is most effective for large networks like the one we were analyzing (for more information, see Pons and Latapy, 2005). We identified communities made up of users that sent or received directed tweets about mental health to each other. Community detection is a computationally intensive task; thus, it was not feasible to perform community detection on the network constructed with directed tweets and retweets. To address this, we created a subnetwork of this network. We eliminated all users with only one connection. This step reduced the size of the network from 1.6 million users with 1.4 million connections to 352,000 users and 418,000 connections, which made the task computationally feasible. The network that we constructed without the use of retweets (534,000 users, 777,000 connections) was computationally tractable without a size reduction.

We used the community structure of networks to understand the characteristics of the mental health–relevant content shared within different communities. We examined how mental health discourse varies among communities and whether there are outlier communities with especially high volumes of a particular type of content, content focused on specific mental health topics, or stigmatizing content. We examined communities with notably high levels of stigma in their posts, as well as high volumes of posts related to the topics of PTSD, depression, substance use disorders, and suicide. In order to understand the kinds of users that the campaigns are reaching, we also explored the distribution of message by type and topic for communities that are engaged with the campaigns.

We also examined some measures of centrality to understand the importance of users within the social network. We opted to explore eigenvector (EV) centrality because it serves as a measure of importance that considers the number of connections a user has, as well as the number of connections that those connections have. Users with higher EV centrality scores are connected to many well-connected users and thus are likely to serve as a central hub for effective distribution of content. This approach aligns well with the notion that effective dissemination of mental health public awareness campaign content on Twitter depends on the ability of a user to propagate messages and influence the conversation around mental health.

Results

In this section, we examine the results of our automated tweet coding models and network analysis to answer the research questions:

- Which mental health topics are characterized by positive and supportive discourse, and which are discussed in a stigmatizing way?
- What are the longitudinal trends in content and sentiment of Twitter conversation around mental health and mental health treatment?
- Do sentiment and topic changes correlate with Twitter activities of the campaigns being evaluated?

Mental Health Discourse on Twitter

Most mental health content on Twitter is self-focused and few tweets share mental health resources. Panel A in Figure E.2 depicts the number of tweets that feature different types of content. We see that the most common type of message is self-focused. Tweets containing informational content accounted for about one-third of total tweet volume; tweets that featured appropriation (that is, using mental health terms to describe things and not people [e.g., "the weather is bipolar"] and using mental health language to describe emotional states [e.g., "I am going insane watching this football game"]) accounted for another third. Few tweets involved the provision of mental health resources. These findings suggest that Twitter users often discuss mental health in a self-relevant way. However, the prevalence of tweets that were informational suggests that Twitter is being used for other purposes as well.

Panel B in Figure E.2 depicts the number of tweets that focus on each of the different topics included in the coding scheme. General mental health (without focus on a specific disorder) is the topic most commonly discussed. Other frequently discussed topics include addiction, bipolar disorder, depression, and suicide.

Approximately 10 percent of mental health–relevant tweets are stigmatizing. We see that most tweets were not coded as being stigmatizing. We found

Figure E.2
Distribution of Tweets, by Type of Content

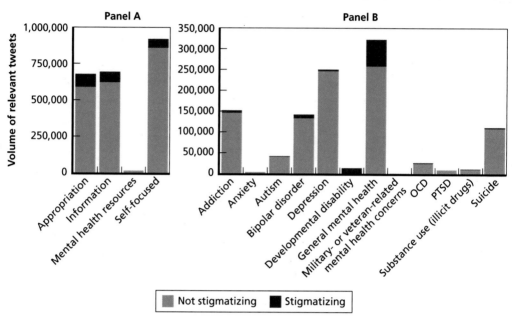

NOTES: Panel A shows the distribution of type of content. Panel B shows the distribution of tweets by topic. The distributions are independent each other, and codes are not mutually exclusive.
RAND RR1612-E.2

that 10 percent of the 2.3 million mental health–relevant tweets were stigmatizing. Panel A in Figure E.2 shows that the proportion of content that was coded as stigmatizing is similar across tweets coded as containing appropriation (13 percent), containing information (10 percent), or being self-focused (7 percent). Panel B shows that most tweets about most topics were not stigmatizing, with the exception of tweets coded as discussing developmental disabilities, of which 99.6 percent were stigmatizing. A larger proportion of tweets focused on general mental health (20 percent) were stigmatizing (when comparing with the proportion of stigmatizing tweets present for most other topics).

We also examined how tweet types and topics were related (Figure E.3) and note several patterns. More tweets about addiction and bipolar disorder contained content coded as containing appropriation than did tweets about other topics. An informal review of tweets about addiction and bipolar disorder suggests that these findings may be driven by casual and colloquial use of such terms as "addicted" and "bipolar" that are not in line with correct clinical use of the terms. We also note that a large volume of tweets about depression are also self-focused, which is likely reflective of the positive correlation between self-focus and negative affect documented in psychological literature (Mor and Winquist, 2002). Finally, we note that tweets focused on general mental

Figure E.3
Relation of Tweets by Type and Topic

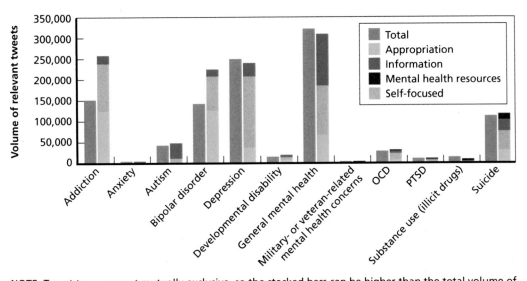

NOTE: Tweet types are not mutually exclusive, so the stacked bars can be higher than the total volume of tweets in that topic.
RAND RR1612-E.3

health are most often coded as informational, which may be reflective of a general conversation about mental health.

Network community conversations about mental health vary in types and topics of tweets, and network communities are highly heterogeneous. Our social network analysis of mental health–relevant tweets revealed more than 126,000 communities, many of which are very small (e.g., pairs of users). Thus, we focus our analyses on communities that had at least 25 members and 150 mental health–relevant tweets. We focused much of our interpretation on these larger communities because we wanted to ensure that there were adequate numbers of members and mental health–related activity to draw conclusions about community conversations. To provide illustrative examples of variation in mental health discourse among different communities, we identified four communities with the highest proportion of tweets related to four mental health– and substance use–related topics (addiction, depression, PTSD, and suicide) that are often discussed in conversations about service member and veteran mental health. The distribution of content for those communities is shown in Figure E.4. These graphs represent the distribution of all content posted by users belonging to communities with the high proportion of the characteristic of interest. Of note, the patterns of tweet types and topics for all four communities differ from the overall patterns indicated in Figure E.3.

Among large communities with mental health conversations, 71 percent demonstrated low levels of stigma in community conversations. We also looked across the 96 larger communities to understand whether the volume of stigmatizing content

Figure E.4
Characteristics of Tweet Types and Topics for Four Communities with High Proportions of Tweets About Addiction, Depression, PTSD, and Suicide

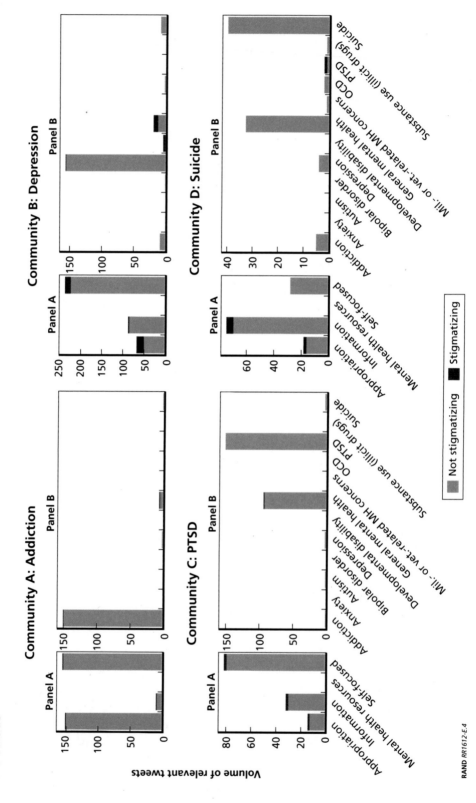

varies across communities. Figure E.5 shows the number of communities with different proportions of tweets coded as being stigmatizing. For 69 of the 96 communities, about 10 percent of tweets are stigmatizing. We manually examined the content of the two outlier communities, for which 45 percent and 75 percent of tweets were stigmatizing. These two communities appear to consist largely of spam accounts that do not represent conversation among typical Twitter users.[7] We identified one additional community with high rates of stigmatizing content (30 percent of total content). Examination of this community indicated that it was largely populated by fans of pop music group One Direction and tweet content was mostly focused on users utilizing mental health terms when expressing strong emotions (e.g., "@Real_Liam_Payne you don't know, but you save me everyday and I don't make a suicide, thank you so much for all, Liam I love you x1178").

We also examined the types and topics of tweets among the four communities with the highest proportions of stigmatizing tweets (excluding the previously mentioned communities that consisted of scam accounts) (Figure E.6). We chose to focus

Figure E.5
Variation in Proportion of Stigmatizing Tweets Across Communities

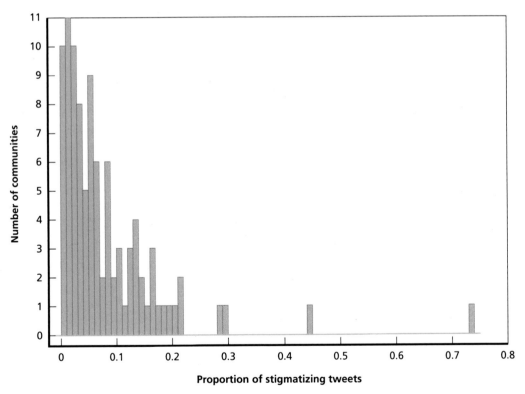

RAND RR1612-E.5

---

[7] The two communities contain many Twitter users that engage in follower trading, in which individuals operate with the goal of creating accounts with a high number of followers that can then be sold or rented for profit.

Figure E.6
Characteristics of Tweet Types and Topics for Four Highly Stigmatizing Communities

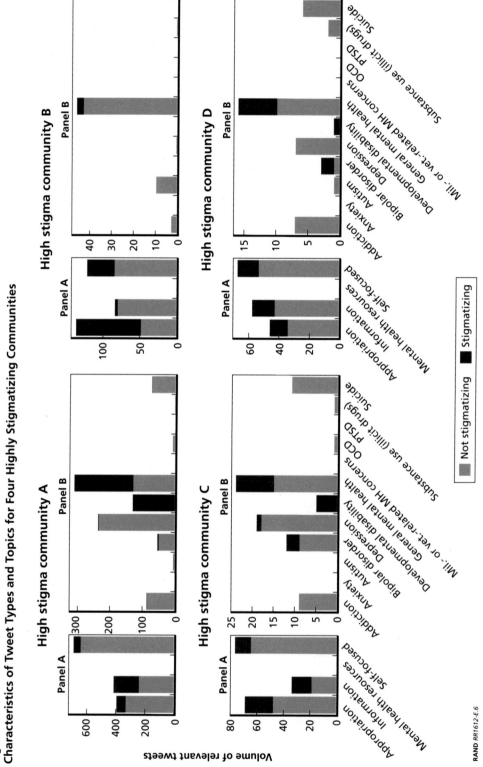

on communities where stigmatizing tweets made up more than 20 percent of the communities' tweets because this allowed us to manually examine a manageable number of communities. Patterns of tweet types and topics seem to largely resemble overall patterns in Figure E.2, suggesting that discourse among the four most highly stigmatizing communities did not differ significantly from overall discourse. This suggests that stigmatizing communities are not type- or topic-focused; rather, stigma is simply part of their discussion of mental health topics.

Longitudinal Trends in Mental Health Discourse on Twitter

Tweet types and topics have changed over time, with increases in informational content and discussion of general mental health and decreases in stigmatizing content. To look at changes in tweet types and topics over time, we conducted a longitudinal analysis of mental health–related tweets from 2009 through 2016 (Figure E.7). To account for changing tweet volumes over time, tweet volumes were normalized by dividing by the total volume of mental health–relevant tweets, and we opted to analyze the proportion of mental health–relevant tweets that were coded as each different tweet type and topic.

We see changes in tweet types over time (Figure E.7, Panel A). The proportions of mental health–relevant tweets that are self-focused or that use appropriation declined over time. Informational tweets slightly decreased until the end of 2012 and have increased since. Despite increases in informational tweets, the proportion of tweets that contain mental health resources has remained steady over time.

We also see changes in tweet topics over time (Figure E.7, Panels B and C). One of the most prominent trends is an increase in the volume of tweets focusing on general mental health, which may suggest increasing engagement among Twitter users with the issue of mental health as a whole—or, perhaps, changes in the prevalence of mental health disorders among the general population. We also note that discussion of PTSD sharply increased in 2012, which may be reflective of the burgeoning discussion of mental health coinciding with the return of troops from Iraq and Afghanistan—e.g., Presidential Executive Order #13625, establishing the Interagency Task Force on Military and Veterans Mental Health (Obama, 2012). Corresponding with this, we see a spike in military- or veteran-related mental health discussion in mid-2012, followed by a decrease. However, we caution that this trend line was derived from very little data and the confidence intervals for the trend line are wider than the full range of values depicted in Panel C. There is very little confidence in the specific pattern of military- and veteran-related mental health discussion. Other trends of note include discussion of depression increasing until 2013 before slightly declining, and discussion of bipolar disorder increasing from 2009 to 2012 before slightly declining.

The change in tweets containing stigmatizing content over time is depicted in Figure E.7, Panel D. We see that the proportion of mental health–relevant tweets that are coded as stigmatizing declines over time, with a steady decline since a peak in 2011.

Figure E.7
Time Trends in Tweet Volume, by Tweet Type and Topic, 2009–2016

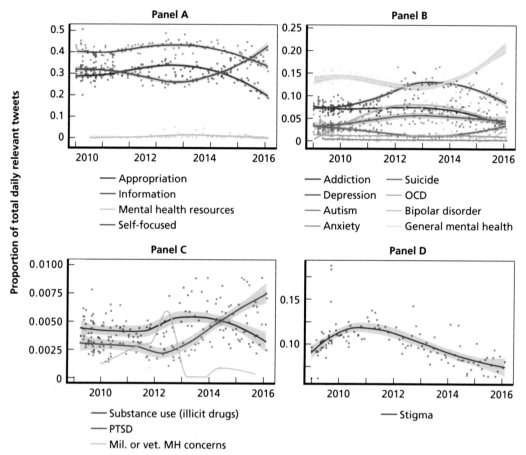

NOTE: Any data point with fewer than ten tweets and any calendar day with fewer than 50 tweets total (across categories) has been excluded. Each data point has been normalized by dividing by the total volume of mental health–relevant tweets. Trend lines were fitted using local polynomial regression (LOESS)—a nonparametric method of fitting a population curve. The shaded areas around the curves represent the 95-percent confidence interval of the estimate.

RAND RR1612-E.7

We also analyzed the decline of stigma for each individual code. We found that stigma is declining for all characteristics analyzed and declining at approximately similar rates.

Campaign Twitter Presence

The volume of campaign-related Twitter activity is too low to assess whether the campaign activity is affecting the overall Twitter conversation about mental health. To better understand how campaign-related tweets were disseminated, we identified tweets as being posted either through official channels (i.e., the Twitter accounts that the campaigns told us were used for dissemination; see Table E.6) or through any

Table E.6
Official Twitter Accounts

Campaigns	Associated Accounts
RWC	**@RealWarriors** @DCoEPage @MilitaryHealth
MTC	@VA_OEF_OIF @VAVetBenefits @DeptVetAffairs @VA_PTSD_Info @VeteransHealth
VCL	@VA_OEF_OIF @VAVetBenefits @DeptVetAffairs @VA_PTSD_Info @VeteransHealth
Recovery Month	**@RecoveryMonth** @SAMHSA

NOTE: Bolded accounts are dedicated accounts for campaigns.

other channel (i.e., an "unofficial" channel). This allows us to distinguish between Twitter activities initiated by the campaign versus activity propagating to other users.

Official and unofficial campaign-related Twitter activity is shown in Figure E.8. Most tweets about the campaigns are from unofficial channels, suggesting that campaign messages are propagating, at least to some degree, through spreading on social media. Between 47 and 670 RWC-related tweets per month occurred throughout the monitoring period, with 16 percent from the official RWC Twitter account. Our search yielded only three MTC tweets through official channels, though, as we noted earlier in the appendix, the common use of "make the connection" as a phrase posed some challenges to identifying this campaign's tweets. More tweets (between 1 and 62) occur each month through unofficial channels. Between 1 and 377 VCL-related tweets per month occurred throughout the monitoring period, with 5 percent tweeted by the official VCL Twitter account. Given Recovery Month's focus on September as National Recovery Month (though events do occur throughout the year), that campaign sees low volumes of Twitter activity with spikes in both official and unofficial activity corresponding with September of each year. The number of tweets in these months ranged from 565 in 2012 to 2,180 in 2015, with 1 percent coming from official channels.

Though we aimed to determine whether trends in campaign-related activity aligned with the trends observed in the previous section, we found that the volume of campaign-related activity was not sufficient to conduct analyses. As noted earlier, there was a general increase in discussion of general mental health and informational content and a reduction in stigmatizing content during the time that these campaigns have been active. However, we cannot conclusively link these broader trends to campaign activities.

Figure E.8
Tweet Volume by Month from Official and Unofficial Channels

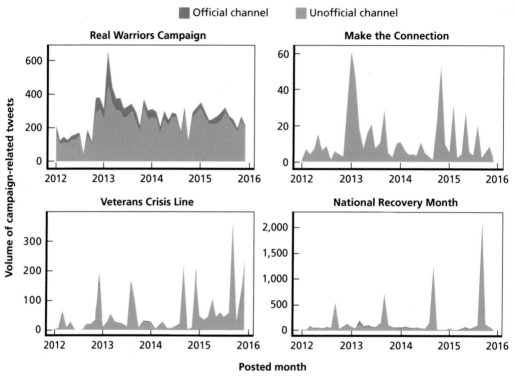

NOTE: These are stacked (not overlapping) charts.
RAND RR1612-E.8

Three of the four campaigns show positive signs of engaging other Twitter users to retweet messages. We also wanted to understand how well the campaigns generate interest in their messages. To do this, we considered all messages posted by official channels and identified any messages with the same content coming from an unofficial channel within 30 days of the initial official post (i.e., a retweet). We consider these retweets to be a good measure of how much engagement the campaign materials are generating. Figure E.9 shows volumes of messages posted by official channels, the portion of messages that were retweeted by unofficial channels, and the average number of retweets of such messages. For RWC, approximately 25 percent of its posts generated some engagement from unofficial channels, and this volume of engagement increased over time even as the volume of official tweets declined. Due to limited official MTC tweets, we were unable to draw conclusions about engagement with those tweets. VCL tweets resulted in high volumes of engagement, with 25 percent of messages being retweeted. Recovery Month tweets resulted in retweeting of 25 percent to 50 percent of the tweets. We are not aware of any common level of retweets for public

Figure E.9
Twitter Engagement with the Campaigns

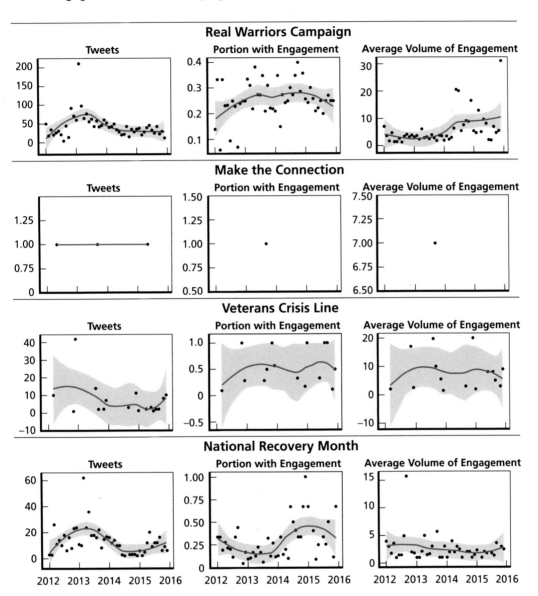

NOTES: "Tweets"(column 1) shows the volume of tweets posted by official channels related to each campaign. "Portion with Engagement" (column 2) shows the proportion of official tweets that generated retweets within 30 days of initial posts. "Average Volume of Engagement" (column 3) shows the average number of retweets generated by an official tweet that creates engagement. The dots indicate data points, the blue lines are trend lines over time, and the gray areas represent confidence intervals.

RAND RR1612-E.9

messaging campaigns, though there is some older evidence that this level of retweets is in line with Twitter as a whole (Suh et al., 2010).

Finally, we wanted to understand the type of Twitter users that were engaging with the military mental health campaigns. We computed EV centrality as a proxy of how important a user is to the network. Those with high scores were central and well connected within the network, and therefore influential. Figure E.10 depicts the distribution of EV scores of users who engaged the campaigns. We see that each of the campaigns are reaching users of similar EV levels, which may be because they are reaching the same population of users. We also see that the users who are engaged with

Figure E.10
Centrality of Campaign-Engaged Users Within Mental Health–Focused Social Network, by Campaign

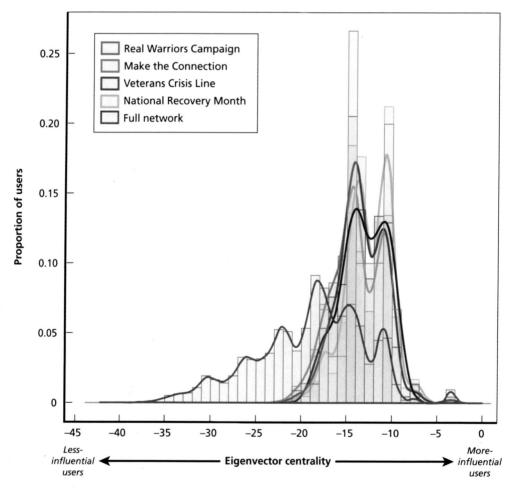

NOTE: The x-axis (labeled "eigenvector centrality") represents a measure of the influence of a node in a network. Higher values (i.e., values closer to 0) indicate that users are more influential. Eigenvector centrality has been log transformed.
RAND *RR1612-6.7*

the campaigns are more influential than the average user in our data set of authors who posted tweets relevant to mental health. The low volumes of official posts from three of the four campaigns combined with the kind of engagement that the campaigns are able to generate suggests that there are opportunities for greater maximization of the Twitter platform for campaign material dissemination.

Engagement with the campaign is visible in the social network. We used the social network we created to understand the characteristics of communities to which campaign-engaged users (i.e., those who mention campaigns in their tweets or retweet campaign-related messages) belong. We then identified campaign-engaged users who were present in our social network. We found that of the 10,134 campaign-engaged users, 6,343 were also present in our network of users who made mental health–relevant tweets.[8] We examined tweet types and topics for campaign-engaged users present in the social network (Panels A and B in Figure E.11). We find that these campaign-engaged users posted primarily informational content but little content containing mental health resources. They also posted about general mental health topics more than any other topic.

Although we could not establish a relationship between trends in mental health discourse and the campaigns, we examined the type and topic of tweets among the "subcommunity" of Twitter users containing the most campaign-engaged users (i.e., those who mention campaigns in their tweets or retweet campaign-related messages). To identify this subcommunity, we first identified that 6,343 of 10,134 campaign-engaged users were also present in our network of users tweeting about mental health. We then examined the community membership of campaign-engaged users tweeting about mental health, finding that 1,127 of 6,343 engaged users belong to a single community of nearly 35,000 users.[9] This community of 35,000 users was the largest community tweeting about mental health and was the community that contained the largest number of campaign-engaged Twitter users. A community is a cluster of Twitter users that tweet and retweet each other (at least once). These users' tweets are similar in type and content to those of campaign-engaged users (Panels A and B). Because this 35,000-member community was so large, it very closely resembled the general population on Twitter. Therefore, we explored subcommunities' users within the body of 35,000 users who are more interconnected (i.e., five or more tweets or retweets), finding 2,698 such subcommunities ranging in size from clusters of two users to clusters of 6,255, with 133 subcommunities having memberships of more than 25 users. We identified the single subcommunity containing the largest number of campaign-engaged users. This subcommunity has 110 members, 36 of whom are campaign-engaged users (Figure E.12). The figure outlines

---

[8] We note that it was expected that not all campaign-engaged users would appear in our network. This is largely because we used a sampling approach to generate each data set, and not a census of all tweets. In addition, the automated coding models used to code tweets are probabilistic in nature, and some false negatives are expected to occur when coding tweets for content.

[9] Exact membership is 34,749 users, but for purposes of discussion, we refer to this community as 35,000 members.

Figure E.11
Centrality of Campaign-Engaged Users Within Mental Health–Focused Social Network, by Community

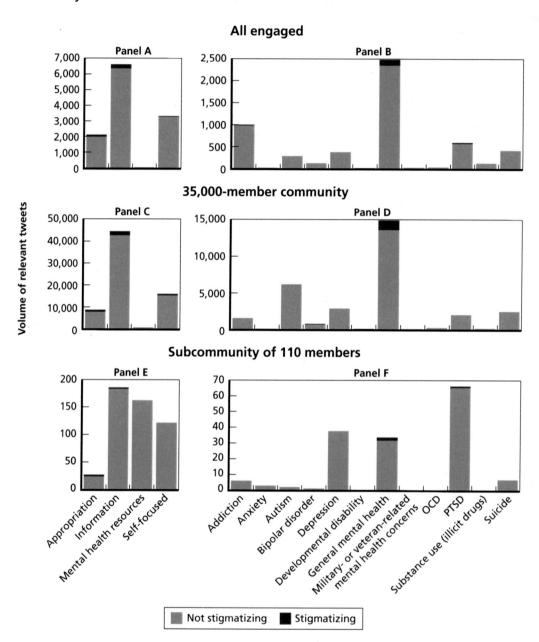

NOTE: The graph shows the content type, topic, and stigma distribution for the population of users engaged with the campaigns, the overall community that most of those users belong to, and the subcommunity that has the largest share of campaign-engaged users.

RAND *RR1612-E.11*

Figure E.12
Identifying a Community of Campaign-Engaged Users

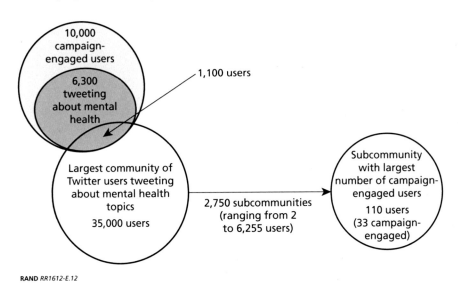

RAND RR1612-E.12

the process of this selection. We characterize the content tweeted by the full community in Panels C and D of Figure E.11.

We examined the type and topic of tweets among the subcommunity containing the most campaign-engaged users (Panels E and F of Figure E.11). These subcommunity members' tweets were largely self-focused and contained informational content and mental health resources. Few of the tweets involved appropriation. In terms of topics, the tweets focused on mental health concerns related to depression and PTSD, along with general mental health topics.

To learn more about this subcommunity, we reviewed user names and their connections within the community (Figure E.13). We visited users' Twitter pages and used their account names, photos, and brief self-entered descriptions to determine which of the following mutually exclusive categories applied:

- official government account (n = 27): Any entity within the federal or state government (including military services and VA locations) is labeled as an official account.
- military- or veteran-related account (n = 29): The user self-identified as a service member or veteran or as having an interest in supporting service members or veterans.
- health-focused account (n = 11): The user self-identified as having a focus on physical or mental health topics.
- other account (n = 43): Users who did not fall into the previous three categories or whose accounts had been deleted or suspended.

Figure E.13
Network of Actively Engaged Users

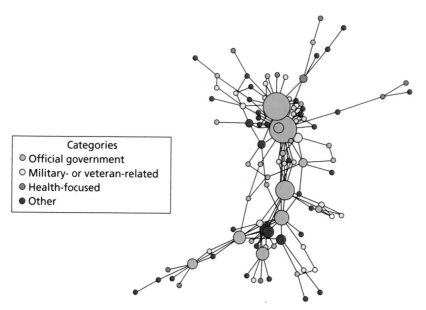

NOTE: This reflects the network of a single subcommunity containing the largest number of campaign-engaged users (*n* = 110). This graph is meant to capture the interaction between clustered active users engaged with the campaigns. The nodes are labeled according to users' Twitter handles and colored according to the category of user account type designated by the research team. Nodes are scaled according to number of connections. All nodes with more than 15 connections are set to 15, and all nodes with fewer than 3 connections are set to 3 for the scaling step only in order to enhance readability.
RAND *RR1612-E.13*

Examining the accounts featured in the network in Figure E.13, we see a mix of accounts of all types, with official government accounts serving as entities with the most connections to other users of diverse types. This network graph suggests that though only one-third of the users in the community were categorized as campaign-engaged users, there is the potential for the rest of the users to see campaign-related activities as they propagate throughout the network.

Development of a Best-Practices Checklist for Mental Health Public Awareness Campaigns

This appendix describes the process of developing a checklist of best practices for mental health public awareness campaigns. We first conducted a literature review of research to develop an initial checklist. We then used a modified version of the RAND/UCLA Appropriateness Method to elicit expert input on the checklist and finalize it. The RAND/UCLA Appropriateness Method (Fitch et al., 2001) is a systematic method for obtaining expert judgment on topics where there are no formalized guidelines to direct practice, such as mental health public awareness campaign design. Finally, expert panelists rated each evaluated campaign against a subset of the checklist items.

Identifying Candidate Checklist Items

The purpose of the checklist is to provide operational guidance, or clear recommendations, about the processes that campaigns should follow to be effective. To identify a candidate set of checklist items, we conducted a literature review of theoretical and empirical sources on health communication campaign evaluation.

The review occurred in two phases. In Phase 1, we began by reviewing the resources used in an earlier literature review on campaign best practices conducted as part of RAND's first assessment of RWC in 2012 (Acosta, Martin, et al., 2012). In Phase 2, we performed a new web-based search of peer-reviewed literature in content-relevant databases, following similar search strategies as were used in the Phase 1 literature review. Returned sources underwent several rounds of screening, including a title and abstract review, followed by a full-text review of potentially relevant sources. The research team abstracted information related to best practices from relevant sources and used these to develop a preliminary list of best practices in mental health public awareness campaign design and dissemination. Figure F.1 illustrates the literature review process.

Identifying Sources for Review

Phase 1 involved searching peer-reviewed literature to identify best practices and empirically defined characteristics and qualities of effective behavioral health media campaigns

Figure F.1
Search Process for Literature Focusing on Best Practices

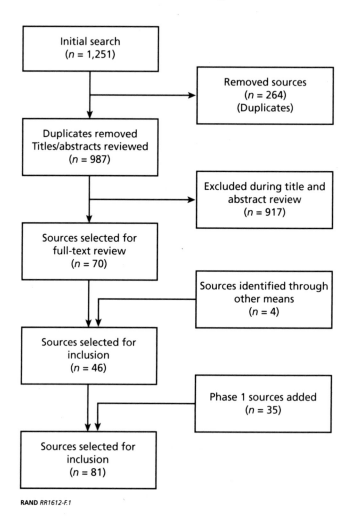

RAND RR1612-F.1

(see Acosta, Martin, et al., 2012; for detailed literature review methods, see Appendix B). The search included content published in English from January 2000 to February 2011. A keyword strategy was used to identify literature focusing on the following priority areas: (1) barriers to mental health care, including mental illness stigma; (2) media campaigns; (3) mental health or substance use disorders, and (4) traumatic brain injury. In total, 35 articles were identified for inclusion in the Phase 1 literature review. This included 21 articles identified in peer-reviewed literature and 14 articles that were recommended by ten experts in (1) barriers to mental health care (including stigma), (2) mental health in the military (PTSD, deployment psychology), (3) effective media campaigns, (4) media campaigns for service members, and (5) psychological resilience. Remaining articles were identified in a supplementary internet search of the gray literature.

Phase 2 of the search process focused on literature published after February 2011 to identify relevant work published after the Phase 1 search. The search focused on citations published in English from February 2011 to December 2015. Databases in this search included PubMed, PsycINFO, and Mass Media and Communication Complete. Citations were identified using a keyword strategy building on Phase 1's priority areas (Table F.1). However, additional search terms were added to the "media campaigns" category to capture new research on social media, and we expanded the mental health category to include search strings related to substance use disorders.

The search strings produced the following results for each database: PubMed (557), PsychINFO (666), and Mass Media and Communication Complete (28) for a total of 1,251 citations. We removed duplicate citations and collected a total of 987 unique articles for review.

Title, Abstract, and Full-Text Review

We examined titles and abstracts of the 987 articles to identify potentially relevant sources. Articles were retained if they described promising, best, or evidence-based practices related to the development or implementation of a media campaign. We specifically defined *best practices* as the "general set of standards, guidelines, norms, reference points, or benchmarks that inform practice and are designed to improve performance" (Seeger, 2006). Articles were excluded if they were not relevant, published in a language other than English, or focused on individuals under the age of 18 years. This stage eliminated 917 articles, leaving 70 articles for additional review. A full-text review eliminated 28 more articles, yielding 42 relevant peer-reviewed sources for data abstraction and further analysis. Four other relevant articles were identified from internet searches of the gray literature and consultation with experts in (1) health communication, (2) mental health and stigma, (3) behavior change, (4) military mental health, and (5) communication campaigns. These supplemented results from the peer-reviewed search. This process yielded a final tally of 46 articles that met our search criteria.

Combined with the results from Phase 1, our search process produced a total of 81 articles for additional analysis. These articles are included in the reference list at the end of this report.

Abstracting Information from Each Source

We created a data abstraction form to extract relevant information from the 46 Phase 2 articles. The form captured (1) article type, (2) content of the media campaign discussed in the article, (3) primary media type discussed in the article, and (4) general best practices. Coders were also provided with an additional open-ended notes field to record additional thoughts or questions as necessary. Each of these categories is described thoroughly in Table F.2.

We conducted a pilot test to ensure that all researchers were abstracting information systematically and the articles were divided among the team for full review.

Table F.1
Search Strings in the Literature Search Process

Barriers to Care (including stigma)	Media Campaigns	Mental Illness and Substance Use	Traumatic Brain Injury
stigma[a]	media[a]	smoking	TBI[a]
stigmas	messag*[a]	smoker	traumatic brain injur*[a]
stigmatize[a]	communicat*[a]	nicotine AND addict*	brain[a]
self-stigma[a]	intervention*[a]	"substance abuse"	
barrier*[a] AND access[a]	social network[a]	"substance use"	
	social networks[a]	alcoholic	
	social networking[a]	"alcohol abuse"	
	social media	"drug abuse"	
	Facebook[a]	"drug abuser"	
	Twitter	"drug addict"	
		"drug addicted"	
		"heroin addict"	
		"heroin addicted"	
		"cocaine addict"	
		"cocaine addicted"	
		"alcohol dependent"	
		marijuana addict	
		marijuana use	
		marijuana abuse	
		marijuana addicted	
		prescription drug abuse	
		prescription drug misuse	
		prescription drug depend*	
		prescription drug addict*	
		nonmedical use	
		extra-medical use	
		painkiller* depend*	
		painkiller* abuse*	
		painkiller* misuse	
		opioid abuse*	
		opioid addict*	
		opioid depend*	
		mental[a]	
		stress[a]	
		anxiety[a]	
		suicidal depression[a]	
		depressive[a]	
		PTSD[a]	
		post traumatic stress[a]	
		posttraumatic stress	
		post-traumatic stress	
		mental health services[a]	
		combat stress[a]	

NOTE: TBI = traumatic brain injury.

[a] Term carried over from Phase 1's search strategy.
* Denotes wildcard search term.

One team member provided oversight and random spot checks of articles from each reviewer to perform quality control. If inconsistency was discovered in a randomly selected article, the article was reviewed again until the RAND staff agreed that all relevant information was recorded on the data abstraction form.

Table F.2
Content of Data Abstraction Form

Element Abstracted from Each Article	Brief Description of the Element
Citation	Reference information for the article reviewed
Type of source	Choices included journal article, book, government source, news article, or other (with an open-ended field for entering more information)
Article type	Article type collected the general purpose of the article and included the following options: evaluation, literature review, theory development, or other (with an open-ended field for entering more information)
Type of media campaign	If the article was about a health communication campaign, the topic of the campaign was captured. Options included mental health, traumatic brain injury, alcohol, tobacco, behavioral health, general health, other substance use, other (with an open-ended field for entering more information)
Primary media discussed in the article	If the article discussed best practices for a specific media channel or channels, we noted the channel. Options included print (newspapers, magazines, brochures), television/movies, radio, websites (including blogs), social media, or other (with an open-ended field for entering more information)
Best practices	General sets of standards, guidelines, norms, reference points, or benchmarks that inform practice and are designed to improve performance

Our goal in creating the abstraction form was to provide a standardized way to review sources and extract relevant details to inform our study. This also allowed us to work simultaneously on reviewing and gathering information from the 46 relevant articles. Each team member recorded his or her data abstractions using Microsoft Excel. When each team member completed his or her abstraction, a master file was created to house all of the information abstracted from the articles.

Findings from the Literature Search and Initial List of Best Practices

We collected best practice excerpts from articles, and subsequently analyzed and sorted excerpts into discrete themes yielding insight into best practices across all articles. After sorting article excerpts into themes, team members who performed data abstraction met to discuss our interpretations of the findings and to collapse or refine the themes. The list of 11 best practices below guided the development of 26 candidate checklist items and represented the distilled findings from all 81 articles reviewed during Phases 1 and 2 of the literature review.

Eleven Best Practices for Mental Health Public Awareness Campaigns Based on Literature Review

This section summarizes the literature supporting each of the best practices identified in the literature review and the candidate checklist items associated with each. The checklist items listed after each best practice reflect the initial list generated by the research team (based on the literature) before the expert panel modified, deleted, or added material.

1. Theoretical Basis

A health communication campaign must have a theory to support its development, and the same theory should serve as a basis for its implementation. Before designing campaign materials, developers must conduct thorough research to identify the knowledge, attitudes, and behaviors of target audiences, as well as identify a behavioral theory that specifies how a campaign might motivate specific audiences to change (White House Office of National Drug Control Policy, 2011). Theories provide critical information on the determinants of behavior (thoughts, feelings, and behaviors) that could lead to the campaign's desired outcomes. Basing a campaign on theory helps developers determine appropriate messages—e.g., Lienemann, Siegel, and Crano (2013) suggest that campaigns targeting depression should address cognitive errors—and vehicles to place messages (Coffman, 2002; Noar, 2006; White House Office of National Drug Control Policy, 2011). A theory will also help to guide campaign goals and outcomes. To be effective, the goals and outcomes of campaign communications must be well defined, be measurable, and guide a defined plan of action (Coffman, 2004). Given that campaigns are focused, time-bound efforts, campaign activities must closely align with stated goals (Evans-Lacko et al., 2010).

Corresponding Checklist Items
- The campaign has a *theoretical basis*, defined as a proposed explanation of empirical phenomena (e.g., behavior change, help-seeking).
- The campaign's guiding theoretical model identifies determinants of the behavior that the campaign is trying to change.
- The campaign has clear goals and objectives.
- The campaign's messages and activities align closely with the goals and objectives of the campaign.
- The campaign communicates messages that are targeted at determinants of behavior (as specified by the campaign theory).

2. Targeted, Simple, and Clear Messages

Targeting messages to specific homogenous audiences helps focus messages so they are simple and clear. For example, the needs of young people at high risk of psychological health problems may be very different from the needs of young people in general, and the preferred style of messages may be very different for young adults and adolescents. Evidence suggests that targeting messages to specific audiences can improve their effectiveness (Tancredi et al., 2013; Corrigan and Gelb, 2006). Such targeting will help ensure that messages are framed in ways that are culturally appropriate, reflect audience values, and are relevant to and resonate with the target audience (Caputo and Rouner, 2011; Noar, 2006). Identifying a specific homogenous audience will also help determine the types of messengers that will be seen as credible to the target audiences (Corrigan and Gelb, 2006). Social marketing national benchmark criteria underscore the importance of avoiding a one-size-fits-all approach (Keller et al., 2014).

Corresponding Checklist Items
- The campaign materials clearly communicate the messages of the campaign.
- The campaign materials are simple enough to be easily understood.
- The messages the campaign is trying to convey are simple and clear.
- The messengers selected in pictures and videos are the types of messengers that will be seen as credible to the target audience.

3. Target Audience Input

The target audiences must have input into the development of campaign messages and strategies for dissemination. A health communication campaign should engage the target audiences early during the campaign development. Input from the target audiences (e.g., through focus groups) should be used to help identify and develop messages that will be relevant to them (Mackert et al., 2014; Noar, 2006). For example, research found that messages to encourage help-seeking behavior in men with depression are different from those for women with depression, with male messages focusing on the fact that getting psychological counseling can help lower the men's health care costs and is courageous or takes strength (Hammer and Vogel, 2010). Through this type of formative research, Pietrzak et al. (2009) found that educating soldiers about the nature and effectiveness of psychological interventions may help decrease stigma and promote help-seeking behaviors.

Health communication campaign developers should also seek input from target audiences about effective dissemination strategies. Various audiences may best be reached through different modes of communication. For example, research suggests that distributing materials through primary care providers is an effective way to reach men with depression (Dew et al., 1991; Hammer and Vogel, 2010), who are more likely to consult with their primary care provider about psychological issues (Andrews, Issakidis, and Carter, 2001). Help-seeking messages may be well received by men with depression if those messages are delivered by peers (e.g., from a similar occupation) or public male figures (Andreasen, 1994; Rochlen and Hoyer, 2005; Rochlen, McKelley, and Pituch, 2006).

Corresponding Checklist Item
- Messages and delivery strategies are targeted based on what is known about the intended target audience.

4. Pilot Testing Messages

Rigorously testing key messages before fully designing and developing campaign materials and pilot-testing campaign materials are key steps in cam-

paign implementation. Qualitative and quantitative techniques can be used to explore understanding of and reactions to campaign messages among individuals from the campaign's target audience (White House Office of National Drug Control Policy, 2011). Some useful items to test include whether the message provides a clear course of action; whether the message is simple, clear, and specific; and whether the message evokes emotion and is thus likely to motivate behavior change (Dorfman, Ervice, and Woodruff, 2002; Hammer and Vogel, 2010). Once messages are determined to be appropriate, campaign materials can be developed and pilot-tested (Noar, 2006). For example, Above the Influence (the National Youth Anti-Drug Media Campaign) pilot-tested ads by showing them to several hundred members of the target audience and assessing changes in drug-related beliefs and attitudes. To be included in the campaign, the ads had to result in greater shifts in drug-related beliefs and attitudes than occurred in a control group that did not view the ads (White House Office of National Drug Control Policy, 2011).

Corresponding Checklist Items

- The campaign messages are rigorously tested among different target audiences before dissemination to ensure that they communicate the intended message.
- Once developed, the campaign materials are rigorously pilot-tested among different target audiences to ensure that they achieve the intended results.
- The campaign messages convey a solution or clear course of action.
- The campaign messages are compelling.

5. Continuous Monitoring and Evaluation

Campaign implementation should include continuous monitoring and evaluation. Campaign monitoring and evaluation procedures may assess campaign exposure, audience response, and preliminary evidence of the campaign on behavior (Smith, 2002). Unanticipated results and side effects, such as inadvertent reinforcement of negative stereotypes, should also be noted (Smith, 2002). This monitoring process allows campaign developers to identify changing audience needs and refine campaign strategy, messages, and materials accordingly (Smith, 2002). This continuous monitoring and refinement also ensures that resources are not wasted if, for example, campaign messages become ineffective or campaign dissemination no longer reaches the target audience as intended (Noar, 2006). In one example, the National Youth Anti-Drug Media Campaign surveyed 100 teens to assess awareness and recall of ads and intentions regarding drug use (White House Office of National Drug Control Policy, 2011).

Corresponding Checklist Items

- The campaign is collecting data on its impact.
- The campaign is using the data collected to regularly assess whether it is meeting its goals and objectives.
- The campaign avoids reinforcing negative stereotypes.

6. Regular and Consistent Message Exposure

For a campaign to be effective, target audiences of campaigns must have adequate exposure to the campaign (Smith, 2002; Rochlen, Whilde, and Hoyer, 2005). Once target audiences are exposed to campaign materials, they notice them, internalize campaign messages, and then react in some form (e.g., by changing attitudes or behaviors) (Pinfold et al., 2005). Campaign developers should use various channels that are likely to be viewed by target audiences, such as use of online messages for younger target audiences (Television Bureau of Advertising, 2008). For example, those with limited literacy skills can take advantage of video, photography, or other visual methods to convey health information (Norman and Yip, 2012). Social media can also facilitate social networks that serve as a conduit for support and information-sharing that can aid in the recognition of mental health problems and access to services (Goodman, Wennerstrom, and Springgate, 2011; Pietrabissa et al., 2015). In a past meta-analysis of public health campaigns, greater campaign reach—that is, a greater number of people exposed to a campaign—was associated with larger campaign effect sizes (Snyder and Hamilton, 2002).

Multiple campaign exposures over time are likely a critical component of effective campaigns (Phillipson, Jones, and Wiese, 2009). The target audience must pay attention to the health communication campaign with enough frequency to be able to recognize and recall campaign messages. A campaign should be expected to run at least six months to affect awareness of the issue, 12 to 18 months to have an effect on attitudes, and 18 to 24 months to influence behavior (Office on Smoking and Health, 2007). Some research suggests that a health communication campaign should strategically aim to reach 75–85 percent of the target audience every three months throughout the campaign, with a more concentrated effort during the initial three to six months of the campaign (Office on Smoking and Health, 2007).

Corresponding Checklist Items

- The campaign uses several different means of dissemination that are tailored to target audiences.
- The campaign's dissemination strategy is designed to provide target audiences with consistent exposure to messages.

7. Audience Segmentation

To reach target audiences efficiently and effectively, campaigns should segment audiences into relevant groups. Segments are based on one or more readily observable factors, such as age, sex, race or ethnicity, income level, occupation, area of residence, or other attributes (Tancredi et al., 2013). Effective campaigns will address mental health–related issues not only in isolation but also in tandem with other relevant cultural and ethnic aspects of the community being targeted for an intervention (Han, Cao, and Anton, 2015). To target messages (see previous section on "Target Audience Input"), campaigns should segment audiences after conducting formative research (e.g., focus groups) (Tancredi et al., 2013). Keller et al. (2014) found that marketing approaches are most successful in reaching diverse and somewhat stigmatized groups when guided by segmentation (Feeley and Moon, 2005; Snyder and LaCroix, 2013) because the segmented audience is more likely to feel the content is relevant to their everyday lives (Caputo and Rouner, 2011).

Individuals with mental health issues are often the primary target audience for mental health public awareness campaigns. However, research has suggested that family members, health providers, and employers are important audiences to include because of their influence (at times both positive and negative) on perceptions of mental health and mental health treatment and on help-seeking behavior (Thornicroft et al., 2014; Acosta, Ramchand, et al., 2012; Henderson et al., 2012).

Corresponding Checklist Items

- The campaign segments audiences by one or more readily observable factors, such as age, sex, race or ethnicity, income level, occupation, area of residence, or other attributes.
- The campaign targets family members, health providers, and employers.

8. Mental Health Communication Campaigns Target Male Audiences

Because both the U.S. military total force and veteran populations are estimated to be more than 80 percent male, it is important to consider how best to target male audiences (Office of the Deputy Assistant Secretary of Defense [Military Community and Family Policy], undated-a; National Center for Veterans Analysis and Statistics, 2014). Designing campaigns for specific target groups can enhance the likelihood of success (Snyder and LaCroix, 2013). In addition, some research suggests that men hold more stigmatizing attitudes and beliefs about mental illness than women and thus may be more likely to benefit from carefully crafted messaging around mental health (Anderson et al., 2015). Research on designing mental health–related messages (often focused on depression) for men suggests that campaigns should discuss symptoms that men are most likely to experience, such as substance use, aggression, and withdrawal (Rochlen, McKelley, and Pituch, 2006; Hammer and Vogel, 2010); emphasize that seeking help promotes strength, health, and autonomy (Andreasen, 1994; Rochlen and Hoyer, 2005); counter the misperception that mental illness is a result of a lack of willpower (e.g., by highlighting the biological underpinnings of depression) (Hammer and Vogel, 2010); use language that is compatible with traditional male gender roles (e.g., "team up," "defeat depression") (Hammer and Vogel, 2010); and show that treatment is cost-effective (Rochlen, McKelley, and Pituch, 2006; Hammer and Vogel, 2010).

Corresponding Checklist Item

- Some of the campaign messages use language and concepts intended to resonate with men (e.g., equating help-seeking with strength and autonomy, countering the idea that mental illness is a result of a lack of willpower).

9. Contact Strategies

Using contact strategies, where members of the target audiences have contact with individuals with mental health challenges, can help reduce stigmatizing attitudes and perceptions of people with mental illness. Contact-based strategies could include exposure to people with mental health challenges on video, in person, or through other channels (Evans-Lacko et al., 2013; Michaels et al., 2014; Yamaguchi, Mino, and Uddin, 2011). Literature suggests that contact strategies yield stronger outcomes than interventions that involve the provision of educational information about mental illness (Michaels et al., 2014; Corrigan, Powell, and Michaels, 2013; Griffiths et al., 2014). Persons who experience contact are more confident to challenge stigma when compared with those who report no contact (Evans-Lacko et al., 2013) and to change their help-seeking behaviors (Yamaguchi, Mino, and Uddin, 2011). Positive role models (e.g., individuals who have recovered from mental illness) can enhance social learning and reinforce messages with direct interpersonal influence (Tancredi et al., 2013). For example, participants in a study exposed to a news article detailing the story of a person who recovered from mental illness experienced reduced stigma and affirming attitudes about individuals with mental illness (Corrigan, Powell, and Michaels, 2013).

Corresponding Checklist Items
- The campaign involves contact with an individual who has experienced mental health challenges.
- The campaign shows positive role models.

10. Suggested Message Content

Literature points to specific message characteristics for promoting public awareness about mental health. Table F.3 includes recommendations from across the literature. Recommendations include designing messages to build social support, decrease feelings of isolation, diminish beliefs that those suffering from mental illness are dangerous, empower care-seeking, emphasize that suicide is everyone's issue, increase health knowledge, promote the possibility of recovery, and discuss the short-term benefits of behavior change. Research results appear to advise against overemphasizing the biological basis of mental health disorders and sharing too many details about mental health symptoms. For example, describing mental illness as a "brain disease" can help audiences understand that mental illness is not a personal choice but rather a physical condition that warrants care. However, biology-based messaging may not generate appropriate emotional responses, reduce stigma, or increase willingness to seek treatment (Boucher and Campbell, 2014). Thus, messages need to be balanced in terms of their focus on biological and psychosocial underpinnings of mental health disorders (Yamaguchi, Mino, and Uddin, 2011).

Table F.3
Evidence-Based Message Recommendations for Mental Health Public Awareness Campaigns

Recommended Message Characteristic	Reference
Build social support to increase help-seeking behavior in target audiences	Clark-Hitt (2012); Snyder and LaCroix (2013)
Encourage individuals with mental illness to reduce isolation and connect with others	Marcus et al. (2012)
Dispel stereotypes that imply that individuals with mental health disorders are dangerous	Yamaguchi, Mino, and Uddin (2011); Anderson et al. (2015); Evans-Lacko et al. (2013)
Present a balanced portrayal of biological and psychosocial factors to target audiences	Boucher and Campbell (2014); Jin (2015); Lee and An (2016); Simmons et al. (2015); Yamaguchi, Mino, and Uddin (2011)
Avoid overemphasizing symptoms of mental health disorders to individuals with mental illness (i.e., to minimize self-stigma)	Han, Cao, and Anton (2015)
Empower those with mental health symptoms to seek care	Marcus et al. (2012)
Communicate that suicide is everyone's issue and not the fault of the individual who attempts or completes suicide	Lee and An (2016)
Illustrate the prevalence of mental illness to target audiences	Jin (2015)
Increase mental health knowledge to target audiences	Calear, Batterham, and Christensen (2014); Del Casale et al. (2013); Henderson, Evans-Lacko, and Thornicroft (2013); Snyder and LaCroix (2013)
Frame messages in terms of recovery from mental illness to the public	Calear, Batterham, and Christensen (2014); Corrigan, Powell, and Michaels (2013); Henderson et al. (2012)
Provide information on the short-term benefits and consequences of behavior change (i.e., help-seeking) to individuals with mental health disorders	Snyder and LaCroix (2013); Tancredi et al. (2013)

Corresponding Checklist Item

- The campaign uses one or more of the evidence-based message recommendations listed in Table F.3.

11. Need for Resources and Supports That Allow Varying Degrees of Anonymity

Campaigns should provide options that allow individuals to seek additional resources and support that involve varying degrees of anonymity. In both face-to-face and computer-mediated interactions, individuals vary in their preferences for anonymity when soliciting resources or support (Wright and Rains, 2013). Although individuals may prefer anonymous options for seeking further resources and support, preferring support from anonymous and low-intimacy sources is associated with higher levels of perceived stigma and distress (DeAndrea, 2015;

Simmons et al., 2015; Wright and Rains, 2013). However, anonymous venues, such as online resources, can also foster helpful connections when offline supports are not available because of geographical, time, mobility, or social network constraints (Stephens-Reicher et al., 2011).

Corresponding Checklist Item

- The campaign offers options for seeking resources and support that allow for varying degrees of anonymity.

Convening the Panel

To vet the checklist items developed based on the literature review, we convened a panel of 26 experts in five key areas that are relevant to mental health public awareness campaigns aiming to influence service member and veteran mental health:

1. applied communication campaigns
2. behavior change
3. health communication
4. mental health and mental illness stigma
5. military mental health.

The experts who served on the panel are listed in the next section. We recruited experts to foster an interdisciplinary, applied, and research-based dialogue during campaign evaluation. Additionally, each topic area provides an important perspective in interpreting the success of a mental health public awareness campaign. The RAND team invited expert participants via email and phone calls in February 2016.

Expert Panelists

Patty Barron is the director of family readiness at AUSA. She supports all AUSA family programs and events by providing management and oversight to all directorate activities. Previously, she served as the director of outreach, Military Family Projects, at ZERO TO THREE and also worked as the director of youth initiatives at the National Military Family Association where she oversaw the association's Operation Purple Camp program.

Ellen Beckjord is the director of population health program design and engagement optimization at the University of Pittsburgh Medical Center Health Plan. For the past ten years, her training and program of research have focused on health communication and consumer health informatics with an emphasis on cancer prevention and control.

Joseph Capella is the Gerald R. Miller Professor of Communication at the Annenberg School for Communication at the University of Pennsylvania. His research has resulted in more than 150 articles and book chapters and four co-authored books in areas of health and political communication, social interaction, nonverbal behavior, media effects, and statistical methods.

Elisia Cohen is a health communication scientist with more than 15 years of experience in community-based participatory research to develop and evaluate communication strategies to improve vaccination and disease prevention outcomes. She is also director of the Health Communication Research Collaborative and a member of the Cancer Prevention and Control Program's Scientific Leadership Committee at the National Cancer Institute–designated Markey Cancer Center (University of Kentucky) and the Research Communication Committee for the Center for Clinical and Translational Science.

Emily Falk is an associate professor of communication at the University of Pennsylvania's Annenberg School for Communication. Her work investigates how to predict behavior change following exposure to persuasive messaging, in addition to understanding what makes successful ideas spread (e.g., through social networks, through culture).

Tony Foleno advises the strategic planning of more than 40 public service communications campaigns at the Ad Council. His primary role is to leverage research-based insights into action, helping to ensure that the Ad Council remains a results-driven organization with a single-minded focus on making a measurable impact in people's lives.

Vicki Freimuth is professor emeritus at the University of Georgia, where she was director of the Center for Health and Risk Communication and held a joint appointment as a professor in the Department of Communication Studies and the Grady College of Journalism and Mass Communication. Before joining the faculty at the University of Georgia, she served as director of communication at the Centers for Disease Control and Prevention.

Howard Goldman is the editor of *Psychiatric Services*, and he served as senior scientific editor of the *Surgeon General's Report on Mental Health* from 1997 to 1999, for which he was awarded the Surgeon General's Medallion. In 1996, he was elected to membership in the National Academy of Social Insurance, and in 2002, he was elected to the Institute of Medicine.

Madelyn Gould is a professor of epidemiology in psychiatry at Columbia University Medical Center (CUMC), is a research scientist at the New York State Psychiatric Institute (NYSPI), and directs a research unit within the Division of Child Psychiatry at CUMC and NYSPI. Her articles on youth suicide risk and preventative interventions laid the groundwork for the development of state- and national-level suicide prevention programs.

Anara Guard has worked in suicide and injury prevention since 1993. For the past five years, she has been a subject-matter expert advising both Know the Signs, the California statewide social marketing campaign to reduce suicide, and the San Diego County suicide prevention campaign It's Up 2 Us.

Nancy Harrington is a professor of communication and associate dean for research in the College of Communication and Information at the University of Kentucky. She also holds an academic appointment in the School of Public Health and is a faculty associate of the Multidisciplinary Center on Drug and Alcohol Research. Harrington's research focuses on persuasive message design for health behavior change.

Kate Hoit is director of communications for the Got Your 6 campaign. She joined the U.S. Army Reserve and served for eight years. She has also worked in digital engagement and congressional communications at VA.

Gary L. Kreps is a university and distinguished professor and director of the Center for Health and Risk Communication at George Mason University. He studies the use of strategic evidence-based communication to promote public health. He was the founding chief of the Health Communication and Informatics Research Branch at the National Cancer Institute at the National Institutes of Health and received the 2015 Research Laureate Award from the American Academy of Health Behavior.

Annie Lang is a distinguished professor of telecommunications and cognitive science at Indiana University. Her research seeks to explore how people process mediated messages, and her work has produced a general data-driven model of mediated message processing.

Tessa Langley is an assistant professor in health economics in the Division of Epidemiology and Public Health at the University of Nottingham. She has expertise in the evaluation of population-level public health interventions, and she is particularly interested in tobacco control mass media campaigns.

Xiaoli Nan is an expert in health and risk communication. Her work addresses the role of persuasive messages and traditional and emerging media in shaping health risk perceptions, attitudes, and behaviors. Her research program at the University of Maryland has been continuously funded by government agencies, including the National Institutes of Health.

Seth Noar is a professor in the School of Media and Journalism at the University of North Carolina at Chapel Hill (UNC) and a member of UNC's Lineberger Comprehensive Cancer Center. He has published more than 100 articles and chapters in a wide range of outlets in the social, behavioral, health, and communication sciences. In 2014, Thomson Reuters recognized him as among the top 1 percent of most-cited researchers in the social sciences.

Mark Olfson is a professor of psychiatry at Columbia University Medical Center and a research psychiatrist at New York Psychiatric Institute. His research focuses on identifying gaps between clinical science and practice in mental health care. He has received numerous federal and private grants and has published more than 350 academic papers.

Ronald Rice is the Arthur N. Rupe Chair in the Social Effects of Mass Communication in the Department of Communication at the University of California, Santa

Barbara. He was elected president (2006–2007) and fellow (2010) of the International Communication Association, won the ICA Chaffee Career Achievement award in 2015, and was a Fulbright Scholar in Finland (2006). He has published more than 120 journal articles and 70 book chapters.

John Roberts served in the U.S. Marine Corps from 1982 to 1996, when he received a medical discharge following a prolonged recovery from wounds suffered in the crash of a helicopter at the beginning of Operation Restore Hope. He went on to become supervisor of the VA regional office in Houston. Since 2007, he has worked with the Wounded Warrior Project, where he currently serves as warrior relations executive vice president.

Karen Roberts is deputy director of communications for the Assistant Secretary of Defense for Health Affairs and the Defense Health Agency. In this position, she is part of the leadership team taking a holistic approach to communications for the Military Health System that includes outreach and education for 9.5 million beneficiaries, all media and social media operations, public and internal communications strategy and planning, outreach, customer service, enterprise publications, and enterprise websites.

Alex Rothman is associate dean for research and graduate programs in the College of Liberal Arts and professor in the Department of Psychology, University of Minnesota. Working across a broad range of health domains, he addresses a range of issues, including how people evaluate and process health-relevant information, why and when different health communication strategies are most effective, and the decision processes that underlie the initiation and maintenance of behavior change.

Barbara Van Dahlen was named to *Time*'s 2012 list of the 100 most influential people in the world and is the president of Give an Hour, a nonprofit organization she founded in 2005 to provide free mental health services to the military and veteran community. She is a licensed clinical psychologist practicing in Washington, D.C.

David L. Vogel is a professor in the Department of Psychology at Iowa State University (ISU), a fellow of the American Psychological Association, and a licensed psychologist in Iowa. He is director of the ISU Interdisciplinary Communication Studies program and serves on the editorial boards for *Stigma and Health* and the *Journal of Counseling Psychology*.

Cynthia Wainscott was a member of the Institute of Medicine committee that released the landmark report, *Improving the Quality of Health Care for Mental and Substance Use Conditions* (Institute of Medicine, 2006). She was nominated by President George W. Bush and confirmed by the U.S. Senate as a member of the National Council on Disability. She has also served as vice president for North America and the Caribbean of the World Federation for Mental Health.

Rick Zimmerman is professor and associate dean for research in the College of Nursing at the University of Missouri–St. Louis. His work focuses on understanding why individuals do or do not engage in risky or protective health behaviors, with much of the work focusing on prevention of HIV/AIDS, sexually transmitted diseases, teen pregnancy, and substance use.

Finalizing Checklist Items

The 26 candidate checklist items were presented as affirmative statements about the characteristics of high-quality mental health public awareness campaigns. The expert panel was asked to rate each candidate checklist item for validity and importance using a nine-point Likert scale ranging from 1 ("definitely not valid/important") to 9 ("definitely valid/important") with the midpoint labeled as "uncertain or equivocal validity." We defined a checklist item to be valid if

- adequate scientific evidence or professional consensus exists to support a link between the item and the effectiveness of health communication campaigns
- a health communication campaign with significantly higher adherence to the checklist items would be considered a higher quality campaign.

We defined a checklist item to be important if

- adherence to the best practice is a driver of health communication campaign effectiveness or has a critical influence on the development or implementation of a communication campaign
- there are serious adverse consequences from not adhering to the checklist item.

In addition to rating each candidate checklist item, expert panel members provided open-ended comments. Comments were used to understand how items should be modified or improved. Additionally, panelists were able to suggest new checklist items.

All panel members submitted ratings and comments for the 26 candidate checklist items. We reviewed the mean, median, and range for each item to determine the panel's collective assessment of each item. Significant disagreement for items was defined as four or more of the 26 panelists rating an item with more than a four-point distance from other panelists. We convened a conference call to discuss the items where significant disagreement emerged, as well as nine new checklist items proposed by experts (Table F.4). Panelists then rerated the two items for which there was disagreement, as well as the newly proposed items. Table F.5 reflects the full list of 26 items with the two revised items (numbers 14 and 21).

After a second conference call, we revised the checklist of best practices, incorporating feedback from the experts, integrating newly proposed items, and using the expert ratings of each items' validity and importance. Based on the expert panel feedback, we revised the five items in Table F.6.

Table F.4
Expert Ratings of the Validity and Importance of the Checklist Items Proposed by the Panel

Item No.	Item	Validity	Importance
1	The campaign uses exemplars, narratives, or evocative imagery to communicate the campaign messages.	M = 6.8 Md = 7 R = 2–9	M = 6.5 Md = 7 R = 2–9
2	The campaign is creative.	M = 3.9 Md = 3 R = 1–9	M = 4.4 Md = 5 R = 1–9
3	The campaign incorporates well-known celebrities, public personalities, and issue champions into campaign materials.	M = 4.9 Md = 5 R = 1–9	M = 4.6 Md = 5 R = 1–9
4	Reliable and valid measures are used to assess campaign impact.	M = 8.1 Md = 8 R = 4–9	M = 7.9 Md = 8 R = 4–9
5	The campaign evaluation is in place (i.e., to collect baseline data) before the campaign is disseminated.	M = 7.9 Md = 8 R = 5–9	M = 7.5 Md = 8 R = 4–9
6	The campaign evaluation is designed to explore potential unintended consequences of the campaign.	M = 6.9 Md = 7 R = 3–9	M = 6.7 Md = 7 R = 3–9
7	The campaign has a logic model that guides the campaign activities and evaluation. A logic model links a goal, behaviors directly related to it, factors that influence those behaviors, and campaign activities designed to change those factors.	M = 7.9 Md = 8 R = 5–9	M = 7.5 Md = 8 R = 3–9
8	The campaign maintains flexibility to capitalize on opportunities that emerge in real time.	M = 6 Md = 7 R = 1–9	M = 6.6 Md = 7 R = 2–9
9	The campaign avoids overly simplistic mental health messages like "help is available" or "recovery is possible" that run the risk of miscommunicating to those whose mental illnesses are intractable, misdiagnosed, or otherwise difficult.	M = 5.3 Md = 6 R = 1–9	M = 5.8 Md = 6 R = 1–9

Based on expert ratings and comparing the list of proposed new items to existing items, we added Item 7 from Table F.4. We deleted items 10, 11, 12, 15, and 16 from Table F.5. The revised checklist included 22 items (Box F.1).

Applying the Checklist of Best Practices to Campaigns

In the next stage of the expert panel, members were assigned a campaign and asked to use the checklist to review the campaign's materials and rate it for alignment with best practices. At least six but no more than seven experts reviewed each campaign. Each campaign was reviewed by at least one panelist from the five key areas of expertise (e.g., applied communication campaigns). Expert panelists were also asked to disclose any potential conflicts of interest prior to campaign assignment. If a conflict was identified (e.g., working for an agency sponsoring a particular campaign), the panelist was assigned to review a different campaign. Once assigned to a campaign, each group received instructions for rating the campaign using the checklist items.

Table F.5
Expert Ratings of the Validity and Importance of Candidate Checklist Items

Item No.	Item	Validity	Importance
1	The campaign has a theoretical basis. *Theoretical basis* is defined as a proposed explanation of empirical phenomena (e.g., behavior change, help-seeking).	M = 7.6 Md = 8 R = 4–9	M = 7.4 Md = 8 R = 4–9
2	The campaign's guiding theoretical model identifies determinants of the behavior that the campaign is trying to change.	M = 7.8 Md = 8 R = 2–9	M = 7.8 Md = 8 R = 2–9
3	The campaign has clear goals and objectives.	M = 8.5 Md = 9 R = 6–9	M = 8.2 Md = 9 R = 0–9
4	The campaign's messages and activities align closely with the goals and objectives of the campaign.	M = 8 Md = 9 R = 5–9	M = 8.3 Md = 9 R = 5–9
5	The campaign communicates messages that are targeted at determinants of behavior (as specified by the campaign theory).	M = 7.8 Md = 8 R = 5–9	M = 7.8 Md = 8 R = 0–9
6	The campaign materials clearly communicate the messages of the campaign.	M = 8.4 Md = 9 R = 5–9	M = 8.5 Md = 9 R = 5–9
7	The campaign materials are simple enough to be easily understood.	M = 7.3 Md = 8 R = 1–9	M = 7.7 Md = 8 R = 1–9
8	The messages the campaign is trying to convey are simple and clear.	M = 7.2 Md = 8 R = 1–9	M = 7.5 Md = 8 R = 1–9
9	The messengers selected in pictures and videos are the types of messengers that will be seen as credible to the target audience.	M = 8 Md = 9 R = 3–9	M = 8 Md = 8.5 R = 3–9
10	Messages and delivery strategies are targeted based on what is known about the intended target audience.	M = 8 Md = 8.5 R = 4–9	M = 8.2 Md = 9 R = 5–9
11	The campaign messages are rigorously tested among different target audiences before dissemination to ensure that they communicate the intended message.	M = 8.4 Md = 9 R = 5–9	M = 8.2 Md = 9 R = 4–9
12	Once developed, the campaign materials are rigorously pilot-tested among different target audiences to ensure that they achieve the intended results.	M = 7.8 Md = 9 R = 3–9	M = 7.6 Md = 8.5 R = 3–9
13	The campaign messages convey a solution or clear course of action.	M = 8 Md = 8 R = 5–9	M = 8.2 Md = 8.5 R = 6–9
14	The campaign messages are engaging and relevant to the target audiences.[a]	M = 7.4 Md = 8 R = 1–9	M = 8 Md = 9 R = 4–9
15	The campaign is collecting data on its impact.	M = 7.8 Md = 8.5 R = 0–9	M = 8.3 Md = 9 R = 5–9

Table F.5—Continued

Item No.	Item	Validity	Importance
16	The campaign is using data collected to regularly assess whether it is meeting its goals and objectives.	M = 7.8 Md = 8.5 R = 5–9	M = 8.1 Md = 9 R = 5–9
17	The campaign avoids reinforcing negative stereotypes.	M = 7.6 Md = 8 R = 3–9	M = 7.8 Md = 8 R = 5–9
18	The campaign uses several different means of dissemination that are tailored to target audiences.	M = 7.6 Md = 9 R = 5–9	M = 7.6 Md = 9 R = 5–9
19	The campaign's dissemination strategy is designed to provide target audiences with consistent exposure to messages.	M = 8.2 Md = 9 R = 5–9	M = 8.3 Md = 9 R = 5–9
20	The campaign segments audiences by one or more readily observable factors, such as age, sex, race or ethnicity, income level, occupation, area of residence, or other attributes.	M = 7.2 Md = 7 R = 5–9	M = 7 Md = 7 R = 5–9
21	The campaign targets relevant social network members (e.g., family members, health providers, and employers) as necessary to support campaign goal(s).[a]	M = 7.4 Md = 8 R = 2–9	M = 7.2 Md = 8 R = 2–9
22	Some of the campaign messages use language and concepts intended to resonate with men (e.g., equating help-seeking with strength and autonomy, countering the idea that mental illness is a result of a lack of willpower).	M = 7.3 Md = 8 R = 1–9	M = 7.4 Md = 8 R = 1–9
23	The campaign involves contact with an individual who has experienced mental health challenges.	M = 7.5 Md = 8 R = 5–9	M = 7.2 Md = 7 R = 5–9
24	The campaign shows positive role models.	M = 7.7 Md = 8 R = 5–9	M = 7.5 Md = 8 R = 5–9
25	The campaign uses one or more of the evidence-based message recommendations listed in Table F.3.	M = 7.5 Md = 8 R = 3–9	M = 7.6 Md = 8 R = 3–9
26	The campaign offers options for seeking resources and support that allow for varying degrees of anonymity.	M = 7.8 Md = 8 R = 4–9	M = 8 Md = 8 R = 3–9

[a] Language reflects changes made after second scoring of items following the conference call.

The Rating Task

Each group received a summary of the checklist items (Box F.1), a background document containing summary information about the campaigns, and instructions for completing the rating assignment. The rating form listed each checklist item, and panelists were asked to rate the campaign using a seven-point Likert scale ranging from 1 ("strongly disagree") to 7 ("strongly agree") with the midpoint labeled as "neither agree nor disagree." The instructions specified that rating a checklist item a

Table F.6
Items Revised Based on Expert Feedback

Item No.	Original Item	Revised Item
5	The campaign communicates messages that are targeted at determinants of behavior (as specified by the campaign theory).	The campaign communicates messages that are targeted at determinants of the desired outcomes the campaign is trying to achieve (as specified by the campaign theory or logic models).
9	The messengers selected in pictures and videos are the types of messengers that will be seen as credible to the target audience.	The messengers selected in pictures and videos are the types of messengers that will be seen as credible to the campaign's target audiences.
14	The campaign messages are compelling.	The campaign messages are engaging and relevant to the target audiences.
21	The campaign targets family members, health providers, and employers.	The campaign targets relevant social network members (e.g., family members, health providers, and employers) as necessary to support campaign goal(s).
23	The campaign involves contact with an individual who has experienced mental health challenges.	The campaign involves contact (on video, in person, or through other channels) with an individual who has experienced mental health challenges.

1 would suggest that most or all of the campaign materials reviewed did not adhere to that checklist item and rating a checklist item a 7 would suggest that most or all of the campaign materials adhered strongly to that checklist item. In addition to the ratings based on their review of all campaign materials, panelists were provided an open-ended field to provide a brief rationale for each rating. For four of the checklist items (items 10–13 in Box F.1), panelists were asked to provide a rating specific to each target population (i.e., service members, veterans, friends and family of service members and/or veterans, or general population) based on their review of the materials for that specific target population.

Campaign Materials Reviewed

Overall ratings reflected an aggregate impression of the extent to which the campaign adheres to the checklist item based on the group review of a subset of campaign materials. Expert panelists were asked to spend 15 minutes reviewing a subset of campaign materials. We chose the subset of campaign materials for review in consultation with campaign staff so that the selected materials represented items viewed by staff as being the key materials associated with the campaign. In addition to the selected subset of materials, experts were instructed to spend 15 to 20 minutes freely navigating the campaign website(s) to replicate the experience of a user arriving at the site. Maintaining a balance of structured and unstructured content for review provided a foundation of core content for consideration while also encouraging experts to interact organically with campaign materials in an unstructured manner. Experts recorded what materials they reviewed during their unstructured review times and submitted their accounts to us. The record of reviewed materials for each campaign is provided in each campaign's respective findings section.

Box F.1
Final Checklist of Best Practices in Mental Health Public Awareness Campaigns

1. The campaign has a theoretical basis. *Theoretical basis* is defined as a proposed explanation of empirical phenomena (e.g., behavior change, help-seeking).
2. The campaign's guiding theory identifies determinants of the behavior that the campaign is trying to change.
3. The campaign has clear goals and objectives.
4. The campaign's messages and activities align closely with the goals and objectives of the campaign.
5. The campaign has a logic model that guides the campaign activities and evaluation. A logic model links a goal, behaviors directly related to it, factors that influence those behaviors, and campaign activities designed to change those factors.
6. The campaign communicates messages that are targeted at determinants of the desired outcomes the campaign is trying to achieve (as specified by the campaign theory or logic models).
7. The campaign materials clearly communicate the messages of the campaign.
8. The campaign materials are simple enough to be easily understood.
9. The messages the campaign is trying to convey are simple and clear.
10. The messengers selected in pictures and videos are the types of messengers that will be seen as credible to the campaign's target audiences.
11. The campaign messages are engaging and relevant to the campaign's target audiences.
12. The campaign uses several different means of dissemination that are tailored to the campaigns' target audiences.
13. The campaign's dissemination strategy is designed to provide the campaign's target audiences with consistent exposure to messages.
14. The campaign segments audiences by one or more readily observable factors, such as age, sex, race or ethnicity, income level, occupation, area of residence, or other attributes.
15. The campaign targets relevant social network members (e.g., family members, health providers, and employers) as necessary to support campaign goal(s).
16. Some of the campaign messages use language and concepts intended to resonate with men (e.g., equating help-seeking with strength and autonomy, countering the idea that mental illness is a result of a lack of willpower).
17. The campaign involves contact (on video, in person, or through other channels) with an individual who has experienced mental health challenges.
18. The campaign shows positive role models.
19. The campaign uses one or more of the evidence-based message recommendations listed in Table F.3.
20. The campaign messages convey a solution or clear course of action.
21. The campaign avoids reinforcing negative stereotypes.
22. The campaign offers options for seeking resources and support that allow for varying degrees of anonymity.

Campaign-Specific Conference Calls

We reviewed the mean, median, and range for each item to determine panelists' collective assessment of each campaign on each item. Significant disagreement for items was defined as two or more of the panelists in each group providing a rating that was more than three points lower or higher than other panelists. For example, items with a range larger than three suggested greater disagreement by expert panelists.

After experts submitted their ratings, we convened a conference call to discuss each campaign and address any questions that arose during the rating exercise. We convened a conference call for each of the four campaigns to discuss experts' ratings of the campaign. During the conference call, we discussed the results from the rating exercise, focusing on items that indicated disagreement and recommendations for each respective campaign.

Across campaigns, experts noted that it was difficult to rate several items pertaining to evaluation or dissemination plans given that the campaign materials they reviewed do not provide sufficient information to make judgments on these topics. These items were 1, 2, 5, 6, 12, and 13 from Box F.1. Considering this feedback, we opted to consider only ratings on the checklist items shown in Box F.2 when judging campaigns' alignment with best practices.

Final Ratings of Campaign Alignment with Best Practices

Following the conference call, expert panelists provided a final rating for items discussed on the call to capture any changes in assessment resulting from the discussion. Summative notes were also compiled following each conference call and reflected key campaign strengths or areas for improvements noted by experts during each call. The final ratings for each campaign are discussed in the subsequent results section. For the remainder of this appendix, item numbers reflect the numbers assigned to items in Box F.2.

Box F.2
Final Checklist of Items Rated by Experts

1. The campaign has clear goals and objectives.
2. The campaign's messages and activities align closely with the goals and objectives of the campaign.
3. The campaign materials clearly communicate the messages of the campaign.
4. The campaign materials are simple enough to be easily understood.
5. The messages the campaign is trying to convey are simple and clear.
6. The messengers selected in pictures and videos are the types of messengers that will be seen as credible to the campaign's target audiences.
   - 6.1. Military service members.
   - 6.2. Veterans.
   - 6.3. Friends and family of service members and/or veterans.
7. The campaign messages are engaging and relevant to the campaign's target audiences.
   - 7.1. Military service members.
   - 7.2. Veterans.
   - 7.3. Friends and family of service members and/or veterans.
8. The campaign segments audiences by one or more readily observable factors, such as age, sex, race or ethnicity, income level, occupation, area of residence, or other attributes.
9. The campaign targets relevant social network members (e.g., family members, health providers, and employers) as necessary to support campaign goal(s).
10. Some of the campaign messages use language and concepts intended to resonate with men (e.g., equating help-seeking with strength and autonomy, countering the idea that mental illness is a result of a lack of willpower).
11. The campaign involves contact (on video, in person, or through other channels) with an individual who has experienced mental health challenges.
12. The campaign shows positive role models.
13. The campaign uses one or more of the evidence-based message recommendations listed in Table F.3.
14. The campaign messages convey a solution or clear course of action.
15. The campaign avoids reinforcing negative stereotypes.
16. The campaign offers options for seeking resources and support that allow for varying degrees of anonymity.

Results

Real Warriors Campaign

Experts reviewed the RWC materials in Table F.7. Out of 16 checklist items, the mean for 12 items scored a 6 or higher on the 7-point scale, indicating that the campaign adhered to most checklist items (Table F.8). The campaign was rated highly for using language and concepts intended to resonate with men (Item 10, M = 6.8,) and employing evidence-based messaging strategies (Item 13, M = 6.8). The expert panel also agreed that RWC emphasized contact (on video, in person, or through other channels) with an individual who has experienced mental health challenges (Item 11, M = 7). The campaign's lowest ratings suggest it should work on making all campaign materials simple and streamlined enough to be easily understood (Item 4, M = 5.7,), improving campaign messages directed toward friends and family of service members and/or veterans (Item 7.3, M = 5.5), segmenting audiences by one or more readily observable factors (Item 8, M = 5.5), and targeting relevant social network members (Item 9, M = 5.5).

Campaign Strengths

Campaign materials clearly align with campaign goals and objectives and communicate campaign messages (Item 1, M = 6.3; Item 2, M = 6.2; Item 3, M = 6.3). Encouraging help-seeking and strengthening support systems are repeated in sufficiently varied ways to clearly reach the campaign's intended audiences. For example, the campaign goal to "reduce misperceptions of mental health concerns and treatment through education" was accomplished by the campaign website and resources (e.g., testimonials, articles). Experts also found that messages and activities aligned with the goals and objectives of the campaign (Item 2). One expert stated that the campaign "has an incredible amount of content, all of which is closely aligned with its goals and objectives." Another expert confirmed this assertion by adding "I cannot think of a

Table F.7
Real Warriors Campaign: Materials Reviewed by Expert Panel

Content	Description
Brochure or folder	Reaching Out Is a Sign of Strength materials (includes six flyers, 16-page booklet, five brochures, one contact card, and external folder)
PSA	I Can, I Will (0:29)
Video profile	Real Warriors Profile–1st Sgt. Simon Sandoval (4:17)
Wallet card	Real Warriors Campaign business card
Webpage	Real Warriors Seek Help 24/7 webpage
Website	Real Warriors Campaign Website

Table F.8
Real Warriors Campaign: Expert Panel Ratings of Campaign Materials' Alignment with Goals

Item No.	Item	M	Md	R
1	The campaign has clear goals and objectives.	6.3	7	5–7
2	The campaign's messages and activities align closely with the goals and objectives of the campaign.	6.2	6.5	5–7
3	The campaign materials clearly communicate the messages of the campaign.	6.3	7	5–7
4	The campaign materials are simple enough to be easily understood.	5.7	5.5	5–7
5	The messages the campaign is trying to convey are simple and clear.	6	6	5–7
6	The messengers selected in pictures and videos are the types of messengers that will be seen as credible to the campaign's target audiences.	6.3	6.2	5.7–7
6.1	Military service members.	6.5	6.5	6–7
6.2	Veterans.	6.5	6.5	6–7
6.3	Friends and family of service members and/or veterans.	5.8	5.5	5–7
7	The campaign messages are engaging and relevant to the campaign's target audiences.	5.7	5.8	4–7
7.1	Military service members.	5.8	6	4–7
7.2	Veterans.	5.8	6	4–7
7.3	Friends and family of service members and/or veterans.[a]	5.5	5.5	4–7
8	The campaign segments audiences by one or more readily observable factors, such as age, sex, race or ethnicity, income level, occupation, area of residence, or other attributes.[a]	5.5	5.5	4–7
9	The campaign targets relevant social network members (e.g., family members, health providers, and employers) as necessary to support campaign goal(s).[a]	5.5	5.5	4–7
10	Some of the campaign messages use language and concepts intended to resonate with men (e.g., equating help-seeking with strength and autonomy, countering the idea that mental illness is a result of a lack of willpower).	6.8	7	6–7
11	The campaign involves contact (on video, in person, or through other channels) with an individual who has experienced mental health challenges.	7	7	7–7
12	The campaign shows positive role models.	6.5	7	5–7
13	The campaign uses one or more of the evidence-based message recommendations listed in Table F.3.	6.8	7	6–7
14	The campaign messages convey a solution or clear course of action.	6.2	6.5	5–7
15	The campaign avoids reinforcing negative stereotypes.	6.7	7	6–7
16	The campaign offers options for seeking resources and support that allow for varying degrees of anonymity.	6	6	5–7

[a] Checklist item discussed during RWC-specific conference call.

way this campaign could have more closely aligned its messages and activities to its goals and objectives."

Messengers in pictures and videos will be seen as credible to the campaign's target audience (Item 6, M = 6.3). Experts found that the messengers are currently most developed for military service members and veterans. An expert explained her high rating and shared that she found the materials to be "appealing to those who serve." Another expert, who rated the campaign a 7 in all groups for Item 6, found the video profiles to be very credible. The expert thought audiences would identify with people in the campaign videos, and particularly noticed the variability in rank, gender, and ethnicity in videos so that audiences could find a credible model to identify with.

The campaign uses language and concepts intended to resonate with men (Item 10, M = 6.8). One expert noted the campaign has a clear emphasis on strength, duty, responsibility, and "hidden wounds," which are intended to resonate with men in the military. Another expert found the campaign to be "male-focused" and thus provided a high rating. Although RWC is focused on men, another panel member shared that even with the high number of male-tailored messages, she felt the campaign did not alienate women. The campaign also received a high rating for Item 13 (M = 6.8), as panelists noted several instances where the campaign employed prescribed messaging strategies.

The campaign uses contact (on video, in person, or through other channels) strategies to expose audiences to positive role models who have experienced mental health challenges (Item 11, M = 7). All experts rated this item a 7, indicating full agreement. Experts noted that the testimonial videos and supporting resources are effective outlets for challenging stigma and encouraging help-seeking behaviors. Individuals in the videos also serve as positive role models (Item 12, M = 6.5) "who share their challenges and express the positive consequences they experience as a result of coming forward to get help." An expert found that role models are "engaging in positive activities (exercise, family time, work) while also emphasizing that they are able to continue in their careers even after acknowledging 'problems' and seeking or receiving help." The panel also took note that the campaign avoided perpetuating negative stereotypes (Item 15, M = 6.7).

Areas for Improvement

Make all campaign materials simple and streamlined enough to be easily understood and navigated (Item 4, M = 5.7). Panelists described many examples of simple messages, but were confounded by the sheer volume of campaign content at times and struggled with website navigability. Another expert echoed this sentiment: "the materials are simple . . . but there is so much content . . . and many of the materials are so text heavy that I am concerned about visitors getting exhausted or overwhelmed by the amount of information." Another expert worried that the videos were long and "would require a high degree of motivation" for users to watch the entire video. Individually reviewed messages may be simple, but as panelists reviewed the campaign holistically, they became increasingly overwhelmed.

Further develop content for veterans and friends and family of service members (Item 7.2, M = 5.8; Item 7.3, M = 5.5). Experts thought that the campaign does best appealing to service members (when compared with family members) and noted that information for families appeared "thin." One expert noted that there is a great deal of content for active duty members and veterans, but materials for the family seem "less extensively developed compared to the videos and materials" for other groups. Family members are a key social network for active duty service members and can be an effective way to reach service members who may not otherwise be able to access resources.

Organize campaign materials to make them more easily navigated based on users' gender, rank, and race. Experts observed that the campaign segmented and clearly organized material by military service members, veterans, and friends and family on the website using tabs on the top of the website allowing users to navigate to content applicable to their role (e.g., family member vs. service member). After further review, experts suggested that the campaign might also segment audiences by gender, rank, and race. For example, "there are videos that address specific experiences and needs of women military members (e.g., the profile of Lt. Col. Mary Carlisle)." However, it was difficult to find content for specific gender, rank, or race when navigating the website. Organizing the content to allow for a more tailored user experience (e.g., similar to MTC's landing page) may remedy this.

Streamline the campaign website and update unrelated or unmoderated website content. Experts suggested that the campaign consider designing the website to be less cluttered and to focus on increasing ease of navigation. Exemplar campaign websites to review for examples include the National Cancer Institute's Smoke Free campaign (smokefree.gov, undated), Centers for Disease Control and Prevention's Tips for Smokers campaign (Centers for Disease Control and Prevention, 2017), and the American Legacy Foundation's Truth Initiative (undated). A first step in streamlining content could be to remove unrelated or unattended website content. For example, users have posted unrelated content on the message board (e.g., some users are using the board to sell items). Other user messages on the message board suggest psychological distress and have received no replies, suggesting that the message board is not well moderated.

Make the Connection

Expert panelists used the campaign materials in Table F.9 to rate the campaign. Out of 16 checklist items, 14 items scored a mean of 6 or higher, indicating that the campaign adhered to most checklist items (Table F.10). The expert panel rated the campaign highly for introducing contact (on video, in person, or through other channels) with an individual who has experienced mental health challenges (Item 11, M = 7) and for showing positive role models (Item 12, M = 7). The campaign received lower ratings

Table F.9
Make the Connection: Campaign Materials Reviewed by Expert Panel

Content	Description
Facebook page	Make the Connection Facebook page
PTSD infographic	Learn About PTSD (1 page)
PSA	Veterans' Voices (1:00)
Shareable social media content	Social media messages for Facebook, Twitter, and Pinterest
Toolkit	#ConnectWith toolkit
Veterans information card	I'm a veteran. I know what it's like. Hear my story. (2 pages)
Video	Treatment Works and Recovery Is Possible (3:30)
Video	Women Veterans' Stories of Strength (3:55)
Website	Make the Connection website

for using messages that convey a solution or clear course of action (Item 14, M = 5.5) and offering options for seeking resources and support that allow for varying degrees of anonymity (Item 16, M = 5.2).

Campaign Strengths

Campaign materials clearly communicate messages (Item 3, M = 6.3). For example, an expert shared, "I really loved the content. All the videos were easy to watch and follow and spoke to experiences, symptoms, help-seeking behaviors, a call to action." Another expert confirmed that the videos were "extraordinarily effective" and "good resources for vets, family, clinicians, all packed with information and driving toward the message that treatment helps and that it is OK to ask for help." Panelists agreed that the campaign materials are also "simple enough to be easily understood" and that messages "the campaign is trying to convey are simple and clear."

Messengers in pictures and videos and campaign messages will be seen as credible to the campaign's target audience (Item 6, M = 6.5). One panelist was impressed by the "array of people involved, the variety of their stories, and their struggles all pretty much ending successfully. . . . They have the credibility of 'insiders' to those in the target audience and people with just a bit of skepticism about treatment being recommended." Another expert agreed, "all spokespersons were very 'real.' Veteran's videos were excellent. The family videos did not 'sugar coat' it, but gave hope and encouragement." Quantitative scores for checklist Items 7 (the campaign messages are engaging and relevant to the campaign's target audiences, M = 6.2) and 8 (the campaign segments audiences by one or more readily observable factors, such as age, sex, race or ethnicity, income level, occupation, area of residence, or other attributes, M = 6) demonstrate that MTC is engaged in selecting appropriate campaign

Table F.10
Make the Connection: Expert Panel Ratings of Campaign Materials' Alignment with Goals

Item No.	Item	M	Md	R
1	The campaign has clear goals and objectives.	6	5.5	3–7
2	The campaign's messages and activities align closely with the goals and objectives of the campaign.	6	6	4–7
3	The campaign materials clearly communicate the messages of the campaign.	6.3	6.5	5–7
4	The campaign materials are simple enough to be easily understood.	6.5	6.5	6–7
5	The messages the campaign is trying to convey are simple and clear.	6.5	6	6–7
6	The messengers selected in pictures and videos are the types of messengers that will be seen as credible to the campaign's target audiences.	6.5	6.7	5.3–7
6.1	Military service members.	6.3	7	4–7
6.2	Veterans.	6.8	7	6–7
6.3	Friends and family of service members and/or veterans.	6.3	6	6–7
7	The campaign messages are engaging and relevant to the campaign's target audiences.	6.2	6.3	5–7
7.1	Military service members.	6	6	4–7
7.2	Veterans.	6.5	7	6–7
7.3	Friends and family of service members and/or veterans.[a]	6	6	5–7
8	The campaign segments audiences by one or more readily observable factors, such as age, sex, race or ethnicity, income level, occupation, area of residence, or other attributes.	6	6	5–7
9	The campaign targets relevant social network members (e.g., family members, health providers, and employers) as necessary to support campaign goal(s).	6.3	6	5–7
10	Some of the campaign messages use language and concepts intended to resonate with men (e.g., equating help-seeking with strength and autonomy, countering the idea that mental illness is a result of a lack of willpower).[a]	6.3	6.5	5–7
11	The campaign involves contact (on video, in person, or through other channels) with an individual who has experienced mental health challenges.	7	7	7–7
12	The campaign shows positive role models.	7	7	7–7
13	The campaign uses one or more of the evidence-based message recommendations listed in Table F.3.	6.5	6	6–7
14	The campaign messages convey a solution or clear course of action.[a]	5.5	6	4–6
15	The campaign avoids reinforcing negative stereotypes.	6.5	7	6–7
16	The campaign offers options for seeking resources and support that allow for varying degrees of anonymity.[a]	5.2	5	3–7

[a] Checklist item discussed during MTC-specific conference call.

messengers, tailoring messages for target audiences, and disseminating content to target audiences appropriately.

The campaign portrays people with mental health challenges as positive role models (Item 11, M = 7; Item 12, M = 7). An expert panel member stated the campaign videos are "extraordinary in-person testimonies." One expert noted that the video library of stories "provides a strong foundation for the campaign" by exposing viewers to individuals who have experienced mental health challenges. Each expert acknowledged that MTC portrayed positive role models in campaign videos.

Areas for Improvement

Allow users to schedule an appointment without leaving the website. Experts suggested that the campaign might help connect users to care by connecting them with an appointment line for a mental health care provider in their area. This more direct connection to care was proposed as a way to mitigate the difficulties that individuals living in isolated or rural locations may face in finding a nearby provider.

Clarify which supports or services are anonymous (e.g., self-assessments) and add content that talks about the challenges associated with maintaining anonymity (Item 16, M = 5.2). This challenge could be addressed by adding clarification to online content to let users know if anonymity is guaranteed (or not). For example, the website's "self-help assessments" section already includes the statement, "These results are completely anonymous and confidential, and none of your answers will be stored or sent anywhere," which could encourage users to complete the assessment. In order to encourage help-seeking, adding a FAQ section on how VA ensures anonymity (or does not) would reduce uncertainty about using VA resources. One expert panelist suggests that a story (i.e., video) should address the challenge of maintaining anonymity.

Further develop the resources webpage to include more self-help resources and resource options to address some of the logistical barriers to care (e.g., transportation). A core element of the campaign is to connect veterans, family members and friends, and other supporters with resources. However, the campaign website offers very basic or introductory suggestions under such subtabs as "self-help" and "self-assessments." A panelist noted that the self-help strategies are not sufficiently developed and additional links and resources need to be provided on this page. Resources that address barriers to care (i.e., transportation, resources) could be beneficial to those who need more information on how to address these challenges.

Create a video game or other unique products to drive people to the campaign website. For example, campaign messages could be embedded in a video game, and video game promotional materials would generate campaign awareness while simultaneously serving as a resource. Video games can deliver health promotion strategies to target audiences and help users learn about prevention and self-care to improve their health. Experts shared that innovative and/or interactive content could help drive users to the website and encourage repeat visits. An expert suggested the "Become an

EX" campaign (EX, undated) as an example of a website that offers resources to drive repeat visits.

Veterans Crisis Line

Experts rated the VCL materials in Table F.11. Out of 16 checklist items, nine items scored a mean of 6 or higher, indicating that the campaign adhered to slightly more than half the checklist items (Table F.12). Experts agreed that the campaign has clear goals and objectives (Item 1, M = 6.4), that messages are simple and clear (Item 5, M = 6.4), the messengers selected in pictures and videos are credible to veterans (Item 6.2, M = 6.4), and the campaign uses one or more of the evidence-based message recommendations (Item 13, M = 6.4). Two items received a mean rating lower than a 5, including Item 7 (the campaign messages are engaging and relevant to the campaign's target audiences, M = 4.9) and Item 9 (the campaign targets relevant social network members [e.g., family members, health providers, and employers] as necessary to support campaign goal[s], M = 4). Five items received a mean rating between 5 and 6, including Item 2 (the campaign's messages and activities align closely with the goals and objective of the campaign, M = 5.6), Item 6 (the messengers selected in pictures and videos are the types of messengers that will be seen as credible to the campaign's target audiences, M = 5.8), Item 8 (the campaign segments audiences by one or more readily observable factors, such as age, sex, race or ethnicity, income level, occupation, area of residence, or other attributes, M = 5.6), Item 12 (the campaign shows positive role models, M = 5.7), and Item 16 (the campaign offers options for seeking resources and support that allow for varying degrees of anonymity, M = 5.4).

Table F.11
Veterans Crisis Line: Materials Reviewed by Expert Panel

Content	Description
Gun Safety video	The Veterans Crisis Line: Gun Safety (2:18)
Power of 1 campaign materials	"The Power of 1—2015 campaign" materials (including editable flyers, posters, web banner ads)
PSA	Lost: The Power of One Connection (1:00)
PSA	1 Act (1:00)
PSA	Veterans Crisis Line "Commitments" (1:00)
PSA	"Waking Up"—A Message from the Veterans Crisis Line
Toolkit	Social media toolkit
Video	Veterans Crisis Line—Behind the Scenes (3:40)
Website	Veterans Crisis Line website

Table F.12
Veterans Crisis Line: Expert Panel Ratings of Campaign Materials' Alignment with Goals

Item No.	Item	Mean	Median	Range
1	The campaign has clear goals and objectives.	6.4	7	5–7
2	The campaign's messages and activities align closely with the goals and objectives of the campaign.	5.6	6	1–7
3	The campaign materials clearly communicate the messages of the campaign.	6.3	6	5–7
4	The campaign materials are simple enough to be easily understood.	6.3	6	5–7
5	The messages the campaign is trying to convey are simple and clear.	6.4	6	6–7
6	The messengers selected in pictures and videos are the types of messengers that will be seen as credible to the campaign's target audiences.	5.8	6.3	2.7–7
6.1	Military service members.	5.4	6	2–7
6.2	Veterans.	6.4	7	5–7
6.3	Friends and family of service members and/or veterans.[a]	5.6	6	1–7
7	The campaign messages are engaging and relevant to the campaign's target audiences.	4.9	5	2.7–6.3
7.1	Military service members.[a]	3.9	4	2–6
7.2	Veterans.	6.3	6	5–7
7.3	Friends and family of service members and/or veterans.[a]	4.4	5	1–6
8	The campaign segments audiences by one or more readily observable factors, such as age, sex, race or ethnicity, income level, occupation, area of residence, or other attributes.	5.6	6	4–7
9	The campaign targets relevant social network members (e.g., family members, health providers, and employers) as necessary to support campaign goal(s).[a]	4	4	1–7
10	Some of the campaign messages use language and concepts intended to resonate with men (e.g., equating help-seeking with strength and autonomy, countering the idea that mental illness is a result of a lack of willpower).	6	7	4–7
11	The campaign involves contact (on video, in person, or through other channels) with an individual who has experienced mental health challenges.	6.3	6	5–7
12	The campaign shows positive role models.	5.7	6	4–7
13	The campaign uses one or more of the evidence-based message recommendations listed in Table F.3.	6.4	7	5–7
14	The campaign messages convey a solution or clear course of action.	6	6	5–7
15	The campaign avoids reinforcing negative stereotypes.	6.1	6	5–7
16	The campaign offers options for seeking resources and support that allow for varying degrees of anonymity.	5.4	5	4–7

[a] Checklist item discussed during VCL-specific conference call.

Campaign Strengths

Campaign materials are easily understood, align with campaign goals and objectives, and clearly communicate campaign messages (Item 1, M = 6.4; Item 3, M = 6.3; Item 4, M = 6.3; Item 5, M = 6.4). The website describes the campaign's goal to connect veterans in crisis and their families with qualified and caring VA responders. An expert shared that the goals to provide assistance to veterans who are experiencing mental health crises is "clearly articulated in the material" (i.e., website, videos, and PSAs). One expert said that the campaign "is clear and easy to understand," making it easy "to access help." Another expert added that the campaign shares not only how to access help but also "the situations in which the services can help and how to access the services."

Messengers in pictures and videos will be seen as credible to veterans (Item 6.2, M = 6.4). The panel also rated campaign messages to veterans as engaging and relevant (Item 7.2, M = 6.3). An expert shared that "the most compelling messengers for veterans were the interviews of counselors in the video. This material conveyed a range of sensitive and understanding individuals who were clearly veterans themselves." A second expert added that the messengers seemed "genuine and credible" and a third shared that "every actor seemed realistic and credible." It was clear that "veterans are the target for this campaign" and most of the content was relevant to veterans.

The campaign uses language and concepts that resonate with men (Item 10, M = 6; Item 13, M = 6.4). Experts observed that the PSAs included content that appeals to men, and one expert identified adherence to this practice as "one of the most successful aspects of the campaign." Another expert noticed the campaign "dispels the idea that mental illness is a lack of willpower," which is an important message for reaching men.

The campaign uses evidence-based message recommendations. Relatedly, VCL successfully uses one or more evidence-based message recommendations (Item 13, M = 6.4). Experts noted "multiple" prescribed strategies noted in the checklist, such as building social support, reducing isolation, and connecting with others.

Areas for Improvement

Further develop materials that highlight the role of family and friends in accessing VCL. The checklist item for whether the campaign targets relevant social network members received a relatively low rating (Item 9, M = 4). While the Power of 1 materials suggest that family and friends are vital to providing support to veterans, experts suggested that the campaign could be strengthened by including additional focus on how network members can help identify signs of crisis and facilitate access to VCL. Experts suggest increasing attention to family and friends, "especially given that some veterans are afraid or view seeking help as weak."

Clarify whether resources offered on the website can be accessed anonymously. An expert noted that "anonymity is not emphasized in the [VCL] messages," and another "didn't see [anonymity] described at great length." While some confidentiality is emphasized on the website, concern emerged about the website's self-help quiz that assures "no follow-up services will be provided unless you request them." However, it is less clear what to expect if a user acknowledges acute suicidal risk. In this instance, an expert questioned whether the confidentiality promise would be honored. Another expert shared that "veterans are scared to reach out because they don't want this on their records, impacting security clearances, etc." The expert continued that users "need to be convinced . . . that it is confidential." Adding an additional question to the FAQs page on how VCL ensures anonymity (or does not) would reduce user uncertainty.

Consider showing users chatting, texting, or calling VCL and the associated benefits in promotional materials. Campaign materials could emphasize that users can call, chat, or text the service to access support by showing someone calling, chatting, or texting the service. The campaign promotional materials should also model positive outcomes from users who contact VCL.

National Recovery Month

Experts reviewed the Recovery Month materials in Table F.13. Out of 16 checklist items, four items had a mean of 6 or higher and 14 had a 5 or higher, indicating that the campaign somewhat adhered to most checklist items (Table F.14). These ratings suggest that the campaign successfully aligned messages and activities with goals and objectives (Item 2, M = 6), clearly communicated messages (Item 3, M = 6), included positive role models (Item 12, M = 6.2), and implemented evidence-based message recommendations (Item 13, M = 6.2). The campaign received lower ratings for selecting credible messengers for target audiences (Item 6, M = 4.8) and using language and concepts intended to resonate with men (Item 10, M = 3.7).

Campaign Strengths

Campaign materials clearly align with campaign goals and objectives and communicate campaign messages. Several experts agreed that the materials clearly conveyed campaign messages (Item 3, M = 6) and that these messages aligned closely with campaign goals and objectives (Item 2, M = 6). For example, one panel member noted that the materials conveyed the messages that "there is hope for recovery, that others have been successful in achieving [recovery], and that there are relevant services and programs available to help."

Positive role models are successfully integrated into the campaign (Item 12, M = 6.2). Experts noticed many examples of individuals who were able to seek help for mental health and addiction services, and found the recovery stories shared in print and video formats to be "very engaging." One expert shared that "one of the strengths of the campaign" was "numerous models of individuals who were able to get help for mental health and additions problems."

The campaign uses evidence-based message recommendations (Item 13, M = 6.2). Experts noted that the campaign employed "many" or almost all of the recommendations included in the checklist recommendations (e.g., present a balanced

Table F.13
National Recovery Month: Materials Reviewed by Expert Panel

Content	Description
Blog post	Access to Behavioral Health Care for Military Service Members, Veterans, and Their Families: Highlights from the Latest Recovery Month Twitter Chat
Facebook page	Recovery Month Facebook page
Facebook post	Recovery Month Facebook post on National Pearl Harbor Remembrance Day providing mental health resources
Facebook post	Recovery Month Facebook post urging returning veterans to visit the MTC website
PSA	Pick Up the Pieces (0:30)
PSA	Rock Climbing (0:30)
Radio series trailer	August 2015 Trailer: Preventing and Addressing Homelessness Among People with Mental and/or Substance Use Disorders (1:23)
Toolkit	Recovery Month Toolkit (Tips and Resources to Plan Events, Distribute Information, and Promote Recovery Efforts)
Tweet	@RecoveryMonth tweet on Veterans Day urging those with PTSD to take time for recovery
Tweet	@RecoveryMonth tweet linking to a SAMHSA web page containing statistics about military and veteran mental health
Twitter page	@RecoveryMonth Twitter page
2015 PSAs	Recovery Month PSAs
Website	National Recovery Month website

portrayal of biological and psychosocial factors to target audiences). The experts specifically noticed that the campaign touched on building social support, connecting with others, dispelling stereotypes, minimizing stigma, and empowering individuals to seek help (among others).

Areas for Improvement

Tailor the campaign to a more targeted audience(s). Experts noted the campaign targeted "everyone," or depicted a "wide range" or mix of audiences. As a result, they felt that the campaign lost its focus on individual groups. One expert shared that when a campaign caters to so many different target audiences, it can be challenging to find the resources to create all the materials needed for a successful campaign. Lack of segmentation is also linked to a lack of content tailored to specific groups. Recovery Month was scored lower by experts on its inclusion of concepts that resonate with men (Item 10, M = 3.7). Improving audience segmentation (Item 8, M = 5.2) could offer more chances to tailor content to specific audiences. One option could be to divide campaign efforts to reach different groups at different points in the year.

Table F.14
National Recovery Month: Expert Panel Ratings of Campaign Materials' Alignment with Goals

Item No.	Item	Mean	Median	Range
1	The campaign has clear goals and objectives.	5.2	6	2–7
2	The campaign's messages and activities align closely with the goals and objectives of the campaign.	6	6	5–7
3	The campaign materials clearly communicate the messages of the campaign.	6	6	5–7
4	The campaign materials are simple enough to be easily understood.[a]	5.3	6	2–7
5	The messages the campaign is trying to convey are simple and clear.	5.7	6	3–7
6	The messengers selected in pictures and videos are the types of messengers that will be seen as credible to the campaign's target audiences.	4.8	4.6	3.3–6.3
6.1	Military service members.[a]	4.7	4.5	3–6
6.2	Veterans.[a]	4.7	4.5	3–6
6.3	Friends and family of service members and/or veterans.	5	5	3–7
6.4	General U.S. population.[a,b]	4.8	4.5	4–6
7	The campaign messages are engaging and relevant to the campaign's target audiences.	5.1	5.6	3–6
7.1	Military service members.[a]	5	5.5	3–6
7.2	Veterans.[a]	5	5.5	3–6
7.3	Friends and family of service members and/or veterans.[a]	5.2	6	3–6
7.4	General U.S. population.[a,b]	5	5.5	3–6
8	The campaign segments audiences by one or more readily observable factors, such as age, sex, race or ethnicity, income level, occupation, area of residence, or other attributes.[a]	5.2	5	4–7
9	The campaign targets relevant social network members (e.g., family members, health providers, and employers) as necessary to support campaign goal(s).	5.2	5	4–7
10	Some of the campaign messages use language and concepts intended to resonate with men (e.g., equating help-seeking with strength and autonomy, countering the idea that mental illness is a result of a lack of willpower).[a]	3.7	3.5	2–6
11	The campaign involves contact (on video, in person, or through other channels) with an individual who has experienced mental health challenges.	5.7	5.5	5–7
12	The campaign shows positive role models.	6.2	6	5–7
13	The campaign uses one or more of the evidence-based message recommendations listed in Table F.3.	6.2	7	4–7
14	The campaign messages convey a solution or clear course of action.	5.5	5	5–7
15	The campaign avoids reinforcing negative stereotypes.	5.6	5.5	4–7
16	The campaign offers options for seeking resources and support that allow for varying degrees of anonymity.[a]	5.7	6	4–7

[a] Checklist item discussed during Recovery Month–specific conference call.

[b] "General population" items are specific only to Recovery Month.

Clearly demarcate outreach materials from resources for individuals with substance use or mental health needs. Greater distinction should also be drawn between resources intended to "help local communities reach out"—such as banners, logos, and flyers—and those intended to reach an individual who is in need of services, such as personal stories of recovery.

Remove technical language and jargon from campaign materials (Item 4, M = 5.3). While campaign messages did align with the goals and objectives of the campaign, an expert found that some materials were "overly technical and not engaging for the average person." For example, the text on the website was particularly "jargon-filled" and overly dense. Currently, the term "behavioral health" is used on the website landing page, the About Recovery Month page, and the Road to Recovery Episodes page. A specific recommendation from the panel is to stop using the term "behavioral health" because this is a technical term that may not be understood by lay audiences. While "behavioral health" is clinically accurate, "very few know what it means." Another way of addressing this concern is to focus on mental health and substance use topics separately. Many of the PSAs use the terms "mental health" and "substance abuse" and are clearer to audiences.

Consider whether a focused month of campaign activity is sufficient, or whether more-sustained messaging is needed to achieve campaign goals. The expert panel questioned whether focusing on an awareness month is an empirically based strategy that is able to compete with other campaigns that operate year-round. An expert shared that there is little support that basing a campaign around a calendar day or month actually improves the effectiveness of the campaign. Days or months could be an occasion to "concentrate" media activities, but, overall, designing a month around an issue does not necessarily affect behavior. Sustained exposure to messages over time is critical, according to another expert, but some change is necessary to keep messages from getting stale and losing attention. Literature supports these observations, noting that campaigns should run at least six months to affect awareness of an issue, 12 to 18 months to have an effect on attitudes, and 18 to 24 months to influence behavior (Office on Smoking and Health, 2007). One option is to use a month as a "focusing event" to showcase a particular help-seeking behavior to allow for more support among others engaging in the same activity.

In summary, Table F.15 contains expert ratings across all four campaigns organized in descending order from the items most highly rated across campaigns to those least highly rated.

Table F.15
Expert Panel Ratings of Each Campaign on a Subset of the Best-Practices Checklist Items

Item	RWC	MTC	VCL	Recovery Month	Combined
The campaign involves contact (on video, in person, or through other channels) with an individual who has experienced mental health challenges.	M = 7 Md = 7 R = 7–7	M = 7 Md = 7 R = 7–7	M = 6.3 Md = 6 R = 5–7	M = 5.7 Md = 5.5 R = 5–7	M = 6.5 Md = 6.4 R = 6–7
The campaign uses one or more of the evidence-based message recommendations listed in Table F.3.	M = 6.8 Md = 7 R = 6–7	M = 6.5 Md = 6 R = 6–7	M = 6.4 Md = 7 R = 5–7	M = 6.2 Md = 7 R = 4–7	M = 6.5 Md = 6.8 R = 5.3–7
The campaign shows positive role models.	M = 6.5 Md = 7 R = 5–7	M = 7 Md = 7 R = 7–7	M = 5.7 Md = 6 R = 4–7	M = 6.2 Md = 6 R = 5–7	M = 6.4 Md = 6.5 R = 5.3–7
The campaign materials clearly communicate the messages of the campaign.	M = 6.3 Md = 7 R = 5–7	M = 6.3 Md = 6.5 R = 5–7	M = 6.3 Md = 6 R = 5–7	M = 6 Md = 6 R = 5–7	M = 6.2 Md = 6.4 R = 5–7
The campaign avoids reinforcing negative stereotypes.	M = 6.7 Md = 7 R = 6–7	M = 6.5 Md = 7 R = 6–7	M = 6.1 Md = 6 R = 5–7	M = 5.6 Md = 5.5 R = 4–7	M = 6.2 Md = 6.4 R = 5.3–7
The messages the campaign is trying to convey are simple and clear.	M = 6 Md = 6 R = 5–7	M = 6.5 Md = 6 R = 6–7	M = 6.4 Md = 6 R = 6–7	M = 5.7 Md = 6 R = 3–7	M = 6.2 Md = 6.0 R = 5–7
The messengers selected in pictures and videos are the types of messengers that will be seen as credible to the campaign's target audiences. *Target audience: Veterans*	M = 6.5 Md = 6.5 R = 6–7	M = 6.8 Md = 7 R = 6–7	M = 6.4 Md = 7 R = 5–7	M = 4.7 Md = 4.5 R = 3–6	M = 6.1 Md = 6.3 R = 6–6.8
The campaign has clear goals and objectives.	M = 6.3 Md = 7 R = 5–7	M = 6 Md = 5.5 R = 3–7	M = 6.4 Md = 7 R = 5–7	M = 5.2 Md = 6 R = 2–7	M = 6.0 Md = 6.4 R = 3.8–7
The campaign's messages and activities align closely with the goals and objectives of the campaign.	M = 6.2 Md = 6.5 R = 5–7	M = 6 Md = 6 R = 4–7	M = 5.6 Md = 6 R = 1–7	M = 6 Md = 6 R = 5–7	M = 6.0 Md = 6.1 R = 3.8–7
The campaign materials are simple enough to be easily understood.	M = 5.7 Md = 5.5 R = 5–7	M = 6.5 Md = 6.5 R = 6–7	M = 6.3 Md = 6 R = 5–7	M = 5.3 Md = 6 R = 2–7	M = 6.0 Md = 6.0 R = 4.5–7
The campaign messages are engaging and relevant to the campaign's target audiences. *Target audience: Veterans*	M = 5.8 Md = 6 R = 4–7	M = 6.5 Md = 7 R = 6–7	M = 6.3 Md = 6 R = 5–7	M = 5 Md = 5.5 R = 3–6	M = 5.9 Md = 6.1 R = 4.5–6.8
The messengers selected in pictures and videos are the types of messengers that will be seen as credible to the campaign's target audiences. *Target audience: Military service members*	M = 6.5 Md = 6.5 R = 6–7	M = 6.3 Md = 7 R = 4–7	M = 5.4 Md = 6 R = 2–7	M = 4.7 Md = 4.5 R = 3–6	M = 5.7 Md = 6.0 R = 3.8–6.8
The campaign messages convey a solution or clear course of action.	M = 6.2 Md = 6.5 R = 5–7	M = 5.5 Md = 6 R = 4–6	M = 6 Md = 6 R = 5–7	M = 5.5 Md = 5 R = 5–7	M = 5.8 Md = 5.9 R = 4.8–6.8
The messengers selected in pictures and videos are the types of messengers that will be seen as credible to the campaign's target audiences. *Target audience: Friends and family of service members and/or veterans*	M = 5.8 Md = 5.5 R = 5–7	M = 6.3 Md = 6 R = 6–7	M = 5.6 Md = 6 R = 1–7	M = 5 Md = 5 R = 3–7	M = 5.7 Md = 5.6 R = 3.8–7

Table F.15—Continued

Item	RWC	MTC	VCL	Recovery Month	Combined
Some of the campaign messages use language and concepts intended to resonate with men (e.g., equating help-seeking with strength and autonomy, countering the idea that mental illness is a result of a lack of willpower).	M = 6.8 Md = 7 R = 6–7	M = 6.3 Md = 6.5 R = 5–7	M = 6 Md = 7 R = 4–7	M = 3.7 Md = 3.5 R = 2–6	M = 5.7 Md = 6.0 R = 4.3–6.8
The campaign segments audiences by one or more readily observable factors, such as age, sex, race or ethnicity, income level, occupation, area of residence, or other attributes.	M = 5.5 Md = 5.5 R = 4–7	M = 6 Md = 6 R = 5–7	M = 5.6 Md = 6 R = 4–7	M = 5.2 Md = 5 R = 4–7	M = 5.6 Md = 5.6 R = 4.3–7
The campaign offers options for seeking resources and support that allow for varying degrees of anonymity.	M = 6 Md = 6 R = 5–7	M = 5.2 Md = 5 R = 3–7	M = 5.4 Md = 5 R = 4–7	M = 5.7 Md = 6 R = 4–7	M = 5.6 Md = 5.5 R = 4–7
The campaign messages are engaging and relevant to the campaign's target audiences. *Target audience: Friends and family of service members and/or veterans*	M = 5.5 Md = 5.5 R = 4–7	M = 6 Md = 6 R = 5–7	M = 4.4 Md = 5 R = 1–6	M = 5.2 Md = 6 R = 3–6	M = 5.3 Md = 5.6 R = 3.3–6.5
The campaign targets relevant social network members (e.g., family members, health providers, and employers) as necessary to support campaign goal(s).	M = 5.5 Md = 5.5 R = 4–7	M = 6.3 Md = 6 R = 5–7	M = 4 Md = 4 R = 1–7	M = 5.2 Md = 5 R = 4–7	M = 5.3 Md = 5.1 R = 3.5–7
The campaign messages are engaging and relevant to the campaign's target audiences. *Target audience: Military service members*	M = 5.8 Md = 6 R = 4–7	M = 6 Md = 6 R = 4–7	M = 3.9 Md = 4 R = 2–6	M = 5 Md = 5.5 R = 3–6	M = 5.2 Md = 5.4 R = 3.3–6.5

NOTE: Each checklist item was rated from 1 (strong disagreement with the item) to 7 (strong agreement with the item).

References

Acosta, Joie D., Amariah Becker, Jennifer L. Cerully, Michael P. Fisher, Laurie T. Martin, Raffaele Vardavas, Mary Ellen Slaughter, and Terry Schell, *Mental Health Stigma in the Military*, Santa Monica, Calif.: RAND Corporation, RR-426-OSD, 2014. As of September 6, 2017: http://www.rand.org/pubs/research_reports/RR426.html

Acosta, Joie D., Laurie T. Martin, Michael P. Fisher, Racine Harris, and Robin M. Weinick, *Assessment of the Content, Design, and Dissemination of the Real Warriors Campaign*, Santa Monica, Calif.: RAND Corporation, TR-1176-OSD, 2012. As of September 6, 2017: http://www.rand.org/pubs/technical_reports/TR1176.html

Acosta, Joie D., Rajeev Ramchand, Lisa H. Jaycox, Amariah Becker, and Nicole K. Eberhart, *Interventions to Prevent Suicide: A Literature Review to Guide Evaluation of California's Mental Health Prevention and Early Intervention Initiative*, Santa Monica, Calif.: RAND Corporation, TR-1317-CMHSA, 2012. As of October 13, 2017: https://www.rand.org/pubs/technical_reports/TR1317.html

American Public Health Association, "Removing Barriers to Mental Health Services for Veterans," webpage, November 18, 2014. As of October 11, 2017: https://www.apha.org/policies-and-advocacy/public-health-policy-statements/policy-database/2015/01/28/14/51/removing-barriers-to-mental-health-services-for-veterans

Anderson, Kristin N., Andrew B. Jeon, Jordan A. Blenner, Richard L. Wiener, and Debra A. Hope, "How People Evaluate Others with Social Anxiety Disorder: A Comparison to Depression and General Mental Illness Stigma," *American Journal of Orthopsychiatry*, Vol. 85, No. 2, 2015, pp. 131–138.

Andreasen, Alan R., "Social Marketing: Its Definition and Domain," *Journal of Marketing and Public Policy*, Vol. 13, No. 1, 1994, pp. 108–114.

Andrews, Gavin, Cathy Issakidis, and Greg Carter, "Shortfall in Mental Health Service Utilisation," *British Journal of Psychiatry*, Vol. 179, No. 5, 2001, pp. 417–425.

Aphinyanaphongs, Yin, Bisakha Ray, Alexander Statnikov, and Paul Krebs, *Text Classification for Automatic Detection of Alcohol Use-Related Tweets: A Feasibility Study*, Proceedings of the 2014 IEEE 15th International Conference on Information Reuse and Integration, August 2014.

Aramaki, Eiji, Sachiko Maskawa, and Mizuki Morita, "Twitter Catches the Flu: Detecting Influenza Epidemics Using Twitter," *Proceedings of the Conference on Empirical Methods in Natural Language Processing*, Association for Computational Linguistics, July 2011, pp. 1568–1576.

Arbisi, Paul A., Laura Rusch, Melissa A. Polusny, Paul D. Thuras, and Christopher R. Erbes, "Does Cynicism Play a Role in Failure to Obtain Needed Care? Mental Health Service Utilization Among Returning U.S. National Guard Soldiers," *Psychological Assessment*, Vol. 25, No. 3, 2013, pp. 991–996. As of September 6, 2017: http://www.ncbi.nlm.nih.gov/pubmed/23544401

Becerra, Monideepa B., Benjamin J. Becerra, Christina M. Hassija, and Nasia Safdar, "Unmet Mental Healthcare Need and Suicidal Ideation Among U.S. Veterans," *American Journal of Preventive Medicine*, Vol. 16, 2016, pp. S0749–S3797.

Benevenuto, Fabrício, Gabriel Magno, Tiago Rodrigues, and Virgílio Almeida, "Detecting Spammers on Twitter," *Collaboration, Electronic Messaging, Anti-Abuse, and Spam Conference (CEAS)*, Vol. 6, 2010.

Ben-Zeev, Dror, Rochelle Frounfelker, Scott B. Morris, and Patrick W. Corrigan, "Predictors of Self-Stigma in Schizophrenia: New Insights Using Mobile Technologies," *Journal of Dual Diagnosis*, Vol. 8, No. 4, 2012, pp. 305–314. As of September 6, 2017: http://www.ncbi.nlm.nih.gov/pubmed/23459025

Bischoff, Britt, "7 Website Analytics That Matter Most," spinutech.com, 2015. As of June 1, 2016: https://www.spinutech.com/blog/digital-marketing/7-website-analytics-that-matter-most/

Bishop, Christopher M., *Pattern Recognition and Machine Learning*, Los Angeles: Springer, 2006.

Boucher, Laura A., and Duncan G. Campbell, "An Examination of the Impact of a Biological Anti-Stigma Message for Depression on College Students," *Journal of College Student Psychotherapy*, Vol. 28, No. 1, 2014, pp. 74–81. As of September 6, 2017: http://search.ebscohost.com/login.aspx?direct=true&db=psyh&AN=2014-02025-009&site=ehost-live

Bowersox, Nicholas W., Stephen M. Saunders, and Bertrand Berger, "Post-Inpatient Attrition from Care 'As Usual' in Veterans with Multiple Psychiatric Admissions," *Community Mental Health Journal*, Vol. 49, No. 6, 2013, pp. 694–703. As of September 6, 2017: http://www.ncbi.nlm.nih.gov/pubmed/23086009

Calear, Alison L., Philip J. Batterham, and Helen Christensen, "Predictors of Help-Seeking for Suicidal Ideation in the Community: Risks and Opportunities for Public Suicide Prevention Campaigns," *Psychiatry Research*, Vol. 219, No. 3, 2014, pp. 525–530.

Campbell, Duncan G., Laura M. Bonner, Cory R. Bolkan, Andrew B. Lanto, Kara Zivin, Thomas J. Waltz, Ruth Klap, Lisa V. Rubenstein, and Edmund F. Chaney, "A Prospective Analysis of Stigma as a Predictor of Depression Treatment Preferences, Mental Health Treatment Engagement, and Care Quality," Philadelphia, Pa., paper and proceedings of the 35th Annual Meeting and Scientific Sessions of the Society of Behavioral Medicine, *Annals of Behavioral Medicine*, Vol. 47, Supp. 1, 2014, p. s.233.

———, "Stigma Predicts Treatment Preferences and Care Engagement Among Veterans Affairs Primary Care Patients with Depression," *Annals of Behavioral Medicine*, Vol. 50, No. 4, 2016, pp. 533–544.

Caputo, Nicole M., and Donna Rouner, "Narrative Processing of Entertainment Media and Mental Illness Stigma," *Health Communication*, Vol. 26, No. 7, 2011, pp. 595–604.

Carpenter, Christopher J., "A Meta-Analysis of the Effectiveness of Health Belief Model Variables in Predicting Behavior," *Health Communication*, Vol. 25, No. 8, 2010, pp. 661–669.

Centers for Disease Control and Prevention, "Tips for Smokers," webpage, July 27, 2017. As of October 16, 2017: http://www.cdc.gov/tobacco/campaign/tips/index.html

Cerully, Jennifer L., Joie D. Acosta, and Jennifer Sloan, "Mental Health Stigma and Its Effects on Treatment-Related Outcomes," *Military Medicine*, 2018.

Cheng, Hong, Philip Kotler, and Nancy Lee, "Social Marketing for Public Health: An Introduction," in Hong Cheng, Philip Kotler, and Nancy Lee, eds., *Social Marketing for Public Health: Global Trends and Success Stories*, Sudbury, Mass.: Jones and Bartlett, 2011, pp. 1–30.

Clark-Hitt, Rose, *Social Support and Persuading Individuals to Encourage Others to Seek Mental Health Help*, dissertation, Michigan State University, 2012. As of September 6, 2017: http://search.ebscohost.com/login.aspx?direct=true&db=psyh&AN=2012-99190-101&site=ehost-live

Clement, Sarah, Oliver Schauman, Tanya Graham, F. Maggioni, Sara Evans-Lacko, N. Bezborodovs, Craig Morgan, Nicolas Rusch, June S. Brown, and Graham Thornicroft, "What Is the Impact of Mental Health-Related Stigma on Help-Seeking? A Systematic Review of Quantitative and Qualitative Studies," *Psychological Medicine*, Vol. 45, No. 1, 2015, pp. 11–27. As of September 6, 2017: http://www.ncbi.nlm.nih.gov/pubmed/24569086

Clifton, Brian, *Advanced Web Metrics with Google Analytics*, 2nd ed., Indianapolis, Ind.: Wiley, 2010.

Coffman, Julia, *Public Communication Campaign Evaluation: An Environmental Scan of Challenges, Criticisms, Practice, and Opportunities*, Cambridge, Mass.: Harvard Family Research Project, May 2002.

———, *Strategic Communications Audits*, Washington, D.C.: Communications Consortium Media Center, 2004.

Cole-Lewis, Heather, Arun Varghese, Amy Sanders, Mary Schwarz, Jillian Pugatch, and Erik Augustson, "Assessing Electronic Cigarette-Related Tweets for Sentiment and Content Using Supervised Machine Learning," *Journal of Medical Internet Research*, Vol. 17, No. 8, 2015, p. e208.

Collins, Rebecca L., Eunice C. Wong, Elizabeth Roth, Jennifer L. Cerully, and Joyce S. Marks, *Changes in Mental Illness Stigma in California During the Statewide Stigma and Discrimination Reduction Initiative*, Santa Monica, Calif.: RAND Corporation, RR-1139-CMHSA, 2015. As of September 26, 2017: http://www.rand.org/pubs/research_reports/RR1139.html

Corker, Elizabeth, Sarah Hamilton, Claire Henderson, C. Weeks, Vanessa Pinfold, Diana Rose, Paul David Williams, Clare Flach, V. Gill, Elanor Lewis-Holmes, and Graham Thornicroft, "Experiences of Discrimination Among People Using Mental Health Services in England 2008–2011," *British Journal of Psychiatry Supplement*, Vol. 55, 2013, pp. s58–s63. As of September 6, 2017: http://www.ncbi.nlm.nih.gov/pubmed/23553696

Corrigan, Patrick, and Betsy Gelb, "Three Programs That Use Mass Approaches to Challenge the Stigma of Mental Illness," *Psychiatric Services*, Vol. 57, No. 3, 2006, pp. 393–398.

Corrigan, Patrick W., Scott B. Morris, Patrick J. Michaels, Jennifer D. Rafacz, and Nicolas Rusch, "Challenging the Public Stigma of Mental Illness: A Meta-Analysis of Outcome Studies," *Psychiatric Services*, Vol. 63, No. 10, 2012, pp. 963–973.

Corrigan, Patrick W., Karina J. Powell, and Patrick J. Michaels, "The Effects of News Stories on the Stigma of Mental Illness," *Journal of Nervous Mental Disorders*, Vol. 201, No. 3, 2013, pp. 179–182.

Corrigan, Patrick W., and Amy C. Watson, "The Paradox of Self-Stigma and Mental Illness," *Clinical Psychology: Science and Practice*, Vol. 9, No. 1, 2002, pp. 35–53.

"Cross-Agency Priority Goal: Service Members and Veterans Mental Health," Performance.gov, White House, undated. As of December 26, 2017:
https://obamaadministration.archives.performance.gov/content/service-members-and-veterans-mental-health.html#overview

Csardi, Gabor, and Tamás Nepusz, "The igraph Software Package for Complex Network Research," *InterJournal, Complex Systems*, Vol. 1695, No. 5, 2006, pp. 1–9.

DeAndrea, David C., "Testing the Proclaimed Affordances of Online Support Groups in a Nationally Representative Sample of Adults Seeking Mental Health Assistance," *Journal of Health Communication*, Vol. 20, No. 2, 2015, pp. 147–156.

De Choudhury, Munmun, Scott Counts, and Eric Horvitz, "Predicting Postpartum Changes in Emotion and Behavior via Social Media," *Proceedings of the SIGCHI Conference on Human Factors in Computing Systems*, April 2013, pp. 3267–3276.

Defense Manpower Data Center, "DoD Personnel, Workforce Reports & Publications," Military and Civilian Personnel by Service/Agency by State/Country, December 2015. As of December 27, 2017:
https://www.dmdc.osd.mil/appj/dwp/dwp_reports.jsp

Del Casale, Antonio, Giovanni Manfredi, Giorgio D. Kotzalidis, D. Serata, Chiara Rapinesi, Federica Caccia, V. Caccia, Chiara Brugnoli, S. S. Caltagirone, Lavinia De Chiara, Stefano M. Tamorri, Gloria Angeletti, Roberto Brugnoli, R. Haghighat, Roberto Tatarelli, and Paolo Girardi, "Awareness and Education on Mental Disorders in Teenagers Reduce Stigma for Mental Illness: A Preliminary Study," *Journal of Psychopathology*, Vol. 19, No. 3, 2013, pp. 208–212.

Denning, L. A., M. Meisnere, and K. E. Warner, eds., *Preventing Psychological Disorders in Service Members and Their Families: An Assessment of Programs*, Washington, D.C.: National Academy of Sciences, 2014.

Dew, Mary Amanda, Evelyn J. Bromet, Herbert C. Schulberg, David K. Parkinson, and E. Carroll Curtis, "Factors Affecting Service Utilization for Depression in a White-Collar Population," *Social Psychiatry and Psychiatric Epidemiology*, Vol. 26, No. 5, 1991, pp. 230–237.

Dietrich, Sandra, Roland Mergl, Philine Freudenberg, David Althaus, and Ulrich Hegerl, "Impact of a Campaign on the Public's Attitudes Towards Depression," *Health Education Research*, Vol. 25, No. 1, 2010, pp. 135–150.

Disability Rights California, *Report on Dehumanizing Terms in California Codes That Foster Stigma Against People with Mental Health Challenges and Policy Recommendations*, Publication #CM36.01, March 2014. As of September 6, 2017:
http://www.disabilityrightsca.org/pubs/CM3601.pdf

Dorfman, Lori, Joel Ervice, and Katie Woodruff, *A Taxonomy of Public Communications Campaigns and Their Evaluation Challenges*, Berkeley, Calif.: Berkeley Media Studies Group, 2002.

Drake, Richard J., Merete Nordentoft, Gillian Haddock, Celso Arango, W. Wolfgang Fleischhacker, Birte Glenthoj, Marion Leboyer, Stefan Leucht, Markus Leweke, Phillip McGuire, Andreas Meyer-Lindenberg, Dan Rujescu, Iris E. Sommer, René S. Kahn, and Shon W. Lewis, "Modeling Determinants of Medication Attitudes and Poor Adherence in Early Nonaffective Psychosis: Implications for Intervention," *Schizophrenia Bulletin*, Vol. 41, No. 3, 2015, pp. 584–596. As of September 6, 2017:
http://www.ncbi.nlm.nih.gov/pubmed/25750247

Duggan, Maeve, *Mobile Messaging and Social Media—2015*, Pew Research Center, 2015. As of September 6, 2017:
http://www.pewinternet.org/2015/08/19/mobile-messaging-and-social-media-2015/

Durantini, Marta R., Dolores Albarracín, Amy L. Mitchell, Allison N. Earl, and Jeffrey C. Gillette, "Conceptualizing the Influence of Social Agents of Behavior Change: A Meta-Analysis of the Effectiveness of HIV-Prevention Interventionists for Different Groups," *Psychological Bulletin*, Vol. 132, No. 2, 2006, pp. 212–248.

Duthaler, Kathryn, phone conversation and email exchange with author about the amount of traffic from Nepal on RWC Facebook, December 21–22, 2016.

Dutta-Bergman, Mohan J., "Primary Sources of Health Information: Comparisons in the Domain of Health Attitudes, Health Cognitions, and Health Behaviors," *Health Communication*, Vol. 16, No. 3, 2004, pp. 273–288.

Edlund, Mark J., John C. Fortney, Christina M. Reaves, Jeffrey M. Pyne, and Dinesh Mittal, "Beliefs About Depression and Depression Treatment Among Depressed Veterans," *Medical Care*, Vol. 46, No. 6, 2008, pp. 581–589.

Evans-Lacko, Sara, Elizabeth Corker, Paul Williams, Claire Henderson, and Graham Thornicroft, "Effect of the Time to Change Anti-Stigma Campaign on Trends in Mental-Illness-Related Public Stigma Among the English Population in 2003–13: An Analysis of Survey Data," *The Lancet Psychiatry*, Vol. 1, No. 2, 2014, pp. 121–128.

Evans-Lacko, Sara, Claire Henderson, and Graham Thornicroft, "Public Knowledge, Attitudes and Behaviour Regarding People with Mental Illness in England 2009–2012," *British Journal of Psychiatry*, Supplement, Vol. 55, 2013, pp. s51–s57.

Evans-Lacko, Sara, Claire Henderson, Graham Thornicroft, and Paul McCrone, "Economic Evaluation of the Anti-Stigma Social Marketing Campaign in England 2009–2011," *British Journal of Psychiatry*, Vol. 55, 2013, pp. s95–s101. As of September 6, 2017: http://www.ncbi.nlm.nih.gov/pubmed/23553701

Evans-Lacko, Sara, Jillian London, Kirsty Little, Claire Henderson, and Graham Thornicroft, "Evaluation of a Brief Anti-Stigma Campaign in Cambridge: Do Short-Term Campaigns Work?" *BMC Public Health*, Vol. 10, No. 1, 2010, pp. 1–6. As of September 6, 2017: http://dx.doi.org/10.1186/1471-2458-10-339

EX, homepage, Truth Initiative, undated. As of October 16, 2017: https://www.becomeanex.org/

Feeley, Thomas Hugh, and Shin-Il Moon, "A Meta-Analytic Review of Communication Campaigns to Promote Organ Donation," *Communication Reports*, Vol. 22, No. 2, 2005, pp. 63–73.

Fitch, Kathryn, Steven J. Bernstein, Maria Dolores Aguilar, Bernard Burnand, Juan Ramon LaCalle, Pablo Lazaro, Mirjam van het Loo, Joseph McDonnell, Janneke Vader, and James P. Kahan, *The RAND/UCLA Appropriateness Method User's Manual*, Santa Monica, Calif.: RAND Corporation, MR-1269-DG-XII/RE, 2001. As of September 6, 2017: http://www.rand.org/pubs/monograph_reports/MR1269.html

Fitzgerald, Britney, "More Women on Facebook, Twitter and Pinterest Than Men," *Huffington Post*, July 9, 2012. As of December 27, 2017: https://www.huffingtonpost.com/2012/07/09/women-facebook-twitter-pinterest_n_1655164.html

Fulgoni, Gian, and Andrew Lipsman, "Numbers, Please: Digital Game Changers—How Social Media Will Help Usher in the Era of Mobile and Multi-Platform Campaign-Effectiveness Measurement," *Journal of Advertising Research*, Vol. 54, No. 1, 2015, pp. 134–142.

Gaebel, W., H. Zaske, A. E. Baumann, J. Klosterkotter, W. Maier, P. Decker, and H. J. Moller, "Evaluation of the German WPA Program Against Stigma and Discrimination Because of Schizophrenia—Open the Doors: Results from Representative Telephone Surveys Before and After Three Years of Antistigma Interventions," *Schizophrenia Research*, Vol. 98, Nos. 1–3, 2008, pp. 184–193.

Glanz, Karen, "Social and Behavioral Theories in Public Health Interventions: Important Theories and Their Key Constructs," *e-Source: Behavioral and Social Sciences Research*, National Institutes of Health, undated. As of February 3, 2017:
http://www.esourceresearch.org/Default.aspx?TabId=736

Goodman, John, Ashley Wennerstrom, and Benjamin F. Springgate, "Participatory and Social Media to Engage Youth: From the Obama Campaign to Public Health Practice," *Ethnicity and Disease*, Vol. 21, No. 3, Supp. 1, Summer 2011, pp. S1-94–S1-99.

Google Analytics, "Analytics Help," webpage, undated. As of March 1, 2018:
https://support.google.com/analytics/answer/2731565?hl=en

Griffiths, Kathleen M., Bradley Carron-Arthur, Alison Parsons, and Russell Reid, "Effectiveness of Programs for Reducing the Stigma Associated with Mental Disorders: A Meta-Analysis of Randomized Controlled Trials," *World Psychiatry*, Vol. 13, No. 2, 2014, pp. 161–175.

Hallgren, Kevin A., "Computing Inter-Rater Reliability for Observational Data: An Overview and Tutorial," *Tutorials in Quantitative Methods for Psychology*, Vol. 8, No. 1, 2012, pp. 23–24.

Hammer, Joseph H., and David L. Vogel, "Men's Help Seeking for Depression: The Efficacy of a Male-Sensitive Brochure About Counseling," *The Counseling Psychologist*, Vol. 38, No. 2, 2010, pp. 296–313.

Han, Meekyung, Lien Cao, and Karen Anton, "Exploring the Role of Ethnic Media and the Community Readiness to Combat Stigma Attached to Mental Illness Among Vietnamese Immigrants: The Pilot Project Tam an (Inner Peace in Vietnamese)," *Community Mental Health Journal*, Vol. 51, No. 1, 2015, pp. 63–70.

Harpaz-Rotem, Ilan, Robert A. Rosenheck, Robert H. Pietrzak, and S. M. Southwick, "Determinants of Prospective Engagement in Mental Health Treatment Among Symptomatic Iraq/Afghanistan Veterans," *Journal of Nervous and Mental Disease*, Vol. 202, No. 2, 2014, pp. 97–104.

Harvard Business School Publishing, "Web Metrics and ROI Advertising Tool," 2007. As of August 25, 2015:
https://cb.hbsp.harvard.edu/cbmp/resources/marketing/multimedia/flashtools/webmetrics/index.html

Hedden, Sarra L., Joel Kennet, Rachel Lipari, Grace Medley, Peter Tice, Elizabeth A. P. Copello, and Larry A. Kroutil, *Behavioral Health Trends in the United States: Results from the 2014 National Survey on Drug Use and Health*, Washington, D.C.: Substance Abuse and Mental Health Services Administration, HHS Publication No. SMA 15-4927, NSDUH Series H-50, 2015. As of June 1, 2016:
https://www.samhsa.gov/data/sites/default/files/NSDUH-FRR1-2014/NSDUH-FRR1-2014.pdf

Henderson, Claire, Sara Evans-Lacko, Clare Flach, and Graham Thornicroft, "Responses to Mental Health Stigma Questions: The Importance of Social Desirability and Data Collection Method," *Canadian Journal of Psychiatry*, Vol. 57, No. 3, 2012, pp. 152–160.

Henderson, Claire, Sara Evans-Lacko, and Graham Thornicroft, "Mental Illness Stigma, Help Seeking, and Public Health Programs," *American Journal of Public Health*, Vol. 103, No. 5, 2013, pp. 777–780.

Herrera, Rhett, email discussion with author, May 13, 2016.

Hinyard, Leslie J., and Matthew W. Kreuter, "Using Narrative Communication as a Tool for Health Behavior Change: A Conceptual, Theoretical, and Empirical Overview," *Health Education Behavior*, Vol. 34, No. 5, 2006, pp. 777–792.

Hoelzel, Mark, "Update: A Breakdown of the Demographics for Each of the Different Social Networks," *Business Insider*, June 29, 2015. As of December 27, 2017:
http://www.businessinsider.com/
update-a-breakdown-of-the-demographics-for-each-of-the-different-social-networks-2015-6

Hornik, Robert C., ed., *Public Health Communication: Evidence for Behavior Change*, Mahwah, N.J.: Lawrence Erlbaum Associates, 2002.

Huang, Jin, and Charles X. Ling, "Using AUC and Accuracy in Evaluating Learning Algorithms," *IEEE Transactions on Knowledge and Data Engineering*, Vol. 17, No. 3, 2005, pp. 299–310.

Hussey, Peter, Jeanne Ringel, Sangeeta Ahluwalia, Rebecca Anhang Price, Christine Buttorff, Thomas W. Concannon, Susan L. Lovejoy, Grant Martsolf, Robert S. Rudin, Dana Schultz, Elizabeth M. Sloss, Katherine E. Watkins, Daniel A. Waxman, Melissa Bauman, Brian Briscombe, James R. Broyles, Rachel M. Burns, Emily K. Chen, Amy Soo Jin DeSantis, Liisa Ecola, Shira H. Fischer, Mark W. Friedberg, Courtney A. Gidengil, Paul B. Ginsburg, Timothy Gulden, Carlos Ignacio Gutierrez, Samuel Hirshman, Christina Y. Huang, Ryan Kandrack, Amii M. Kress, Kristin Leuschner, Sarah MacCarthy, Ervant J. Maksabedian, Sean Mann, Luke J. Matthews, Linnea Warren May, Nishtha Mishra, Lisa Kraus, Ashley N. Muchow, Jason Nelson, Diana Naranjo, Claire E. O'Hanlon, Francesca Pillemer, Zachary Predmore, Rachel Ross, Teague Ruder, Carolyn M. Rutter, Lori Uscher-Pines, Mary E. Vaiana, Joseph Vesely, Susan D. Hosek, and Carrie M. Farmer, *Resources and Capabilities of the Department of Veterans Affairs to Provide Timely and Accessible Care to Veterans*, Santa Monica, Calif.: RAND Corporation, RR-1165/2-VA, 2015. As of December 27, 2017:
https://www.rand.org/pubs/research_reports/RR1165z2.html

Ilic, Marie, Jost Reinecke, Gerd Bohner, Hans-Onno Röttgers, Thomas Beblo, Martin Driessen, Ulrich Frommberger, and Patrick William Corrigan, "Managing a Stigmatized Identity-Evidence from a Longitudinal Analysis About People with Mental Illness," *Journal of Applied Social Psychology*, Vol. 44, No. 7, 2014, pp. 464–480.

Institute of Medicine, *Improving the Quality of Health Care for Mental and Substance Use Conditions*, Washington, D.C.: National Academies Press, 2006.

Java, Akshay, Xiaodan Song, Tim Finin, Belle Tseng, "Why We Twitter: Understanding Microblogging Usage and Communities," *Proceedings of the 9th WebKDD and 1st SNA-KDD 2007 Workshop on Web Mining and Social Network Analysis*, New York: ACM, 2007.

Jin, Hyun Seung, "Antidepressant Direct-to-Consumer Prescription Drug Advertising and Public Stigma of Depression: The Mediating Role of Perceived Prevalence of Depression," *International Journal of Advertising*, Vol. 34, No. 2, 2015, pp. 350–365. As of September 6, 2017:
http://dx.doi.org/10.1080/02650487.2014.994802

Jorm, Anthony F., Helen Christensen, and Kathleen Margaret Griffiths, "The Impact of Beyondblue: The National Depression Initiative on the Australian Public's Recognition of Depression and Beliefs About Treatments," *Australian & New Zealand Journal of Psychiatry*, Vol. 39, No. 4, 2005, pp. 248–254.

Kaczmarek, Sarah, "You Have the Data, Make the Most of It," DigitalGov, June 27, 2014. As of December 27, 2017:
https://www.digitalgov.gov/2014/06/27/you-have-the-data-make-the-most-of-it/

Kaushik, Avinash, "Standard Metrics Revisited: #3: Bounce Rate," *Occam's Razor*, blog post, August 6, 2007. As of June 1, 2016: http://www.kaushik.net/avinash/standard-metrics-revisited-3-bounce-rate/

Keller, Colleen, Sonia Vega-López, Barbara Ainsworth, Allison Nagle-Williams, Kathie Records, Paska Permana, and Dean Coonrod, "Social Marketing: Approach to Cultural and Contextual Relevance in a Community-Based Physical Activity Intervention," *Health Promotion International*, Vol. 29, No. 1, 2014, pp. 130–140.

Kelley, Christie L., Thomas Watson Britt, Amy B. Adler, and Paul D. Bliese, "Perceived Organizational Support, Posttraumatic Stress Disorder Symptoms, and Stigma in Soldiers Returning from Combat," *Psychological Services*, Vol. 11, No. 2, May 2014, pp. 229–234. As of October 5, 2017: http://www.ncbi.nlm.nih.gov/pubmed/24364593

Kessler, Ronald C., Steven G. Heeringa, Murray B. Stein, Lisa J. Colpe, Carol S. Fullerton, Irving Hwang, James A. Naifeh, Matthew K. Nock, Maria Petukhova, Nancy A. Sampson, Michael Schoenbaum, Alan M. Zaslavsky, and Robert J. Ursano, "Thirty-Day Prevalence of DSM-IV Mental Disorders Among Nondeployed Soldiers in the U.S. Army: Results from the Army Study to Assess Risk and Resilience in Servicemembers (Army STARRS)," *JAMA Psychiatry*, Vol. 71, No. 5, May 2014, pp. 504–513.

Khazaal, Yasser, Anne Chatton, Sophie Cochand, Olivier Coquard, Sebastien Fernandez, Riaz Khan, Joel Billieux, and Daniele Zullino, "Brief DISCERN, Six Questions for the Evaluation of Evidence-Based Content of Health-Related Websites," *Patient Education and Counseling*, Vol. 77, No. 1, 2009, pp. 33–37.

Kohavi, Ron, and Foster Provost, "Glossary of Terms," *Machine Learning*, Vol. 30, Nos. 2–3, 1998, pp. 271–274.

Landis, J. Richard, and Gary G. Koch, "The Measurement of Observer Agreement for Categorical Data," *Biometrics*, Vol. 33, No. 1, 1977, pp. 59–174.

Lee, Hannah, and Soontae An, "Social Stigma Toward Suicide: Effects of Group Categorization and Attributions in Korean Health News," *Health Communications*, Vol. 31, No. 4, April 2016, pp. 468–477.

Lewis, Seth C., and Oscar Westlund, "Actors, Actants, Audiences, and Activities in Cross-Media News Work: A Matrix and a Research Agenda," *Digital Journalism*, Vol. 3, No. 1, 2014, pp. 19–37.

Lienemann, Brianna A., Jason T. Siegel, and William D. Crano, "Persuading People with Depression to Seek Help: Respect the Boomerang," *Health Communications*, Vol. 28, No. 7, 2013, pp. 718–728.

Livingston, James D., Michelle Cianfrone, Kimberley Korf-Uzan, and Connie Coniglio, "Another Time Point, a Different Story: One Year Effects of a Social Media Intervention on the Attitudes of Young People Towards Mental Health Issues," *Social Psychiatry and Psychiatric Epidemiology*, Vol. 49, No. 6, 2014, pp. 985–990. As of September 6, 2017: http://www.ncbi.nlm.nih.gov/pubmed/24401914

Livingston, James D., Teresa Milne, Mei Lan Fang, and Erica Amari, "The Effectiveness of Interventions for Reducing Stigma Related to Substance Use Disorders: A Systematic Review," *Addiction*, Vol. 107, No. 1, 2012, pp. 39–50.

Lobo, Jorge M., Alberto Jiménez-Valverde, and Raimundo Real, "AUC: A Misleading Measure of the Performance of Predictive Distribution Models," *Global Ecology and Biogeography*, Vol. 17, No. 2, 2008, pp. 145–151.

Luoma, Jason B., Magdalena Kulesza, Steven C. Hayes, Barbara S. Kohlenberg, and Mary Larimer, "Stigma Predicts Residential Treatment Length for Substance Use Disorder," *American Journal of Drug and Alcohol Abuse*, Vol. 40, No. 3, 2014, pp. 206–212. As of September 6, 2017: http://www.ncbi.nlm.nih.gov/pubmed/24766087

Luty, Jason, Daniel Fekadu, Okon Umoh, and John Gallagher, "Validation of a Short Instrument to Measure Stigmatised Attitudes Towards Mental Illness," *The Psychiatrist*, Vol. 30, No. 7, 2006, pp. 257–260.

Luty, Jason, Harish Rao, Sujaa Mary Rajagopal Arokiadass, Joby Maducolil Easow, and Arghya Sarkhel, "The Repentant Sinner: Methods to Reduce Stigmatised Attitudes Towards Mental Illness," *BJPsych Bulletin*, Vol. 32, No. 9, 2008, pp. 327–332.

Luty, Jason, Okon Umoh, Mohammed Sessay, and Arghya Sarkhel, "Effectiveness of Changing Minds Campaign Factsheets in Reducing Stigmatised Attitudes Towards Mental Illness," *BJPsych Bulletin*, Vol. 31, No. 10, 2007, pp. 377–381.

Lysaker, Paul H., Louanne W. Davis, Debbie M. Warman, Amy Strasburger, and Nicole Beattie, "Stigma, Social Function and Symptoms in Schizophrenia and Schizoaffective Disorder: Associations Across 6 Months," *Psychiatry Research*, Vol. 149, Nos. 1–3, 2007, pp. 89–95. As of September 6, 2017: http://www.ncbi.nlm.nih.gov/pubmed/17156853

Lysaker, Paul H., Chloe Tunze, Philip T. Yanos, David Roe, Jamie M. Ringer, and Kevin L. Rand, "Relationships Between Stereotyped Beliefs About Mental Illness, Discrimination Experiences, and Distressed Mood over 1 Year Among Persons with Schizophrenia Enrolled in Rehabilitation," *Social Psychiatry and Psychiatric Epidemiology*, Vol. 47, No. 6, 2012, pp. 849–855. As of September 6, 2017: http://www.ncbi.nlm.nih.gov/pubmed/21603968

Mackert, Michael, Erin E. Donovan, Amanda Mabry, Marie Guadagno, and Patricia A. Stout, "Stigma and Health Literacy: An Agenda for Advancing Research and Practice," *American Journal of Health Behavior*, Vol. 38, No. 5, 2014, pp. 690–698.

Make the Connection, homepage, undated. As of October 12, 2017: http://maketheconnection.net/

Marcus, Madalyn A., Herry A. Westra, John D. Eastwood, and Kirsten L. Barnes, "What Are Young Adults Saying About Mental Health? An Analysis of Internet Blogs," *Journal of Medical Internet Research*, Vol. 14, No. 1, 2012, p. e17.

Marczyk, Geoffrey R., David DeMatteo, and David Festinger, *Essentials of Research Design and Methodology*, Hoboken, N.J.: John Wiley & Sons, 2005.

Mehta, Nisha, Aliya Kassam, Morven Leese, Georgia Butler, and Graham Thornicroft, "Public Attitudes Towards People with Mental Illness in England and Scotland, 1994–2003," *British Journal of Psychiatry*, Vol. 194, No. 3, 2009, pp. 278–284.

Meredith, Lisa S., Andrew Parker, Ellen Burke Beckjord, Sarah J. Gaillot, Manan M. Trivedi, and Mary E. Vaiana, *Educating Military Personnel and Their Families About Post-Deployment Stress*, Santa Monica, Calif.: RAND Corporation, WR-544-CCF, 2008. As of September 6, 2017: http://www.rand.org/pubs/working_papers/WR544.html

Michaels, Patrick J., Patrick W. Corrigan, Blythe Buchholz, Jennifer Brown, Thomas Arthur, Clarissa Netter, and Kim L. Macdonald-Wilson, "Changing Stigma Through a Consumer-Based Stigma Reduction Program," *Community Mental Health Journal*, Vol. 50, No. 4, 2014, pp. 395–401.

Mor, Nilly, and Jennifer Winquist, "Self-Focused Attention and Negative Affect: A Meta-Analysis," *Psychological Bulletin*, Vol. 128, No. 4, 2002, p. 638.

Myslín, Mark, Shu Hon Zhu, Wendy Chapman, and Mike Conway, "Using Twitter to Examine Smoking Behavior and Perceptions of Emerging Tobacco Products," *Journal of Medical Internet Research*, Vol. 15, No. 8, 2013, p. e174.

National Center for Veterans Analysis and Statistics, "Veteran Population," Projection Model, 2014 (VetPop2014), data from 1L_VetPop2014.xlsx, U.S. Department of Veterans Affairs, 2014.

National Recovery Month, homepage, Substance Abuse and Mental Health Services Administration, undated. As of October 16, 2017:
http://www.recoverymonth.gov/

Nevo, David, "Experts' Opinion: A Powerful Evaluation Tool," Chicago: Annual Meeting of the American Educational Research Association, March 1985.

Noar, Seth M., "A 10-Year Retrospective of Research in Health Mass Media Campaigns: Where Do We Go from Here?" *Journal of Health Communication*, Vol. 11, No. 1, 2006, pp. 21–42.

Noar, Seth M., Philip Palmgreen, Melissa Chabot, Nicole Dobransky, and Rick Zimmerman, "A 10-Year Systematic Review of HIV/AIDS Mass Communication Campaigns: Have We Made Progress?" *Journal of Health Communication*, Vol. 14, No. 1, 2009, pp. 15–42. As of September 6, 2017
http://www.ncbi.nlm.nih.gov/pubmed/19180369

Norman, Cameron D., and Andrea L. Yip, "eHealth Promotion and Social Innovation with Youth: Using Social and Visual Media to Engage Diverse Communities," *Studies in Health Technology and Informatics*, Vol. 172, 2012, pp. 54–70.

Obama, Barack, "Improving Access to Mental Health Services for Veterans, Service Members, and Military Families," Executive Order 13625, White House, August 31, 2012. As of October 16, 2017:
https://www.gpo.gov/fdsys/pkg/CFR-2013-title3-vol1/pdf/
CFR-2013-title3-vol1-eo13625.pdf

Office of the Deputy Assistant Secretary of Defense (Military Community and Family Policy), *2014 Demographics: Profile of the Military Community*, Washington, D.C.: U.S. Department of Defense, undated-a. As of September 6, 2017:
http://download.militaryonesource.mil/12038/MOS/Reports/2014-Demographics-Report.pdf

———, *2015 Demographics: Profile of the Military Community*, Washington, D.C.: U.S. Department of Defense, undated-b. As of December 26, 2017:
http://download.militaryonesource.mil/12038/MOS/Reports/2015-Demographics-Report.pdf

Office on Smoking and Health, *Best Practices for Comprehensive Tobacco Control Programs–2007: Section A: Health Communications Interventions*, Atlanta, Ga.: U.S. Department of Health and Human Services, Centers for Disease Control and Prevention, National Center for Chronic Disease Prevention and Health Promotion, 2007.

Paek, Hye-Jin, Thomas Hove, Yumi Jung, and Richard T. Cole, "Engagement Across Three Social Media Platforms: An Exploratory Study of a Cause-Related PR Campaign," *Public Relations Review*, Vol. 39, No. 5, 2013, pp. 526–533.

Phillipson, Lyn, Sandra Jones, and Elizabeth Wiese, "Effective Communication Only Part of the Strategy Needed to Promote Help-Seeking of Young People with Mental Health Problems," *Social Marketing Quarterly*, Vol. 15, No. 2, 2009, pp. 50–62.

Pietrabissa, Giada, Gian Mauro Manzoni, Davide Algeri, Luca Mazzucchelli, Alice Carella, Francesco Pagnini, and Gianluca Castelnuovo, "Facebook Use as Access Facilitator for Consulting Psychology," *Australian Psychologist*, Vol. 50, No. 4, 2015, pp. 299–303. As of September 6, 2017:
http://search.ebscohost.com/login.aspx?direct=true&db=psyh&AN=2015-33280-009&site=ehost-live

Pietrzak, Robert H., Douglas C. Johnson, Marc B. Goldstein, James C. Malley, and Steven M. Southwick, "Psychological Resilience and Postdeployment Social Support Protect Against Traumatic Stress and Depressive Symptoms in Soldiers Returning from Operations Enduring Freedom and Iraqi Freedom," *Depression and Anxiety*, Vol. 26, No. 8, 2009, pp. 745–751. As of September 6, 2017: http://dx.doi.org/10.1002/da.20558

Pinfold, Vanessa, Graham Thornicroft, Peter Huxley, and Paul Farmer, "Active Ingredients in Anti-Stigma Programmes in Mental Health," *International Review of Psychiatry*, Vol. 17, No. 2, 2005, pp. 123–131.

Pons, Pascal, and Matthieu Latapy, "Computing Communities in Large Networks Using Random Walks," in Pinar Yolum, Tunga Güngör, Fikret Gürgen, and Can Özturan, eds., *Computer and Information Sciences-ISCIS 2005*, Germany: Springer, Berlin, Heidelberg, 2005, pp. 284–293.

Ramchand, Rajeev, Rena Rudavsky, Sean Grant, Terri Tanielian, and Lisa Jaycox, "Prevalence of, Risk Factors for, and Consequences of Posttraumatic Stress Disorder and Other Mental Health Problems in Military Populations Deployed to Iraq and Afghanistan," *Current Psychiatry Reports*, Vol. 17, No. 5, 2015.

Rashtchy, Safa, Aaron M. Kessler, Paul J. Bieber, Nathaniel H. Schindler, and Judith C. Tzeng, *The User Revolution: The New Advertising Ecosystem and the Rise of the Internet as a Mass Medium*, New York: Piper Jaffray, February 2007. As of December 27, 2017: http://people.ischool.berkeley.edu/~hal/Courses/StratTech07/Lectures/Google/Articles/user-revolution.pdf

Real Warriors Campaign, "Applying for a Discharge Upgrade," webpage, undated-a. As of October 11, 2017: http://www.realwarriors.net/veterans/discharge/upgrade.php

———, homepage, undated-b. As of October 11, 2017: http://www.realwarriors.net/

———, "Navigating the Disability Evaluation System," webpage, undated-c. As of October 11, 2017: https://www.realwarriors.net/active/disability/disability.php

———, "Sharing Messages of Strength," webpage, undated-d. As of March 2, 2018: https://www.realwarriors.net/materials/one-pager-sharing-messages-of-strength

———, "Video Profiles," webpage, undated-e. As of October 11, 2017: http://www.realwarriors.net/multimedia/profiles.php

Reger, Mark A., Derek J. Smolenski, Nancy A. Skopp, Melinda J. Metzger-Abamukang, Han K. Kang, Tim A. Bullman, Sondra Perdue, and Gregory A. Gahm, "Risk of Suicide Among U.S. Military Service Members Following Operation Enduring Freedom or Operation Iraqi Freedom Deployment and Separation from the U.S. Military," *JAMA Psychiatry*, Vol. 72, No. 6, 2015, pp. 561–569.

Ritsher, Jennifer B., and Jo C. Phelan, "Internalized Stigma Predicts Erosion of Morale Among Psychiatric Outpatients," *Psychiatry Research*, Vol. 129, No. 3, 2004, pp. 257–265. As of September 6, 2017: http://www.ncbi.nlm.nih.gov/pubmed/15661319

Rochlen, Aaron B., and Wayne D. Hoyer, "Marketing Mental Health to Men: Theoretical and Practical Considerations," *Journal of Clinical Psychology*, Vol. 61, No. 6, 2005, pp. 675–684. As of September 6, 2017: http://dx.doi.org/10.1002/jclp.20102

Rochlen, Aaron B., Ryan A. McKelley, and Keenan A. Pituch, "A Preliminary Examination of the 'Real Men. Real Depression' Campaign,' *Psychology of Men and Masculinity*, Vol. 7, No. 1, 2006, pp. 1–13.

Rochlen, Aaron B., Margaret R. Whilde, and Wayne D. Hoyer, "The 'Real Men. Real Depression' Campaign: Overview, Theoretical Implications, and Research Considerations," *Psychology of Men and Masculinity*, Vol. 63, No. 3, 2005, pp. 186–194.

Rogers, Everett M., and J. Douglas Storey, "Communication Campaigns," in Charles R. Berger and Steven H. Chaffee, eds., *Handbook of Communication Science*, Newbury Park, Calif.: Sage, 1987, pp. 817–846.

Rose, Diana, Graham Thornicroft, Vanessa Pinfold, and Aliya Kassam, "250 Labels Used to Stigmatise People with Mental Illness," *BMC Health Services Research*, Vol. 7, No. 97, 2007.

Rosen, Craig S., Mark A. Greenbaum, Julie E. Fitt, Charlene Laffaye, Virginia A. Norris, and Rachel Kimerling, "Stigma, Help-Seeking Attitudes, and Use of Psychotherapy in Veterans with Diagnoses of Posttraumatic Stress Disorder," *Journal of Nervous and Mental Disease*, Vol. 199, No. 11, 2011.

Rüsch, Nicolas, Mario Müller, Karsten Heekeren, Anastasia Theodoridou, Sibylle Metzler, Diane Dvorsky, Patrick W. Corrigan, Susanne Walitza, and Wulf Rossler, "Longitudinal Course of Self-Labeling, Stigma Stress and Well-Being Among Young People at Risk of Psychosis," *Schizophrenia Research*, Vol. 158, Nos. 1–3, 2014, pp. 82–84. As of September 6, 2017: http://www.ncbi.nlm.nih.gov/pubmed/25086660

RWC—*See* Real Warriors Campaign.

Sadilek, Adam, Henry A. Kautz, and Vincent Michael Bernard Silenzio, "Modeling Spread of Disease from Social Interactions," International Conference on Weblogs and Social Media, 2012.

SAMHSA—*See* Substance Abuse and Mental Health Services Administration.

Sanders Analytics, "Twitter Sentiment Corpus," webpage, 2011. As of November 20, 2015: http://www.sananalytics.com/lab/twitter-sentiment/

Schultz, Don E., and Heidi Schultz, *IMC, The Next Generation: Five Steps for Delivering Value and Measuring Financial Returns*, New York: McGraw-Hill, 2004.

Seeger, Matthew W., "Best Practice in Crisis Communication: An Expert Panel Process," *Journal of Applied Communication Research*, Vol. 34, No. 3, 2006, pp. 232–244.

Simmons, Leigh Ann, Qishan Wu, Nancy Yang, Heather M. Bush, and Leslie J. Crofford, "Sources of Health Information Among Rural Women in Western Kentucky," *Public Health Nursing*, Vol. 32, No. 1, 2015, pp. 3–14.

Smith, William, "From Prevention Vaccines to Community Care: New Ways to Look at Program Success," in Hornik, 2002.

smokefree.gov, homepage, National Cancer Institute, undated. As of October 16, 2017: https://smokefree.gov

Snyder, Leslie B., and Mark A. Hamilton, "Meta-Analysis of U.S. Health Campaign Effects on Behavior: Emphasize Enforcement, Exposure, and New Information, and Beware the Secular Trend," in Hornik, 2002.

Snyder, Leslie B., and Jessica M. LaCroix, "How Effective Are Mediated Health Campaigns? A Synthesis of Meta-Analyses," in Ronald E. Rice and Charles K. Atkin, eds., *Public Communication Campaign*, Thousand Oaks, Calif.: SAGE Publications, 2013.

Sponder, Marshall, *Social Media Analytics: Effective Tools for Building, Interpreting, and Using Metrics*, New York: McGraw Hill, 2012.

Spoont, Michele R., David B. Nelson, Maureen Murdoch, Thomas Rector, Nina A. Sayer, Sean Nugent, and Joseph Westermeyer, "Impact of Treatment Beliefs and Social Network Encouragement on Initiation of Care by VA Service Users with PTSD," *Psychiatric Services*, Vol. 65, No. 5, 2014, pp. 654–662. As of September 6, 2017:
http://www.ncbi.nlm.nih.gov/pubmed/24488502

Spoont, Michele R., David B. Nelson, Maureen Murdoch, Nina A. Sayer, Sean Nugent, Thomas Rector, and Joseph Westermeyer, "Are There Racial/Ethnic Disparities in VA PTSD Treatment Retention?" *Depression and Anxiety*, Vol. 32, No. 6, 2015, pp. 415–425. As of September 6, 2017:
http://www.ncbi.nlm.nih.gov/pubmed/25421265

Statista, "Distribution of Twitter Users in the United States as of December 2016, by Age Group," 2016. As of December 27, 2017:
https://www.statista.com/statistics/192703/age-distribution-of-users-on-twitter-in-the-united-states/

Stephens-Reicher, Justine, Atari Metcalf, Michelle Blanchard, Cheryl Mangan, and Jane Burns, "Reaching the Hard-to-Reach: How Information Communication Technologies Can Reach Young People at Greater Risk of Mental Health Difficulties," *Australasian Psychiatry*, Vol. 19, Supp. 1, July 2011, pp. S58–S61.

Substance Abuse and Mental Health Services Administration, *Results from the 2013 National Survey on Drug Use and Health: Summary of National Findings*, Rockville, Md., U.S. Department of Health and Human Services, 2014.

Suh, Bongwon, Lichan Hong, Peter Pirolli, and Ed H. Chi, "Want to Be Retweeted? Large Scale Analytics on Factors Impacting Retweet in Twitter Network," *Proceedings of the 2010 IEEE Second International Conference on Social Computing*, IEEE, 2010, pp. 177–184.

Tancredi, Daniel J., Christina K. Slee, Anthony Jerant, Peter Franks, Jasmine Nettiksimmons, Camille Cipri, Dustin Gottfeld, Julia Huerta, Mitchell D. Feldman, Maja Jackson-Triche, Steven Kelly-Reif, Andrew Hudnut, Sarah Olson, Janie Shelton, and Richard L Kravitz, "Targeted Versus Tailored Multimedia Patient Engagement to Enhance Depression Recognition and Treatment in Primary Care: Randomized Controlled Trial Protocol for the AMEP2 Study," *BMC Health Services Research*, Vol. 13, 2013, p. 141.

Tanielian, Terri, and Lisa H. Jaycox, eds., *Invisible Wounds of War: Psychological and Cognitive Injuries, Their Consequences, and Services to Assist Recovery*, Santa Monica, Calif.: RAND Corporation, MG-720-CCF, 2008. As of September 6, 2017:
http://www.rand.org/pubs/monographs/MG720.html

Television Bureau of Advertising, *2008 Media Comparisons Study*, New York: Nielsen Media Research, 2008.

Tenhula, Wendy, email discussion with authors on goals of the Make the Connection campaign, October 26, 2016.

Thornicroft, Calum, Allan Wyllie, Graham Thornicroft, and Nisha Mehta, "Impact of the 'Like Minds, Like Mine' Anti-Stigma and Discrimination Campaign in New Zealand on Anticipated and Experienced Discrimination," *Australian & New Zealand Journal of Psychiatry*, Vol. 48, No. 4, 2014, pp. 360–370.

Truth Initiative, homepage, undated. As of October 16, 2017:
http://truthinitiative.org/

U.S. Census Bureau, *Current Population Survey, 2015 Annual Social and Economic (ASEC) Supplement*, Washington, D.C., 2015a.

————, "Facts for Features: Veterans Day 2015, Nov. 11, 2015," November 17, 2015b. As of December 26, 2017:
https://www.census.gov/newsroom/facts-for-features/2015/cb15-ff23.html

U.S. Department of Veterans Affairs, "National Campaigns & Partnerships," June 3, 2015. As of December 26, 2017:
https://www.va.gov/QUALITYOFCARE/improving/campaigns-and-partnerships.asp

U.S. Government Accountability Office, *VA Mental Health: Clearer Guidance on Access Policies and Wait-Time Data Needed*, Washington, D.C.: Government Printing Press, 2015.

U.S. Marine Corps, *Combat and Operational Stress Control*, MCRP 6-11C, NTTP 1-15M, Washington, D.C., December 2010. As of February 3, 2017:
http://www.marines.mil/Portals/59/Publications/
MCRP%206-11C%20%20Combat%20and%20Operational%20Stress%20Control.pdf

VA—*See* U.S. Department of Veterans Affairs.

van het Loo, Mirjam, and James P. Kahan, *The RAND Appropriateness Method: An Annotated Bibliography Through June 1999*, Leiden, Netherlands: RAND Europe, RE-99-010-EC/DG/XII, 1999. As of February 3, 2017:
https://www.rand.org/pubs/rand_europe/RE99-010.html

Veterans Crisis Line, "Create a Message of Hope," undated-a. As of October 12, 2017:
https://www.veteranscrisisline.net/GraphicGenerator.aspx

————, homepage, undated-b. As of October 12, 2017:
https://www.veteranscrisisline.net/

————, "Videos," undated-c. As of October 12, 2017:
https://www.veteranscrisisline.net/Resources/Videos.aspx

Watson Institute for International and Public Affairs, "Costs of War: US Veterans and Military Families," 2015. As of August 25, 2015:
http://watson.brown.edu/costsofwar/costs/human/veterans

Weiss, Janet A., and Mary Tschirhart, "Public Information Campaigns as Policy Instruments," *Journal of Policy Analysis and Management*, Vol. 13, No. 1, 1994, pp. 82–119.

White House Office of National Drug Control Policy, *National Youth Anti-Drug Media Campaign*, Washington, D.C., 2011.

Wong, Eunice C., Rebecca L. Collins, Jennifer Cerully, Beth Roth, and Joyce Marks, "Stigma, Discrimination, and Well-Being Among California Adults Experiencing Mental Health Challenges," *RAND Health Quarterly*, Vol. 5, No., 2, p. 11, Santa Monica, Calif.: RAND Corporation, 2015. As of October 5, 2017:
https://www.rand.org/pubs/periodicals/health-quarterly/issues/v5/n2/11.html

Wright, Annemarie, Patrick D. McGorry, Meredith G. Harris, Anthony F. Jorm, and Kerryn Pennell, "Development and Evaluation of a Youth Mental Health Community Awareness Campaign—The Compass Strategy," *BMC Public Health*, BioMed Central, Vol. 6, 2006, p. 215. As of September 6, 2017:
http://www.ncbi.nlm.nih.gov/pubmed/16923195

Wright, Kathleen M., Thomas W. Britt, and DeWayne Moore, "Impediments to Mental Health Treatment as Predictors of Mental Health Symptoms Following Combat," *Journal of Traumatic Stress*, Vol. 27, No. 5, October 2014, pp. 535–541. As of October 5, 2017:
http://www.ncbi.nlm.nih.gov/pubmed/25322883

Wright, Kevin B., and Stephen A. Rains, "Weak-Tie Support Network Preference, Health-Related Stigma, and Health Outcomes in Computer-Mediated Support Groups," *Journal of Applied Communication Research*, Vol. 41, No. 3, 2013, pp. 309–324. As of September 6, 2017: http://search.ebscohost.com/login.aspx?direct=true&db=psyh&AN=2013-32682-006&site=ehost-live

Wroblewski, Angela, and Andrea Leitner, "Between Scientific Standards and Claims to Efficiency: Expert Interviews in Programme Evaluation," in Alexander Bogner, Beate Littig, and Wolfgang Menz, eds., *Interviewing Experts*, London: Palgrave Macmillan, 2009, pp. 235–251.

Wyllie, Allan, and James Lauder, *Impacts of National Media Campaign to Counter Stigma and Discrimination Associated with Mental Illness: Survey 12: Response to Fifth Phase of Campaign*, Auckland, New Zealand: Phoenix Research, 2012. As of August 25, 2015: http://www.likeminds.org.nz/assets/Uploads/Impacts-of-national-media.pdf

Yamaguchi, Sosei, Yoshio Mino, and Shahir Uddin, "Strategies and Future Attempts to Reduce Stigmatization and Increase Awareness of Mental Health Problems Among Young People: A Narrative Review of Educational Interventions," *Psychiatry and Clinical Neuroscience*, Vol. 65, No. 5, 2011, pp. 405–415.

Yang, Shuang-Hong, Alek Kolcz, Andy Schlaikjer, and Pankaj Gupta, "Large-Scale High-Precision Topic Modeling on Twitter," *Proceedings of the 20th ACM SIGKDD International Conference on Knowledge Discovery and Data Mining*, New York: ACM, 2014.

Yanos, Philip T., Paul H. Lysaker, and David Roe, "Internalized Stigma as a Barrier to Improvement in Vocational Functioning Among People with Schizophrenia-Spectrum Disorders," *Psychiatry Research*, Vol. 178, No. 1, 2010, pp. 211–213. As of September 6, 2017: http://www.ncbi.nlm.nih.gov/pubmed/20417973

Yanos, Philip T., Michelle L. West, Lauren Gonzales, Stephen M. Smith, David Roe, and Paul H. Lysaker, "Change in Internalized Stigma and Social Functioning Among Persons Diagnosed with Severe Mental Illness," *Psychiatry Research*, Vol. 200, Nos. 2–3, 2012, pp. 1032–1034. As of September 6, 2017: http://www.ncbi.nlm.nih.gov/pubmed/22763091

Yen, Cheng-Fang, Yu Lee, Tze-Chun Tang, Ju-Yu Yen, Chih-Hung Ko, and Cheng-Chung Chen, "Predictive Value of Self-Stigma, Insight and Perceived Adverse Effects of Medication for the Clinical Outcomes in Patients with Depressive Disorders," *Journal of Nervous and Mental Disease*, Vol. 197, No. 3, 2009, pp. 172–177.